AF609317

PARACOUSTICS

Sound & the Paranormal

PARACOUSTICS

Sound & the Paranormal

edited by

STEVEN T. PARSONS &

CALLUM E. COOPER

www.whitecrowbooks.com

Paracoustics

Sound & the Paranormal

Published and printed in the United States of America and the United Kingdom
by White Crow Books; an imprint of White Crow Productions Ltd.

For information, contact White Crow Books
at 3 Hova Villas, Hove, BN3 3DH United Kingdom,
or e-mail to info@whitecrowbooks.com.

Cover Designed by Butterflyeffect
Interior design by Velin@Perseus-Design.com
Translation by Textcase, Utrecht, Netherlands

Hardback ISBN 978-1-910121-53-5
Paperback ISBN 978-1-910121-32-0
eBook ISBN 978-1-910121-33-7

Non Fiction / Body, Mind & Spirit / Death & Dying

www.whitecrowbooks.com

ACKNOWLEDGEMENT

With gratitude to the Society for Psychical Research's
Survival Research Committee
in supporting the production of *Paracoustics*

CONTENTS

Contributed Chapters

ABOUT THE EDITORS

In 2012, The *Wall Street Journal* Called Steve Parsons *"The Gold Standard of Ghost Hunting."*

Steven T. Parsons is a unique investigator of ghosts, hauntings and related phenomena whose background, peer recognition, experience, and knowledge separate him from a domain full of pseudo-scientific amateur ghost hunters. He has hunted for ghosts since childhood and has been a full time investigator for more than 20 years. Peers and leading academic parapsychologists currently acknowledge him to be one of the best paranormal investigators in the UK. He has been involved in many areas of psychical research and has developed and pioneered several new methods of investigating ghosts and haunting phenomena and he remains at the forefront of true scientific ghost hunting. His work on infrasound and the paranormal led him to design and build specialist equipment to precisely measure & record location based Infrasound. Using newly applied digital photographic techniques, he was the first person to finally demonstrate and prove that the much debated orb phenomenon has a mundane explanation.

Steve has contributed to, and participated in, numerous documentaries for broadcasters worldwide including productions for The Discovery Channel, National Geographic Channel, Japanese TV and for both the BBC and other UK broadcasters. In addition, he has worked as the paranormal investigator on the hit TV shows Most Haunted and I'm Famous & Frightened, cleverly balancing the entertainment aspect of such shows with his highly technical & informative approach to investigations. Whilst co-hosting his own paranormal show for BBC radio, Steve also made regular expert contributions on radio stations throughout the UK and for broadcasters in the UK, USA and Australia. A regular contributor to the news media, books & magazines, his prolific work has featured and has been cited in many books, peer reviewed journals, as well as popular magazines and newspapers.

His forthright and no nonsense approach is well known throughout paranormal investigation circles and he has a hard won reputation for producing results. Steve is also currently studying for a parapsychology focused Ph.D. that examines the role of **Infrasound** as a possible cause for various haunting experiences.

Steve is the co-founder of Para.Science, which in 2014 celebrated 21 years of active spontaneous case investigation. Investigations that have in some instances lasted tens of thousands of man-hours and taken several years to fully undertake. A commitment to quality that will continue into the future.

In addition to his work with Para.Science, he is often asked to act as an independent advisor on many other investigations offering training, support and analysis of subsequent evidence. He is a Member of the Spontaneous Case Committee of The Society for Psychical Research and an Advisor to The Ghost Club.

Callum E. Cooper is from Nottinghamshire in the Mansfield area, and throughout his early life was fascinated by stories of local ghosts and hauntings in and around Nottingham. This interest came from spending a lot of time throughout his childhood visiting Newstead Abbey (the former home of the poet Lord Byron) and visiting his local library through schooling, to read the various books on paranormal phenomena, particularly the haunting investigations of the notorious ghost-hunter Harry Price.

Having spent over ten years investigating haunting type phenomena to date, it was this interest which led him into psychology, and more so, to investigate questions about the mind and its capabilities: Is psychic phenomena a reality? Does the mind persist after death?

He read for a psychology BSc degree at the University of Northampton and then an MRes in social science research methods (psychology) at Sheffield Hallam University. In 2012 he became a PhD candidate within the *Centre for the Study of Anomalous Psychological Processes* (CSAPP) at the University of Northampton, where his research focuses on anomalous experiences during bereavement. CSAPP is currently the largest research centre in the world for parapsychology, transpersonal psychology and consciousness studies, with the university teaching modules in these areas and taking on research students.

At the University of Northampton, Callum is a lecturer on parapsychology, thanatology (dying, death and bereavement), positive psychology, and human sexual behaviour and has given guest lectures throughout the UK and in the USA on parapsychology and his research projects. His research interests within the paranormal have mainly involved issues of survival of consciousness beyond bodily death and field investigations of spontaneous phenomena, particularly hauntings. Owing to this, he has contributed to various radio and TV shows (including BBC radio and ITV's This Morning) and was involved in a well-received Japanese documentary on haunting investigations alongside Steve Parsons.

Throughout his research and teachings he has received various awards related to parapsychology, these include the 2009 Eileen J. Garrett Scholarship (Parapsychology Foundation), the Alex Tanous Scholarship Award – numerous times since 2011 – (Alex Tanous Foundation for Scientific Research) and the 2014 Dr Gertrude Schmeidler Outstanding Student Award (Parapsychological Association). Alongside this, he is a Chartered Psychologist of the British Psychological Society and a Fellow of the Higher Education Academy, and a member of various organisations such as the Society for Psychical Research (and is on their Survival Research Committee), the Parapsychological Association, and a Graduate Researcher of Hope Studies Central (University of Alberta).

He has published numerous articles and research reports on parapsychology, such as in the *Journal of Parapsychology*, the *Australian Journal of Parapsychology*, the *Journal for Spiritual and Consciousness Studies, Paranthropology Journal, Anomaly*, and the *Christian Parapsychologist*. He is also the author of *Telephone Calls from the Dead* (Tricorn Books) and, alongside the late Dr Alex Tanous, he is the co-author and editor of *Conversations with Ghosts* (White Crow Books).

INTRODUCTION

Our sense of hearing is one of the first senses that we develop; even before we are born we are listening to the sounds of our Mother and the world around us. From around 16 weeks of gestation it is likely that the foetus is capable of hearing.

Our sense of hearing continues when other senses have shut down; a simple example is our daily alarm clock, which wakes us even when we are oblivious to other sensory signals such as touch or smell. When someone is in a deep state of unconsciousness or coma they retain their sense of hearing, as many people report upon regaining full consciousness.

It is therefore hardly surprising that sounds are some of the most commonly reported features of paranormal experiences. The realm of the paranormal is not a silent realm, ghosts rarely glide silently along empty corridors; they are frequently accompanied by the swish of a spectral dress or the sound of ghostly footsteps treading the empty floorboards. Poltergeists are, as their name suggests, inherently noisy affairs. In Ireland, the Banshee is said to wail or scream in lament as an omen of a forthcoming death. Communicating spirits knock and tap during séances, they ring bells, play musical instruments and speak with disembodied voices to the living. Writing in first century BC Athens, Pliny the Younger gives us one of the earliest accounts of a haunting and it is complete with a fearful noise of rattling chains:

> It happened that Athenodorus the philosopher came to Athens at this time, and reading the bill ascertained the price. The extraordinary

> cheapness raised his suspicion; nevertheless, when he heard the whole story, he was so far from being discouraged, that he was more strongly inclined to hire it, and, in short, actually did so. When it grew towards evening, he ordered a couch to be prepared for him in the forepart of the house, and after calling for a light, together with his pen and tablets, he directed all his people to retire within. But that his mind might not, for want of employment, be open to the vain terrors of imaginary noises and apparitions, he applied himself to writing with all his faculties. The first part of the night passed with usual silence, and then began the clanking of iron fetters; however, he neither lifted up his eyes, nor laid down his pen, but closed his ears by concentrating his attention. The noise increased and advanced nearer, till it seemed at the door, and at last in the chamber. He looked round and saw the apparition exactly as it had been described to him: it stood before him, beckoning with the finger. Athenodorus made a sign with his hand that it should wait a little, and bent again to his writing, but the ghost rattling its chains over his head as he wrote, he looked round and saw it beckoning as before. Upon this he immediately took up his lamp and followed it. The ghost slowly stalked along, as if encumbered with its chains; and having turned into the courtyard of the house, suddenly vanished. Athenodorus being thus deserted marked the spot with a handful of grass and leaves. The next day he went to the magistrates, and advised them to order that spot to be dug up. There they found bones commingled and intertwined with chains; for the body had mouldered away by long lying in the ground, leaving them bare, and corroded by the fetters. The bones were collected, and buried at the public expense; and after the ghost was thus duly laid the house was haunted no more.

In addition to the noisy attempts of Athenodorus' spectral visitor it is interesting to note that even 2,000 years ago some individuals were aware of our human characteristic of fear linked to imagination. More often than not, sounds are benign and unlikely to have a paranormal origin; some would argue that all sound must have a normal explanation, as there is no such thing as the paranormal. Be that as it may, for many, sound is inexorably linked with ghosts, hauntings and other similar anomalous experiences.

Sounds have been recorded and presented as evidence, from modern day Electronic Voice Phenomena (EVP) to the earliest attempts by psychical researchers. In the 1890's a group, including members of the

Society for Psychical Research, spent some months investigating an alleged haunting in a Scottish hunting lodge. Their experiences were published in 1899 in *The Alleged Haunting of B-House* written by Ada Goodrich-Freer and the Marquess of Bute. The book is full of references to peculiar and unexplained sounds; shrieks, raised voices, footsteps and loud explosions. Some sounds were inaudible to anyone except a single individual, others were heard collectively:

Monday, August 15th. Father H—— went away after luncheon.

> Lord Bute recalls that Father H—— told him that he had been at B—— for the purpose of giving a Retreat [a series of sermons and meditations] to some nuns, who were charitably allowed by Mr S—— to take a sort of holiday, at a house called B—— Cottage, which had been originally built and occupied by the late Major S——, when he first took up his residence at B——, which at the time was let.
>
> Father H—— told Lord Bute that in consequence of the disturbance his room had been several times changed, and he expressed surprise that the sounds did not appear to be heard by anybody except himself. He also said that he had spoken of the matter to Mr S——, who expressed an idea that the disturbances might be caused by his uncle, the late Major S——, who was trying to attract attention in order that prayers might be offered for the repose of his soul. The sounds occurred during full daylight, and in a clear open space between his bed and the ceiling. He did not know to what to compare them, but as he said they were explosive in sound, Lord Bute suggested that they might be compared to the sounds made by petards, which are commonly used in Italy for firing feux de joie. Father H—— answered, "Yes perhaps, if they were continuous enough." He said that the sound which alarmed him more than any other was as of a large animal throwing itself violently against the bottom of his door, outside. A third noise which he had heard was of ordinary raps, of the kind called "spirit-raps." He mentioned a fourth sound, the nature of which Lord Bute does not remember with the same certainty as the others, but believes it was a shriek or scream. Such a sound is described by other witnesses during the subsequent occupation of the house by the H—— family. The fact that the sounds appear to have been inaudible to everyone except Father H—— is a strong argument in favour of their subjective, or hallucinatory, character. It will be found that this was very often the case with the peculiar sounds recorded at B——, and even when

> they were heard by several persons at the same time, there does not appear to be any ground for refusing to recognise them as collective hallucinations.

The group were aware of seismic activity in the area and made use of a seismographic instrument in an attempt to record any vibrations due to localised tremors. They also planned to use a phonograph in order to record the sounds, but this plan was forestalled by the early end of the investigation due to a very public quarrel in The Times newspaper with the owner of the property.

In compiling this book, the editors and contributors are not seeking to write a complete history of sound and the paranormal, nor are we trying to write a definitive work dealing with every aspect of sound and the paranormal. Such a book would be prohibitively long winded and ultimately not needed. The accounts of psychical research, ghost investigation and paranormal study (historical and modern) are bursting at the seams with descriptions of sound related phenomena and the reader is urged to seek out these accounts and read widely of these experiences, be they real or imagined. We have provided some suggestions for further reading but they cannot ever hope to be complete – such a book of reference would exceed the limits of modern printing. Instead, we have sought to consider several of the key aspects of sound and its relationship with paranormal experiences. In addition, we have included within the appendices additional guidance gained from our own and others work.

It is our hope that "Paracoustics" will provide the foundation for further work and research by those who are studying sound and the paranormal for themselves and that it will go at least part-way toward answering some of the questions that will be raised by those who are merely interested in discovering more about this fascinating aspect of our human experience.

STP, *On behalf of the Editors*
& Contributing Authors

Section 1

WORKS AND RESEARCH BY THE EDITORS

THE PHYSICS OF SOUND

Steven Parsons

Sound

Sound is a commonly reported feature of many paranormal experiences and these experiences may relate to sounds that are both real and imagined. In this chapter we will consider only those sound events that are externally produced by the vibration of matter and that can be objectively measured and observed.

The vibration of matter causes sound waves to be formed. When the cone of a loudspeaker vibrates, the air adjacent to it is pushed to and fro. This creates a series of pressure waves and rarefactions in the air as the loudspeaker pushes and pulls the adjacent air molecules. The same principle may be observed when the string of a musical instrument is vibrated. The sound waves radiate outwards from the source in all directions. Our interest and investigation into the nature of sound dates back almost to our earliest recorded history. Ancient writings show that Aristotle (384-322 B.C.) observed two things regarding sound: first that the propagation of sound involved the motion of the air, and second that high notes travel faster than low notes. Since in the transmission of sound air does not appear to move, it is not surprising that other philosophers later denied Aristotle's view. Disagreements continued until 1660 when Robert Boyle in England concluded that air is an effective medium for acoustic transmission.

Wavelength, Frequency and Velocity

Sound waves are simply changes in air pressure. A sound wave can be described in terms of having a wavelength (frequency) and amplitude (power or loudness). Sound waves are therefore just small and rapid changes in air pressure.

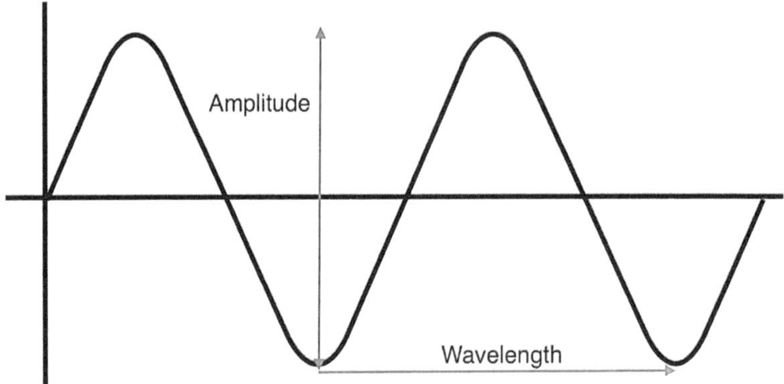

Our most common experience of sound is in air, but sound is able to travel through any solid, liquid or gaseous medium. Sound is normally produced by anything that is vibrating and causing the surrounding molecules to vibrate in sympathy with the source. These vibrations travel in the form of waves, which can be defined as a travelling disturbance consisting of coordinated vibrations that transmit energy with no net movement of matter. Sound waves take the form of alternating compressions and rarefactions; this is known as a longitudinal wave. A good example of a longitudinal wave can be seen travelling along a spring or 'slinky' as it is alternatively stretched and released and the adjacent coils move further apart and closer together.

In air, sound waves travelling past a fixed point cause the atmospheric pressure to vary slightly above and below the steady barometric pressure. The distance between any two corresponding points on successive pressure waves is termed the wavelength. Frequency refers to the number of successive waves that are emitted from the source in one second. Frequency is stated in units of Hertz (Hz), i.e. 100 wavelengths per second are expressed as 100 Hz. In 1635, Pierre Gassendi, made measurements of the speed of sound in air; he calculated a speed of around 478 metres per second (m/s). Later, French Philosopher, Marin Mersenne, often referred to as the 'father of acoustics', corrected this to about 450 m/s. Gassendi also demonstrated conclusively that the speed of sound is independent of frequency, forever discrediting Aristotle's view. In 1656, the Italian Borelli and his colleague Viviani made careful measurements of the speed of sound and reached a figure of 350 m/s. However, it is now recognised that all these values suffer from a lack of reference to the temperature, humidity, and wind velocity conditions. The first measurement judged precise in the modern sense occurred under the direction of the Academy of Sciences of Paris in 1738, where cannon-fire was used. The speed of sound varies both with the temperature and the density of the medium through which it is passing. Changes in temperature and humidity of the air will also significantly affect the speed at which sound is transmitted. Sound waves are able to pass more quickly through warm air than through colder air. Sound waves also pass more easily through air that has a higher humidity. For example: in dry Air (0% relative humidity) at 0°C, the speed of sound is 331.45 m/s whilst at 20°C the speed of sound increases to 343.37 m/s. As the humidity increases, the speed of sound also increases. As an example, using the previous temperature of 20°C, an increase in the relative humidity (RH) from 0% to 50% will increase the speed of sound by 3.75% to 356.25 m/s. Wavelength, velocity and frequency of a sound wave are linked by a simple mathematical formula:

Wavelength = Velocity ÷ Frequency

Using this formula we are able to determine the wavelength for any given frequency. For example, in normal air, for a frequency of 20Hz, (20°C, 50% RH), the wavelength would be 356.25 ÷ 20 = 17.81 metres. The same formula allows the calculation of frequency, as a function of the velocity divided by the wavelength, which in this case gives 356.25 ÷ 17.81 = 20 Hz.

Note that in materials such as solids that have a higher molecular density, sound waves will have a higher speed, such as Water-1480 m/s, Glass-5200 m/s, Steel-5000 to 5900 m/s (depending upon the composition of the metal). The sound waves themselves are also different within solids than in air. In solids they are a combination of the longitudinal waves (described previously) and transverse waves in which there is displacement of the medium at right angles to the direction of the sound transmission. A good example of transverse waves can be observed in the ripples on the surface of a pond.

Sound Waves, Transmission and Attenuation

Sound waves are absorbed, reflected and diffracted by any obstacles in their path; this may also include the medium through which the sound waves are passing. Any interference to the sound wave will reduce the amount of energy it is able to transmit to the listener, which will reduce the loudness of the sound. Interference to the sound wave may also cause attenuation to the distance that the sound waves can travel or alter the direction from which the sound appears to originate from. Energy from the sound wave is given up to the air or other medium it is passing through, this is known as the inverse square law. Simply stated, the inverse square law means that every time the distance from the source doubles the amount of energy carried by the sound wave is cut by a factor of four (6dB).

For reflection of the sound waves to occur, the wavelength must be smaller than the dimensions of the reflecting object. For example, if an obstacle such as a wall is 1 metre high and 2 metres long, its dimensions will have an appreciable effect upon the reflection of sounds with wavelengths of less than 1 metre. This corresponds to a frequency of around 340Hz and sounds above that frequency will be readily reflected. Further strong reflection of sound waves with a wavelength of 2 metres (172Hz) will also take place. If sound waves with a lower frequency and correspondingly longer wavelength encounter the same obstacle they will not be reflected but will instead bend around the obstacle, a process called diffraction. If the wavelength is much greater than the obstacle size, then there will be increased bending around the obstacle. At very low frequencies where the wavelengths are considerable, sometimes exceeding hundreds or thousands of metres in length, comparatively little of the sound wave energy is attenuated in this manner, as the sound waves are able to bend around even large obstacles. Low frequency sound waves are therefore capable of travelling greater distances from the source without significant attenuation.

At higher frequencies, the energy is much more readily absorbed reflected and attenuated by the environment through which it passes, high frequency sounds will therefore travel a much shorter distance before becoming completely dissipated and undetectable. The effect of increasing frequency upon the distance a sound is capable of being heard is easily demonstrated. A person shouting may only be heard over a distance of several hundred metres at best, the frequency of the normal human voice being between about 300 Hz and 4,000 Hz (4 kHz), whilst traffic roar might be heard over a much greater distance as its general frequency range is much lower lying between 20 Hz and 1,000 Hz (1 kHz).

Sound waves are also affected by atmospheric conditions; movement of the air itself (wind) causes refraction or an alteration in the direction of the sound waves. The moving air causes the sound waves to bend and so someone standing downwind of the sound source will hear higher sound levels than someone who is standing upwind of the source. Sound can also be perceived to alter its frequency when the source of the sound is moving with respect to a stationary observer. This is called the Doppler effect, named after the Austrian Physicist Christian Doppler who first proposed it in 1842. The Doppler effect is the apparent change in frequency produced by a moving source of waves in which there is an apparent increase in the sound frequency for observers when the source is approaching and an apparent decrease in frequency for observers from whom the source is receding. It is important to note that the effect does not result because of an actual change in the frequency of the source, which remains unaltered.

As already discussed, sound can be altered by the physical medium it is passing through and by the immediate environment. Within an enclosed space such as a room or building, all these factors will combine to affect the way in which sound is perceived and recorded. As an example, when someone pops a balloon in a room the direct sound is heard after a very short delay, as these direct sound waves will have travelled the shortest distance from the source to the listener, they have the least amount of attenuation and so are the loudest. Shortly afterwards, waves that have been reflected off the various surfaces within the room will be heard, sometimes in the form of an echo. Finally, after the first reflected waves reach the listener, additional sound waves from multiple reflections and interactions between the sound waves themselves will arrive. In fact, there are so many sound waves bouncing back and forth, interfering with one another that the overall sound becomes extended and distorted, an effect known as reverberation. The time taken for this reverberation to subside is related to the size of the room and the materials used. Small rooms have shorter reverberation times and reflections are reduced by sound absorbing materials such as wood and fabric used in the construction of the room and it's furnishings.

A final consideration is that of standing waves. Standing waves occur when sound waves from a continuous source are reflected between surfaces that are an exact multiple of half the wavelength apart. The reflected energy is then added to the energy of the original sound, resulting in their energies being combined. This has the effect of increasing the loudness of the sound and is called resonance. Non-parallel surfaces reduce the incidents of standing waves being formed and for most purposes standing waves may be considered as not occurring for sounds of very short duration such as bangs or claps.

Basic Units of Measurement used for Sound

Sound waves are periodic oscillations in atmospheric pressure and their amplitudes are proportional to the change in pressure during each oscillation. There are several ways of expressing the amplitude or intensity of sound waves. However, it is commonly expressed as sound pressure level (SPL). In scientific terms this is defined as the force acting on a unit of area. Thus sound pressure waves are normally expressed as Newtons per square metre (N/m^2). More recently it has become the official practice to refer to the N/m^2 using the S.I. (Système International d'Unités) term, Pascal (Pa). The sound pressure variations that are detectable by a typical human ear are immense. For example, the quietest sound that can be detected has a sound pressure level (SPL) of 0.00002 Pa and the loudest sound has an SPL of around 200 Pa.

In order to simplify the expression of sound pressure levels, the decibel (dB) is more commonly used. This is a unit of comparison and so must be stated against a reference value in order for it to be meaningful. Formally expressed, the number of decibels represents a ratio of two powers using the formula dB = 10 log (power ratio). An SPL of 0.00002 Pa is referred to as 0dB, and this is the reference value against which all comparisons of SPL are expressed.

This standard allows any sound pressure to be quoted as (x) dB above that reference pressure value and is expressed as dB(SPL) or more often simply dBS. Thus a sound that is 10 times more powerful than the reference SPL is expressed as 10dBS, a sound 100 times more powerful is 20 dBS, a sound 1,000 times more powerful is 30 dBS, etc. For instance, a sound with an SPL of 140 dB (200 Pa), such as might be found in some industrial locations, is 100,000,000,000,000 more powerful than the reference and is considered to be able to cause rapid ear damage and aural pain.

Although not used for sound measurement, the expression volume is often encountered when dealing with sound. In acoustic terms, volume is related to the amplitude, sound pressure level and frequency of the sound. Another expression that is common is loudness. Loudness refers to the primary psychological correlate of the amplitude of a sound source. It is worth noting that the loudness control found on some consumer audio equipment alters only frequency response curve of the sound to better correspond to the characteristics of the human ear and is intended to make recorded sounds appear more natural when played at lower sound pressure levels.

Sound Physics Relating to Hearing and Measuring Sound

In the foregoing section we have learned something about the physics and nature of sound and its measurement but how does this affect those who are interested in observing sound in the context of a paranormal investigation?

Hearing Sound

Sound waves are rarely simple and straightforward events that reach the listener by a direct path without interference by the environment. Whenever a sound event occurs multiple sound waves will be created, having a wide range of frequencies, both within and outside of the audible frequency range and at a range of intensities that vary in loudness between the imperceptibly quiet and the very loud. The human ear is a remarkable piece of bioengineering capable of discerning sounds over a range of around 120 dB which is equivalent to an amplitude range of around 1 million times. The frequency range of human hearing is generally considered to be from around 20 Hz to 20,000 Hz. Sounds that lie within the audible range of human hearing i.e. 20 Hz to 20 kHz regardless of whether or not they are of sufficient amplitude to he heard are referred to as audible sounds or more often simply sound. Sounds that are above 20 kHz and therefore generally considered to be inaudible are referred to as ultrasound, whilst sounds below 20 Hz and again considered inaudible are known as infrasound. The human ear is most sensitive to sounds that have a frequency of between 1 kHz and 4 kHz. Outside this range, the sensitivity of the ear decreases and a corresponding increase in the amplitude is required in order for sound to be heard. As an example, most people will be able to hear a sound as low as 0 dB SPL at 3 kHz but will require an increase in amplitude to 40 dB SPL (a factor of 100x increase) in order to hear a sound at 100 Hz. In many instances it is actually possible for individuals to 'hear' sounds that have a frequency that is considered to be outside of the normal hearing range. This ability is a function of the amount of energy that is present within the sound waves but, simply put, if the sound is loud enough some people might be able to hear it. Our ability to hear sounds changes with age and according to other factors such as damage to hearing from work and leisure pursuits or from disease. Age, damage, and disease affect both amplitude and frequency of the sounds we are able to hear, with higher frequency sounds generally being the first to be affected in all cases. Our ability to discern direction is also adversely affected when any hearing loss is not uniform in both ears.

Humans have the ability in most instances to be able to identify the direction from which a sound emanates as we have two ears. Most people can identify the difference between two sound sources positioned about half a metre apart at a ten metre distance, which corresponds to an angular separation of around 3 degrees. This directional information is obtained in two ways. First, frequencies above about 1 kHz are strongly shadowed by the head, the ear nearest the sound receiving a stronger signal than the ear on the opposite side of the head. The second method used to determine directionality is that the ear on the far side of the head hears the sound slightly later than the near ear, due to its greater distance from the source. Directionality works best for sound frequencies below about 1 kHz. Directional information is also greatly aided by the listener's ability to turn their head and observe the change in the signals. While human hearing can quickly determine the direction a sound is from, it is generally poor when trying to identify the distance to the sound source. This is because there are few clues available in a sound wave that can provide this information. Human hearing perceives that high frequency sounds are nearby, while low frequency sounds are distant. Reverberation does provide some weak clues about distance and provides a perception of the room size. For example, sounds in a large auditorium will have a longer reverberation time (perhaps 100 milliseconds) while less than 10 milliseconds is a more typical reverberation time for a smaller room or office. Hearing is based on the amplitude of the frequencies, and is very insensitive to the phase of the sound wave. This insensitivity to phase can be understood by examining how sound propagates through the environment, for example, when you listen to a person speaking across a room whilst you move about. In these circumstances, most of the sound reaching the ears is reflected from the walls, ceiling, and floor, with different frequencies reaching the ears via different paths. These multiple pathways mean that the relative phase of each frequency changes as you move about the room. Our hearing for the most part disregards these phase variations; the voice is perceived as unchanging regardless of the position of the listener. From a physics standpoint, the phase of an audio signal becomes randomised as it propagates through a complex environment.

Measuring Sound

Sound is measured by the use of devices that are able to register the amount of sound energy and the frequency of the sound waves passing the device. The type of device that is used may vary depending upon the nature of the sound waves that are being measured. For very low frequency sounds, such as those created by earthquakes and other natural events, or by man-made explosions, a sensitive vibration-sensing device called a seismometer is usually preferred. For higher frequency sounds, and those that lie within the audible range, then a microphone is normally used. In some instances a barometer can be used to detect to changes in air pressure and therefore may be used to measure passing sound waves.

Seismometers work by responding to the physical vibrations of the sound wave, most often as they travel through a solid medium such as rock or building materials. Early seismometers used some form of heavy weight that was suspended from a fixed support. The passing vibrations caused the weight to move relative to its support and these movements were then translated by mechanical means, or in later devices by electrical signals, which could be used to record and observe the passing vibrations. More recent designs use highly sensitive electronic sensors and can be both highly sensitive and incredibly small. Depending upon the actual design, seismometers can be used to measure vibrations vertically and in two horizontal planes, the lateral and longitudinal that lie at right angles to one another. Such devices are known as 3-axis seismometers. Seismometers are insensitive to sound waves passing through the air and are optimised for the measurement of very low and low frequency vibrations between around 0.01Hz and 500Hz. Accelerometers are related to seismometers although the primary aim of an accelerometer is to measure acceleration forces. The measurement of sound is not the primary function of this type of sensor, and its sensitivity to sound waves is much reduced, accelerometers have been used for sound measurement, especially for measurements relating to low frequency sounds or short duration sonic events such as jolts, thumps, and knocks.

Microphones are the most commonly encountered devices used for the measurement of sound waves in air. As already described, passing sound waves cause extremely small variations in air pressure to which a microphone is capable of responding to a greater or lesser extent. Microphones may therefore be considered as highly sensitive barometers. Depending upon the actual design, the microphone may be more or less sensitive to a range of sound frequencies and amplitudes. There are numerous specialist designs of microphone depending upon the type of sound they are designed to measure, including the ribbon microphone, fibre-optic microphone, and the piezoelectric microphone, but most of the commonly encountered types can be placed in two broad categories, the dynamic microphone, and the condenser or capacitor microphone.

The dynamic microphone uses the principle of electromagnetic induction to turn sound waves into electrical signals that are proportional to the amplitude and frequency of the sound waves. In this design, a thin diaphragm moves in direct response to the air pressure changes of passing sound waves. Attached to the diaphragm is a coil of fine wire or other electrically conductive material and this conductive coil is mounted in close proximity to a fixed magnet. As the diaphragm and the coil move back and forth in the magnetic field, a tiny electric current is induced into the coil. This induced current is directly related to the magnitude and direction of the motion of the diaphragm and is therefore an electrical representation of the passing sound waves. Dynamic microphones require no additional power in order to operate but, due to the additional components attached to the diaphragm, they may be slow to respond to transient changes in sound and exhibit lower sensitivity to sound waves that lack sufficient amplitude to properly move the diaphragm / coil assembly.

The capacitor microphone also uses a thin diaphragm, but in this design the diaphragm is coated on one side with an electrically conductive material, usually gold. The conductive face of the diaphragm is mounted in close proximity to a fixed conductive surface or back plate. The two conductive surfaces are separated by an air gap and form an electrical component called a capacitor. As the diaphragm moves, its motion corresponding to passing sound waves, the size of the air gap changes and the capacitance of the device changes in proportion to the passing sound waves. Capacitor microphones require a power source in order to work, as it is necessary to maintain an electrical charge on the diaphragm at all times. Because it is not necessary to mount or attach additional components such as a coil to the diaphragm, capacitor microphones can generally respond more quickly to rapid changes in the passing sound waves and so normally have a greater degree of sensitivity to low amplitude sounds.

We have already mentioned that barometers can be used for the measurement of sound and there are certain instances where these devices might be desirable; these include the measurement of small changes in air pressure associated with airborne sound generating events which include atmospheric explosions and sonic booms, but their use in general sound measuring is limited. Regardless of the type of microphone or device that is used to detect sound, the resulting electrical signal that is produced is tiny and some form of additional amplification is required in order to increase the signal to a useable degree.

Microphones react to sound in a very different way to the way our hearing does. Microphones do not process the sound but merely respond to the passing sound waves to produce an electrical representation of the acoustic frequency and amplitude; this is a single step process. Hearing always involves processing of the sound by the brain and is therefore a multi-step process, the sounds we hear are not the same as what our ears respond to. Few microphones can even hope to match the enormous range of human hearing in either frequency or amplitude. This means that when a human observer hears a sound and the same sound is recorded and later played back, it may appear very different. Quiet sounds that may be heard by a listener might not be picked up by a microphone, likewise loud sounds might contain more energy than the microphone is designed to handle leading to distortions in the subsequent electrical signal from the microphone. Most microphones simply produce an amalgam of all the passing sound waves with no particular emphasis being given to the direction of the sound source; these are called Omni-directional microphones. Other designs can in effect reduce the amplitude of some sounds coming from certain directions, making them more effective at responding to sounds from a given direction; these are known as directional microphones. Microphone designs can be tailored for specific applications and frequency ranges and sound pressure levels. They may be used for sound measurement, environmental noise monitoring, speech, music applications such as vocals or musical instruments, in fact anywhere that sound needs to be recorded or measured.

Most investigators select a microphone that is designed for general applications, i.e., speech and music. They may also make their selection based upon cost. Whilst on paper, the specifications relating to the frequency range and power handling (SPL range) of two microphones may appear similar in practice, this is normally not the case. Cheaper microphones will rarely do as well in accurately reproducing the passing sound waves as one that is more expensive. Better materials and components will allow a more faithful reproduction of the sound to take place. Better design will allow for the removal of unwanted noise, i.e., electrical (generated within the microphone circuitry) and physical (from handling and vibrations passing through the microphone body.)

Recording Sound

Once the information from the sound waves has been turned into an electrical signal by the microphone or other device, it may then be used in a number of different ways in order to obtain information about the nature of the sound. That information is in the form of the frequency, amplitude, and sound pressure level of the sound. It may simply be recorded to an audio recording device for later playback and listening, or used by a device that can display and record the different parameters of the sound, such as a spectrum analyser, or oscilloscope. The electrical signal from the microphone etc., can be utilised by an audio recorder or sound analyser using either analogue or digital techniques. Whilst both techniques are still actively employed in sound measurement, digital techniques have become more prevalent.

Analogue and Digital Recording

Analogue

Analogue recording has been the technique used since Edison patented the first sound recorder in 1878. The recording is a direct representation of the signal coming from the microphone. Analogue recordings contain all the information coming from the microphone. Electrical noise is also recorded. With every successive copy that is made, the ratio of the noise to the original information is increased. Techniques, such as Dolby recording, which uses a combination of selective frequency cutting and amplification, may be employed to reduce the impact of the noise.

These days, the only analogue recorderos likely to be found in the paranormalist's kit are the standard cassette and micro-cassette recorders that some investigators still use. Available at low cost, and straightforward to use, they allow sound to be recorded with varying degrees of quality. Many of these recorders have their own built in microphones that are sufficient for use when recording something like a personal memo or perhaps an interview with a witness, but analogue machines do have some serious drawbacks as they are very prone to noise and hiss on the recording and this may mask quieter sounds. Using a higher quality machine improves this signal to noise (S/N) ratio. Some analogue recorders can make use of specialised electronic circuits to reduce hiss and noise, such as those developed by the Dolby Labs. Unfortunately, noise reduction works by boosting and cutting the levels of some recorded frequencies, thus altering the nature of the sounds that have been recorded and reducing the quality and usefulness of the subsequent information obtained. Noise reduction and other similar enhancements offered by the equipment manufacturers must therefore be used with great care and, if used, must be noted and considered in any subsequent analysis or interpretation of the recording. Analogue machines do, however, have some advantages. Many digital recorders heavily compress the amount of information that is recorded in order to make effective use of the space available on the disc or memory. Generally speaking, digital recorders do this by removing those parts of the audio spectrum above and below the range we humans can hear, typically 20Hz to 20,000Hz, and if the compression process in the recorder removes the audio information, then it is gone forever. Analogue machines do not use audio data compression, so the information recorded onto the tape is full-spectrum (within the already mentioned limits of noise and the frequency range of the microphone) and therefore analogue recording may be a better choice in some investigation situations. Cassette tapes are cheap but have limitations. For instance, it may not be possible to completely erase earlier recordings, potentially making it possible to hear previous recordings underneath a newer one. This can, and has, fooled unwary researchers into thinking they had recorded something other than actually was the case. In order to prevent this from happening, each cassette should be used only once for important sound recording tasks. However, once used, a tape may be re-used for less important recordings and perhaps interviews a few more times. The Micro-Cassette tape format uses a smaller cassette than the standard cassette and results in a much smaller, highly portable device. However, the smaller tape format also means that the signal to noise ratio is usually higher and the physically smaller recording head can also create further noise issues. In all analogue recorders, any physical distortion or misalignment of the tape as it passes the head will create additional audio problems that may fool some into thinking they have recorded an anomalous event. A very small number of researchers still favour the larger reel-to-reel tape recorders for specialist applications. They offer the advantage of generally lower signal to noise ratios and overall higher quality recordings, but all of the aforementioned drawbacks may still apply.

Analogue: Successive copies increase the noise and obscure the definition

Digital

Digital recording techniques sample the electrical signal from the microphone or other device many thousands of times every second. This is done using an Analogue to Digital (A/D) converter. The digital output is then recorded as a stream of data in much the same way that a computer writes information to its memory. Digital techniques make use of error checking and other methods to remove much of the noise that analogue methods suffer from, resulting in an improved quality of sound. Digital sound recording can generate huge amounts of data. This can use the available recording media at an astonishing rate and for some high quality audio recorders this can be several Megabytes every second. This is obviously not very practical as, in order to obtain a useful recording time, a recorder would need a vast amount of memory, which is costly. The huge files would also be unwieldy and can make editing a nightmare. Digital audio compression uses a number of techniques to reduce the amount of memory needed to record the audio. All of the techniques for compressing the amount of data degrade the sound in some way. The almost universal .mp3 format, for example, discards most sound frequencies that lie outside the audible range. Other methods include reducing the number of times the audio signal is sampled, or only writing information to the memory when there are changes to the audio signal, such as alterations to frequency and amplitude. As mentioned, digital recorders sample the sound many thousands of times per second. Most models offer the user the option of changing the sample rate; the lower the sample rate, the more data can be stored on the media. This is often expressed in terms of either the available recording time or in terms of sound quality, such as HQ (High Quality), SP (Standard Play) and LP (Long Play). The standard audio sample rate for CD audio is 44.1 kHz (i.e. 44,100 samples per second) Some digital audio recorders can exceed this; sample rates of more than 200 kHz are possible on some machines fitted with small hard drives or large amounts of solid state memory. In addition to the sample rate, which is simply the number of times per second the electrical signal is sampled, the recording also needs to contain information about the amplitude of the signal. This is called the bit depth. The greater the bit depth or rate, the more accurately the amplitude of the sound wave will be represented within the resulting data. Standard CD audio has a total of 65,536 bits. This is referred to as 16-bit audio (2 to the 16th power). In general terms, the greater the bit depth the better overall will be the quality of the sampled sound wave. 8-bit is sometimes used in more basic recorders in order to save on memory space. There are some digital recorders that offer a 24-bit recording option, often combined with the option of a high sampling rate. This provides an excellent representation of the original electrical signal from the microphone. Such techniques require very large amounts of memory in order to store the data and, whilst they may offer little advantage for general listening, the increased data can provide more accurate information when any form of analysis or editing is required. Some compressed audio formats such as .mp3 have no requirement for the bit depth information and so the only variable is the sample rate. In order to ensure that the widest range of frequencies are recorded, it is essential to make certain that the sample rate and the bit rate are sufficient to accurately represent the electrical signal from the microphone. The Nyquist-Shannon sampling theorem states that a sample rate of twice the maximum frequency of the original signal being sampled is needed to describe the frequency of the sampled signal. To put it more simply, in order to ensure that all the frequencies within the normal human hearing range of 20 Hz to 20 kHz are represented accurately, the sample rate must be at least 40 kHz.

Before being written to the media, the data normally needs to be compressed in some way as the amount of original data can be very large. The compression rate is also something that the user can adjust in some models. Progressively lowering the sample rate or bit depth can also achieve longer recording times for any given amount of memory. The result of an increased recording time (without increasing the storage memory) is always a reduction in the quality of the audio and an increase in the noise levels, sometimes to the point of making the audio almost worthless for later analysis, although this may not be initially noticed when one is simply listening to the playback. If a longer recording time is required, the only option is to increase the amount of memory available. Digital recording media can be safely erased and therefore be re-used almost indefinitely. Digital recordings can sometimes suffer when previous recordings 'bleed through' onto subsequent recordings, but this is rare and can usually be overcome by reformatting the media between use, instead of merely erasing the previous recording. Re-use of the recording media means that digital is a cost effective method; memory cards, for example can be re-used thousands of times therefore they are very economical to use, in fact, the makers claim they can be used up to 2,000 times and still be used to record cleanly and clearly. In recent years there has been an increase in studio grade digital recorders. These machines are capable of recording using an uncompressed audio format such as .BWF (Broadcast Wave File) or .WAV (Wave file) in addition to the more usual compressed .mp3 format. Until very recently there were no solid state or hard drive digital recorders that offered a high quality built-in microphone. Zoom, Tascam, and Marantz have all released digital recorders designed primarily for the musician and have excellent in-built stereo microphones in addition to sockets for plugging in external microphones. Some of these types of recorder do not offer an uncompressed file format option but instead use high sample rate .mp3 compression. An interesting potential drawback of these newer generation digital recorders is that the recording quality is so good, that unless you have a very high quality microphone, your recordings will show up the weaknesses of the microphone itself.

Still being used, but becoming increasingly uncommon, are early digital recorders such as the Minidisc, which was in effect a small Compact Disc (CD) with similar audio properties to the CD i.e. 44.1 kHz

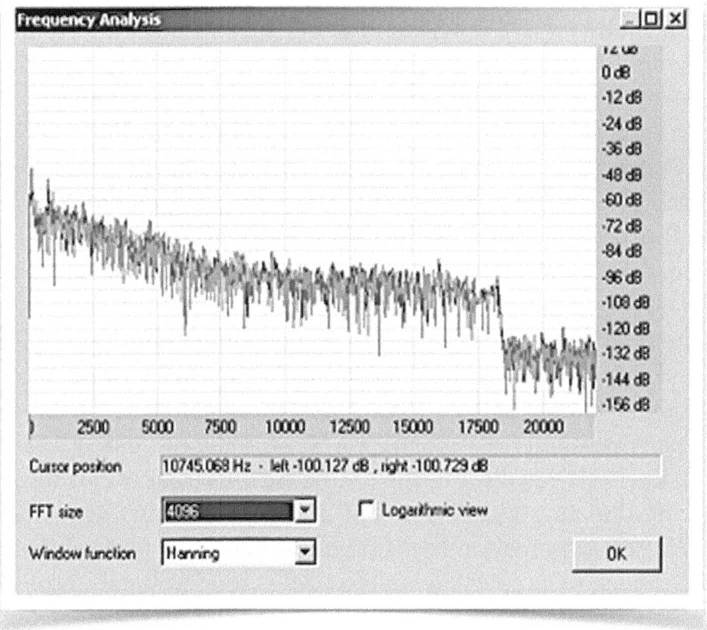

Compression removes frequencies outside the audible range (mp.3 spectrogram)

16-bit audio. Minidisc recorders are capable of surpassing the recording quality of many more recent digital recorders. They have the advantage of being small and portable and the discs can be reused many times without degradation. Another early type of digital audio recorder is the Digital Audio Tape or DAT recorder, which uses digital recording techniques and utilises a small form cassette tape. DAT recorders have now been largely replaced by solid state recorders and the use of a tape recording medium does mean that for the highest quality recording to be obtained, each tape can only be used a couple of times and must be properly erased between each use. DAT recorders also have a limited lifespan before the recording heads need to be replaced.

Sound Analysis

Beyond simple listening there is a great deal of other information that can be obtained from recorded sounds, but this requires both knowledge and understanding of the nature of sound and also the way in which the sound information can be examined. Sound rarely consists of a single pure tone or note, but instead takes the form of a complexity of different frequencies, amplitudes, and phases. One technique that is used to obtain information about the recorded sound is frequency analysis. The primary means of obtaining frequency information is by use of the Fourier transform method, devised in the 1820's by Mathematician Jean-Baptiste (Joseph) Fourier. There are a number of derivations of the Fourier transform but the most commonly encountered is probably the Fast Fourier Transform or FFT. As the name suggests, this is just a fast way of carrying out a Fourier transform. Fourier transforms take the recording and express it in terms of the different frequencies that make up the recording. Fourier analysis provides a great deal of information about the frequencies and the amplitudes of the different frequencies and the information is normally presented in a visual form known as a spectrogram with the various frequencies separated out along the horizontal (x) axis of a graph and their various amplitudes shown as points on the vertical (y) axis. This technique is generally referred to as spectral analysis. Most modern analysis of sound is carried out using computer software in the form of a spectrograph, which performs a series of spectral analyses continuously and displays them using a three-dimensional display of frequency, amplitude, and time. This should not be confused with the more simple representation of the amplitude of a recording being represented instantaneously or over time as is used in oscilloscope for instance. With the advent of powerful modern computers, it is now possible to perform Fourier transform analysis using personal computers or even handheld devices. Many sound editing programmes also include the capability to examine a recording as a spectrogram. Analysis may take the form of a mathematical comparison between the recorded sound and a known reference sound, or it might simply be used to separate out frequencies of particular interest within the recording. Filters may be applied to the recorded sound in order to block or permit specific frequencies. A Low Pass (LP) filter, for instance, will permit only those frequencies below a specified frequency to be passed; frequencies above this specified point are blocked. A High Pass (HP) operates by only allowing those frequencies that lie above a specified frequency to pass whilst blocking all those that lie below. Band Pass filters specify both the upper and lower frequency limits and permit only those sounds that lie within the specified limits to pass unaltered. Filters may be progressive in their action and can progressively attenuate frequencies that lie outside the specified range rather than simply blocking them entirely. Gain or amplification may also be applied to the whole recording or selectively to specific frequencies; this has the effect of increasing or reducing the amplitude of the recording wherever it is applied. Within any sound analysis or sound editing programme there is usually a large range of filters that are offered, many of which are just variations of these basic filter parameters. For example, noise reduction filters may, depending upon the complexity of the software algorithm used, either simply remove all those frequencies where the majority of the signal noise exists, or it may sample the recording to determine those frequencies which are more likely to contain noise and attenuate them, whilst at the same time increase the amplitude of those frequencies that lie within the range of speech or music. Any changes that are applied to the recording in the form of filters or adjustments to the amplitude will have the effect of altering the recording permanently unless one is working from a copy. Any alteration to the recording will inevitably change the way it sounds when played back and appears when the spectrogram is viewed. These changes can sometimes radically change the way a recording is interpreted and may lead to mistakes being made in the analysis of what the recording actually represents. Just as it is a simple matter to alter a photograph, change colours or add and remove components within photo-editing software, so it is an easy matter to do the same with a recording either intentionally or unintentionally. Such actions (intended or unintended) may be undertaken to support the case for a recorded sound being anomalous or may be used to misrepresent a sound recording and present it as being anomalous, as in a hoax for example.

Another method of analysing sound is by the process of listening to the recording with or without any adjustments being made to the amplitude or frequencies. Listening to a sound may allow comparisons to be made between the recorded audio and the sound that was heard and reported at the time the sonic event occurred. This can be used to verify that such an event actually took place but it may be less reliable in determining that the two events are actually the same. As stated, listening (hearing) involves many steps and is more fully considered within the chapter dealing with the Psychology of Sound.

Either the sound recording equipment or the method of its use can lead to errors in interpreting the recorded sounds. Some years ago I was re-playing a tape recording from an investigation and was surprised to discover what sounded like heavy footsteps rapidly descending a bare wooden staircase. The portable cassette recorder had been located on the 2nd step from the bottom and had been left unattended for a period of about 40 minutes. The recorder was an expensive model with a high quality microphone built-in. The footsteps certainly sounded convincing as they seemingly rushed headlong down the stairs, the sound getting louder as it neared the recorder. More than a little intrigued, I checked through the notes of nearby investigation team members and found that two of the team located at the head of the staircase had reported nothing untoward at that time, yet the sound was clearly loud and I was surprised that they had not heard anything. At that time there was nobody on the lower floor, but there was a video camera located near to the bottom of the stairs with a good view of the entire staircase. Upon examining the footage, I saw immediately the cause of the phantom footsteps. One of the investigators at the top of the stairs had dropped his pen, which had bounced down the entire flight. This small plastic pen had been the cause of the loud footsteps. The reason was the recorder had been placed on the bare, hard surface of the step, and the sound of the pen as it bounced its way down had been picked up by the internal microphone as a series of vibrations through the body of the recorder and rendered as a series of loud rhythmic thuds which I had subjectively concluded were footsteps. Without saying anything about the actual cause, I later played the tape to several others who all reached the same conclusion – what sounded like footsteps, must have been footsteps!

This was an important lesson and a timely reminder of the way that a recorder fitted with an internal microphone picks up sounds, both from sound waves travelling through the air and also through the body of the device. Our method of using these recorders was quickly altered and we simply placed them onto a bath sponge as a cheap and simple means of removing at least some of the problems of body-induced vibrations. I also learned a valuable lesson about the way in which sounds are interpreted. The recorder was on a staircase, so I made the assumption that any sounds that resembled footsteps were most likely footsteps. The team member who dropped the pen didn't make note of the loss because he didn't consider it noteworthy and, as he was carrying a spare pen, he just continued with his work. Afterwards, we made some changes to our note writing protocols too!

Sound analysis, as a means of extracting information by examining its frequency and amplitude, was not available to Price or other early psychical researchers, the technology only becoming available during the 1940's with the advent of the personal computer. True sound analysis is the domain of the professional audio forensic analyst such as those employed in air accident investigations in which the sounds on the Cockpit Voice Recorder (CVR) may be used to glean many details about the operation or malfunction of the aircraft – the engine sounds and cockpit alarms being an example, together with the conversations of the crew. Such analysis is a highly skilled art and even then can still be somewhat imprecise.

It largely remains the case to this day that few investigators undertake little more than the most basic analysis of their audio recordings; no doubt this is in no small part due to the complexity of the task and the general lack of specific expertise that is required. Some investigators claim that they have undertaken such analysis and that their work demonstrates conclusively the paranormality of the sounds they have recorded, but unfortunately this is rarely actually the case. When questioned regarding their techniques and protocols, they all too often resort to vague responses such as "we handed the recording to an (unnamed) expert" or reveal that the analysis involved little more than adjusting the noise and gain settings within the sound editing software and listening to the results.

THE PSYCHOLOGY OF SOUND

Callum E. Cooper

For humans, in particular, sound and sight are our most prominent senses for surviving in the world. From the recognition of someone's voice, to sounds of danger, and enjoyable rhythmic music, it is a pretty difficult task for the brain to consciously ignore the sounds we hear around us, and practically impossible for the brain to stop the unconscious processing of sound. We need sound for communication through speech, either in person or on the telephone, and even for entertainment through music, radio, cinema, and television. All of these forms of 'sound-waves' are received by our ears and then processed into meaningful information by the brain. But *how* and *why* does this happen? How and why does sound interact and influence us in our everyday lives? Let us briefly consider the processes involved and the impact sound has on the mind.

Auditory Perception – How We Process Sound

The phenomenon of sound splits into two distinguishing features which we perceive as *tones* and *noises*. We distinguish sounds by pitch and understand words by letters. Tones and music tend to please us, while noise generally displeases us. All of these forms of sound are created by changes in air pressure; in the case of speech, this is achieved when air from the lungs passes through the muscles in the throat thereby stretching the *vocal cords* which vibrate. The air is then forced through a narrow slit called the *glottis*, as we change the structure of our mouth, tongue, and lips, thereby producing various words and sounds. A healthy person uses around seventy-two different muscles in order to produce speech.

With sounds such as a musical tone or a soft to loud noise, these changes in air pressure form the production of waves, which are created through the influence of one object on another. For example, when pots and pans crash against the floor when dropped, this creates sound waves primarily through the structural vibrations of the fallen objects. When we pluck a guitar string, the string vibrates when the string is released, thus causing micro vibrations within the string. Sounds are created from the force of one object (i.e. the solid floor against the pans, or a finger plucking the guitar string) being applied on another object. The vibrations expand and travel as sound waves which reach the human ear where processing begins. However, the further the sound waves travel, the weaker they generally become, thus the sound is often stronger and clearer at the source. The frequency, or rate of vibration, can be interpreted by the human brain so long as those waves fall within the range of 20-20,000 hertz (1 Hz = 1 cycle per second). Frequencies outside of this range are not heard by humans, but can be heard by some animals. Those waves too low to be heard are known as infrasound, and those too high are known as ultrasound, and although we may not be able to hear these sound waves, they can still have an evident impact on the body, given that we're still *exposed* to sounds that we can't hear.

Every person's perception of sound is different depending on the health of the individual ear. We *listen* with the ear but *hear* with the brain, and it is the brain's task to make sense of the information that sound brings. Therefore, the ear merely acts as a microphone in the receiving of sound waves. The sound waves we receive follow a particular path to be processed by the brain which is as follows:

Fig. 1: The process of sound perception

As the sound is processed by the brain, our memory then steps in and recalls past experiences of various sounds. These sounds are then perceived either negatively or positively, depending on past experiences of that sound. It may frighten us, or sooth and comfort us, or it may even be mundane and neutral to us. It could be rhythmic and addictive, depending on our individual connection with rhythm and music and the structure of musical acoustics. A powerful aspect of sound is its instant ability to tap deep into our unconscious and produce memory recall. Sounds and songs can recover memories from decades ago in our personal lives, all the way back to childhood memories. It can remind us of various times and experiences and make us think of people we've known in our lives at some point. Sounds can even be hypnotic and induce in us a meditative state in which our mind allows us to let go of reality and experience an altered state of bliss, harmony, and relaxation. Taking all of this into account, how we recognise and perceive sound depends on individual experience and memory and therefore can be highly individualistic, which explains why we all have different tastes in music.

Thus a particular form of sound that most of us can relate to is that of music and harmonics. Music is all about the pitch of a note on a musical scale, in other words, a series of notes of 'definite and different frequencies'. The sensation that a pitch produces for the mind and body depends on the frequency with which the impulses of sound waves succeed one another at the point of reaching the ear. Frequency is the objective rate of the vibrations and sound being produced (e.g. the speed at which a drum is hit), while pitch is a subjective sensation determined by the brain, with the listener identifying the note as high or low (this variation would depend on how hard or softly we beat the drum). It is possible for two notes of slightly different frequencies to have practically the same pitch since it is subjectively determined.

Music comes in various forms and genres as we all have individual taste as to what particular type of music and sound pleases us. For example, music can make us happy, relaxed, or can even promote an energy that makes us want to dance. Rao (1918/2008, p. 50) stated the following with regards to the psychology of music:

> Music stimulates the nerves of a person very mildly and regulates the flow of blood. It creates a power of concentration in the mind, and spreads an agreeable massive sensation all over the body. The person feels, under the influence of music, disposed to receive impressions from outside. It tills his frame and furrows it, and renders it fertile for the reception and growth of ideas.

This description of music and its influence describes an altered state of consciousness that music and sound can induce – opening the mind to ideas and mental imagery by focusing more clearly than normal on our thoughts. This is why harmonic sounds are often used to help induce meditative states. Visit any spa, for example, and you will often hear gentle harmonic sounds being played by the pool, in the steam rooms, and other relaxation areas. These tunes normally involve windpipes, chanting of various forms, string instruments such as harps, and are sometimes accompanied by the sounds of running water. Jonathan Goldman refers to harmonics as *healing sounds*, which indeed allow us to enter a calm and relaxed state. So much so that harmonics have a strong relationship with altered states of consciousness which are found to be psychically conducive (often termed as psi conducive states).

With sounds that we can hear clearly, such as harmonics, they have demonstrated psychological healing properties, by assisting us to relax and in turn regulate blood flow. Sounds that fall outside of the range that we can hear have also demonstrated healing properties. For example, ultrasound has been used to treat muscular sprains and other injuries, accelerating healing within the body. On the other hand, sound can also be used to cause harm in extreme cases. For example, in policing and the armed forces, sonic and ultrasonic weapons (USW), such as the Long Range Acoustic Device (LRAD), have been used in crowd controlling situations. This use of sound waves has the ability to injure, incapacitate, and even kill, when focused on particular people in groups and crowds.

Though we may use music in a number of social situations, from parties and weddings, to various ceremonies and funerals, it is clear that sounds have varying influences on us, making us happy, sad, and inducing various forms of motivation and emotion. They may excite us, scare us, or make us relaxed and become deep in thought. Sound can also affect our bodies in various ways, either when it is unconsciously processed, or when we are exposed to infrasound and ultrasound, which in turn alters our perception to varying degrees. So what links does the psychology of sound have to parapsychological experiences?

Sound and Parapsychology

As described at the beginning of this chapter, when we are exposed to music and certain sounds, there is a large shift in our state of mind

– our awareness. It impacts on memory, emotion, mood, and motivation and helps us to see and interact with the world in different ways. Hence harmonics and the relaxing feelings produced by the exposure to such sounds allows us to focus our thoughts inwards, perhaps even allowing us to see what may be psychic impressions received by our minds on a daily basis but which are never clear enough to consciously reach the surface of our awareness.

Psychic experiences and impressions are often spontaneous but when our thoughts are altered in some way, especially by sound, such experiences and impressions can be induced. For example, in an experiment known as the *ganzfeld* (often credited to Charles Honorton for its introduction to parapsychology in the mid-1970s), participants are placed in a state of sensory deprivation. The experiment involves sitting back in a large comfy reclining chair wearing eye shields (halved ping-pong balls). A red light is shone onto the face, producing a warm pink haze to the participant's vision under the shields. Headphones are worn continuously playing pink noise (this is often termed as white noise – static – but in the case of the ganzfeld, this static contains a slightly reduced hiss to make the sound comfortable to listen to). In listening to the static, water is normally the first *interpretation* of the

Fig. 2: The ganzfeld, inducing sensory deprivation
(photograph: Callum E. Cooper)

sound that jumps into the mind of the participant, as it is easily related to the sound of fast flowing water. But continuous exposure to the sound allows the participant to tap further into their mind and think beyond the sound they are hearing, which then allows the participant's thoughts to perhaps unlock information from the unconscious. In doing so, and from the vast majority of findings in ganzfeld studies, sensory deprivation appears to allow potential psychic impressions of the mind to become more evident thereby facilitating conscious exploration. In other words, psychic impressions are to some extent temporarily controlled in the form of daydream like imagery and sounds.

The ganzfeld is just one instance where sound has some form of connection with altered states of consciousness and psychic phenomena. But, what about the séance room? What about hearing footsteps going up the stairs in a reputedly haunted location, and what about poltergeist raps? What causes these phenomena? Are they natural sounds of the environment misinterpreted by us, often quite innocently, as communication from the dead? Or is it indeed, the surviving consciousness of deceased people trying to communicate? There is no certain answer within science at present or a universal theory to explain all such phenomena. However, in one particular case of a séance device created in the 1940s to allegedly contact the dead (recently investigated by the editors of this book), it appears the mystery of its mechanisms and effect on people was solved – regarding its unique use of sound!

A piece of machinery named the Scammell device had been sitting in the office of the Society for Psychical Research in London for a number of years and was donated by the Scammell family. I had been made aware of it by the SPR secretary, Peter Johnson, as he understood my interest in researching electronic communication with the dead. I was given permission to take the device away with me and shed some light on what it was, and how it worked. This required Steve Parsons' input on electronics. There was no escaping the psychology and physics of sound with this device given that one of its main components was a large speaker fixed to the lid of the device (see figure 3 below).

After some re-wiring and the initial firing up of the machine (quite literally, as it produced smoke from a combination of hot vacuum tubes and bee's wax being melted by them from the wooden panels), it was clearly capable of producing a variety of humming noises when the dials on the front of the device were altered. Its components are effectively different radio parts of the late 1930s to early 1940s, and yet it is

Fig. 3: The Scammell Device (photograph Steven Parsons)

incapable of picking up radio-waves without additional components. Effectively, it is assumed that the original sitters of any séance where the device was used were to act as the aerial, in receiving messages from their deceased loved ones from the astral plane. This astral plane of existence for consciousness beyond death has been described by several early Spiritualists and psychical researchers (such as Hudson Tuttle, Sir Arthur Conan Doyle, and Professor Robert Hare) as being somewhat like that of radio-waves.

When the device was left on, it produced such a repetitive tone that for some people it appeared to induce discomfort (in the form of headaches). Steve Parsons worked further on the device, investigating its circuitry and operation. In listening to some of the varieties of tones that the device was able to produce, he noticed that in listening to a single frequency for around 5-10 minutes, the device appeared to have the potential to create a tinnitus effect. With that, sitters would experience the fluctuation of sound waves (i.e., audible humming) and become accustomed to the sound as a dull hissing/ringing in their ears. In turn, when a sitter reported hearing a name and asked out for it (e.g. "did anyone just hear the name Sarah?"), group conformity, suggestion, and especially the tinnitus effect, would contribute to making this experience very real.

Picture the scene of this particular séance. The sitters would be sat in a semi-lit room, the curtains closed, doors and windows shut. The device is turned on and the sitters are informed that the Scammell device has the ability to contact their deceased relatives. The sound waves produced by the device are effectively trapped within the closed room. The sound waves are projected from the lid speaker, reach the walls, and return to the sitters, much like ripples of water in a bath. Once they reach the edge, they have nowhere else to go but to return and repeat. The sitters are therefore continually exposed to this and, as a result, their own sense of hearing becomes distorted by the sound waves that are produced and subsequently mixed with the various other suggestions the séance room may bring. In this case, it appears an impressive use of sound was responsible for producing what seemed to be contact with the dead. From our investigation, at least, it was the likeliest explanation, although perhaps not the only explanation.

Summary

This brief chapter has presented a few examples of how sound and psychology interrelate and how sound plays a large part in our perception and understanding of the world around us. To understand the vast complexities of sound and its link to paranormal experiences, and to answer some of the questions raised here, the chapters throughout this book will focus on various prominent aspects of sound and how it has been the focus of numerous paranormal events. In some instances, some natural environmental aspects of sound might confuse our senses and lead us to interpret something as being paranormal. However, in other instances, sound appears to be produced via some form of anomalous process leaving us void of any psychological or physical explanation for its production. All such phenomena within this book have, to date, been researched as far as possible and continued research will produce new findings. Therefore, beyond the conclusions of the researchers/authors of each chapter, it is down to 'you', the readers of this book, to make reasonable and educated conclusions as to whether the answer to such sounds and experiences lie within psychology or parapsychology.

SOME NOISY GHOSTS

Steven Parsons

Ghosts are not a silent phenomenon. Haunted houses are the domain of many sounds, some real, some imagined, and many are explainable in terms of natural and normal occurrences such as the creaking of settling floorboards, or the rattling of windows on a windy night. Although there are some who would argue differently, the history of ghost hunting and psychical research is replete with sounds that seemingly defy explanation. In the introduction to this book, mention was made of one of the earliest written accounts of a haunted house in 1st century BC Athens, an account of a particularly noisy phantom that rattled it's chains with increasing frustration in an attempt to be acknowledged. However, the history of ghosts and hauntings has numerous other examples of noisy phantoms that are worth considering.

In 1661, incessant drumming together with disembodied voices, plagued the home of John Mompesson, along with animal sounds. The sounds formed a significant part of the haunting, which included a ghostly figure, terrible smells, objects moving, and the levitation from their beds of Mompesson's children. Joseph Glanvill, a member of the clergy and a Fellow of the Royal Society, investigated the case and wrote about it in his book *Sadiucismus Triumphatus or, Full and plain evidence concerning witches and apparitions. In two parts. The first treating of their possibility. The second of their real existence.* Published in 1681, the book is a complete account of the haunting. Glanvill, claimed to have heard several of the noises for himself, including being present when the entity spoke for the first time. This case has been cited in many works on ghosts and haunted homes and is well known throughout psychical research as The Drummer of Tedworth.

Seemingly, the affair began when Mompesson, a landowner and magistrate, brought a lawsuit against an itinerant drummer for extorting monies. Upon winning the case the drum was confiscated, whereupon the drumming and the other phenomena commenced. Sometime later, the drummer apparently confessed to summoning the drumming entity by using witchcraft, a crime for which he was tried and convicted. A Royal Commission was established to examine the case but they failed to witness any of the disturbances for themselves and there are many, both contemporary and modern, who consider the case to be either a hoax brought about by Mompesson, confederates of the drummer, or both, although why Mompesson would seek out such notoriety by being party to this is quite another question.

The noted antiquary and Fellow of The Royal Society, John Aubrey included a number of brief accounts of knockings that he related to the world of spirits in his book *Miscellanies Upon Various Subjects* published in 1697. He also gave similarly brief accounts of voices and sounds that had been reported to him.

The Scots journalist Charles Mackay, writing in 1841, considered another well-known noisy spirit to be "an absurdity". In his book *Extraordinary Popular Delusions and the Madness of Crowds* the author gives an account of the Cock Lane ghost which was the topic of much conversation in 18th century London. In 1760, number 33 Cock Lane was the home of Richard Parsons and his family. It was also the lodging of William Kent and his lover Frances (Fanny), the sister of Kent's wife who had died in childbirth. While Kent was absent on business, Fanny reported hearing strange noises and the sighting of a ghostly figure. The noises were at first attributed to a cobbler working next door, although this was soon discounted. Shortly afterwards Fanny died after contracting smallpox. In 1762, the ghost of Fanny commenced haunting Cock Lane, announcing her presence by a series of knocks and scratching sounds. Shortly thereafter, word of the ghost spread and nightly crowds would gather to witness the phenomena for themselves. The ghost seemed to perform only in the presence of Parsons' daughter Elizabeth and would, by a series of knocks and raps, answer questions put to it by the family maid Mary Frazer. A simple code was established whereby one knock was given to signify 'yes' and two knocks for 'no'. Amongst the nightly chaos, a local clergyman assembled a group of people which included Dr Samuel Johnson who was intent on testing the case along with the claims by Fanny that she had been murdered by William Kent. The ghost continued to accuse Kent who was forced to endure the accusations of the ghost and the crowd without legal redress. Various methods to prevent fraud were tried including suspending Elizabeth in a hammock with her hands and feet extended and, indeed, the sounds ceased. The investigators suspected the child was producing the sounds and threatened both Parsons and his daughter with imprisonment should the ghostly knocks and scratches not re-occur. Elizabeth apparently made an attempt to conceal a small wooden board and used it to make noises in response to the enquiring group. Her attempt to conceal the board and to replicate the sounds produced by the ghost both failed. Parsons, the maid, and several others were eventually tried and jailed for conspiracy. Modern psychical researchers might do well to question the conclusion reached by their 18th century counterparts, indeed the case has been the subject of debate for the past 250 years. In *Cock Lane and Common-Sense (1894),* the folklorist Andrew Lang notes that the noises began before Fanny's death and that the child was driven by threats in her attempt to reproduce the knocks, the sounds of which she herself and others stated were completely unlike those produced by the ghost. Lang also noted the inadequacy of the séance, which lasted little more than an hour. The case is perhaps noteworthy for the use of a coded series of knocks in order to elicit answers, a method still favoured by some spiritists and one that is usually attributed to the Fox sisters in Hydesville, New York State, in 1848 and a case that led to the birth of the Spiritualist movement. In fact, neither case can claim the distinction of being the first to establish communication with ghosts or spirits by using a sound code. Who was the first remains in doubt, but Jacob Grimm records a case in his book *Deutsche Mythologie (1835)* that occurred in 858 in which a spirit uses rapping communication in a similar fashion and there are several other earlier cases of responsive sounds in the records of psychical research and folklore.

Both of the foregoing examples of noisy ghosts will be recognised as having many of the features of what is now termed a poltergeist. Appropriately named, a poltergeist derives its name from the German for 'noisy ghost'. Poltergeist cases are characterised by their disruptive nature with frequent sounds. Banging, loud percussive knocks, scratching sounds and, in some instances, vocalisations, are all elements of the poltergeist. So too is their association with children, disturbed and highly stressed individuals, and situations. The great psychical investigator Harry Price described the poltergeist as an, "Alleged ghost, elemental, entity, agency, secondary personality, intelligence, power, spirit, imp or familiar, with certain unpleasant characteristics".

His 1945 book *Poltergeist Over England* is an account of more than three centuries of such cases. It is clear from Price's own introduction to the subject that poltergeists are extremely difficult to characterise in terms of their cause and nature, a question we do not need to consider here. What is apparent is that, almost without exception, such cases feature numerous and wide-ranging sound phenomena associated with them. However, sounds are not restricted to poltergeist cases and it may be misleading to try and classify cases in which sound is a prominent feature into a separate category. In 1572, in his book *Of Ghostes and Spirites Walking by Nyght*, Lewes Lavater provides examples of the range of sounds that are encountered, "There are those who heare the dores and windows open and shut, that some thing runneth up the stairs or walketh up and downe the house or doth someone or other such like thing".

Lavater also cautions that many of these sounds are natural and are not to be taken as ghosts, citing examples such as the crying of rats or other beasts, or the knocking of trees against walls.

Sound associated with haunting may appear to emanate from outside or inside. In Hampton Court Palace, the screams of Queen Katherine Howard's ghost are said be heard, together with the sounds of her running footsteps in the corridor that led to King Henry the Eighth's private chapel, re-enacting an event supposed to have taken place immediately prior to her execution for treason and adultery. Other sounds associated with a haunting are less dramatic but no less interesting. In *Ghosts Vivisected (1957)*, Anna Stirling describes a firsthand account given to her by her cousins of an event that took place during the Second World War in a large country house:

> Twelve hours later, at 1a.m. in the stillness of the quiet country night, Mr and Mrs M. were both roused from sleep by hearing what sounded like a ponderous van drive up to the front door. To their further amazement they heard what sounded like a party of men enter the house and begin noisy operations down below. In the reception room where the crates were stacked they heard these being dragged across the floor, banged about, apparently during efforts at removal, and even dropped occasionally with a resounding thud owing to their unexpected weight.

Being alone, Mr and Mrs M decided it was unwise to investigate further and continued to listen to the commotion. After a time they heard the van depart and ventured downstairs and were amazed to discover that the room was completely undisturbed and that the front door remained locked and barred from the inside. Near to Clouds Hill in Dorset local people have reported the ghostly sounds of a powerful motorcycle. The location is close to the spot where T. E. Lawrence, better known as Lawrence of Arabia, was killed in 1935 in a fatal accident whilst riding his Brough Superior motorcycle. The sound ceasing before anything is seen.

I could continue to give examples of ghostly sounds almost ad-infinitum, but it would serve little purpose except to perhaps illustrate the sheer number of ghost cases in which sound is a key component of the witness's experience. Pick up any book about ghosts and hauntings and you will soon see that sound is perhaps more frequently reported than any apparition or other sensory anomaly. I myself have heard sounds where no cause was apparent both whilst alone and in the presence of others, some of these sounds where coincident along with a visual experience such as that which took place during a day visit to a haunted Welsh manor house. On that occasion, my companion and myself (herself a highly experienced investigator) both heard the distinct sound of footsteps walking across a room above us which we knew, with certainty, was empty. As we both looked up the stairs toward the empty room, we briefly glanced the lower part and legs of a person. Quickly we ascended the short flight of stairs and without much surprise discovered the room was empty and, unless someone had leapt out of a window and 40 feet to the ground below, had been empty throughout our brief encounter. Not a word had passed between us and, before we spoke of the incident, we both made some hasty notes which showed that we had shared a common experience of both the sound and the apparition.

Most accounts of ghostly sounds go no further than simply reporting the event, describing the sounds, and likening them to other sound events as the witness seeks to make sense of their experience. This can lead to descriptions that might be more or less accurate but often the description is highly coloured by the witness with respect to any belief, expectation, or prior knowledge they may have. In some instances this can result in some unusual analogies being given. In a case of a haunting I was personally involved with, one of the investigation team noted that periodically they could hear a sound "Like someone dragging a heavy body across the floor above them". I asked if they had ever heard a heavy body being dragged across wooden floorboards, to which they replied 'No". Their analogy was merely an attempt to portray what they had heard. No murder had ever taken place in that location as far as we were aware and the sound was afterwards traced to the emptying of a water sluice located on an outside wall. Without investigation, the sound might have been simply documented and reported as the witness had subjectively perceived it. The question of whether a sound actually occurred, or the witness simply imagined it in order to supplement another experience such as a visual event, is a question that can be readily answered by the use of recording apparatus. What the recorded sound might actually be is entirely another question however.

Before the later years of the 19th century, investigators were entirely reliant upon the witness's descriptions of what they had heard and the accuracy of how they described the experience. It was not possible to do anything other than accept what they were told and what others claimed to have heard, they had no ability to record the sounds. The phonograph, invented by Thomas Edison in 1877 changed that situation. It used two needles, one for recording and another for playback. The sound was recorded as grooves indented onto a tinfoil-covered cylinder. In the introduction to this book the case of B- House was mentioned. This case was perhaps the first suggested attempt to record sound within a haunted location for the purpose of aiding the investigation. Ultimately, due to legal wrangles, a phonograph was never used in this case, but it could have been an early guide to those who followed and sought out explanations for ghostly sounds. Had the investigators been able to record the sounds, they would no doubt be hard pressed to have obtained sufficient recording cylinders given the extensive number of sound events contained within their journal covering the period between February and May 1897. The list, which is included in the book *The Alleged Haunting of B – House (1898)*, fills almost 6 pages and includes a wide range of different sounds. Some were heard only by a single witness and some by multiple witnesses. The sounds included loud percussive bangs or explosions, voices as if in conversation, footsteps, groans, blows to doors and walls, the clanging of metal, heavy objects falling, and even the sound of cannon being fired. More than thirty people claimed to have heard this range of sounds over the four-month period. The group kept a detailed journal of their experiences and throughout it they note many of the sounds in detail:

> February 4th, Thursday: I awoke suddenly, just before 3 a.m. Miss Moore, who had been lying awake over two hours, said, "I want you

to stay awake and listen." Almost immediately I was startled by a loud clanging sound, which seemed to resound through the house. The mental image it brought to my mind was as of a long metal bar; such as I have seen near iron foundries, being struck at intervals with a wooden mallet. The noise was distinctly as of metal struck with wood; it seemed to come diagonally across the house. It sounded so loud, though distant, that the idea that any inmate of the house should not hear it seemed ludicrous. It was repeated with varying degrees of intensity at frequent intervals during the next two hours, sometimes in single blows, sometimes double, sometimes treble, latterly continuous. We did not get up, though not alarmed. We had been very seriously cautioned as to the possibilities of practical joking; and as we were alone on that floor in a large house, of which we did not even know the geography, we thought it wiser to await developments. We knew the servants' staircase was distant, though not exactly where.

About 4.30 we heard voices, apparently in the maid's room, undoubtedly on the same floor. We had for some time heard the housemaids overhead coughing, occasionally speaking, and we thought they had got up and had come down to her room.

February 18th, Thursday: This morning's phenomenon is the most incomprehensible I have yet known. I heard the banging sounds after we were in bed last night. Early this morning, about 5.30, I was awakened by them. They continued for nearly an hour. Then another sound began in the room. It might have been made by a very lively kitten jumping and pouncing, or even by a very large bird; there was a fluttering noise too. It was close, exactly opposite the bed. Miss Moore woke up, and we heard it going on till nearly eight o'clock. I drew up the blinds and opened the window wide. I sought all over the room, looking into cupboards and under furniture. We cannot guess at any possible explanation. Further experience of these curious hallucinatory sounds, combined with visual hallucination in the same room, taking also into consideration the interest which our own dogs always displayed in these phenomena, led us to the conclusion that our first deductions had been wrong, and that the sounds were those of a dog gambolling.

Even following the invention of sound recording equipment, investigators of haunted houses seemed to have largely missed the opportunity to document the sound occurrences by using equipment that, at the very least, would have been capable of demonstrating that many sounds reported by a witness were not the result of some auditory hallucination on their part. A sound recorder lacks any ability to hallucinate, it simply records sound as it is picked up via the microphone, and if a real sound takes place with sufficient volume and frequency to be heard, then it is reasonable to presume that a suitable recorder placed nearby should be capable of recording that sound. Harry Price certainly used audio recording equipment in his various experiments with mediums, but he failed to use the same equipment to record the many sound events that were reported by the numerous witnesses over an almost 20 year investigation of Borley Rectory. Price himself reported hearing footsteps and other apparently anomalous sounds but it never seemed to occur to him that he might record them. Perhaps his decision was based upon practical constraints, the equipment was complex and the process was difficult, even in the confines of a laboratory or studio. Perhaps Price realised that, apart from confirming that a sound actually occurred, a recording might add little to the overall investigation. After all, the sounds of footsteps are just that; there is no information within the recording about who or what made them.

Sound recording apparatus was used throughout the Enfield poltergeist case. The location for this extraordinary case was a council house in the London suburb of Enfield. One of the leading investigators, Guy Lyon Playfair, later wrote an account of the complete investigation in *This House is Haunted (1980).*

The ordinary and unassuming house was home to a single mother and her four children, the eldest thirteen, and the youngest seven. Events began in August 1977, sounds being the almost obligatory opening salvo of phenomena associated with this type of haunting. At first it was just a shuffling, like someone moving across the floor wearing slippers, which was soon followed by a series of loud knocks. Investigators from the Society for Psychical Research soon picked up the case and, almost from the outset, used tape recorders to document the sounds and also the voice, which was seemingly being produced by the entity. The voice followed on from a series of communications using the time-acknowledged systems of coded knocks or raps in response to questions put to the entity by the investigators. Sometime later, sounds described as "whistling and barking" began to be heard coming from the direction of the eleven year old girl. Initially the investigators were unimpressed and considered it possible that the child was in some manner responsible, despite her assurances she was not. The investigators, decided to challenge the entity to speak. It did, and over the coming days and weeks the voice could be clearly heard by the investigators responding to their questions, sometimes helpful, often abusive, and for much of the time recorded by the investigators. It seemed to be a male voice and quite unlike that which the investigators expected a young girl to be able to produce. The voice and the other noises continued. The investigators were hampered in trying to understand where or by what means the voice was being produced as it would refuse to 'speak' whilst they were observing the girl. They did experiment to try and eliminate fraud such as ventriloquism or other tricks by having the girl drink water whilst they questioned the entity which subsequently responded, and getting the child to sing whilst persuading the entity to join in. In early 1978, the team brought in a professional speech therapist and took her to the house so that she might hear the voices for herself. After listening to the voice for around half an hour, and also conducting some simple tests on the girl, the therapist was asked for her conclusions:

> I can only say I don't know where the sound is coming from or how it is being sustained......As far as I am concerned, it's a sound. I wouldn't identify it as a voice, because when I say a voice, I'm thinking in terms of phonation created by the vocal cords and I can't identify this with that.

No further substantive work was done with the recordings of the voice, although the recordings remain archived. For those wishing to hear for themselves examples of the voice and several other of the recordings made during the Enfield investigation, a search using terms such as 'Enfield Poltergeist Sound Recording' will suffice. The recordings did however permit some interesting studies to be undertaken on the communicating knocks and raps. Dr Barrie Colvin carried out this work and is dealt with elsewhere in this book by Dr Colvin. In time, the incidents at Enfield subsided and finally ceased altogether in 1979.

In writing this chapter I am reminded of an intriguing personal experience in which sound featured prominently. At the time, we were conducting an investigation of a former school building at the invitation of staff working there. It had been converted into a series of units for small start-up business ventures and a majority of those working there had approached us with a view to trying to explain a number of their anomalous experiences. These included apparitions but also sounds and noises, such as the sound of a piano being played and also of children rushing about, shouting and playing. During one of our investigations, which spanned almost a year and comprised more than thirty visits to the location, we were joined by several of the people who worked in the building. Each of the visitors (four in all) was paired with an investigator to make up a team of two. In total, there were eight people on site that particular evening. After several hours, the notes and reports from several of the teams mentioned unusual sounds, described as musical, and like a piano playing. During the session that followed, additional audio recorders were placed on both the ground and first floor of the two storey building, together with the equipment already in use which comprised four video cameras (with sound) on each floor, and one stereo audio recorder (Minidisc) per floor. Following the reports of the musical sounds in the previous session, this was increased by one additional Minidisc recorder per floor. All the recorders were fitted with external stand mounted stereo microphones. As the session got underway, I began to play back one of the recordings from the earlier session to hear if anything had been recorded that substantiated the claims of the investigators and our guests. Throughout the session that followed, I was wearing headphones, concentrating on the task in hand. When the session ended forty minutes later and the teams returned, it was immediately apparent that something had transpired, although the investigators were prevented from talking openly about their experiences. A glance through the various notes revealed that every team had heard sounds they were reported as being 'the sounds of children at play', 'playground sounds', and 'children shouting and singing'. The tapes from all the devices, video and audio were immediately collected and fresh replacements installed whilst two of the investigators were dispatched immediately to conduct a search for radios or tape recorders that might be responsible for the sounds being produced. Many of the offices did indeed have radios, but all were found to be turned off and the thorough search revealed no tape recorders, hidden or otherwise, in the building except our own.

The night progressed without further reported incident. The following day, upon playing the sound from the audio recorders it was apparent that each machine had recorded the same sound event; the recorders were time coded so we could be certain that it was the same event. The event lasted almost ten minutes in total, the sound sometimes fading and growing in volume before finally it faded away completely. What was perhaps the most important discovery was that each sound recording was of the same general amplitude within a margin of 3dB. If we had been dealing with a hidden device this should not have happened as the sound recorders were positioned on two separate floors and spaced well apart toward either end of a very long corridor. At this point we examined the video camera footage and were surprised to discover that the stereo audio track of each of the eight machines also contained exactly the same sound event. The video cameras were placed well apart, again over the two floors and the stairwells. Again, the audio amplitude for the sound was very similar for each recording, which supported the information we had already from the audio recorders. One possibility we considered was a public address system, and that the sounds were being played from an undetected device being piped throughout the building. This was quickly discounted, as no such system existed in the building. The following night, and over several nights in the ensuing weeks, we tried every conceivable thing we could think of in order to replicate the sounds. The equipment in each case was placed exactly as on the night the anomaly was recorded. Investigators were positioned at various points inside and outside the building, they ran about, shouted, and generally did all they could to simulate the sound and it's very unusual property of being at same level regardless of which machine recorded it. In each of our attempts, it was very apparent from the amplitude of the recording if the source was nearer or further from the recorder or if it was coming from inside or outside the building. We failed miserably in all our attempts to replicate the sounds and were forced to conclude that we could also find no apparent cause or reason why the sounds had been recorded so uniformly. One other test we were able to carry out with the recordings involved examining them with a spectrum analyser. Our team does not have the luxury of having a forensic acoustic analyst but it was a straightforward matter to compare the frequency information on the recordings with information relating to frequency ranges of the human voice and we found that there was a very strong correlation between the sound frequencies on our recordings and those that might be expected to be produced by pre-teen children and young adolescents. The sounds were recorded on every item of recording equipment and were heard and reported in the notes by everyone who was present that night with one single exception – me!

I was happily sat wearing over-ear headphones and listening to a recording from the previous session. At least the musical sounds that had been recorded were quickly recognised as being a phone ring-tone coming from one of the offices. We have archived the recordings and an extract of the sound that was recorded that night has been placed online.

Modern investigators continue to record sound extensively as part of their investigations of haunted locations but predominantly their interest has changed in recent times from merely recording the sounds as a document of what transpired acoustically, to using sound recording apparatus in electronic voice (EVP) communication experiments. Such experiments are claimed to be producing interesting results that those same claims provide conclusive evidence for the existence of intelligent discarnate entities.

SOME NOISY SPIRITS

Callum E. Cooper

What are some of the first words you hear being asked at a séance or similar form of vigil? "If there is anyone there, please make a sound, a rap, or tap the table" or "please knock once for yes and twice for no". In this chapter we are particularly concerned with the activity of the séance room and phenomena which appears to centre around the sitters and Spiritualist mediums involved. The latter being a person who claims to be able to communicate with the dead and pass on messages from our deceased loved ones.

Mediumship typically splits into two distinct categories. Firstly, with mental mediumship, which may take the form of a medium speaking to the dead and passing on messages verbally to the living, or they enter some form of trance and take on the personality of the deceased, in which case, the deceased supposedly takes temporary control of the medium's body. Secondly, with physical mediumship, communication with the dead typically takes the form of the production of physical effects within the séance room. This is much like poltergeist activity but the medium has, it seems, some limited control of the phenomena. In other words, items begin to move around, sitters claim to be touched by unseen hands, responsive knocks and bangs are heard and, in rarer cases, ectoplasm is reported to be seen (this, purportedly being a smoke like substance which creates the physical form of spirits/ghosts and is popularly understood, though very rarely ever reported as a slimy substance). In his book *The Enigma of the Poltergeist*, Raymond Bayless describes the typical sounds of spirit raps as follows (p. 5):

> Rappings, poundings, and scratching are common effects of the poltergeist. The rappings can range from light tappings and creaks to

> violent blows that literally shake the house. During many cases, the rappings have answered questions, showing intelligence, but on the other hand, cases exist where houses have been subject to mysterious poundings and rappings which were apparently aimless in their nature.

To understand these *noisy spirits* further, let us delve back into the history of it all. The beginnings of Spiritualism tell us a lot about their involvement. In fact, noise appears to be the dominating feature of physical mediumship and the séance room. It was also the first thing noticed with the eminent Fox sisters. On 11 December 1847, John D. Fox, his wife and their daughters Margaret (aged 14) and Catherine (Kate, aged 12) set up home in a small wooden building in Hydesville, New York, (there was a third sister Leah, who at this point was married and living in a neighbouring town.) Their house had already gathered a reputation for being haunted. However, the case that sparked a large step forward in Spiritualism, and indeed psychical research, began in March 1848, when loud repeated banging sounds were heard on the walls and floor of the home. On 11 April, Mrs Fox reported that, on retiring to bed, the family once again heard the raps. The children tried to imitate the sound and responsive raps were received. The girls also discovered that the raps would produce other things on command, such as asking them to rap out numbers, and thus using a code they could also answer simple questions.

The Fox family were so convinced by the rapping noises that they called in neighbours to witness the sounds. They too heard the noises, and posed questions to the spirits. Their questions were answered, even with specific and private information. One witness, Chauncey P. Losey, believed that it wasn't possible for all of the raps to be caused by humans through trickery, given the specific questions which had been asked and answered.

The family were initially upset by the noises, and spent the night with the neighbours, all but Mr Fox, as he and Mr Redfield (one of the neighbours) stayed behind to question the raps further. In doing so, it appeared the spirit communicating was of Charles Rosma, a former salesman when alive, and had been murdered in the cottage and robbed by the former occupant named John Bell. A former maid of the Bells, Lucretia Pulver, came forward and verified the spiritual messages as she had heard similar sounds herself. John Bell denied the entire story and so the events were never confirmed. However, a newspaper article reported that a partial skeleton had been found in the cellar when an old wall had given way. But all of these events, like many initial claims through the Spiritualist movement, had very little corroborative evidence besides second-hand statements and word of mouth.

Maggie and Kate appeared to be the focus of the raps, as the activity would always appear centred around them. There has always been a massive amount of controversy as to whether the girls were creating the raps themselves through trickery and it has been noted that the girls became skilled at cracking their toes inside their shoes to produce "spirit noises" in response to questions. And yet, the rappings occurred both when they were home and when they were away. They were later joined by their older sister Leah, with all three of them preaching the new gospel of Spiritualism. They travelled the country giving demonstrations of the raps and discussing communication with the dead, renting halls in which to give these demonstrations. Although some hounded the commercial gain the sisters had achieved, others were paid to investigate their abilities during these events with little or no evidence for fraud.

These demonstrations carried on for years. Two of the sisters resorted to alcoholism. At one point when the family were apparently destitute, Maggie and Kate confessed to the newspapers that they created all of the noises themselves and demonstrated their ability of toe clicking. They reaped the financial rewards of making such a confession, but at the cost of destroying their reputation. Leah continued to give demonstrations, while Maggie and Kate attempted to retract their statements, but it was too late, the damage had been done and was irreversible. Even so, some witnesses came forward publicly and stated that the toe clicking demonstrated by the sisters held no resemblance to the raps *they had heard* during demonstrations/séances.

Whatever the cause of the spirit noises surrounding the Fox sisters, their reports of such activity and public demonstrations were an incredible driving force behind the Spiritualist movement. People became more open in discussing such matters, and engaging in séances themselves, particularly where families had lost loved ones in war and never had the chance to say goodbye. Equally, haunting type phenomena became more frequently reported and discussed. And so, the latter part of the 19th century saw the establishment of the Society for Psychical Research (1882, UK) and the American Society for Psychical Research (1884). Both organisations were formed of various eminent scholars who were interested in investigating the claims produced by Spiritualism, particularly concerned with such questions as "does personality persist after the physical body has died?" and if so, "is it this spiritual essence which is responsible for apparitions, mediumship, and responsive raps of the séance room?"

The Society for Psychical Research were (and are) certainly aware of the fraudulent and/or perfectly natural environmental factors that could be responsible for noisy spirits. In *Phantasms of the Living*, published in two volumes in 1886, the authors Edmund Gurney, Frederic Myers, and Frank Podmore stated that non-vocal noises and shocks of haunted houses or the séance room deserve "more jealous scrutiny, since odd noises are often due to undiscovered physical causes in the vicinity" adding that:

> Odd noises, especially at night, are very common phenomena; and though the particular cause of them is often hard to detect, the physical conditions of our indoor life are prolific of possible causes. Most of us are in constant proximity to wind that may blow through crevices, and rattle or flap or dislodge loose parts of our windows and walls and chimneys; and to water in pipes or cisterns that may leak, or burst, or may contain bubbling air; and to slates that may fall; and to wooden furniture and floors that may crack and creak. And if anyone should say that he has heard a noise which, from its nature or its position, could not be accounted for by any such ascertainable cause, he might be reminded that sounds are the hardest things in the world to localise; and that no one who has not given special attention to the subject can realise how easy it is to mistake the source and character of an auditory impression. (Gurney, Myers, & Podmore, 1918, pp. 434-444)

Thus, psychical researchers by no means have assumed instantly that the raps of the séance room must be caused by spirits of the dead, but they at least knew that they must have a cause, and many such researchers were, and still are, open to the possibility of the survival of personality beyond death if all conventional explanations can be reasonably assessed and ruled out. The main assumption at the time was that, in cases of haunted locations and séances where "non-vocal sound-phantasms" were encountered, consisting of noises and shocks, that perhaps such phenomena, being a subjective experience, is a telepathic phenomenon, if no conventional explanation applies. For example:

> There is no doubt that surprising noises and crashes, though often due to undiscovered external causes, are also a form of purely subjective

> hallucination – which make it at least probable, if telepathy be a reality, that they will be a form of telepathic hallucination. (ibid, p. 444)

This assumption on the nature of the sounds is completely dependent on the manner in which the sounds are experienced. For example, are these non-vocal sounds, raps and shocks occurring in a purportedly haunted location, and occurring without pattern or any recognisable intelligence? Or are they occurring within a séance setting? Were multiple people present who also need to be accounted for in terms of their experience and honesty? Were the sounds objective and able to be recorded? And were the sounds responsive, intelligent, and able to convey meaningful and specific information relating to the known dead? Let us explore such cases further.

Louis Henderson presents in his book *Strange Experiences*, the account of a trumpet séance which he was witness to in the mid-twentieth century. It was during this time that many mediums were beginning to use specialised tools in the séance room to establish communication with spirit. These séances were often conducted in semi-lit conditions, and the tools would include chalk slates, tables, cabinets, and trumpets. A trumpet séance involves the use of a horn-shaped speaking tube, which would typically be formed of several metal pieces. These trumpets are allegedly meant to magnify the faint voices of spirits, which are not normally audible to our hearing range. Typically, the trumpet may be placed on a table surrounded by a circle of sitters and therefore in full view of everyone, although this would depend on the lighting conditions used.

The séance took place at the London Spiritualist Mission, where Mr Henderson arrived at 3pm with a friend and colleague, Mr Alain Raffin, finding several other people their waiting to sit in on the séance. All were unknown to Henderson, apart from a Miss Crocker. In any séance or investigation of a purportedly haunted location, it is best to be acquainted with the people there. If they are known to you, to an extent you can vouch for their honesty, but if not known to you, they may be in on the act or an assistant to the medium – perhaps? This is an important question to critically consider. Even so, the medium arrived, of whom Henderson could not recall her name, but described her as a "stout lady, a little below medium height, and a most happy smile". Everyone became seated, curtains were drawn, lights were extinguished, and the long trumpet stood in the middle of the table. Short prayers were said, and the medium went into trance. As Henderson recounts:

> Several loud knocks were heard on the door and in various parts of the room. When the first distinct knock sounded, I automatically looked around. Miss Crocker smiled – I could faintly see her in the dim light, and then she explained to me 'They are Spirits who wish to make their presence known to us'. She turned slightly and added in a louder tone, 'God bless you, friends. Thank you for coming. We heard you clearly'. (Henderson, 1955, p. 105)

The knocks were repeated. Miss Crocker asked the spirits in gentle tones not to make a disturbance. Henderson reports that he then heard "deep breathing" coming from the medium and "strange noises", although exactly what the strange noises that were coming from the medium were is left to the imagination. From this point on, the knocks were overcast by the medium speaking in trance, firstly in a male voice, and where the majority of the communications were focused during the séance.

Henderson recalled being initially bored of the event, with some sitters noting a "pathetically sorry" look on his face until, to his "horror", the trumpet moved. He thought it was perhaps on wires, and yet, it moved several times. It jerkily rose and wandered around the table, and levitated in front of some of the sitters. A strange "guttural voice" answered as is from nowhere and the sitters replied. The trumpet suddenly fell to the floor and then lifted again, this time a girl's voice distinctly saying "Mother! O Mother! How are you? Are you any better?" To which one of the sitters answered, noting that her deceased daughter's voice sounded somewhat different, with her spirit daughter being equally shocked that her voice was not the same as it was when alive.

The whole séance continued in this manner with different sitters receiving messages, with some being quite specific and accurate in their messages, enough at least to make Henderson more open-minded to the events. Of course we can begin to ponder the conventional explanations for what was witnessed (of which I believe there are several) but, at face value, this is a typical example of the noises encountered in the séance room with the addition of spiritual amplification equipment.

In a report from 1921 by F.R. Melton, an inventor and amateur psychical researcher from Nottingham (England), he mentions an instance of some curious but impressive raps during a séance he held at his home on Good Friday evening. There present, were his wife, his youngest son, and a friend who was staying for the Easter period with them. It should be noted that his eldest son, who was not present at first, was quite cynical of psychical researcher and spiritual phenomena. He had been working for army schools and colleges teaching radio, telephone electronics, and communication after being injured in the First World War. There was a particular electronics shop where he would purchase items he needed for the classes he taught. It was there that he fell in love with a lady whom he intended to marry. They often sent messages (as we do now via texting) using the wireless telegraph and Morse code, in fact, his sweetheart was very skilled with tapping out Morse code messages. They both had particular messages that they would send each other and a private code. However, she was soon taken by a brief illness which shocked everyone, especially Melton's eldest son.

On the evening of the séance, which was already underway, Melton's eldest son entered the room at 10:30pm. He was somewhat amused by what everyone was engaged in and mocked the entire procedure. The sitters had already begun to receive messages from a "J.F.", the initials of the deceased lady whom Melton's son had loved and lost. He made a few "jocular remarks" to the sitters, when his younger brother exclaimed "Shut up! We are getting a message from J.". The older son smiled and shook his head, whilst doubting the accuracy of the messages being spelt out on the table through lettered cards. Melton states (p. 534):

> We had during the evening been having a series of little taps that sounded between the card and table, and my eldest son at once said, 'If you are J. at the table you can rap me out a message?' Instantly came the reply, 'Yes.' My boy sat down and in a few seconds they were dot-and-dashing it as fast as they could go! I saw my son's face change colour, and his whole manner became serious. At last he uttered a favourite expression of his when anything occurs to astonish him. He said, 'Well, it's a devil.' 'No!' rapped the table, 'It's J.' My son then told us it was J. indeed. She had given him their own private code signal, and had answered questions on matters only known to themselves.

Following this event, J. became a regular spiritual visitor to the Melton home, rapping out responsive and apparently accurate Morse code. Not only is that somewhat unique of spirit sounds within the séance room, it also demonstrated a large degree of intelligence to the entity, whatever it may be. In addition to the Morse code raps, additional séances led to sitters seeing J.'s apparition. Melton's eldest son felt J. sit next to him, and Melton described J. as bringing them "beautiful flowers that fill the room with their perfume", meaning that the family reported spontaneous smells of flowers following the events of the Good Friday séance.

The Morse code system of tapping out messages has been reported in a few séances. Another particular instance of note is that of a séance attended and reported by John Logie Baird, the famous engineer and inventor of the world's first mechanical television. The séance occurred in the mid-1930s, and was not a one-off event for Mr Baird, as he was indeed interested in psychical research and was well acquainted with Sir Oliver Lodge, a well noted psychical researcher and past president of the SPR (1901-1903), yet mostly known as a successful physicist with his involvement in the development of wireless telegraphy.

Baird's involvement in the séance began when a gentleman asked him to examine the invention of an electric motor controlled tuning fork. The machine didn't work, and Baird asked the man to return when it did. The man was then preparing to leave when he asked Baird a most unusual question completely out of the blue: "Would you care to have definite and irrefutable evidence of the survival of the personality after death?" Baird said "Yes" and the gentleman said he could give it to him if he was prepared to make the journey. He was prepared to travel anywhere for such evidence. Even so, this journey only took him to West Wimbledon of all places (London).

The séance was arranged and Baird arrived at the address given which was, as he describes, "a small highly respectable villa" where he was welcomed by a party of elderly ladies and gentlemen and was given tea. The medium arrived, "a neurotic, nervous looking woman of about 35" and everyone gathered in the séance room where they were faced with a circle of chairs with a small box in the centre, draped in black, resting on a chair. The medium was handcuffed to a chair and the audience sat around her in the chairs provided, including Baird, with everyone holding hands and placing a foot on top of each neighbour's foot. This was done so that any reported movement could not be explained as the actions of the sitters. The lights went out and the singing of hymns began, followed by a prayer (as was traditional then for Spiritualism and still is now within the Spiritualist National Union churches and their demonstrations.) In the darkness and silence Baird heard a humming sound, which he learned afterwards was the electrical tuning fork. Apparently, the rhythmic sound assisted the manifestations, although Baird believed that perhaps this sound masked any noises made by the medium and to some extent disorientated some of the sitters, as many sceptics, including myself, would deduce from such use of the instrument.

After some time of waiting, an elderly lady who was sat next to Baird squeezed his hand and whispered, "Look, it's coming". In front of the booth in which the medium sat, a very faint purple coloured cloud began to form. It grew denser, and then the silence was broken by an unusual tapping, "the spirit was signalling by tapping in Morse code". The message was directed at Baird, and was allegedly the spirit of the late Thomas Edison, who besides being a famous inventor, was fascinated by psychical phenomena, was raised by Spiritualist parents, and employed several laboratory assistants who were Spiritualist mediums. It appeared from the translated Morse code that Edison had been experimenting with noctovision (Baird had been experimenting with infrared rays several years beforehand and the ability to photograph images in the dark) in his home in the astral place, and he was convinced that it would, in time, prove of great use in assisting communication between the living and the dead. But now was not the time, as to use it at that moment would have caused "grave danger". He informed Baird that he would contact him again when the time was right. The séance drew to a close soon after the messages from Edison had ended.

Beyond the intelligence of Morse code rapping, it seems that *spirits* also have a good sense of rhythm or at least musical knowledge. For example, in 1971, Dr Alan Gauld briefly reported in the *Proceedings of the Society for Psychical Research* on other unique spirit noises that he was personally witness to, or at least noises of the séance room. In this case, he was somewhat impressed and at the same time amused, as during the table sitting (in good lighting conditions), it was suggested that the rapping noises already being heard by the sitters, "might like to rap out the National Anthem". A few moments later, after the conversation had moved on, Dr Gauld realised that the raps were doing just that, slowly, but unmistakably. All of this was recorded on tape, and those people who the tape was played to at a later date recognised the rapping sounds as the tune of the National Anthem without any hint or suggestion.

***

It has been just over ten years now since I actively began investigating reported experiences of hauntings, and in doing so I have personally witnessed dozens upon dozens of examples of séances with the use of mediums, Ouija boards, glass moving, automatic writing, etc., with a select few instances being somewhat impressive compared to the majority that were not. When I say they weren't impressive, I simply mean that nothing was conveyed that I could not present a conventional explanation to, without the need to assume paranormal processes being present. Certainly, in many of these modern day séances, bangs, taps, and creaks were heard, but due to their random and naturally sounding acoustical properties, such sounds of the séance room were likely to be nothing more than the natural sounds of the building. This was highlighted by Gurney, Myers and Podmore in *Phantasms of the Living*, with regards to non-vocal sounds. Natural sounds of a building happen all the time but we rarely consciously register them. It is only whilst sitting in silence and carefully listening that sounds may be ascertained.

However, there is one personal instance I feel I must relay here which is highly appropriate for *Paracoustics*, although some of you reading this may question whether my curious account can be more likened to that of a noisy ghost, rather than a noisy spirit, if indeed there is a difference between the two. Nevertheless, in 2005 I first began investigating reports of haunting type phenomena at Clifton Hall in Nottingham, England. At the time, the building was highly run down, and displayed the traits of a typical motion-picture haunted mansion, with an abandoned reception, paintings and statues still in place but gathering dust, and the old lights flickering occasionally revealing the odd few spider-webs. The house had last been occupied as an all-girls school several decades before and was now empty with one security guard overseeing the building and grounds by day and night.

In these early visits a few strange experiences occurred, such as loud banging sounds which were heard at one end of the hall which was not occupied, or dragging sounds heard on the floor above which, when investigated, nothing was found. At one point, infrared beam-barriers which are typically used for home security were set off several times, suggesting something had passed through them and broken the infrared beam to then activate its alarm system in the corridor where they were set up. Needless to say, everyone was accounted for and no-one was in the vicinity of the beam-barriers which were set up on the top floor outside of the old nursery, and no-one was on the top floor at the time. I recall running up two large flights of stairs when the alarm went off to check what had happened, only to find no-one there and the alarms blaring.

The strangest instance of perhaps a 'noisy-spirit' occurred on my return to Clifton Hall in 2007, during a two-year long investigation (beginning in 2007 and ending in 2009.) After having spent the day in the hall with a few colleagues, some of them went home as others turned up for a night shift. Cameras were set up throughout the day and night, and every hour a routine walk-round was done whilst notes were taken. In the late evening, around mid-night, I was undertaking a walk-round with Karen Doxey, who at the time was involved in law enforcement, as were several other members of the team. We were just about to head down to the cellar from the kitchen area, when the strange sound of a two-toned whistle occurred. We stopped at the gate which led down to the cellar in a bid to listen out for the whistle again. I then decided to whistle back in another two-toned whistle (somewhat like a wolf whistle) to which we received a different whistle back. I hastily went to the kitchen thinking it was water pipes under the sink. However, the sound then came from one of the living rooms. On entering the living room, the whistle appeared to come from the first floor. We stopped, listened, and gave a whistle in reply, and then a second or two later the whistle appeared to come from the dining room. We then headed back down stairs. At this point I should inform the reader that Clifton Hall by this point had been renovated. New carpets, newly painted walls, and so on, but *all* of the rooms were empty!

Recalling this event from memory was supported by re-viewing the video footage of the entire event and it was deemed that the activity perfectly fit the rough translation of poltergeist, "noisy spirit" or "boisterous ghost" (along with several other colloquial translations from German). Reports and literary works on poltergeists and those who have given serious study on the matter have said that such phenomena is typical of poltergeists. In particular, I recall Maurice Grosse mentioning a case in one of his many interviews where he had experienced strange sounds and walked over to the wall where he perceived the sounds to be coming from. Upon inspection, the same sound was suddenly coming from the opposite wall, which would then move again and again, as often as the investigator moved.

With the cases presented here, it certainly demonstrates once again that early psychical researchers such as Gurney, Myers, and Podmore were correct in their conclusions, that it is difficult to locate the source of non-vocal sounds. However, just because we can't find the source, this does not necessarily mean that the sounds are being produced by paranormal means, but it does limit the conventional explanations to which we can apply. For example, in the Clifton Hall case, why was the whistling sound responsive? There was no one else in that area of the hall except for Karen and myself and everyone else was accounted for, and yet, each time I gave a different whistle, the whistle replied with a different two-toned whistle to the one I gave. The sounds were heard by both of us, and were recorded on video footage in the audio. To this day, it is one of the few cases where I am unsure as to what caused the phenomena we witnessed. By no means is it anything new, as throughout this chapter, and throughout psychical research literature, there are numerous accounts of strange noises being heard which, when subjected to serious investigation, display no obvious conventional cause. I invite the reader to seek out further reading on this matter, especially from the references for this chapter in the back of this book, as here we have discussed only a few cases of *some noisy spirits.*

A BRIEF HISTORY OF EVP RESEARCH

Callum E. Cooper & Steven Parsons

Electronic voice phenomenon (EVP) is the occurrence of voices, utterances, raps and taps that appear on audio recording devices without the operator being aware of them at the time the recording is taking place. In many cases, the voices heard on playback can be very distinct, yet most are barely coherent at all. Typically, they are assumed by many people to be the disembodied voices of the dead. In this chapter we will consider some of the most prominent research that has taken place within EVP, due to its rapid growth since the 1970s, although it would not be possible to include here every single aspect of the history and those researchers involved. There are however, numerous texts devoted to EVP that cover information on some of the lesser known researchers and parts of the history, which are recommended in the reference section for this chapter. Exponents of EVP claim that almost everybody who is really interested in the phenomenon can, with practice and persistence, get positive results.

Around the turn of the twentieth century, there were various fragments of documentation of psychic phenomena which briefly mention what we could call EVP. For example, in the 1920's, during a studio radio session with the psychical researcher Hereward Carrington, an unnamed medium, Carrington, and others described hearing a disembodied voice asking: *"Can you hear me?"* This voice came from a microphone that had been left switched on in a sealed room. The rest of the building was empty. No explanation could be found as to its source.

In 1928, Thomas Edison was said to be working on equipment incorporating chemicals, including potassium permanganate, which he hoped would permit spirit communications. An interviewer from *Scientific American* asked Edison in 1921 about the possibility of contacting the dead. Edison responded:

> That nobody knows whether our personalities pass on to another existence or sphere but it is possible to construct an apparatus which will be so delicate that if there are personalities in another existence or sphere who wish to get in touch with us in this existence or sphere, this apparatus will at least give them a better opportunity to express themselves than the tilting tables and raps and Ouija boards and mediums and the other crude methods now purported to be the only means of communication.

Despite a number of claims to the contrary, there is no evidence that Edison ever designed or tried to construct such a device.

The publication *Psychic News,* carried a series of reports discussing an event that took place at Wigmore Hall in London in the 1930's in the presence of around 600 people. During the séance, more than fifty disembodied voices were said to have spoken through a microphone placed at a distance from the medium and wired to loudspeakers in the hall. Two of the technical staff from the company who provided and installed the public address system, and who were present at the time, also claimed to have heard the voices and stated that the voices must have definitely come from the microphone and that no human was close enough to have been within recording distance of the microphone during the sessions. Both men later signed a statement, published in *Psychic News,* that they had become Spiritualists as a result of their experiences on that occasion. Also during the early 1930's, strange unidentified voices were picked up by Swedish and Norwegian military radio monitoring stations. In March 1934 they ceased abruptly. At the time, they were attributed to stray Nazi transmissions. The voices were 'Polyglot' – containing several languages within a single message. However, after the war when archives were searched, no evidence of German involvement was discovered.

In 1949, a Spirit Electronic Communication Society was formed in Manchester, England. It was here that Mr Zwaan demonstrated a device (then called the Super Rays and later renamed Zwaan Ray in honour of the inventor), using spirit guidance in order to discover a means of scientific communication with the dead. The Zwaan Ray evolved into the Binnington model, developed in 1952, and then into the Teledyne model. It was claimed that direct spirit voice communication was eventually obtained by a medium with the help of this machine.

Revealed in 1990 was possible further evidence for EVP that occurred back in 1952, when two Italian Catholic priests, Father Ernetti and Father Gemilli, were collaborating on a musical research project. Ernetti was a respected scientist, physicist, philosopher and music lover, and Gemilli, President of the Papal Academy. In September 1952, the two priests were recording a Gregorian chant but the wiring in their equipment kept breaking. Exasperated, Gemilli looked up and exclaimed aloud for his dead father to help. To his amazement his father's voice was heard saying,"Of course I shall help you. I'm always with you".

They repeated the experiment, and the voice was again heard using the name that Gemilli's Father called him as a boy. Gemilli was astounded; no one knew the nickname his father had teased him with when he was a boy. After further experiments, the two men sought an audience with Pope Pius XII. Gemilli told the Pontiff of his experience and was, to his very great surprise, immediately reassured. According to accounts of his meeting, the Pope is reported to have told Gemilli:

> You really need not worry about this. The existence of this voice is strictly a scientific fact and has nothing whatsoever to do with Spiritism. The recorder is totally objective. It receives and records sound waves from wherever they come. This experiment may perhaps become the cornerstone for a building for scientific studies which will strengthen people's faith in a hereafter.

These brief examples mentioned above are all fragments of a long history of attempted or accidental apparent communications which have suggested the possibility of discarnate voices being capable of being heard over electrical devices or even being recorded. However, the turning point of EVP research is attributed to a psychic and astral projector by the name of Atilla von Szalay, known to his friends and family as Art. It was in 1936 in Schenectady, New York, in a photographic darkroom studio at 1am, that von Szalay heard an independent (aka, aerial, or direct) voice. What he heard appeared to be the voice of his deceased brother Edson, loudly saying "Art!" After that he regularly heard direct voices, especially after taking classes in yoga, meditation, and pranayama exercises, thus developing his ability to alter his state of conscious awareness. In the fall of 1941, he attempted to record the voices he allegedly heard using a radio cutter on old 78 r.p.m. records.

These initial informal experiments were not very successful, and were also expensive to carry out. His experiments continued until 1945, in which time he had only managed to record faint and intangible voices. He later moved to California, where he met the artist and psychical researcher, Raymond Bayless, and began more developed experiments under Bayless' direction.

Through practical research and investigation, EVP was *formally* discovered in 1956 during the Bayless / von Szalay experiments. In a rented studio in Hollywood, Bayless began the experiments with Atilla von Szalay. Bayless aimed to see if he could record these independent voices. Within the studio, a large wooden cabinet was built in which a microphone was placed (leading to a tape recorder outside of the cabinet), and von Szalay would sit inside the cabinet to try and produce the voices. Once they began to occur he would leave the cabinet with the hope that they would continue in his absence and subsequently be recorded. The first experiments began in November of 1956, with von Szalay describing them as follows (see Smith, 1977, p. 46):

> When Bayless and the Marros sat with me the following day for a recording session, we were astounded and pleased to hear a masculine voice declare, 'This is G!' The microphone was locked in the clothes closet and we sat outside in the lighted studio. We followed this technique of recording for years to ensure that the voices were genuinely paranormal and not fraudulently produced by any of us.

These experiments continued for several years until Bayless published a report on the findings. On many occasions, after von Szalay had left the cabinet, or while he and Bayless were sitting in the studio in silence, the tape recorder on playback produced scratching noises, bangs, taps, raps, voices, and utterances, which could not be accounted for by any person present. This report was published in 1959 as a correspondence in the *Journal of the American Society for Psychical Research*. Although the report went unnoticed within the parapsychological community and credit for the discovery of EVP was given to Friedrich Jürgenson (which we shall later discuss), the von Szalay research continued.

Raymond Bayless
(Photograph: Parker Publishing, 1967)

In 1967, a young D. Scott Rogo (aged 18-19 years) began to be mentored in psychical research by Raymond Bayless and assisted in the Art von Szalay experiments, which he documented as "The von Szalay Affair" in a chapter of his book entitled *In Search of the Unknown*. The research had become slow due to a lack of interest from the parapsychological community. Rogo temporarily took over the von Szalay experiments, which were among his very first experiments, alongside the investigation of spontaneous paranormal music.

The first somewhat amateur report by Rogo, which was possibly the first report he ever wrote, was published in 1969 in the *Journal of Paraphysics* alongside an editor's note highlighting the need for better control in the von Szalay experiments. Rogo adhered to the editor's requests, and in 1970 further reported on the recorders he used and how he had taken along brand new sealed tapes to von Szalay's photographic studio, where the experiments were now being conducted, whilst still making use of the recording cabinet. The results of these studies still demonstrated inexplicable tapping and whistling sounds being recorded in von Szalay's presence, even a voice saying "Hi-ya, Art" which was recorded in the first of the second sittings. Rogo was always in von Szalay's company and they never sat in the dark. In some instances, the direct voices were objectively heard by both sitters and thus recorded on the tape, rather than being imprinted (with the latter meaning that the recorders/experimenters would not hear the sounds at the time of recording but would only discover the sound on playback, as is the case of most EVPs). During this time, Rogo discovered that the American Society for Psychical Research was still hostile towards supporting any formal investigation of the von Szalay voices, and he felt he should have learnt from Bayless' first attempt to draw attention to the case through the ASPR in 1959.

At one point, Rogo did gain the attention of parapsychologist Dr Ian Stevenson, who was greatly interested in survival and became well known for his work on reincarnation accounts. Dr Stevenson suggested to Rogo that voice prints were to be done on the von Szalay recordings, ruling out fraud from sitters and demonstrating some form of paranormality if the voices did not match (voices prints being the acoustical version of fingerprints, whereby a recorded voice pattern can be matched to a particular person). However, Dr Stevenson soon withdrew his interest in the case due to his commitments to other projects. Therefore, private investigation of EVP continued in California, carried out by Rogo and Bayless, and were submitted to the journals of the Toronto Society for Psychical Research and the California Society for Psychical Research.

D. Scott Rogo, conducting recordings with
Attila von Szalay and Raymond Bayless
(Photograph: retrieved from www.evp-experiments.nl)

Raymond Bayless began researching and publishing on EVP again in the mid-1970s. This time the medium involved in his research was a gentleman by the name of Wesley Frank, who Bayless used for several studies in identifying anomalous acoustical raps on tape which appeared to be paranormal in origin – as Bayless concluded. As before with Bayless' recordings, sounds were reported to be heard on playback, but not during recording by the sitters. In the experiments with

Mr Frank, chimes were heard on playback which seemed to be intelligently patterned. Most of the raps, voices, and chimes were recorded while the microphone was *not* shielded, which suggested to Bayless that they were acoustical in their nature, air vibrations, which become imprinted on the magnetic tape. And yet, if the microphone were to be sound proofed and anomalous sounds were still recorded, it was assumed to be a psychokinetic (PK) effect on the part of the medium involved, given Bayless had taken precautions to avoid fraud or error leading to false recordings or misinterpretation.

Not a single recording with Mr Frank was devoid of raps. Bayless used both new tapes and erased old tapes for his recordings, of which he made a point of mentioning in his reports, especially stating that he checked for stray sounds left on the tapes and that they truly were blank before recording began. Every session conducted was recorded in 10 minute intervals in an attempt to capture EVP and rapping sounds. From the result of two reports submitted to *New Horizons* (Journal of the Toronto SPR), it was stated that the quality of the recordings varied in tone and quality, and yet every session produced results with what appeared to be intelligent raps, chimes, whispers, and clear voices.

In Bayless' second report, published in 1977, precautions were taken and noted strongly to enforce the impossibility, in his opinion, that the raps could have be caused by any conventional means. In one particular experiment attempted by the researchers, Bayless placed a bell and microphone inside a small wooden box at the other end of the room away from Mr Frank, to see if via PK Mr Frank could influence the bell and the sounds to be recorded. Sure enough, on playback, a variety of sounds were heard including "tings", bell-like sounds, and whispering. The precautions involved a variety of shielding efforts, where in some cases the microphone was shielded, and in other cases it wasn't. Thorough details of what tapes were used, and when, and whether they were brand new or erased tapes were noted, and the variety of tape recorders that were used were also noted. Even surface vibrations were tested as a possible cause for the recordings with the help of a fellow EVP researcher, William Welch, who published the book *Talks with the Dead*, for which Bayless provided the forward. Additionally, Bayless and Mr Frank maintained silence during recordings and an agreement of no contact, so their movements or unconscious coughing, sighing, and so on, was not recorded and misinterpreted. The main conclusion was that PK must have had some involvement in the recording of these sounds, given that everything recorded was almost never heard whilst recording was taking place.

This appeared to be a popular theory for the recordings at the time, and a researcher named Riley presented a report to *New Horizons* in 1977, looking into whether a group of people 'trained' in PK could produce EVP. Fifteen sittings were conducted in total, and one took place in an electrically shielded sound proofed room. The results found that anomalous sounds were indeed recorded, involving raps and spoken words. However, Riley withheld any conclusions for this study, considering it to be a pilot study, and making no claim as to the nature of the sounds or their origin. With what seemed to be the researcher presenting some much needed scepticism, and wishing to ask more questions of the study he had conducted before committing to what some would consider controversial conclusions, he stated that he would conduct further experiments. However, Riley submitted no further reports to *New Horizons.*

The final report on EVP produced by Bayless was a further study involving Mr Frank, this time published in the *Journal of the Southern California Society for Psychical Research* in 1979. This paper outlined around a dozen EVP trials held at Mr Frank's home, with the aim of assessing the nature of the anomalous rapping sounds, but this time focusing on target objects such as the bell in the wooden box which had been used before. Bayless wished to question whether conventional explanations and stray sounds could really be ruled out in order to place a confident conclusion of PK being responsible for the recorded sounds. Several of these sittings were observed and assisted by D. Scott Rogo and Dr Elizabeth McAdams (the latter being President of the Southern California SPR at the time). Once again, the reports for these rigorous experiments outline the meticulous details of the sittings, such as: the position of people present, the type of recorders used, the tapes used, the target objects used, how long each recording lasted, notes on what sounds were heard during recording, what was heard on play back that didn't match the sounds heard on recording, and so forth. Bayless concluded that when controls are put in place, certain people, perhaps those more prone to psi experiences, are likely to be responsible for some of the recorded effects, stating:

> It is now clearly seen that the acoustical tape recorded voice phenomenon is frequently accompanied by many other psychokinetic effects including telekinetic phenomena, raps, whistles, 'scratching'

> sounds, bell tones, tuning bar tones, etc. The taped voices, then, are only part of a complex overall effect. (Bayless, 1979, pp. 16-17)

It was at this point that Bayless shifted his interests slightly. During the time that he and Rogo were conducting EVP experiments, various people that they had met and explained the EVP research to then stated that they had experienced what they believed to be phone calls from the dead. As they began their EVP research together in the late 1960s, it wasn't until around 1977 that they began to take such accounts seriously and pursue investigation of such phenomena, which we shall discuss in the following chapter. However, it seems that the 1979 report with Wesley Frank was possibly Bayless' final presentation of his EVP experiments, to which he could find no conventional explanation for the sounds recorded. It also seems evident that no-one else involved could find conventional causes and "extreme care", as they called it, had be taken to rule out any form of error or fraud accounting for the sounds. To Bayless, it was a parapsychological milestone and worth all the effort, which demanded further attention.

Many consider Friedrich Jürgenson to be the first to discover electronic voices, a claim that is often repeated in articles dealing with EVP. Whilst this is certainly not the case, no discussion of EVP can ignore his contribution and the subsequent influence his work had on modern studies of electronic communications. Only some three months after Bayless published his report in 1959 in the Journal of the ASPR regarding EVP, the Swedish filmmaker, Friedrich Jürgenson, announced that he had discovered anomalous voices and raps whilst working on a project recording wild bird songs in the forest near to his home. These recordings also included anomalous voices appearing within normal recorded conversation, which seemed to mention "nocturnal bird songs". He further experimented and recorded more bird songs in the hope of additional voices appearing on playback, and these produced what appeared to be more human voices, with some claiming to be deceased friends and relatives. After months of unsuccessful attempts, the first voice reported was that of a mature woman. The woman spoke several words and Jürgenson insisted it was the voice of his deceased mother calling his name. He was also reported to have received voices which were concluded to be that of his deceased father. In his continuation of the research, he received regular words and speech such as "Friedrich, you are being watched!" and various other EVPs in Swedish, German, and Latvian.

Fourteen years after his initial announcement, he claimed that the voices were not discovered accidentally at all, but that he had an intuitive desire at the time to make electronic contact with the dead via the tape recorder. He didn't know why, he simply claimed it to be an inner urge. His initial attempts were without success. However, when he finally succeeded and listened closely to the voices, Jürgenson found that they spoke in different languages, often changing in mid-sentence. Also, phrases frequently had incorrect structure or grammar and, in some cases, syllables were stretched or compressed in a way that made it difficult to comprehend the messages. The strangest aspect of all was the uncanny way the voices seemed to respond to his comments. Jürgenson began to converse with the voices, recording his questions and afterwards searching the tape for answers. After four years of experimental recording, he announced his discovery at a press conference in 1963 and his book, *Roesterna Fraen Rymden (Voices from the Universe),* was published the following year. His conclusion was that the tape recordings were acting as a form of electronic communication link to the realm of the dead. In 1967, he produced another book with the translated title of *Radio Contact with the Dead.* Neither of these books have yet been published in English.

Jürgenson's attempts at EVP were largely ignored in parapsychology, much like the von Szalay experiments. Professor Hans Bender, a German parapsychologist, based at the University of Freiburg, travelled to Sweden and experimented with Jürgenson extensively. Observed and controlled sittings were conducted, with several other experimenters present in some cases. Two methods had been adopted and Jürgenson was using tape-recorders and the radio to produce anomalous sounds and voices. The latter he referred to as 'the inter-frequency method' and was based upon radio reception. This radio would often produce voices saying "conditions are bad" or "we will speak today". Reports suggested the voices to be clear and articulate. Professor Bender first reported on these experiments in 1970 in the *Zeitschrift für Parapsychologie und Grenzgebiete der Psychologie.* The report was recently translated into English and published in the *ITC Journal* in 2011.

Jürgenson himself was convinced, after dozens of recordings were carried out, that the voices were paranormal in origin and were specifically "voices of the dead". Professor Bender and the Freiburg Institute were aware of Jürgenson's opinion on the recordings, but were officially undetermined as to whether the voice phenomena were normally explainable or were evidence of paranormal effects. After two experiments with Jürgenson and the recordings, Professor Bender's report concluded that the paranormal hypothesis of the origin of the voices was highly probable, but less likely to be the voices of discarnate entities. The voices were definitely human and different voices appeared on tape each time. He was also keen to investigate further whether some form of PK effect was responsible for the recordings whilst Jürgenson still held his opinion to the contrary, stating "I believe without and beyond a shadow of doubt that I am communicating with those many call dead" (Smith, 1977, p. 14).

Through this accidental discovery, EVP indeed began to gain further recognition, and the subject was picked up by one of Jürgenson's experimenters. This particular experimenter was Dr Konstantin Raudive, through whom Jürgenson's voices are better known in popular EVP literature. Raudive was a Latvian psychologist and philosopher living in Germany, a former student of the eminent Professor Carl Jung in Germany and at Oxford University. He announced that he had also managed to replicate EVP and had found an electronic method for contacting the dead. Inspired to make his own recordings after reading Jürgenson's books and later meeting with him, Raudive's EVPs were reported to be similar to that of Jürgenson's recordings, in which additional voices would appear on the playback of normal conversations, and sometimes these additional voices would comment on the conversation.

More than four hundred people participated in his voice recordings, including prominent physicists, psychologists, electronic engineers, as well as medical doctors and teachers. None of them could explain the origin of the voices produced before them. The tests, in Raudive's opinion, demonstrated that the voices originated outside the experimenter and were not subject to autosuggestion or telepathy.

His claims were not so well known in the UK or USA. However, 1969 marked a turning point for EVP. At the Frankfurt Book Fair, Colin Smythe was handed a copy of Raudive's book, and was encouraged that its translation and publication would be a worthy project. The book, entitled *Unhörbares Wird Hörbar* (*The Inaudible Becomes Audible*) was considered by Smythe's colleague, Peter Bander, who translated a chapter 'on obtaining the voices'. At first it didn't seem likely to go ahead for a full translation until Smythe, without Bander's knowledge, read the translation and attempted the recordings for himself. Bander then became fascinated and also attempted the recordings (which a few years later led to his own book on the subject entitled *Carry on Talking: How*

Dead are the Voices?) and was particularly impressed by the amount of noted professionals and scholars who supported Raudive's research, most notably, Professor Gebhard Frei and Professor Hans Bender. As a result of their own efforts, Smythe and Bander invited Raudive to England to demonstrate the phenomenon to a group of selected witnesses. The demonstration was a success and *Unhörbares Wird Hörbar* went ahead for a full English translation and publication.

In 1971, the book, now re-titled *Breakthrough: An Amazing Experiment in Electronic Communication with the Dead* was released. Initial copies came with an accompanying record of examples of the recordings for the reader's consideration. This attracted a lot of attention from physicists and electronics experts. Lay investigators also became fascinated by the work of Raudive, even to the present day many EVP commentators and researchers still refer to the various recorded voices as "Raudive voices". Several parapsychologists also began to show increasing interest in EVP, but most were equally extremely wary of it. Many of Raudive's recordings are, and indeed were from the very beginning, considered to be highly questionable, and some said that Raudive's best EVPs were comparable to von Szalay's worst, such as unclear speech and utterances. Raudive spoke several languages and he interpreted the sounds, as had Jürgenson before him, as being a mix of different languages. This opened up a wide range of possible interpretation and a lot of criticism. For example, he received voices in a variety of languages, such as, Latvian, German, Swedish, Russian, Spanish, French, and English. With this polyglot of languages taken into account, in which many words in the various languages have similar phonetic patterns, the interpretation and translation become open to the experimenter and sitter, and this was highly unsatisfactory. An example of this would be a noise being heard such as "mer", which could be English (a female horse) or French (mother or sea). Trawling through a variety of familiar languages, as Raudive did, it is indeed possible that the more unclear voices and whispers were over-interpreted, misinterpreted, or may just have been plain wrong, the sounds heard being nothing more than random noise and not speech.

Several methods were employed by Raudive to obtain the voices. The most simple method involved placing a brand new blank tape into the recorder and setting up a live microphone which picked up his voice and that of the observers engaged in conversation, and when played back, during conversations and periods of silence, additional voices would be heard. Some would even respond to questions asked.

In other sessions, a radio was used. This was wired up to the recorder. The tuner on the radio was kept between stations so that a vague background noise was heard. On playback, additional voices became present above the carrier frequency noise.

There has been extensive criticism and a number of alternative explanations for the "Raudive voices". Dr Lester Smith produced one particular in-depth criticism, which received a lot of criticism in itself by readers of the *Journal of the Society for Psychical Research* in 1972. In this critical review, he argued that alternative explanations could be put forward due to the methods applied to the recordings and the analysis, and also the trustworthiness of the experimenters was questionable and their actions during recording could be responsible, albeit via innocent or purposeful action. It was clear that Smith was not convinced that *Breakthrough* contributed anything towards the issue of survival. Rogo commented on this review, finding it to be a careless analysis of the "Raudive voices" with very weak, or more so, illogical assumption. As he stated, "In his paper Smith merely stated since we have no conceptual model to explain paranormal voices, no such voices were likely to exist. This was a ridiculous declaration since we have no conceptual model for ESP either" (1976, p. 172). Smith firmly believed that the source of the noises on playback was from the recording device (mechanical), static, or background noise during recording (unconsciousness noises from the sitters or natural sounds of the room they were in).

Other arguments against Dr Smith were expressed immediately. For example, Manfred Cassirer replied to the *JSPR* in 1973 and found the review to be poor, in that Smith had not bothered to listen to any of the recordings even though they were available on record which accompanied copies of *Breakthrough*. Furthermore, he was confused as to why Smith asserted that a critical review of *Breakthrough* was long overdue, when at this time it had become common knowledge within psychical research that David Ellis was conducting a formal investigation of the voices. Overall, Cassirer was not impressed, and certainly wasn't convinced by the conclusions drawn from Smith's review. Equally, Richard Sheargold replied to the *JSPR* in 1973 (and published a pamphlet on techniques for obtaining the voices in that same year), pointing out that Smith failed to explain the mass of voices obtained or the verification methods used by the experimenters to confirm the voice. Smith's reply to this was that he was not impressed to learn of other people's success of obtaining EVP, believing anyone could do it, and that there are too many conventional explanations to blame for the effect, closing with the comment:

> Perhaps I should add that I am not just a hard-headed biased scientist. I believe in life after death, and I sincerely wish there were some reliable mode of communication with the departed. What I cannot accept is that Raudive and others involved with electronic phenomena have found one. (Smith, 1973, p. 209)

On reflection, Smith was right in some of his assumptions about EVP, audio electronics, and human psychology, as research was beginning to reveal. However, various other criticisms were produced against Raudive, while those who criticised often supported the work being conducted by David Ellis on a formal examination of the voice recordings. Some such criticisms were that electronic engineering was already aware that white noise could produce voice effects and it was therefore illogical to assume them to be the responsive voices of the dead, as S.N. Gaythorpe wrote to the journal *Light* in 1972. While in other opinions, such as that of Dr Alan Vaughan, the Raudive voices were indeed paranormal in origin, but not a product of the dead attempting to communicate. He believed that it had been experimentally demonstrated by Raudive that transmission of sub-conscious thoughts and speech are capable of being impressed upon magnetic tape via some form of PK effect. Raymond Bayless previously held this same theory, as we have discussed.

It has been briefly mentioned already, that during the time of Raudive's rise to fame with EVP and the instant backlash of criticism, a serious review and examination of the phenomenon was being conducted within psychical research. It took place during the period of 1970-72 at Cambridge University. Perrott-Warrick student, David Ellis, who at the time was new to the psychical research scene, undertook a two-year research project that set out to test some of the claims of Raudive and EVP in general, in an attempt to gain an understanding of the recordings and their possible causes.

David J. Ellis
(Photograph published by Woman's Own magazine, 18 August 1973)

At first, Ellis was required to submit progress reports during this study to his supervisor, but began duplicating them for interested colleagues and researchers, a practise that escalated. Soon, Ellis found himself posting over 250 copies of his progress reports. He outlined a number of hypotheses he wished to explore in investigating the origin of the voices, and his studentship even sent him on several trips to Germany to visit Raudive and observe the recording sessions carried out. Ellis found Raudive reluctant to be tested, or to let others test his tapes, and yet he was very eager to add interpretation to every sound and whisper that was produced on playback, and was above all devoted to their study. After the thorough two year examination of the voices, Ellis compiled all of his progress reports and additional information, and subsequently self-published a book on his findings in 1978 entitled *The Mediumship of the Tape Recorder*. The project went from a positive high to a disheartening low for Ellis, given that the project initially presented so much potential for a new phenomenon to be controlled and understood, especially the prospect of communication with the dead through something as simple as a tape recorder. As Ellis' research progressed, he frequently found people "deluding" themselves in their interpretation of the sounds, or 'voices'. He concluded in his book (p. 145):

> There is thus no reason to postulate anything but natural causes: indistinct fragments of radio transmissions, mechanical noises and unnoticed remarks, aided by imaginative guesswork and wishful thinking, to explain the 'voice phenomenon'.

Ellis was unconvinced by the end of his research that anything paranormal was responsible for the 'voices' with only conventional explanations accounting for their occurrence. This even excluded the possibility of PK being involved in producing the voices on the magnetic tape. He later commented that he turned from believer to sceptic by the end of his studentship. Ellis' overall conclusions pointed toward the psychology of the experimenters and the sitters in their interpretations of the sounds heard. Even several years after his study with new developments in EVP having taken place, his opinion stayed the same within his postscript. Dr Susan Blackmore was very impressed by the study, and its thoroughness. In reviewing Ellis' book for the *Journal of Parapsychology* in 1979, Blackmore believed that not everyone would be happy with Ellis' conclusions, adding that a few strange effects still required further investigation and a few experiments were left undone at that point, but overall she supported Ellis' conclusions as being the most reasonable after thorough examination.

Scott Rogo found Ellis' work to be generally negative of EVP and questioned whether he had really demonstrated anything at all. At the very least, Ellis had highlighted some of the conventional explanations for EVP, such as: fragments of radio transmission, mechanical noises and unnoticed remarks, aided by "imaginative guess work and wishful thinking". With these latter comments, Ellis did indeed highlight an interesting psychological component of EVP, that being the pareidolia effect. This is a natural psychological phenomenon whereby when we see vague images or hear unclear sounds, our brain instantly tries to form recognition with that sensory input without much conscious effort. In other words, in a darkened room we could relate a shadow like form to be that of a human figure, and a mumbled sound could be interpreted as a particular word, name, or phrase. Both instances could be neither and purely random shapes and sounds without clarity, but we innocently and unconsciously interpret them into something which we can relate to. This might not be the absolute explanation for EVP, but it certainly applies to *a lot* of cases.

In 1995, Ellis wrote a further report on his thoughts on EVP. In this reflection on his time investigating the voices, he stated "my studies showed that the voices recorded were not quite clear enough to be heard accurately, and when you can't quite hear something you have to resort to guesswork, but when you do this you tend to find more meaning than the evidence warrants – and so the argument of paranormality from meaning is not valid". This final report further highlights the time and effort put into the investigation of the voices thereby dispelling paranormal theories. Ellis was disappointed that, regardless of his two-year research project and production of a book on the whole study; many individuals both inside and outside of the science community, either ignored the work or were not aware of it. Subsequently, EVP research has continued with many of the documented errors of the recordings, and the continued use of discredited methods and the assumed evidential value that is placed upon the recordings remains a significant problem for current research in EVP.

The pareidolia effect is clearly evident in the concluding explanations for the interpretation of many of the voices in Ellis' work, although not specifically mentioned or explained, but it concerns suggestion and interpretation of the sounds heard. During the time of Ellis producing reports on his research, Professor Charles Tart was casually testing something similar which related to the pareidolia effect in EVP research, as he reported in a correspondence to the *JSPR* in 1974. He had experimented with tape loops of human voices repeating a single word (the word could be anything) over and over again. He tested this on himself and his students. With the student group, anywhere from one to forty different words were reportedly heard by the listeners in a twenty-minute period. The reality of such situations is that nothing has actually changed on the tape and the sitters are still hearing one word over and over again being played to them. Our brains become too familiar with the words heard, thus the acoustical structure of the sounds become reshaped and are therefore interpreted in different ways. (Have you ever thought of a word for too long and then, due to repetition, it does not make sense to you any more in its phonetic structure? It is very common!). In 1975, Sheargold replied to Professor Tart's letter regarding the psychology of EVP and how the mind can play tricks on the sounds we hear, arguing that Professor Tart misunderstood how EVP research was carried out, and that researchers don't use tape loops. Seemingly, Sheargold had entirely missed the point of Professor Tart's argument and what his experiment demonstrated.

Dr Konstantin Raudive passed away in 1974. By that time, he had claimed to have recorded and catalogued at least 100,000 voices. For years he spent up to 12 hours a day at his recorder, until warned by his doctor that this could damage his hearing permanently. Most of his lecture fees and book royalties were spent on blank tapes. It is certainly clear that from the time and devotion taken over the recordings that he was serious about their importance. The legacy that he left behind has however been met with mixed feelings. Some believe his studies are an important contribution to parapsychology, while others are not impressed by the findings whatsoever. In Ellis' 1995 reappraisal note, he mentioned that Dr Eric Dingwall commented on Raudive's passing, and stated "Poor fellow, what a waste of time!" Following his death, Raudive's followers claimed that he became a regular spirit communicator via his own equipment. British psychologist George Gilbert Bonner began using a reel-to-reel recorder and a battery radio tuned to static or white noise to act as a carrier for discarnate voices to conduct an experiment in 1972, after reading Raudive's book. He asked into his microphone, "Can anyone hear me and would anyone like to speak to me?" not expecting any response. He received the answer in a hiss and rush of sound "Yes". Ultimately, Bonner claimed to have recorded more than 50,000 spirit voices up until 1997.

During the mid-1970's, at around the same time that Ellis was conducting his extended study, Raymond Cass, an audiologist by profession with wide experience in sound projection and detection (specialising in hearing aids), was producing what was argued to be some of the finest quality EVPs. Based in Hull, England, Cass spent his evenings and whenever his free time permitted at the Hearing Aid Consultancy, experimenting with EVP. Being familiar with the Jürgenson / Raudive work, he was aware how much time, effort, and patience such recordings required. From a young age he had been open to the paranormal, and later in life he joined a psychic society in Hull which led to the discovery that an ancestor of his, Robert Cass (died 1898), was a founder of the Spiritualist movement in Hull. Robert Cass claimed that amongst his numerous psychic feats, there was an alleged event in which he levitated a table with three men on top, all the way to the ceiling. Apparently the men wrote their names on the ceiling with pencils as evidence. Raymond Cass' own exploration of EVP was apparently foreseen in 1938, at a Helen Duncan séance in Bridlington, where the prediction came that Mr Cass would develop direct voice mediumship.

Raymond Cass
(Photograph: retrieved from www.raymondcassfoundation.co.uk)

For a while, Cass' scepticism for EVP led him to feeling foolish for talking "to thin air" whilst waiting to receive a reply on tape, this being a direct response method previously employed by Jürgenson. He had kept up to date with European research, due to being fluent in German, which also kept him ahead of the research in England (Peter Bander was another). By 1976, not only had Cass been receiving voices with clarity (which other witnesses verified), but also he had made it his aim to try and contact the surviving personalities of deceased EVP researchers, specifically Raudive. His recording methods also employed the use of radio frequencies, as had previous studies. In August 1976, Cass, using a small multi-band radio together with a battery operated cassette recorder, tuned to the aircraft communications band, and claimed that he had recorded the hoarse voice of Raudive (who had died two years earlier) shouting in German, "Here's Raudive...waiting at the bridge".

Ultimately, Cass claimed to have recorded thousands of clear discarnate voices over the years speaking and singing. He theorised that the proximity of his office, close to a mass public health X-Ray unit around 30 yards away, produced an emanation which was interacting with the selected aircraft band frequency thereby producing a transient condition enabling the voices to manifest.

Raymond Cass was certainly a patient and dedicated EVP researcher, although unfortunately he is now rarely discussed with regard to EVP. This is mainly owing to his lack of published material. Though he documented his efforts, he did not publish them as reports or indeed in book form as other people had done. The most detailed discussion of Cass' work is in Harold Sherman's book *The Dead Are Alive*, in which Cass contributed a chapter of his own work simply entitled 'The Raymond Cass Report'. In this, he outlined his methods used and transcriptions of some of his best voice recordings. He also used portable tape recorders for field investigations of EVP. Cass was very much in touch with members of the parapsychological community, especially those involved in EVP research throughout the 1970s-80s. It is fortunate now, however, that through simple internet searches, information on Raymond Cass is available to the serious EVP researcher, and a website dedicated to his life and work is also available.

George Meek, a retired engineer, with a lifelong interest in the paranormal became fascinated with EVP and established his own laboratory in 1971 to study the phenomenon. He was convinced that if electronic communication with the dead were to become truly effective, then more sophisticated techniques and equipment would be needed. He claimed to enlist the help of "departed scientists and engineers" in order to develop such a device. Meek also wrote to the American magazine, *The Psychic Observer*, following which he was put in touch with Bill O'Neil, an electronics engineer who was also a clairaudient and clairvoyant. In October 1977, and working in collaboration with Bill O'Neil, technology was developed between them in order to form a communication with the dead.

Together with O'Neil, Meek established the Metascience Foundation, and claimed to have made contact with a man who had been dead for five years and who was a medical doctor while on earth. "Doc Nick", as he became known, proposed that the team should use particular audio frequencies instead of the white noise traditionally used by EVP researchers. This, he said, would serve as an energy source against which the sounds produced by his vocal cords could be played. Apparently it worked, as shortly afterwards a spirit calling himself Dr George Jeffries Mueller announced he had come to join the team after materialising one afternoon in O'Neil's living room. Mueller was a deceased university professor and NASA scientist who had died in 1967. Meek and O'Neil said that Mueller gave them numerous facts with which to verify his identity including his security number and intimate details of his life and scholastic achievements. Dr Mueller began communicating regularly, helping to design a new piece of electromagnetic equipment that would convert spirit voices into audible voices. In October 1977, his first words were recorded on the new system that the Spirit / Living team jointly developed and which Meek named Spiricom.

The device consisted of a series of 13 tone generators, producing a range of tones equivalent to that of a typical adult male voice, i.e., from 130Hz-710Hz. The output from the tone generators was then transmitted at frequencies of around 29MHz to an adjacent radio receiver. The resultant audio was fed to a loudspeaker and together with the questions of the experimenter was recorded to a tape via a microphone. Spiricom voices had a typically synthetic almost robotic quality. Over the years, Meek and O'Neil made additional modification and improvements to Spiricom and made the details of the device openly and freely available to other researchers.

Tapes of conversations with Dr Mueller were released to the public and indeed made fascinating listening. Dr Mueller could be heard joking with Meek and O'Neil and discussing his favourite foods and the view of time from the perspective of the spirit world. Dr Mueller provided unlisted telephone numbers and asked that Meek should call the number and confirm the identity of the subscriber, which Meek states they were able to do successfully. It was claimed that Dr Mueller also gave O'Neil precise directions with which to help build experimental video equipment. George Meek never patented the Spiricom device in the hope that science would carry on his work and take it to the next step. In 1982, he held a press conference in Washington, USA, and revealed Spiricom's secrets. Before Mueller ceased communicating with Meek and O'Neil, the team had been working to develop spirit communications using video techniques, but with little success. It seemed the device required O'Neil to be present. Meek invited others to try out the device, including the founder of the American Association of Electronic Voice Phenomenon (AA-EVP), Sarah Estep. Yet, replications of the communications achieved by O'Neil were not repeated.

Estep established the aforementioned AA-EVP in 1982. The organisation produced a newsletter/journal called *AA-EVP News*, providing news and updates on EVP research. In the past, Estep had been more or less certain that death was the end of life, having had family working in the funeral industry. She had personally seen dead bodies laid out on a few occasions, without her family knowing, but was not scared of the experience and thus reached her own conclusion that a corpse is bereft of life. However, it was in later life, after becoming qualified as a social worker, that she explored and investigated her interests into the reincarnation experiences of children. After this research came to an abrupt end, she found other interests by reading the work being done in EVP. This led to her own attempt at recording such voices to see if personality really does continue in some form beyond death. She gave the phenomenon a chance and gave herself one week in which to find some credibility to EVP. On the sixth day, in desperation for something to happen, she asked "Please tell me what your world is like" a voice replied on tape "Beauty".

This research continued on the basis of trial and error. She communicated with various EVP researchers for help and guidance. Raymond Cass suggested to her that she should try using a radio in a manner similar to other researchers, whereby an area of static between stations is found and held whilst recording takes place and questions are asked. Estep's most popular book published on the topic of EVP is entitled *Voices from Eternity*, in which accounts are discussed where she attempted to record EVP in purportedly haunted locations. In the year 2000, Estep decided to retire and entrusted AA-EVP to Tom and Lisa Butler, who themselves had been researching EVP since 1988. Their work in EVP and communicating this work to the public and the AA-EVP's members still continues to this day.

In 1986, Klaus Schreiber, a Swiss electronics engineer, claimed to have obtained pictures of the dead on television by means of an apparatus he called a Vidicom. This consisted of a specially adapted television which was switched on but not attached to an aerial and with a video camera in front of it forming an opto-electrical feedback system to capture images on the screen. He stated that by using this method he had made audio/video contact with his two deceased wives. Perhaps the best-known experimenters receiving visual-audio communication are Maggie and Jules Harsch-Fischbach of Luxembourg. They developed and successfully operated two electronic systems in 1985 which they claimed could produce results that could be reliably duplicated. In 1987, they received their first TV picture sequences and, a year later, they claimed to have established sustained computer contact in which messages were found on unattended computer screens and photographs of dead friends and co-workers were uploaded onto their computers that were not connected to any external network. A further case of instrumental trans-communication (ITC) using a computer took place in Doddleston, Cheshire, England, between 1984 and 1986. The homeowner, Ken Webster received messages from a man named Thomas Harden who claimed he was writing from the year 1545, during the reign of Henry VIII. The language of his messages appeared to be pre-Shakespearean but this has been disputed by a number of linguistics experts. Webster received more than 250 messages, whilst at the same time reporting poltergeist phenomena in the family home. In addition to the messages from Thomas Harden in the 16th century, there were a series of messages from a group calling themselves 2109, who were apparently communicating from the future. After the communications at Doddleston ceased, it was reported that the 2109 group began communicating with the Harsch-Fischbach group in Luxembourg. Webster detailed his experiences in a book published in 1989 entitled *The Vertical Plane.*

In 1999, Dr Anabela Cardoso, a senior diplomat, established the *ITC Journal,* which is an international journal for anomalous electronic communication and is still going strong today, encouraging such research to be carried out and published. Dr Cardoso began her own research in 1997 under the guidance of Carlos Fernández. Her main breakthrough was during some experiments in 1998 when, sitting on her floor at home using radio frequencies for communication, a loud and clear voice came through. In shock of the clear result, Cardoso managed at least to pick out the words 'difícil' (difficult) and 'outro mundo' (another world). Carlos Fernández turned up later the next morning to examine the voices for himself but, besides other utterances, the words recorded by Cardoso were clear and certain. The voices had answered in reply to questions asked by Cardoso and therefore appeared responsive and not due to misinterpretation of voices from radio stations.

Some of the main communications established by the *ITC Journal Research Centre* have involved contacts from the Rio de Tempo. A popular theory, which has been posed in various areas of EVP communication history, suggests that in another plane of existence there is a group composed primarily of Portuguese and Brazilians, known as the Landell Group. Their aim is to communicate with the living world through the Rio do Temp Station and is thus where Cardoso's first communications of 'difícil' and 'outro mundo' came from, with communications still continuing to this day. This belief is supported by several researchers in EVP/ITC.

Additionally, the *ITC Journal Research Centre* has hosted two successful international conferences thus far with a variety of leading authorities gathering together to discuss their research and findings on electronic communication. Cardoso has also followed a similar tradition of EVP history which was introduced with the books of Jürgenson and Raudive Accordingly, Cardoso's own book, *Electronic Voices,* is accompanied by an audio CD of examples and translations of EVPs which have been recorded by herself and the *ITC Journal Research Centre.*

For some scholars/researchers, typically based within the field of psychology, EVP has been the topic of their degree thesis, although these often go unpublished and therefore are rarely heard about in the documented literature. However, to discuss a few examples, in 1980 Patricia Clancy completed a Master of Arts degree in counselling psychology at the University for Humanistic Studies (San Diego, CA), with her thesis topic being an analysis of paranormal sounds which occur on electronic recording equipment. Using an experimental research design, a cassette recorder was used to make recordings over a seven month period, whereupon fifty-one unexplained sounds were detected, twenty-six of which resembled voices. All the voices were listed in the appendix and included phrases such as "okay", "all right", "how are you" and "allow time", which were interpreted from the recordings. The recordings also included whistling, bird like sounds, and sounds of an electronic quality. Two tape recorders were used in alternation and during seven recording sessions, a Faraday Cage, which is an electrically earthed box surrounding the experiment and used to prevent any unwanted radio waves or electrical interference, was employed as an additional control measure. Vocal and non-vocal sounds were recorded even when the Faraday Cage was in use. The conclusion was that sounds do appear to be recorded via paranormal means, even when methods are put in place to exclude the recording of conventional sounds. The conclusions, including the common conclusions of early studies, also leaned towards the suggestion of a psychokinetic effect being produced from the experimenter manipulating the magnetic tape and information recorded, which is then heard only on playback. In recommendations for taking the study further, Clancy suggested further work with the Faraday Cage in a sound proofed room, the use of voiceprint analysis, and applying Kirlian photography to the participants of the recording.

Ross Friday who has more recently become involved within the parapsychological community and who is now conducting doctoral research on 'the sense of being stared at' at the University of Greenwich, focused his psychology undergraduate dissertation on EVP and individual differences in the perception of sounds heard. Using 106 participants in total, all of them filled in questionnaires to measure their temporal lobe lability, levels of expectation, and schizotypy, before undertaking a listening test to see if they could detect voices at a predetermined volume. All recordings were presented to participants as genuine EVPs, and all of their perceptions from the recordings and voices they believed they heard in the random audio samples were documented. Some recordings were just random white noise (static) others were pseudo-EVPs, created for the purpose of the study. The findings of this study suggested that the *combination* of temporal lobe lability, schizotypy, and expectation within participants, significantly correlated with the detection of voices in the recordings. No single cognitive trait or neurological factors were accurate predictors of voice detection amongst participants, but they are important issues to consider within other paranormal experiences.

At present, Ann Winsper (co-founder of Para.Science alongside Steve Parsons) remains the most active parapsychologist in EVP research. Her undergraduate psychology dissertation, conducted within the psychology department at John Moores University, Liverpool, focused on the effects of paranormal belief and positive schizotypy on response bias in an auditory EVP task (conducted a few years before the work of Ross Friday). Winsper's current doctoral research has focused on the psychology of EVP even further, and is now possibly the most in-depth psychology study of EVP to date. Winsper herself discusses this elsewhere in this book.

In 2002, American EVP researcher, Frank Sumption, created a device that he claimed had been developed with assistance from the spirit realm and was said to be able to facilitate real-time communications with spirit voices. Originally, this comprised a white noise generator and an AM radio that continuously tuned through the frequency band. The combined audio outputs from the two were output via a loudspeaker contained inside a small chamber that also contained a microphone connected to a recorder. The units built by Sumption became known as Ghost-boxes which have been continually developed over a number of years by Sumption who has also made circuits and plans for the devices openly available online via a number of internet sites: i.e. http://www.keyportparanormal.com/images/theghostbox_1_.pdf

Sumption's Ghost Box spawned a series of other designs generically referred to as Frank's Boxes. Many of these are much less complex in their design and functioning, many (all) relying solely upon a continually scanning tuning circuit and often built using a modified cheap digital AM / FM radio receiver. They are available to buy on a number of internet stores and auction sites. These devices are actually far removed from the original Ghost Box and are in fact more akin to the early detuned radios used by Raudive. In operation, they produce short staccato snatches of radio broadcasts and noise which is recorded, together with any questions from the experimenter, using a separate recorder (these days usually digital). They are relatively inexpensive, although much more expensive than the modified donor radios which typically cost $20 or $30 unmodified and this has made them popular with ghost hunters, particularly after they were shown in use on several TV ghost investigation shows in the USA and UK. In the past five years, there has been an increase in the number of EVP gadgets being offered to ghost hunters – the MiniBox, Steve's Box, the Shack Hack, and others, all being based on some form of continuously scanning radio receiver. Devices such as the EVP listener use a simple electromagnetic coil that replaces the microphone, originally used for placing on telephone handsets for (often covert) recording of conversations by means of electromagnetic induction, and will readily produce responses in proximity to any nearby electromagnetic field. This close association with EMF has no doubt helped with their popularity with ghost hunters.

Many current EVP experimenters still use the simple methods of microphone recording with and without the use of an additional background radio or white noise source with much claimed success. Others are working with Spiricom derivatives. Researchers at the German Association for Transcommunication Research (VTF) developed the radio "Sweeping" method in 1991, which was subsequently described in their journal:

> Sweeping a radio receiver now is done by moving the scale pointer back and forth over a defined (small) frequency band.
>
> An example: The receiver is tuned to Radio Vatican (1530 kHz). By using a sweep amplitude of ± 10 kHz, the tuning of the receiver would move back and forth between 1520 and 1540 kHz, i.e., over Radio Mainflingen and Radio Kosice. This happens with a speed of 4 Hz, which is adjusted to four times a second. Now assume that these three radio stations all transmit voice transmissions at the same time. You would hear a mixture of Italian, Slovakian, and German, and all these languages would alternately blend into each other.
>
> In this mixture, EVP are formed very often – voices independent from the background, the mode of speaking peculiarly linked to the sweep rhythm. The voices arise through the actual sweep movement, and it's a misunderstanding to believe that it's possible to produce a "sweep cassette" for subsequent application. This can be done just as little as one can spare somebody gymnastics by watching a gymnastics video.

> Now how is it done technically? What you need are two very simple constructions:
>
> 1. A receiver with a sweep connector, i.e. an input that allows varying the tuning by applying a voltage.
> 2. A sweep generator. This is a device, which provides a slowly increasing and decreasing voltage and thereby can alter the receiver tuning by a certain amount and with a certain speed (sweep amplitude and sweep frequency).
>
> To do an EVP recording, you first find a radio station or a mixture of stations; preferably all voice transmissions, with the sweep amplitude turned to the minimum. Next you slowly increase the sweep amplitude, and maybe alter the sweep frequency. The whole thing requires some experience, but after a few attempts it will work very easily. (VTF-Post Issue 2/91 p. 63)

The technical term "sweeping", which is well known in electronics, means to automatically move the tuning between two fixed frequencies back and forth. The distance between these frequencies is called "sweep amplitude" and the speed of the back and forth movement is called sweep frequency. Both of them are usually adjustable within certain limits.

It may be noticed that this technique is remarkably similar to and predates the development of Sumption's Ghost-Box and the Frank's Boxes by over 10 years.

Summary

The history of EVP has rapidly grown and it is too lengthy to discuss every single element of it in full here, including all the various researchers involved. However, as it currently stands, there are many active researchers, from professional scientists to keen amateurs. Many ghost hunters also maintain an extremely active interest in EVP, producing recordings during various nights spent in haunted locations or even within their own homes. These recordings are often destined for the internet, with hundreds of internet sites showcasing EVP and other methods of ITC with the results, equipment, and merchandise. An internet search conducted in 2012, using the search term "electronic voice phenomenon" produced a staggering 863,000 results! The same search term in YouTube will produce well over 6000 results. All of the researchers mentioned throughout this chapter involved in EVP research were/are trying to better understand and explain what it is we are actually hearing. Looking at the available information on EVP as a whole, on the internet or otherwise, some results are more thorough and honest than others, and this is evident on simple close inspection of the *methods* and *motives* for conducting the research and its place of publication. Research and interest for EVP remains strong and active, with steady and patient research progressing toward a greater understanding of the nature of the voices. No discussion of EVP can hope to cover the subject in absolute depth and much of the earliest research is now probably lost forever and we are left with only fragments and sometimes hearsay descriptions of the pioneers of electronic communications with the dead. Included in these it is worth mentioning at least in passing:

> American Spiritualist, Jonathan Koon (1852), claimed to have devised a machine for communicating with deceased spirits. The plans of which have never been discovered.
>
> Inventor, Nicola Tesla (1888), suggested radio could be used to communicate with the dead.
>
> Father Landell de Moura (1893), Priest and early radio pioneer described the possibility of radio communication with the dead and was said to have built a prototype spirit radio device. No plans or notes have ever been found.
>
> Brazilian Oscar D Argonnel (1925), publishes his book *"Voices From Beyond By Telephone"* describing contacts from other dimensional beings using the telephone.
>
> Brazilian Cornelio Pires (1923-1928), worked on equipment intended to communicate with spirits.

INFRASOUND AND THE PARANORMAL

Steven Parsons

In 1998, researchers Vic Tandy and Tony Lawrence published their paper 'The Ghost in the Machine' in the *Journal of The Society for Psychical Research* that stated a case for infrasound as a causal factor in the production of certain subjective paranormal-like experiences in some people. Their work specifically pointed toward a frequency close to 19Hz as being key in creating such experiences, which included a sense of presence, depression, chills and sweating and vague peripheral apparitions. Since then, infrasound has become an established explanation within paranormal research as a causal factor in the production of personal experiences that may be interpreted by the percipient as having a paranormal origin. This chapter, based upon the author's published research (see appendix) examines the case for infrasound and its association with paranormal experiences.

What is Infrasound?

Infrasound is generally considered to be audio-frequency energy that lies below the range of normal human hearing; typically 20Hz. Ambient infrasound within the environment is produced by both natural and man-made sources. Natural sources include weather-related effects, e.g., wind and storms, surf and wave action, volcanic eruptions, and upper atmospheric phenomena, e.g., the jet stream and meteors. Man-made infrasound is associated with vehicles, aircraft, machinery, and the interactions of weather with buildings and other structures. Ambient infrasound levels from natural and man-made causes are variable in intensity, and there have to date been a limited number of measurements of ambient environmental infrasound. From these few studies, however, and the author's own survey of ambient infrasound levels at more than 40 locations in the UK, it is clear that ambient infrasound is often to be found at levels of 50–80 dBS in rural locations, and frequently in excess of 90 or 100 dBS in suburban areas and close to industry and major transport routes. All of the various surveys showed that the amount of infrasound rose markedly as a result of increased weather interactions with structures (particularly wind). Because of its low frequencies and long wavelengths, infrasound is capable of travelling long distances with little attenuation. Consequently, much of the infrasound energy, even from sources that produce sound energy across the entire sound-frequency spectrum, will be apparent at considerable distances from the actual source. The infrasound shockwave or sonic boom from Concorde travelling between London and New York at supersonic speed was measured at up to 75 dBS several hundreds of kilometers away in the North of Sweden. The infrasound from volcanic and other seismic events can be recorded as it travels around the Earth numerous times, losing only a small percentage of its total energy on each circuit. It is therefore clear that infrasound is not only present almost everywhere but it is also present at considerable amplitudes, although it is largely undetectable by normal hearing and un-measurable by the majority of available sound-level measuring equipment. In 1975, J. B. Westin noted in a review paper dealing with the effects of infrasound on man, that the amounts of natural and man-made infrasound that man is subjected to is larger than generally realised, and commented that few studies have concerned themselves with the physiological effects of moderate-to-high levels of infrasound exposure.

Paranormal Interest in Infrasound

Early investigators of the paranormal recognised that vibrations were a component in some reported haunts and poltergeist cases. The pioneering psychical investigator Harry Price, for example, included a bowl of mercury in his personal ghost-hunting kit for the detection of tremors in a room or passage. Price was also aware of the ability of certain notes and sounds to cause a sympathetic vibration in other objects. For example, he observed that in one case, a particular pealing of nearby church bells caused the wires of a piano in a haunted house to vibrate in sympathy, leading to the residents reporting that ghostly music was at times being played by unseen hands.

Other early psychical researchers, including Sir Oliver Lodge and Nandor Fodor, also noted that sound vibrations played a mysterious part in the production of psychic phenomena. Whilst none of the early investigators directly mention infrasound, as the concept of low-frequency sounds that exist below the normal human hearing range did not gain general scientific recognition until the 1940's, it is clear that they considered that sound energy that could not be directly heard was potentially significant in cases of hauntings and poltergeists. Later research also failed to show familiarity with infrasound and continued to focus upon the direct physical effects of the sound pressure waves on structures rather than people. In an experiment that was set up to examine vibrations and jolts associated with poltergeist activity, SPR members Alan Gauld and Tony Cornell used a powerful mechanical vibrator attached to a group of abandoned houses that were scheduled for demolition. This created powerful vibrations throughout the structure of the building and could be set to vibrate at frequencies between 45 Hz and 12 0Hz. The aim of the experiment was to test the claim that geophysical forces might be responsible for some aspects of poltergeist activity. The experiment would have produced large amounts of infrasound within the building as the powerful machinery vibrated the structure. The investigators did not report or look for any anomalous physiological or psychological subjective experiences during any of these experiments and confined their reporting of results to observed physical effects upon the structure. In 1974, Canadian Professor, M. A. Persinger, made the first direct claim of a possible causal link between infrasound exposure and reported anomalous experiences. He stated that:

> Infrasound, however, is an excellent candidate for at least some types of precognitive experiences. Weak infrasound energy from ambient sources could evoke vague responses and lead to reports of feelings of foreboding, depression, or impending doom ahead of natural phenomena such as earthquakes or storms.

However, exploration of the potential link between infrasound and subjective paranormal experiences was not undertaken for many years, possibly because of the perceived technical difficulties in properly measuring infrasound energy within a haunt location, and a general lack of data relating to levels of ambient infrasound within the environment. In the past decade and a half, infrasound has captured the attention of investigators of the paranormal. This interest follows studies that have postulated a causal link between infrasound energy and the appearance of apparitions. Tandy and Lawrence proposed that exposure to infrasound close to 19Hz was instrumental in the production of psycho-physiological experiences that were subjectively reported as being paranormal in their origin. As a result of their paper, and a second published in 2000, paranormal investigators have begun to take a keen interest in infrasound. Tandy's suggestion was based upon his own personal experiences and existing studies carried out on behalf of the United States space programme and military weapons research. These research programmes were set up to study the physiological and psychological effects of infrasound exposure on astronauts and military personnel. The experiments used high infrasound exposure levels (150dBS–170dBS) - levels much higher than might be expected in homes, industry, or from environmental sources.

The secrecy surrounding lethal and non-lethal acoustic weapon development, and the general lack of information detailing the effects of high levels of infrasound exposure has periodically resulted in dramatic, even alarmist claims being made within the media about infrasound and its effects – 'The Silent Sound Menaces Drivers' (*The Daily Mirror*, 19th October 196), 'Brain Tumours caused by noise' (*The Times*, 29th September 1973), 'The Silent Killer All Around Us' (*London Evening News*, 25th May 1974). As a result of these distorted claims, infrasound has developed a popular mythology and has been blamed for many ailments and misfortunes for which no other explanation could be forthcoming. These have included brain tumours, cot death, and road accidents. In 1973, Lyall Watson published '*Supernature: A Natural History of the Supernatural*', in which he repeated a series of claims originally made by French weapons scientist Vladimir Gavreau, including:

> ...that "in an experiment with infrasonic generators, all the windows were broken within a half mile of the test site", later adding that "two infrasonic generators focused on a point five miles away produce a resonance that can knock a building down as effectively as a major earthquake".

Gavreau's original claims have never been substantiated and many subsequent researchers have disputed them. However, these sometimes extraordinary and frequently misleading claims about the physical and physiological effects of infrasound, combined with a general lack of research into the effects of exposure both to naturally occurring and to man-made infrasound, have permitted many to popularise the idea that infrasound is the cause of many paranormal experiences.

Many researchers have developed their own theories and explanations of a relationship between infrasound and the paranormal. Some of these appear to be the work of a creative rather than a logical mind. On their internet site one established and well-known paranormal group claim that:

> Infrasound is caused by ghosts and spirits as they use electromagnetic energy to move things or materialise, just as lightening which is moving energy creates thunder which is infrasound, this can be recorded and used to prove that spirits are present.

Another respected team of investigators claims to have recorded many infrasonic EVPs (electronic voice phenomena) using handheld digital dictation recorders, devices that are completely incapable of recording infrasound. There also seems to be a generally poor understanding of the original work by Tandy and of the technical constraints and limitations to making infrasound measurements within the broad paranormal community by both parapsychologists and amateur investigators alike. This has led to a general misunderstanding of any actual relationship between infrasound and paranormal experiences and accounts.

Psychological and Physiological Effects of Infrasound

A number of studies have been conducted to study the psychological and physiological effects of infrasound on individuals. Such studies have used a range of pure infrasound tones at high sound-pressure levels to examine the effects of infrasound exposure upon subjects. Individuals subjected to infrasound at high sound pressure levels (SPL's) reported ear pressure, headaches, and tiredness; they also described feeling uncomfortable or 'troubled'. Other studies reported effects on the cardio-vascular and respiratory systems, including changes in heart rate, blood pressure, and respiratory rate. Although the effects of infrasound exposure have been objectively demonstrated, the results obtained from these experiments have shown highly variable effects, with different individuals experiencing different responses to the infrasound exposure. Infrasound exposure has also been reported to include effects on the inner ear, leading to vertigo and imbalance, intolerable sensations, incapacitation, disorientation, nausea and vomiting. Subjects exposed to infrasound at 5Hz and 10Hz with levels of 100dB–135dB reported feelings of fatigue, apathy, depression, pressure in the ears, a loss of concentration, drowsiness, and vibrations of the internal organs. In a study on airline pilots, it was found that long-term exposure to infrasound of 14Hz–16Hz at levels around 125dB caused decreased alertness, a faster decrease in the electrical resistance of the skin, and an alteration in time perception. Other researchers have reported that infrasound exposure produced sensations of apprehension, visual effects, nausea and dizziness, depression, fatigue, and headaches. Furthermore, it has been observed that ordinary man-made sources of infrasound such as fans and defective air conditioners might produce similar effects.

Anecdotally, many people report adverse physiological and psychological effects, which they claim, result from exposure to man-made infrasound. In response to a series of articles about the possible dangers of low-frequency noise, *The Sunday Mirror* received over 700 letters from readers describing a wide range of adverse health and psychological effects that they attributed to low-frequency sounds, including severe headaches, nausea, palpitations, dizziness, extreme fatigue, visual hallucinations, disturbed sleep, nightmares, and suicidal thoughts. From the various studies of the biological effects, it would appear that the effects of exposure to infrasound are highly variable from individual to individual. Studies carried out using animals have also reported adverse effects from exposure to infrasound.

Infrasound Waves and Structures

As previously stated in the chapter relating to the physics of sound, sound waves are absorbed, reflected, or diffracted by any obstacles in their path. Absorption or reflection of a sound wave reduces the amount of energy it is able to transmit. This will reduce the loudness of subsequent sounds and will also cause an attenuation of the distance that the sound waves can travel. For reflection of the sound waves to occur, the wavelength must be smaller than the dimensions of the reflecting object. For example, if the side of a building is 10m high and 20m long, the dimensions of the building will have an appreciable effect upon the reflection of sounds with wavelengths of less than 10m. This corresponds to frequencies of around 34Hz. Sounds above that frequency will be more readily reflected. If sound waves with a lower frequency and correspondingly longer wavelength encounter the same obstacle, they will not be reflected but will instead bend around the obstacle, a process called diffraction. If the wavelength is much greater than the obstacle size, then there will be marked bending around the obstacle. At infrasonic frequencies where the wavelengths are considerable, sometimes hundreds or thousands of metres in length, very little of the infrasound wave energy is reflected. Absorption of the infrasound wave may also be significantly lower than for audible sounds. Therefore infrasound waves are able to travel greater distances from the source without significant attenuation; in air infrasound may be detectable over tens or even hundreds of kilometres and even further through liquid or solid media.

Acoustic pressure waves reflected and refracted by the structure of a building from man-made infrasound sources such as machinery and vehicles either externally, internally, or both, may also combine with naturally produced infrasound from wind and weather interactions upon the structure. This will have the effect of creating regions within the building that have significantly higher and lower levels of infrasound. Such regions may be highly localised and depend upon the actual acoustic wave and structural interactions. Additional factors that will affect the local levels of infrasound and must be considered include the dimensions, shape, and construction materials of a building, together with the frequency and amplitude of the infrasound. If the infrasound is produced by weather and other natural sources of infrasound, these too must be acknowledged and understood. Local infrasound levels will vary over time because of variations in the ambient infrasound sources, natural or man-made, and the resultant change in their structural interactions. When measuring infrasound within any location, a single measuring point will rarely produce an accurate overall result for that location. When measuring potential human infrasound exposure, the measurements should be made as close as possible to the position of the percipient, as a difference of just a few feet can create a significant difference within the local infrasound levels.

Measuring Low Frequency Sound and Infrasound

A number of techniques are available to detect and measure low-frequency sound and infrasound. At the lowest frequencies, i.e. below 1.5 Hz, seismometers are normally used for measuring infrasound in the form of structural vibration. These may be from tectonic sources such as earthquakes and volcanoes and man-made mining explosions. Micro-barometers are preferred for the detection and measurement of infrasound transmitted through the air. These devices are highly accurate and were originally developed for the detection of infrasound generated by atomic bomb tests. They have also been used for the study of meteors, thunderstorms, and weather-related phenomena, mainly in the range 0.1–5 Hz. For higher infrasound frequencies, typically those above 5Hz, microphone-measuring systems are commonly employed, such as the Bruel and Kjaer Type 2209 sound-level meter. This meter employs a microphone that is sensitive to 1Hz and can be connected to a fast fourier transform (FFT) analyser to allow spectral analysis measurements to be made. Many of these systems have been developed to permit environmental noise measurement and the subsequent measurements generally use some form of electronic filtering in order to replicate as closely as possible normal thresholds of human hearing, a technique known as 'weighting'. This has led to the development of a series of weighting filters that have been optimised to cover a range of different environmental and acoustic conditions. The most commonly used is the 'A' filter, which is designed for general environmental monitoring. However, a major drawback of the 'A' weighting scale is that it underestimates the importance of frequencies below 100Hz. Alternative weighting filters have been developed for specialist measurement of sounds having a significant low-frequency component, these include the 'C' filter, which is recommended for artillery noise, and the 'D' filter, which is used for aircraft noise measurement. Both of these commonly used filters are based on extrapolations into the lower frequencies and are not based upon empirical low-frequency data. The best noise weighting for infrasound remains to be settled but many infrasound researchers now believe that the most effective method predictor for human reaction to infrasound is the equal energy units method, sometimes called Zero or 'Z' weighting, in which no additional weighting is applied to the sound pressure measurement. These un-weighted measurements are normally quoted in units of dB suffixed with 'Z', or more commonly 'S', thus dBZ or dBS. Professional environmental sound monitoring systems are generally prohibitively expensive for many researchers. Additionally, no single standard for the measurement of environmental low-frequency sound and infrasound has been adopted as yet, a situation, which can result in difficulties when trying to make direct comparisons between existing studies.

Testing the Case for Infrasound and the Paranormal

The first paper by Tandy and Lawrence, *The Ghost in the Machine* (see appendix), suggested a causal role for infrasound in some instances of haunt phenomena and apparitions. This suggestion was based entirely upon the observed effects on a metal sword blade and the anecdotal reports of paranormal experiences within the same location. The source of the infrasound was traced by trial and error to a defective fan within the haunted workplace. The actual frequency and amplitude of the infrasound were never directly measured but they were estimated from the authors' personal experiences, mathematical calculations, and the observation of the effects. The authors noted similarities in psycho-physiological effects reported by workers exposed to low-frequency fan noise. A key suggestion of this paper was that infrasound at a specific frequency range (around 19Hz) was causing eyeball vibration and leading to visual effects that may subsequently be interpreted as apparitional encounters. Tandy later conducted a series of field infrasound measurements in a 14th-century cellar beneath a tourist information centre in Coventry. In this experiment, objective measurements of the ambient infrasound were made using contemporary environmental monitoring equipment. He observed that a frequency close to 19Hz was present within the location, confirming his earlier idea. Tandy's infrasound hypothesis was quickly picked up by the media and the paranormal community, and seems to have become the catalyst for many of the claims now being made for infrasound involvement in paranormal cases.

Without exception, infrasound exposure studies carried out by researchers (other than by those having any paranormal interest) have been for the purposes of seeking to establish whether there are any adverse human health or performance implications for people who are exposed to infrasound in the workplace. These studies have predominantly used pure-tone infrasound at high or very high amplitudes or long exposure periods in their experimental design. The use of pure tones in many of the infrasound exposure studies may severely restrict the applicability of their findings to real-world situations, since ambient infrasound from both natural and man-made sources is almost without exception in the form of broadband noise consisting of a range of fundamental notes, harmonics, and resonant frequencies. The findings from these studies, as previously mentioned, describe feelings of anxiety or dread, nausea, sickness, and the sudden onset of headaches. Many of these effects are notably similar to those reported in spontaneous paranormal cases. Initially, this similarity of experience may seem impressive and should certainly not be dismissed, but a number of problems remain to be addressed. For example, a study carried out in 1991 found that long-distance truck drivers who were exposed to infrasound at around 115 dB showed no statistically significant incidence of fatigue, subdued sensations, or cardiovascular changes.

Studies by those interested in the possible links between reported paranormal experiences and infrasound exposure have so far tended to focus most of their experiments on infrasound frequencies of close to 19 Hz (interest in this frequency range being as a direct result of the work by Tandy and Lawrence). The frequency was identified by a mathematical calculation.

> The following day V.T. was entering a fencing competition and needed to cut a thread onto the tang of a spare foil blade so that he could attach the handle. He had all the tools necessary but it was so much easier to use the engineer's bench vice in the lab to hold the blade that he went in early to cut the thread. It was only a five-minute job, so he put the blade in the vice and went in search of a drop of oil to help things along. As he returned, the free end of the blade was frantically vibrating up and down. Combining this with his experience from the previous night, he once again felt an immediate twinge of fright. However, vibrating pieces of metal were more familiar to him than apparitions, so he decided to experiment. If the foil blade was being vibrated it was receiving energy, which must have been varying in intensity at a rate equal to the resonant frequency of the blade. Energy of the type just described is usually referred to as sound. There was a lot of background noise but there could also be low-frequency sound or infrasound, which V.T. could not hear. As it happens, sound behaves fairly predictably in long thin tubes such as organ pipes and ex-garages joined end to end, so V.T. started his experiment. He placed the foil blade in a drill vice and slid it along the floor. Interestingly the vibration

> got bigger until the blade was level with the desk (half way down the room); after the desk it reduced in amplitude, stopping altogether at the far end of the lab. V.T. and his colleagues were sharing their lab with a low frequency standing wave! The energy in the wave peaked in the centre of the room indicating that there was half a complete cycle. Once V.T. knew this, he calculated the frequency of the standing sound wave.

Tandy's mathematical calculation of the standing wave within the lab is however based solely upon a single room dimension, specifically its length, which is given as 30ft, and a wavelength of twice the length of the room, i.e., 60ft.

Tandy used the formula Wavelength = Velocity ÷ Frequency to compute frequency as the velocity of sound (1139ft/sec) divided by wavelength (60ft), which equals 18.89Hz. In the calculations contained within the paper, it appears that no account was taken of either the height or width of the room, the dimensions of which are not provided. However, in order to properly determine the acoustic properties of any space and accurately calculate the frequency of standing waves within the space, calculations involving all three dimensions of the space must be used.

Broadly speaking, three types of standing wave will exist inside any space. The most powerful of these are the axial waves, which involve any two parallel surfaces, such as opposing walls, or the floor and ceiling. With axial waves there are always sound-pressure maxima at the walls. In addition, there will be tangential waves that involve any two sets of parallel surfaces - all four walls, or two opposing walls and the ceiling and floor. These are about half as strong as the axial modes, and also give maxima at the walls. Finally, there are oblique waves that involve all six surfaces (four walls, the ceiling, and the floor) and are about one quarter as strong as the axial waves and half as strong as the tangential waves. Oblique waves, which are rarely of much relevance, also give sound pressure maxima at the walls.

It is noteworthy that with all three types of standing wave within a room or space there is always a pressure maximum at the walls - something which seems to be contrary to the observation made by Tandy:

> Interestingly, the vibration got bigger until the blade was level with the desk (half way down the room); after the desk it reduced in amplitude, stopping altogether at the far end of the lab.

In order to calculate the frequencies of the axial, tangential and oblique waves, the following formula may be used: -

$$f = \frac{c}{2}\sqrt{\left(\frac{Nx}{L}\right)^2 + \left(\frac{Ny}{B}\right)^2 + \left(\frac{Nz}{H}\right)^2}$$

f = Frequency of the standing wave in Hz.
C = Speed of sound in air at C.
Ny = Order of standing wave for room width
Nx = Order of standing wave for room length
Nz = Order of standing wave for room height
L, B, H = Length, Width, Height of the room

Using the above formula and assuming the stated room length of 30ft, and estimating a reasonable width of 12ft and a height of 10ft for the laboratory, in the Tandy and Lawrence's original paper, we are presented with a range of fundamental (first order) low-frequency standing waves below 100Hz that would be expected to be present inside the lab room: -

18.8Hz (x axial wave)	50.7Hz (x-y tangential wave)	75.9Hz (x-y-z oblique wave)
47.1Hz (y axial wave)	59.6Hz (x-z tangential wave)	
56.5 Hz (z axial wave)	73.5Hz (y-z tangential wave)	

As may be clearly seen, there is no single standing wave existing inside the laboratory room but in fact several, all of which to a greater of lesser degree may have affected the sword blade. Furthermore, the authors do not provide any information regarding the dimensions, i.e. the length, width, and thickness, of the blade that was seen to be vibrating, thus it is impossible for us to calculate the resonant frequency of the blade itself and to know which standing wave(s) might therefore have been responsible for producing the observed vibrations within it.

Without extensive measurements being undertaken, it will be practically impossible to predict all the various effects that acoustic vibrations might produce within structural systems. Tandy's mathematical modelling of the standing wave within the lab also assumes that the source of the standing infrasound was a new fan fitted to the lab's extraction system. Certainly he observed that turning off the fan caused the sword blade to cease vibrating and the untoward experiences to also cease, which might indicate that the fan was indeed the source of a standing wave. However, this could equally indicate that an infrasound standing wave of unknown frequency or frequencies had been formed by the interactions of the fan noise with another undetermined external or internal infrasound source. We have seen that infrasound is capable of travelling large distances without significant attenuation, and as no actual infrasound measurements were made within the lab, either with or without the fan, it is not possible to know here which is the case. Taking the above into consideration, it could be argued that the case for a 19Hz standing wave effect is not as strong as it first appeared. This likelihood is further borne out by a mass infrasound exposure study carried out in Edinburgh at the Real Mary King's tourist attraction and within concert applications of infrasound applied to unknowing audiences, neither of which produced the visual hallucinations or the apparitional experiences that Tandy suggested were caused by a 19Hz infrasound exposure.

Are Paranormal Researchers Measuring Infrasound Properly?

In his subsequent paper, *Something in the Cellar* (see appendix), Tandy reports finding an infrasound standing wave at 19Hz with amplitude of 38dB in the haunted cellar. Unfortunately, he does not specify what weighting filter (if any) was applied to his measurements. As has already been described, the use of a filter weighting scale (i.e. A, B, C, or D) when obtaining infrasound measurements of the ambient levels of infrasound within the environment, may result in the erroneous under-reporting of the actual levels present. Given the type of equipment used by Tandy (a Bruel & Kjaer Type 2209 sound-level meter), if one of the standard weighting filters was applied to the data, either 'C', or more likely the 'A' weighting its use could lead to a serious underestimate of the infrasound pressure levels. In 1978, The Journal of Sound Vibration described a case in a London home where infrasound, which was causing annoyance to the wife but not the husband, was measured to be only 32 dB using 'A' weighting, but the actual SPL was actually measured at 63dB – around 1,000 times more powerful in terms of acoustic energy being measured.

In September 2006, immediately before its closure, I was able to undertake a series of infrasound measurements at the haunted cellar in Coventry using the 1st version of ARID to repeat the experiment carried out by Tandy. Replicating Tandy's placement, of the microphone, infrasound measurements were made automatically at one-minute intervals in the empty cellar. The measurements did not support Tandy's claim of finding a 19Hz standing wave within the cellar, although infrasound-exceeding 30dBS was found to be present across a broad range of frequencies between 2Hz and 20Hz, together with a strong peak of 44dBS at 5.7Hz. However, it is difficult to make any further comparisons between the two infrasound surveys because of the variability of location of infrasound production on account of changes in the ambient sources, plus not knowing what, if any, filter weighting Tandy used for his measurements, and the lack of proper calibration for the ARID system at that time.

Tandy acknowledges that his measured value of 38dB within the cellar is substantially lower than those previously reported to have effects on people but suggests that, as the effects are rather less spectacular, this may simply be the result of the lower amplitudes found. Others, such as Braithwaite and Townsend also make the point that there are no published studies that have found any implications for cognition or experience of infrasound as weak as this. In fact, as already noted, depending upon the type of filter weighting used (if any), the actual levels of infrasound present may have been substantially higher and therefore much closer to those demonstrated in other studies to produce effects. This difference in measuring and quoting infrasound levels between field and laboratory studies may also provide an explanation for the results of other experiments where low-amplitude infrasound has been suggested to have effects.

Another difficulty in determining infrasound amounts from field measurements is the sampling period used. In his published experiments using the haunted cellar, Tandy reports using a sample time of just 20 seconds. Although we are informed that the measurements were repeated a number of times, it is not made clear whether the resultant data came from a single sample period or were the average of a number of measurements. A short sampling period of 20 seconds will inevitably mean the overall measured infrasound values are likely to be affected by transient high-energy events, for example, a passing bus or other vehicle, or by the slamming of a nearby door. Weather effects and weather interactions, with the structure of the location being measured (such as a wind gust), might also generate transient infrasound frequencies during such a short sampling period. Using a longer sampling period would have permitted any such transients to be taken into account and would have allowed a more realistic assessment of the true ambient infrasound levels to be made. My own measurements at the haunted cellar showed that there were indeed short-duration infrasound events caused by passing vehicles, including buses, construction traffic, and delivery vehicles. Interestingly, it was also discovered that the presence of people within the cellar contributed significantly to the production of infrasound. Increases in the measured infrasound levels of between approximately 15 and 30dBS were recorded as members of the experimental team moved and walked about within the cellar. Tandy records that he vacated the cellar prior to his measurements being carried out. However, the original incidents took the form of visitor's personal anomalous experiences during tours of the historic cellar, suggesting that vacating the cellar may not have provided an accurate reflection of the prevailing conditions at the time of the original incidents. Following the death of Tandy, there had been little effective research into the possible involvement of infrasound in the production of paranormal experiences. However, since 2006, I have undertaken a series of broadband infrasound measurements using ARID (1&2) at a number of locations around the UK, and have conducted a number of experiments to study the link between infrasound exposure and reports of anomalous and paranormal experiences.

A pilot study was carried out at the former Cammell Laird shipyard on Merseyside in 2006. The location had a reputation among staff of being haunted, and paranormal investigators also reported unusual sensations and experiences. Many of the reported sensations were similar to the physiological and psychological effects that are known to be associated with infrasound exposure. Results of this pilot study suggested that there was a strong link between high ambient levels of infrasound (up to 80dBS), at frequencies of between 7Hz and 15Hz, and reports of anomalous experiences in the percipients. The source of the powerful ambient infrasound was eventually traced to the engines and associated equipment on ships berthed in an adjacent dock. Of further interest, were the noted impressions of a psychic medium who conducted an independent walk through the location. The medium reported that he sensed areas where the "psychic energy" (medium's words) was dense or strong. These reported changes within the psychic energies at the location corresponded closely to the objectively measured regions of high levels of ambient man-made (ship) infrasound.

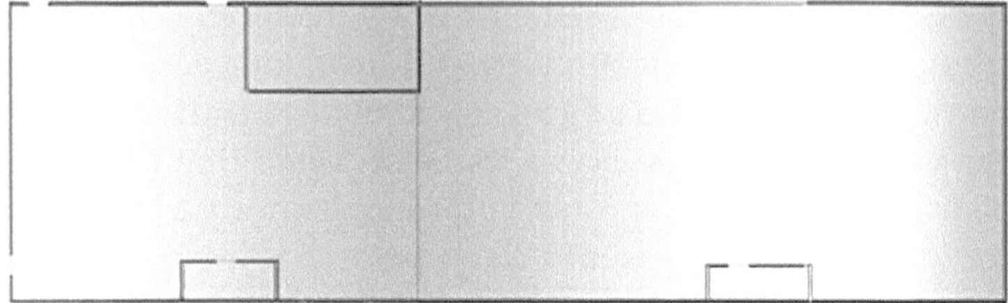

Shipyard: Regions of higher ambient infrasound

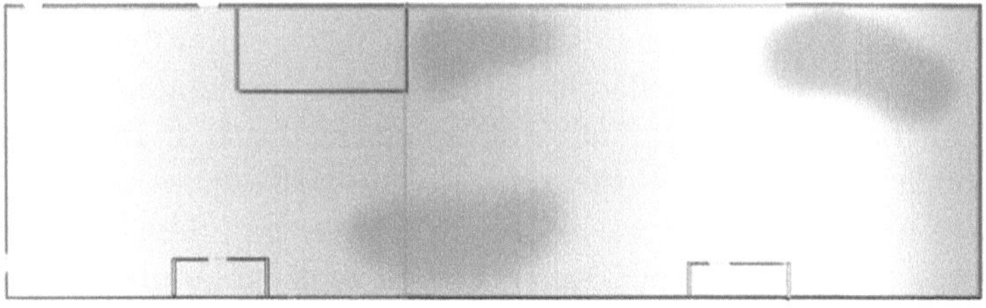

Shipyard: Areas of 'dense psychic energy' as reported by medium

During 2007, I led a team which conducted a pilot study at the Real Mary Kings Close tourist attraction in Edinburgh as part of their annual *GhostFest* event. A controlled level of infrasound was produced using a purpose-built infrasound generator given the acronym ARIA (Acoustic Research Infrasound Array). Throughout the study period, ambient levels of infrasound were measured using ARID2. Hourly tour groups to Mary Kings Close were unknowingly subjected to either only the ambient infrasound that is normally present, or the ambient infrasound plus experimenter-produced high-level infrasound (more than 100dBS) at a frequency of 18.9Hz. The route of the tours and the commentary of the tour guides were observed and were consistent for all the tour groups. The physical conditions, such as lighting and temperature within the location, were measured and constant throughout the period of the study. Upon completion of the tour, the subjective anomalous experiences of 439 individuals were surveyed by means of a questionnaire. The results obtained strongly indicated that infrasound exposure played a significant role in the production of subjective paranormal experiences for around one-third of the total survey. However, the study failed to demonstrate any of the visual disturbances and resulting apparitional experiences that Tandy had suggested would be created by exposure to the frequency range around 19Hz.

ARIA has also been used in two public performances (2006, 2010) in which a frequency of 18.9Hz was produced at an SPL exceeding 90dBS, measured using the calibrated ARID2 equipment. Anecdotal accounts from participants and audience members did indicate a significant number of psycho-physiological effects, such as feeling ill at ease, anxiousness, and physical discomfort being experienced whenever ARIA was in use. For example, during the first performance at the 2006 Silent Sound performance held in Liverpool's St George's Hall, a number of the musicians within the auditorium reported feeling unwell and nauseous and were subsequently unable to play their instruments ultimately abandoning the room during a rehearsal session as the output level of ARIA was being set. During this set-up test, infrasound levels of more than 90dBS were measured at 10 metres from the infrasound generator. During a break following the initial ARIA set-up tests, we learned that on the ground level, three floors below the auditorium, a security guard had also reported feeling suddenly unwell and had left the building. None of these unfortunate side effects of the infrasound exposure lasted more than a few minutes and they ceased once the infrasound generator was switched off. For the actual performance, infrasound levels not exceeding 60dBS (18.9Hz) were used (10 metres from the infrasound generator). Following the performance, audience members and several musicians anecdotally reported unexpected sensations, including vertigo, pressure in the ears, and the sensation of 'having something pressed tightly over the head'. Similar experiences were reported during the 2010 Silent Sound concert held in Middleborough. At neither performance were any visual or apparitional experiences reported.

Tandy's hypothesis that infrasound may be responsible for inducing anomalous sensations was also tested in 2008. *The Haunt Project* used infrasound and electromagnetic fields to investigate the possibility of creating an artificially haunted room. Specifically, it set out to investigate whether exposure to infrasound, complex electromagnetic fields, or both in combination, would lead to an increased reporting of anomalous sensations in participants compared with a baseline condition. The room was a circular chamber of wood, fabric, and canvas built inside an empty room approximately 4m × 4m (based upon the plans of the experimental area). To produce the electro-magnetic fields, a pair of electromagnetic coils was hidden outside the chamber. Infrasound was produced using a single infrasound speaker positioned outside the

Silent Sound: ARIA infrasound generators
(photograph: Steven Parsons)

chamber in a corner of the main room. The infrasound was generated by combining two sine waves at 18.9Hz and 22.3Hz output via a purpose-built cabinet. These frequencies were chosen to be representative of the infrasound recorded by Tandy in the Coventry cellar. Participants each spent 50 minutes in the chamber and recorded on a floor plan a brief description of any anomalous sensations they experienced, noting their position within the chamber, and the time the sensation was experienced. The participants were randomly allocated to experimental conditions according to the presence or absence of infrasound and electromagnetic field.

Many of the participants reported having anomalous sensations, a number of which have previously been linked to infrasound exposure: dizzy or odd feelings (79.7%), spinning around (49.4%), tingling sensations (32.9%), and pleasant vibrations through their bodies (31.6%).

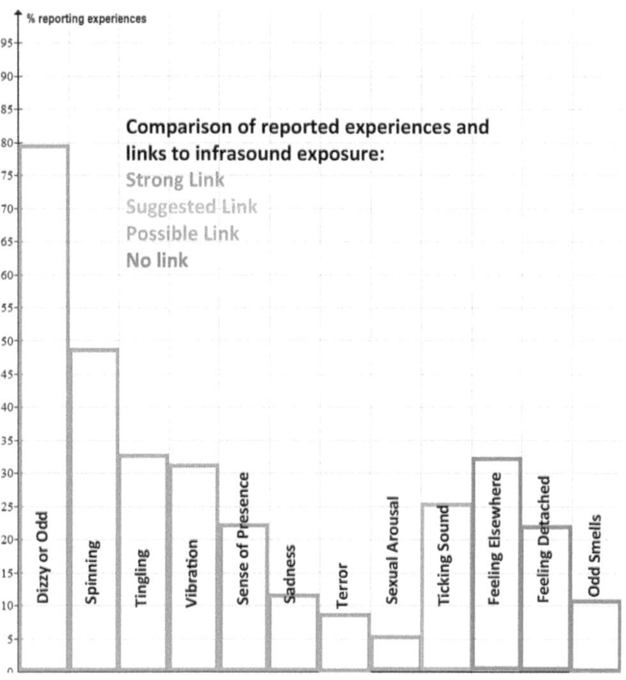

Other sensations linked to infrasound exposure were also reported, including the sense of presence (22.8%), sadness (11.4%), terror (8.9%), and sexual arousal (5.1%). Sensations that may be associated to infrasound were additionally reported such as hearing a 'ticking sound' (25.3%). This may have been the result of changes within the air pressure caused by the infrasound acting on the ear or acting upon some structural component within the room or chamber and causing resonance. Sensations were also reported that have no known association with infrasound exposure, such as the participants feeling they were somewhere else (32.9%), feeling detached from their bodies (22.8%), and odd smells (10.1%).

The researchers reported that they had failed to find any support for a link between the presence of infrasound and the experiencing of anomalous sensations, suggesting, "The case for infrasound inducing haunt-type experiences now appears to be extremely weak". However, as this experiment failed to properly address a number of issues relating to the physics of infrasound, so this conclusion seems potentially weak.

In order to establish undetectable levels of infrasound within the chamber a series of pilot trials were carried out, participants being asked to indicate when they became aware of the infrasound stimulus at a range of frequencies: 15Hz, 17Hz, 19Hz, 21Hz, 23Hz and 25Hz. During this pilot it was determined that "No participant was able to perceive infrasound at a level below 75dB".

It is not stated what equipment or method was used to obtain these sound-level data, or what (if any) filter weighting was applied to the measurements. As previously discussed, it is perfectly possible that significantly higher amplitudes of low-frequency ambient sound and infrasound may have been present throughout the entire experiment without being measured by the experimenters. Moreover, the use of two combined sine waves (18.9Hz and 22.3Hz) will result in the production of secondary frequencies as a result of inter-modulation between the two primary signals. These secondary tones (harmonics) are equal to the sum and difference of the two primary frequencies, i.e. $f1 \pm f2$ (3.4Hz and 41.2Hz). Other harmonic frequencies, well within the region of normal human hearing, might also be expected to be present and the masking effect of audible frequencies upon the perception and reporting of low-frequency sounds was not considered. The experiment also did not consider interactions of the infrasound within the room itself caused by reflected and refracted sound waves bouncing off the walls, floor and ceiling, and the possible effects upon the participants as they walked through what might have been large variations in the sound frequencies present (although interestingly the experimenters did note the effects of field variability in relation to the electromagnetic field.) "The nature of the field itself can vary infinitely and the participants' movements through the field will add an extra level of complexity to the field as experienced".

Measurements that were made are stated to be "50dB with all the equipment turned off, 65dB with the air-conditioning switched on, and 75dB" when the infrasound was switched on. No information was provided about the sound-measuring equipment that was used or any indication whether or not any frequency weighting was applied to the measurements or information about the sampling rate and period. Without this crucial information about the ambient infrasound levels present, the experimenter's argument against the role of infrasound as a causal factor in the production of anomalous sensations reported by the participants must be seriously questioned.

Should Paranormal Researchers be Interested in Infrasound at all?

The work by Tandy and Lawrence remains the only real basis for the assumption of an infrasonic involvement in personal experiences at haunt locations. Inevitably, such primary studies are flawed because there is little or no preceding data for the authors to make use of when developing their arguments. However, there are clear similarities between the reported experiences and sensations of those people who have experienced infrasound and those reporting paranormal experiences and sensations. My own preliminary studies in the former shipyard and in Mary Kings Close, together with the anecdotal reports from the infrasound concerts, do strongly suggest that infrasound is a component in the production or enhancing of reported paranormal experiences. The suggestion of a link between infrasound and reported paranormal experiences was also tested in 2003 in a series of 'Soundless Music' concerts that took place in Liverpool and London. Questionnaires handed to the audience elicited a range of reported experiences. Many unusual experiences were reported during the concerts, ranging from the emotional (e.g. sense of sorrow), brief moment of anxiety and excited, to the physiological (e.g. increased heart-rate), headache, tingling in neck and shoulders, nausea, and a sense of coldness. The Soundless Music concerts used an infrasound frequency of 17Hz. However, from the experimenter's own low frequency and infrasound measurements it was clear that infrasound was present at all frequencies below 20Hz at considerable intensity.

Susceptibility to the psycho-physiological effects of infrasound exposure seems to be linked to both exposure duration and overall sound-pressure level. Prolonged exposure to low infrasound pressure levels has been suggested as a likely cause of adverse psycho-physiological effects. Although the current research does not directly indicate it, it might be fair to assume that short-duration exposure to high infrasound pressure levels may cause similar effects. Existing research does indicate that exposure to high levels of low-frequency sound at concerts and within some industries does cause aural pain and other physical effects; such effects may be temporary or permanent.

A key problem for paranormal research lies with the lack of information about levels of ambient infrasound at haunt locations. Ambient infrasound studies that are available have been made either following noise complaints or for the establishment of safe exposure limits and thresholds within high noise environments. This lack of baseline data is a crucial problem for paranormal researchers seeking to test or develop the case for an infrasound involvement and must be addressed urgently if meaningful research is to continue. My own on-going survey measures infrasound at similar or co-located control (i.e. non-haunted) sites in order to ascertain whether there are any significant differences in the ambient infrasound frequencies and amplitudes at haunt locations compared with the control sites. Such a survey must also undertake measurements of the ambient infrasound at a wide range of locations, regardless of any paranormal association or reports, in order to establish a set of baseline ambient infrasound data to support future infrasound studies. Other researchers interested in environmental influences, including infrasound upon paranormal witnesses, have also highlighted the need for such baseline data.

Initial Conclusions and Suggested Possibilities

From the limited studies conducted to date and the knowledge that infrasound is produced by so many natural and man-made sources, it now seems highly likely that infrasound is just one of many factors that may lead to the reporting of anomalous or paranormal experiences by some individuals. The research to date has suggested a number of possibilities which I am currently examining further:

(i) That infrasound alone does not produce anomalous and paranormal experiences.

(ii) That infrasound presented at a range of frequencies is more likely to produce reports of anomalous and paranormal experiences than single-frequency infrasound.

(iii) That a rapid variation in the infrasound frequency and/or amplitude i.e. > 1Hz per second or 3 dB per second is more likely to contribute to the reporting of anomalous and paranormal experiences than infrasound that is constant or is slowly changing.

(iv) That a small variation in the infrasound frequency and/or amplitude, i.e. ±2Hz or ±3dB, is more likely to contribute to the reporting of anomalous and paranormal experiences than greater variations.

Further developments and upgrades of both ARID and ARIA are planned which will permit better measurements of the ambient infrasound to be made and to support further studies of infrasound exposure experiences and explore more fully the potential links to reported paranormal experiences.

TELEPHONE ANOMALIES

Callum E. Cooper

Ever since the introduction of the wireless telegraph, there have been reports of irregular and unsettling messages being received over such communication devices. The device of focus within this chapter is the familiar telephone, of which the vast majority of people today own and use every day. The term "telephone" is derived from Greek with "tele" meaning "far/distance" and "phone" meaning "voice" (distance voice). Several individuals are disputed to be given the credit for the invention of the telephone, including Charles Bourseul, Antonio Meucci, Elisha Gray, Johann Philipp Reis, and Alexander Graham Bell – the latter of whom was the first to be awarded with a patent for the electric telephone by the United State Patent Office and Trademark Office in March 1876.

Unlike electronic voice phenomena (EVP), telephone anomalies are spontaneous in their nature, thus occurring without expectation and intent to experience them. The two most common reports of paranormal telephone calls are either: 1) calls from a person who was confirmed to be elsewhere at the time *they* purportedly made the call, and 2) accounts of phone calls from the dead.

In trawling through the available literature on psychical research and electrical apparatus producing unusual messages, strange telephone events can be traced as far back as 1897! In Volume 4 of the psychical research journal *Borderland*, an account was submitted and published entitled 'Did the ghost use the telephone?' The account discussed a gentleman referred to as Mr B. One summer (assumed to be between 1895-96) Mr B. and his wife were looking after their daughter after she had been sent home by her husband for a few days rest – her condition was not serious. Mr B. owned a local business several miles from his home. The office at his place of business had a telephone which connected to the house of his son, also being several miles away. One Sunday, Mr B. junior, heard the telephone ring. He picked up the handset and asked what the matter was and received an unsettling reply: "Go to your father's house at once. Poor Nelly is dead".

Mr B. junior immediately caught the next train. Upon arrival he found the family in distress as his sister had died quite suddenly. What astonished him more was that nobody had sent any message of Nelly's death (or at least no one confessed to) and few people had access to a telephone anyway. The telephone call took place at the very moment his sister passed away. He claimed that he had not been thinking of his sister at the time, and the bell was heard by others in the room. On returning home, he went straight to the office to check the telephone and realised that the call could not have been placed by any natural means. He discovered that wires to the telephone has been disconnected and had been so since the Saturday.

This account is possibly the earliest on record of a paranormal telephone call where the source of the ghostly caller appears untraceable. And yet, the caller relayed a message of urgency, as is often the case, which no one appeared to have actually made. There are several instances beyond this case of amateur psychical researchers and inventors who allegedly started plans to create a telephone that was able to contact the dead, some of whom claimed they successfully did so. Among these claimants are Francis Grierson, F.R. Melton, Harry Gardner, and J. Gilbert Wright, and most famously, although in rumour alone, Thomas Edison. Edison was fascinated with Spiritualism, and reported his intention to build a trans-communication machine to *Scientific American* in 1920. This was around the same time that most other claimants had actually produced something and reported on it, and perhaps Edison wanted to be in on this scene too. Although rumours of blueprints were produced following his death in 1931, no such telephone device to contact the dead was ever recovered (see Cooper (2012) Chapter 3, for a full historical outline).

Research on Strange Phone-Calls

To skip forward some fifty years, Raymond Bayless and a young D. Scott Rogo had been gathering data on the rapidly developing phenomenon of anomalous electronic voice recordings. During this time (mid-1970s) more and more people began approaching the two researchers to report events that they thought Rogo and Bayless would be interested in, given their rigorous study of EVP. These events were what the witnesses claimed to be "phone calls from the dead". At first, Rogo and Bayless paid little attention to such accounts, given that they had never really come across any such instances in their psychical studies. However, given that accounts began to trickle in, they felt it was worth investigating what seemed to be a new parapsychological phenomenon and additional form of potential evidence for survival of personality beyond death.

In what turned out to be a two-year long study into the collection and investigation of accounts of telephone anomalies, Rogo and Bayless collectively compiled fifty cases for analysis. They then carried out a content analysis on the case collection, which is a process by which all of the accounts were thoroughly read through by the researchers, and familiar themes and characteristics of the accounts were identified. This found several types of call characteristics. The majority of the calls were reported to be communication with the dead, as interpreted by the recipient due to specific information mentioned by the caller, and/or their recognisable voice characteristics. The categories of call types found by Rogo and Bayless are as follows:

1. Type 1: *Simple Calls* – These are the most commonly reported phone calls from the dead. Typically, the dead caller says only a few words and is unresponsive to any questions asked. At this point the caller may say nothing at all and the line will go dead without any sound of the caller hanging up or the phone being cut off.

2. Type 2: *Prolonged Calls* – These calls last for some time (30 minutes or so) and involve a conversation like any other telephone call. The recipient does not realise until after the call that the caller was in fact dead at the time. Due to the recipient of the call not knowing the caller is dead, this somehow seems to allow the conversation to last longer. Simple calls show that the shock of knowing the caller is dead somehow leaves the conversation short, or the dead caller unresponsive.

3. Type 3: *Answer Calls* – These are cases where a living person makes a call to someone they do not realise is dead (or someone who simply wasn't home at the time the call was made) and yet

> they get an answer from what seems to be that very person. These calls are usually prolonged.

To get an idea of what typically occurs within these telephone calls, below is an example of a Type 1 call (reported by Cooper, 2012, p. 56):

> My wife's mother has just died 11 July 1978 from cancer. It was just about a week after she passed away we were getting ready to visit my wife's grandmother in West Virginia. I had gone to the store and my wife was out back in our garden picking vegetables to give away so they wouldn't go to waste while we were gone. She heard the phone ringing, she said it rang several times and she didn't think she would get to it in time but it kept ringing. When she answered it the voice on the other end said:
>
> 'Jessy [only her mom and brother called her that] this is mommy don't you worry about me now cause I'm all right.'
>
> At the time my wife went into hysterics and we thought someone was playing a very sick joke… (Mr D. Byrd - June, 1981)

A fourth type of call was found by Rogo and Bayless in which people would intend to make a call but changed their mind at the last minute. However, the person they intended to call insisted that the call still took place. These were labelled *Intention Calls.* Below is a case that happened to Rogo, during data collection of the original 1979 study by Rogo and Bayless (Rogo, 1986, pp. 116-117):

> It was 4 o'clock on a bright Thursday afternoon, and I was lying on my living room couch thinking about making a phone-call to a psychologist I knew at the U.C.L.A Neuropsychiatric Institute. Although I intended to make the call, I never did. About six that evening, though, I got the shock of my life when a call came in from the Institute and from the office of the very psychologist I had thought about calling. The call was from her research assistant saying that he was 'answering my message'. When I asked what in blazes he was talking about, he told me at 4pm a call had come in to them from me. The caller had left my name, and had asked the call be returned!

All of these findings were compiled into a book by Rogo and Bayless entitled *Phone Calls from the Dead,* which has become a well-known and sought after piece of research, written for the attention of both an academic and public audience to raise awareness of all such related phenomena. Both researchers were in agreement that some form of paranormality was present within many of the accounts that they had gathered, firmly believing that they suggested that the dead *can* and *have* indeed made contact through the telephone.

D. Scott Rogo
(Photograph: *Fate* magazine, Volume 43(12) 1990)

Following their landmark work, they continued to collect cases but never produced any further analysis. Two years later, Bayless contributed a chapter on 'mysterious phone calls' to what was to be his final book concerning psychical research and survival entitled *The Case for Life After Death*, co-authored with Dr Elizabeth McAdams in 1981, and Rogo did the same, but in more detail, in one of his later books *Life After Death* in 1986.

A follow-up study by Dr Massimo Biondi was conducted in Italy regarding anomalous telephone calls in 1984. This study took a year to carry out. The collection of accounts was similar to the previous method used by Rogo and Bayless, through advertising on radio shows, newspaper articles, and specialist publications (i.e. *Fate* magazine). All of these methods asked people to come forward with accounts of "exceptional experiences involving the telephone" so as not to cause a bias in people just presenting instances of "phone calls from *the dead*" rather than strange instances involving living callers. This was important, as it helped avoid any criticism that the sampling method was bias – which it wasn't – in leading participants to report one form of telephone anomaly (dead calls) more than another (living calls).

Around 40 accounts were gathered by Dr Biondi. These accounts were then investigated by interviewing percipients and following up information with telephone companies. This was done to clarify the accounts and to rule out conventional explanations for the events as far as possible. This subsequently led to a smaller sample of accounts which presented few, if any, normal explanations for their occurrence (15 accounts in total). The study found that the Italian sample of anomalous call cases could be fit into the categories of call types generated by Rogo and Bayless from their content analysis. Yet, as Rogo later argued against criticisms of the research, these patterns do not suggest paranormality, but they at least demonstrate some form of internal consistency and suggest how such events occur. Dr Biondi believed that it is doubtful that such experiences present evidence for survival of death, however, this still leaves room for the possibility of some form of psi process being present. He further noted that the majority of the calls he collected fell into the category of impossible calls from *living* people (i.e., *Answer Calls* and *Intention Calls*), rather than cases of communication with the dead. He concluded that the evidence is too limited to verify that these calls are what they appear to be, owing to the numerous conventional explanations that could apply (e.g., misinterpretation, fraud, hypnogogic and hypnopompic states, electrical faults).

However, Dr Biondi still felt such phenomena were worthy of further study in order to attempt to identify the nature and origin of the calls. In 1996, just over a decade later, in an article submitted to *Luce e Ombra*, Dr Biondi once again encouraged a serious examination of telephone anomalies, but he doubted that further research would be carried out in the near future. This was for several reasons: (a) even though the study was advertised to thousands of radio listeners on mainstream stations, no more than 50 respondents were recruited, (b) the study took time and effort, taking a year to collect the data and do follow-up interviews, and (c) the study required more than one researcher to gather more accounts, absorb the financial commitment, and produce serious and meaningful results.

Around thirty years on from the original study by Rogo and Bayless, new research was presented also in the form of a publicly accessible book entitled *Telephone Calls from the Dead: A Revised Look at the Phenomenon Thirty Years On.* This was done following several previous articles on the matter presented by myself in 2010. Similar methods of data collection were also applied in which advertising on social media websites was employed, radio and newspaper advertising, and advertising in relevant academic journals. It was discovered that, following the untimely passing of D. Scott Rogo in 1990, that his files were donated to the California Institute of Integral Studies. Through contacting the Institute and library staff, they kindly assisted the research by sorting through Rogo's files. In doing so, they discovered a file labelled "new cases". This contained investigated cases of telephone anomalies which were unpublished, as they had been submitted after 1979 following the publication of the book *Phone Calls from the Dead.* Some of these accounts were included in the analysis of modern day accounts where telecommunication technology has developed to the common mobile phone, which a vast majority of people now carry, compared to the 1970s when landline and payphone were all that was available. Therefore, the new analysis involved a mixture of Rogo's and Bayless' unpublished and researched accounts (from 1979-1982), and new accounts collected between 2010-2012 (approximately 20% old accounts and 80% new accounts).

All of these accounts were investigated as far as possible and lengthy correspondence was kept with many modern day percipients to strange telephone calls in order to establish the best memory recall of the events in question. In some cases not only were substantial witness statements provided, but also diary extracts from the time the calls took place were provided, and in some cases, actual recordings of voicemail messages – allegedly from the dead.

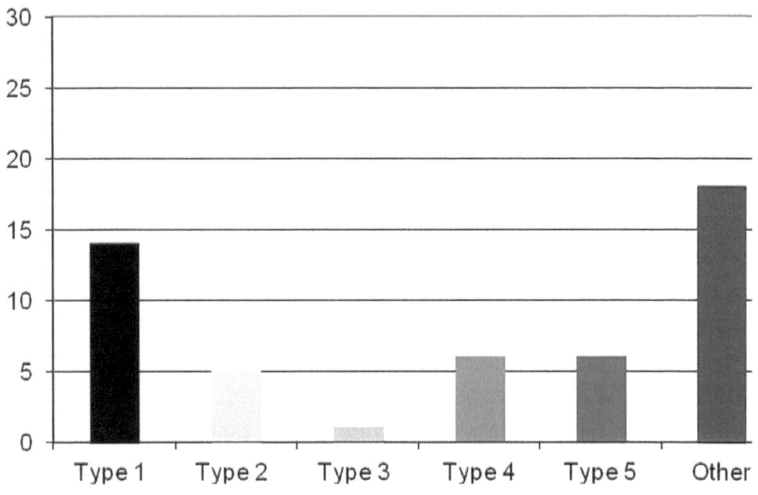

Table 1: *Frequency of Call Types from an Analysis of 50 Cases (Cooper, 2014)*

Type 1 – Simple Calls	Type 4 – Mixed Calls
Type 2 – Prolonged Calls	Type 5 – Intention Calls
Type 3 – Answer Calls	Other – Miscellaneous

So how did the analysis take place? This was done in the same manner as the previous studies. A content analysis is a common research method of the social sciences. It is often used when exploring uncharted territory of human experiences. In this case, strange telephone calls. Given that we cannot jump to conclusions as to what caused the experience, we need to know in what circumstances the calls take place, common themes, the possible source, how they are interpreted, and the content of the calls. Such basic information is essential in attempting to understand the possible – (psychic?) – mechanisms involved. All of the accounts were read over several times to become familiar with the general theme of accounts reported. Once this was done, each case was read through, again noting characteristics of the telephone calls and then placing them into piles of similar overall themes. The frequency of call types is demonstrated in Table 1, and the full methodology and analysis for this study was summarised in a paper published by myself in the Fall 2014 issue of the *Journal of Parapsychology.*

This most recent analysis of telephone anomalies produced another call type, this being Type 4 – *Mixed Calls.* This call category simply highlights calls which contain elements of both Type 1 and Type 2 calls, for example, a person might receive a call from someone they know to be dead, but the call is prolonged and in some rare instances they might receive more than one call from the deceased. One classic example of this involved a mother receiving multiple calls from her childhood sweetheart over a 3 year period! This case was re-examined by her son, a doctor of psychology and sociology, and myself, within a long period of correspondence to establish the facts of the case. This led to no solid conclusion as to the source of the calls thus leaving general speculation, yet is still an extensive and detailed account outlined in *Telephone Calls from the Dead.*

Several other instances of strange telephone calls were noted which had never really been brought to light in previous studies (listed in Table 1 as "Other"). There were cases where people reported "haunted telephones", these being properties which housed a telephone which would ring when disconnected. When the phone was answered, strange messages were heard, warnings, utterances, and static. Some people reported dreaming of a telephone call from the dead, which in some studies on bereavement have found this to be a common dream scenario for bereaved individuals. In no more than 2-3 cases, as was also the finding of Rogo and Bayless, there were precognitive messages of warning given by the deceased caller. In other words, they may have called to warn the living of not taking a particular car journey on a certain day. That journey is then avoided and it is later discovered that there was a major car accident on the very route that would have been taken, and the caller could have been involved if they had not taken the advice of the unknown (or deceased) caller.

Laboratory Experiments

Is it possible to research telephone anomalies in a controlled environment such as the laboratory? To a certain extent, yes! The obstacle of the spontaneity of telephone anomalies has been overcome in a few cases, through investigating what remains besides an eyewitness account. For example, with voicemail messages, an actual recording of the alleged deceased caller remains. Following the death of the EVP researcher Dr Konstantine Raudive, there were reports in the USA, France, and Germany that he had been telephoning people from beyond the grave to confirm his own survival of death and his continued experimentation of transcommunication on the 'other side'. Several of these communications were recorded, and recordings of his voice when alive also exist.

Paolo Presi took this opportunity to compare the recordings of Dr Raudive's voices before and after his death, the results of which were published in the *ITC Journal* in 2001. The samples that Presi analysed were taken from audio contact received by the couple Harsch-Fischbach in 1988 when Raudive first made his alleged discarnate call. It was stated that the voice of Raudive was exceptional in quality, as it sounded perfectly like him when alive. Other samples were used from recorded telephone calls received in Germany (by Friedrich Malkhoff) and in the USA (by Mark Macy). The voice samples used for comparison were extracted from the vinyl record of EVP examples which accompanied Raudive's book *Breakthrough*, obviously recorded at a time when he was alive and well. An audio-acoustical analysis was conducted to see if the voices of the living Raudive matched that of the recordings of the deceased version recorded from telephone conversations.

The results found that the quality of the deceased Raudive's voice were so good that it was instantly recognisable and in perfect quality, however, the acoustical analysis found that the voices of the living Raudive did not match that of the deceased recording. Therefore it was concluded that it simply could not be considered the same. However, this does raise a further issue. The recordings of Raudive's voice when he was alive were being produced from the biological structure of the human voice box and lungs, and projected through sound waves, and subsequently recorded. The second set of recordings via the telephone is also meant to be Raudive, deceased, in a disembodied form. Therefore, the latter voice would need to somehow be created through manipulation of electrons within the telephone to produce a recognisable voice, or produced via Rogo's and Bayless' *paraphysical theory,* and therefore created within the room but from no certain locality via some form of psi process for people to hear and record. Evidently, the audio acoustical properties would not match, as both voices are produced by two entirely different means. Putting parapsychological theories aside, if the telephone calls were discovered to be a deliberate hoax, and therefore someone was imitating Raudive, then clearly the voice patterns would not match – which makes one possible conclusion.In 2012, Mark Boccuzzi, parapsychologist and co-founder of the Windbridge Institute, created a closed loop telephone system (that is, a phone system that is not connected to the public telephone network) in order to see if anomalous telephone calls might occur in a controlled environment (what we would consider a laboratory experiment of the phenomenon). By using a closed system, the possibility of outside confounds, such as wrong numbers, bad connections, crossed lines, etc., are removed from the equation of likely conventional explanations if a call were to be produced.

The system consists of a standard phone base and handset, a regulated power supply to power the phone, and a data logger attached to a computer running custom software that monitors the phone's line voltage and manages recording of any incoming calls. If there is a change in the voltage (this would happen if a phone on a normal network were to receive a call), the software causes the computer to play a ring tone.

The person answering the phone can then click the record button on the computer's software interface. This starts recording the call (an acoustic tap placed on the phone receiver is plugged into the computer microphone input). Once the recording starts, the phone receiver can be picked up and answered. Any words spoken or sounds heard through the handset are recorded by the computer and saved in an audio file. An automated system could have been used for the recording and answering procedure, but Boccuzzi wishes to mimic the physical process of answering a phone.

All of this, at present, is just a pilot study, therefore Boccuzzi has not presented any theory as to what potential parapsychological mechanism(s) may be involved if the telephone were to ring and produce a voice. As this study develops, Boccuzzi acknowledges that blinding, randomisation, statistical tests, and the source-of-psi problem, will later have to be considered within the study.

During data collection sessions, the system is turned on and "discarnates" are invited (with the help of a medium) to try to call. As this study is still on-going, findings will be discussed at a later date. It must be duly acknowledged that this is a unique attempt at adding control, in some respects, to strange telephone call phenomena which is almost always experienced spontaneously and therefore only a memory of the event within the percipient remains in most circumstances. This in itself presents a problem in terms of evidentially, and was also an issue raised by Dr John Palmer, who states:

The weakness is attributable in large part to the very nature of this type of phenomena. Like most cases of spontaneous psi, "death calls" occur infrequently and at times when they are unexpected. People usually do not wait around for a phone call from a departed relative! This, in contrast to laboratory experiments and certain "recurrent" spontaneous phenomena such as poltergeists, there is unlikely to be a trained investigator on hand when the phenomena occur. (Rogo & Bayless, 1979, p.152)

Boccuzzi's study may actually be the *second* time that such a controlled experiment has been conducted. Between 1930-1932, the well-known ghost hunter Harry Price built a replica of F. R. Melton's psychic telephone device in order to attempt to repeat the results of alleged communication with the dead. Although Price managed to build a replica of the device, it didn't work. He even tried to get the device to work with the assistance of a medium being present, and still no results were produced as he reported back to Melton.

What Causes the Calls?

When it comes to the topic of paracoustics, we have an obvious issue of what appears to be an impossible voice being heard over the telephone. This being a) the recognisable voice of the dead, or b) a person who was verified to have been elsewhere at the time, and could not possibly have made the call. We also have the issue of the telephone ringing in the first place. If, as in many cases, the telephone company have no record of a call being placed at the reported time, what did cause the event of the telephone call to take place?

In exploring conventional explanations first for what might produce the effect of a telephone call from the dead, we have several possibilities to investigate and illuminate in pursuit of a parapsychological, or paracoustical, phenomena. For example, fraud is certainly one of the most possible alternative explanations for the calls. Someone could receive a prank call from someone pretending to be someone they know, or someone they knew, who is dead. A horrible thought, but the late biologist and psychical researcher, John L. Randall discussed this possibility with me some years ago, stating: "There is also the possibility of deliberate hoaxes although, as you say in your paper, that would be very cruel. Unfortunately some people *are* naturally cruel." What might motivate someone to do this? Some people being naturally cruel might target telephone numbers at random to place a prank call and, in other cases, particularly where the caller is perceived to be the dead, the prankster might be known to the receiver of the call. In other words, following possible personal disputes, the prankster may well seek revenge, and find the perfect means of doing this when learning of a recent bereavement for the person who upset them. They then pretend to be the deceased, placing a prank call that is perceived to be one "from beyond the grave". Some might find this a farfetched explanation, but I would agree with Mr Randall that it is an important explanation to consider, investigate, and rule out.

Other events could be a case of coincidence and misinterpretation. For example, parents grieving the loss of their child have in some cases reported receiving a telephone call with a child's voice simply saying "Mum..." or "Dad..." and then the line cutting off. For the parents, this is accepted as confirmation of survival and rarely in such cases is it checked with the telephone companies or the call traced. It could be a simple case of a wrong number with a young person genuinely calling home and realising they have the wrong number thereby hanging up without apology. It could be that simple, especially in some cases where so little information is relayed over the telephone.

Electrical faults are also something to investigate. Often the brief voices of Type 1 calls are reported to be accompanied by the sound of static on the line, which occurs in around 30% of cases, as well as the voices sounding distant or hollow. It was common for some landlines to have crossed wires and to pick up the telephones from the same street and hear a conversation being had several houses away by neighbours, or hear a third voice on the line talking about typical day to day things. This could account for some early instances, though rarely occurs today. These super-imposed voices clearly do not relay information of 'what it's like to be dead' or present 'a message of the future', therefore, such errors should be fairly apparent. These problems were discovered as far back as the 1930s, when an amateur psychical investigator by the name of Hunt, discovered that when contact is established between two telephones, the production of sound waves can sometimes create a super-imposer of the voices speaking, thus producing a third ghostly voice. These are perfectly natural sounds caused by a recognised technological fault, but have often been interpreted by those engaged in conversation at the time they occur as paranormal. It was an early attempt to explain such experiences, but obviously does not account for all strange telephone experiences.

There have been just a few cases submitted for analysis where the recipient of the call claimed they were in bed at the time the call took place. If they were alone in bed when this occurred it is more or less impossible to know what really happened. It could be argued that the person slipped off to sleep and dreamt the experience. It is also possible that the percipient encountered the telephone call when going to sleep (the hypnagogic state) or while waking up (the hypnopompic state), both being an altered state of consciousness where we might confuse dreams with reality.

However, we are aware that altered states of consciousness are psi conducive, therefore, in such instances we must focus on what the content of the call revealed regardless of whether the experience was dreamt or not. The caller may reveal information which might not have been previously known to the recipient of the call. If the experience was nothing more than a dream, how would they have gained access to this information? It could only lead to two things, such as some form of psi process being involved, or discarnate communication.

Some critiques of *Phone Calls from the Dead* by Rogo and Bayless went to great lengths to suggest conventional explanations for the calls, Anderson argued in a review to the *Journal of Religion and Psychical Research* that such events may involve expectancy or hallucinations. Rogo replied and was not satisfied with such suggestions, as even in current research, no percipient claimed to have been *expecting* a paranormal telephone call. Few people, if any, knew such events had ever been reported. The idea of hallucinations being involved is a controversial issue in itself. We cannot assume that we regularly hallucinate telephone calls and normally there has to be psychological, physiological, and environmental changes for us to hallucinate anything. Thus, it has been suggested that perhaps being in a state of extreme grief is the explanation for some of the telephone calls – at least in those cases where the caller is purported to be dead. Robert Baker in his book *Hidden Memories* considered such experiences to be a psychological projection of grief. He believed the bereaved would experience "selective amnesia" when a regular telephone call to the house came through, thus, upon answering, the bereaved would assume the caller to be whomever they desired (i.e., the deceased). Although many psychologists and parapsychologists might find this explanation more farfetched than a conclusion of survival. I for one, find Baker's theory an incredibly weak argument for the vast majority of telephone accounts.

It is clear when exploring conventional explanations that there is a minefield of possibilities which could account for the calls (and indeed many forms of paranormal encounter), but through careful investigation they can be considered, and in some cases ruled out.

Psi or Survival?

It is at this point that we have stretched the limits of the most likely conventional explanations that could produce what appears to be a paranormal telephone call. If we can satisfactorily rule out the likelihood of these being involved in each individual case that is investigated, what then are we left with? At the very least, the calls suggest some form of psi process being involved and produced by the living, and at the very most, they suggest survival for human personality beyond death, and psi being employed by the disembodied mind. What is meant by this is that we have two parapsychological events to consider:

1. The call was created via a psychokinetic (PK) effect by someone alive making the telephone ring in order for the percipient to be alerted to answer it. And then the caller's voice was either hallucinated, or a further product of ESP and/or PK by someone living somehow acting on the telephone itself (which would explain why some calls were not registered with the phone company as having been made).

2. Whatever form consciousness may take beyond bodily death, if indeed it does continue, it is responsible for physically manipulating the telephone to (a) ring and (b) produce a recognisable voice.

Certainly we have extensive evidence demonstrating the common factor of hallucinations of the dead being present during bereavement. This phenomenon became more accepted within the mainstream setting following Dr Dewi Rees' publication of his MD thesis on this very topic in the *British Medical Journal* in 1971. However, we also have cases of physical effects being present that we might label as poltergeist activity during the bereavement period which have been given extensive study by Dr Sylvia Wright. In interviewing the bereaved about their experiences of poltergeist type activity during a period of personal loss, a variety of electrical disturbances have been noted, including lights playing up, radios and televisions, and most notably, the telephone randomly ringing and producing static and scrambled voices. These events don't really provide any clear communication or information that would lead to a logical conclusion of the dead trying to communicate. However, the spontaneous unusual behaviour of these electrical items might suggest grief being unleashed from the mind (presumably if the emotions are intense and harboured by the bereaved) into psychokinetic effects. Perhaps on an extreme scale, they cause the telephone to ring and voices to be heard.

Rogo and Bayless were convinced that, when conventional explanations for the telephone calls can be accounted for, some calls seem to demonstrate evidence for survival. They found that 22% of cases occurred after six months of the death of the phantom caller, or even longer. Therefore, it was concluded that there would be no psychological reason as to why a person would be unconsciously motivated to then produce a paranormal telephone call after such a long interval. They postulated that perhaps at the time of a loved one's death (within a 24 hour period/crisis period), the witness unconsciously receives a telepathic message about the death and then produces the telephone call via a form of PK, as a means to bring this information to conscious attention.

The mechanics of the calls were also considered by Rogo and Bayless, and a theory as to how the calls are produced was developed. They asked the question:

> Are they genuine incoming calls – i.e., calls produced from some distant location which are then routed to the witnesses' homes through a central phone exchange – or are they psychically produced directly over the individual telephones on which they are received? This may not strike you as a particularly important question, but it is critical as far as we are concerned. If these calls are incoming signals, then the phantom telephone voices would have to be an electromagnetic phenomenon. In other words, our witnesses really heard only a pattern of electrical oscillations that imitated human speech. We've come to call this the "electromagnetic theory." If, however, these voices are somehow being produced over or within the 'specific instruments on which they are received', their nature might be very different. They might be some sort of human speech or "independent voice" (that is, a disembodied voice created out of thin air) speaking directly over the amplifier in the receiver. This might be called the 'paraphysical theory'. (Rogo and Bayless, 1979, pp.73-74)

Here we have an assumption that via some form of psi process, the dead are able to manipulate the electrons within the telephone to produce a pattern of recognised speech, especially in those cases where the call is not recognised by the telephone company as having been made. Rogo and Bayless found cases that supported both theories.

However, the electromagnetic theory was certainly not a new hypothesis and Carlos G. Romas in 1925, under the pen name of Oscar D'Argonnel, published a book of his accounts of receiving phone calls from the dead (the translated book title being *Voices from Beyond by Telephone*, although never published in English). It was in fact the voices on the telephone that told Romas that the only reason he could hear them and the spirit world was due to *power*, and a manipulation of *electrical currents* down the telephone line during the conversations.

The deeper we delve into exceptional events, the more questions they raise than answers. Are we really being contacted by the dead who can manipulate sound waves from electrons to produce a voice we recognise? Or are we creating the illusion ourselves through our own unconscious psychic potentials? The issue of separating psi from survival has been noted for a long time, and Dr William Roll noted this issue very well in what he called the "catch-22 of survival". We can only *prove* that the calls were created by the deceased, if we can *disprove* that some form of psi from the living created the call. When we investigate spontaneous phenomena, especially telephone calls, and try to retrace the footsteps of the event as it happened, at best we can be left only with evidence to *suggest* that some form of psi process was involved. But certainly, in some few cases, no conventional explanations adequately apply.

Summary

At present, it seems the source of these telephone calls is unlikely to be traced once we have considered the conventional explanations and ruled them out. Currently our best option is to ensure that the spontaneous case collections we continue to gather are not accepted as pure anecdotes and that every case is researched to its full capacity, with additional eyewitnesses, following up leads, and alternative possibilities. It is the duty of any serious investigator to not leave any stone unturned before allowing such cases to be included in a file of collected cases for analysis. Just like the experience of ghosts, it is a certainty that these telephone experiences actually occur and, due to the volume of reports, there is no denying that. But are we actually experiencing a call that could not conventionally be made? And hearing voices of the dead, or is it something conventional which is just not apparent? The methods and findings of the few initial studies on this topic suggest that such calls involving psychic phenomena and discarnate personalities are a likely reality in certain cases. Right now, these experiences are only just being brought to light in terms of our basic understanding of *how* they occur and possibly operate. Continuing such research with persistence, professionalism and an open mind may reveal more about their nature and origin.

Section 2

CONTRIBUTED CHAPTERS

THE PSYCHOLOGY OF EVP

Ann R. Winsper

According to a poll conducted by Gallup UK in 2005, 40% of the UK population believe houses can be haunted, with 27% believing people can hear from or communicate mentally with someone who has died. There is considerable debate as to whether these apparent paranormal phenomena are genuine manifestations of the dead, or simply misperceptions of natural phenomena. The possibility of "life after death", or the continuation of the personality after death, has been an ongoing theme in human history, both in a religious and non-religious context. The main world religions subscribe to some idea of life continuing after death, whether that is in heaven, reincarnation, or continuation of the soul in another dimension. Spiritualist mediums claim to communicate directly with the deceased. However there have been a number of techniques for contacting the spirit world described over the years. One technique of apparently contacting the spirit world is via Electronic Voice Phenomena (EVP), most commonly understood to be the apparent presence of anomalous voices and sounds appearing on magnetic tape recordings (although in recent years this has expanded to include phenomena that appear on other electronic devices, such as televisions and computers). There have been a number of attempts by researchers over the years to explain this phenomenon, both by amateurs and by academic parapsychologists, however the debate over the source of these recordings still continues.

Recently a new discipline has emerged in the academic world called anomalous psychology, with a number of UK universities setting up departments devoted to the discipline. Anomalous psychologists attempt to find a non-paranormal explanation for apparent paranormal experiences, in contrast to the previous parapsychological research which assumes that there may be a paranormal explanation, although using rigorous methods to rule out misperception and fraud. Regarding EVP, the current thinking by psychologists appears to be that the phenomenon is simply misperception, and therefore not worthy of study. However there have been few experiments to demonstrate this, and whilst it may prove that EVP has a non-paranormal explanation, without research to back this up it cannot be assumed.

There have been a number of suggested explanations to account for EVP voices appearing, including stray radio transmissions, tape noise, and the innate tendency of people to interpret ambiguous sounds as speech. But we need to understand how these processes work, and what would cause people to misinterpret sounds in this way. Of course, once we can identify sounds and voices that are not paranormal, we may then find that there are still some sounds that we cannot readily explain, and this will enable researchers to concentrate on these as yet unexplained voices to try and discover their origin.

There are a number of serious EVP researchers in the world currently looking into the phenomenon, and there have been a number of experiments described that attempt to factor for these suggested explanations. For example, carrying out recordings within Faraday cages to remove the risk of stray radio broadcasts. A number of these experiments appear to show quite impressive results. However a faster growing field recently has been the use, by paranormal investigators, of so-called "Ghost Boxes", and subsequent refinements of the same technique. As described in the previous chapter, these consist of a radio receiver that constantly scans the airwaves, the theory being that spirit entities utilise fragments of voices, music and noise picked up as the radio sweeps through the stations, and assemble these fragments into words, phrases or sentences to communicate with the living. There are a multitude of clips of these EVPs available for listening on the internet, yet the results on the whole are far from impressive. A cursory analysis shows that the random sounds are being interpreted to say what the investigator wants them to say, and the actual sounds when analysed do not bear much relation to what is being described. The more serious EVP research foundations also dismiss these recordings and interpretations, so the interesting question is why do people want to believe that these clips are the voices of spirits communicating with them, and also what factors make them think that they are hearing the sounds of spirit voices?

Psychological and Neuropsychological Accounts of EVP

Interpreting Sounds

There has been a considerable amount of research into how people can misinterpret events as paranormal, with a lot of focus on people who believe in the paranormal and what connects their belief with a hypothesised tendency to misinterpret events. When we hear a sound, or a collection of sounds, we can normally identify instantly what the sound is. For example if you hear the two tones of a police siren, rather than experiencing it as two separate and unconnected sounds, you interpret it as "a police siren", a whole sound built up of components. This is because you have a template in your mind about what a siren sounds like. In normal circumstances, this works well and we identify the world around us correctly. However if you are in a noisy environment, or the sound is very quiet, it is more difficult to pick out and interpret sounds from the general background noise. In these situations, you use what psychologists call top-down processing, the sound is interpreted according to your beliefs, expectations, and what you expect to hear. Human beings are very good at picking out sounds from the background noise, for example there is a well-known effect called the "cocktail party effect", where you can be in a very noisy situation but still pick out someone saying your name at the other end of the room. However due to the influence of our prior expectations and beliefs, we can misinterpret sounds and either create meaning out of random noise or hear something different to the original sound. A famous example of this has been termed a "mondegreen", commonly where lyrics to songs are misheard, for example the most famous of these must be the Jimi Hendrix lyric to Purple Haze, originally sung as *"'Scuse me while I kiss the sky"* which was misheard so many times as *"'Scuse me while I kiss this guy"* and apparently Hendrix was known to sing the misheard version at live gigs.

Research has shown that people will rate ambiguous speech as much clearer if they are given a transcript to follow whilst listening. This mimics the process used by numerous paranormal investigators, where listeners are prompted as to what they *should* be hearing.

This prompting effect can be seen very clearly when listening to sine wave speech. Sine wave speech was developed in the 1970's by Rubin and Remez, and consists of frequency modulated sine waves which retain the frequency and amplitude of normal speech, whilst lacking a lot of the normal acoustic cues present in speech (see appendix for links to on-line sine wave demonstrations). Acoustic cues in speech enable us to decide not only that it is speech that we are hearing, but also characteristics of the speaker such as gender, age, etc. Listeners who are played sine wave speech and not told that it is based on speech will usually not recognise the sounds as speech sounds. However, if these people are told that the sounds are manipulations of natural speech, they will immediately interpret the sounds as words, and provide quite accurate transcriptions of the speech.

In 2004, Alexander McRae published details of his experiments with his Alpha Interface System. This was initially designed to test for mediumistic abilities being a factor in the production of EVP. The system was designed to measure the electrical conductance of the skin, then use the voltage produced by the skin to control an oscillator, which was set in the same range as a general voice pitch. Faster electrodermal changes controlled a second oscillator, which simulated the resonant sounds of the vocal cavity. These two oscillator outputs were then mixed together to give the final output. Following initial experimentation, a radio receiver was used to detect the sounds rather than using direct output, and noise reduction was applied. Apparent voices were recorded using this method, and MacRae argues that the results were not due to stray radio broadcasts or other non-paranormal sources. The results from using this method are remarkably similar to sine wave speech. To verify the results, MacRae sent copies of his audio files to a number of participants, along with a list of five possible interpretations for each one. Participants had to choose which interpretation they thought was the correct one. As MacRae's samples are both similar to sine-wave speech, and were post-processed in a number of ways, with the participants additionally being given interpretations to choose from, it would seem likely that an incorrect conclusion may be that a number of apparently genuine EVPs exist on the recordings.

Humans are "tuned-in" to distinguish acoustic signals that are consistent with sounds that the human voice producing mechanism can produce, so non-vocal sounds that mimic speech sounds (even if only small segments of sound) are likely to be interpreted as speech.

Suggestion

The role of suggestion in EVP interpretation is two-fold, firstly suggestion can be classed alongside expectation when people are listening for EVP voices, both the expectation and suggestion that apparently paranormal voices may be present on a recording may be enough to cause a paranormal believer to report hearing voices, even when none are present. Secondly, when listening to recordings, if people who are listening to sound clips are told what they should be expecting to hear before listening to the sound clip, they are far more likely to interpret ambiguous clips in the manner they have previously been prompted.

Wiseman, Greening and Smith found that under séance room conditions, paranormal believers are more suggestible than non-believers, but only when the suggestion is consistent with the existence of paranormal phenomena. This does not hold true where suggestions are not consistent with the existence of paranormal phenomena. This may suggest that believers would be more likely to report the hearing of voices if paranormal terms (such as the voices being EVP) are used.

Paranormal Belief

If EVP proves to be nothing more than misperception, there must be a psychological reason why people interpret and believe that the sounds they hear are the voices of the dead. Research has been carried out for many years into how individuals may misinterpret events as anomalous, particularly how those who believe in the paranormal are more likely to misinterpret events. Henry Irwin describes a 'top-down' cognitive process whereby people maintain their paranormal belief by making use of deficient reality testing processes. This means that they attribute a paranormal explanation to an unusual event without testing whether such an explanation is logically plausible or not. Thus, each apparently paranormal experience reinforces their *a priori* belief which in turn reinforces their paranormal interpretation of subsequent events. According to this model, believers would be more likely to report hearing EVPs, particularly if they report having already experienced hearing them previously (for example during ghost hunts).

Blackmore & Moore showed that paranormal believers were more willing to report seeing forms in a noisy visual image and they suggest that this may apply to auditory tasks as well as visual ones. Brugger, Landis & Regard (in French and Wilson) found believers are more likely to report the presence of 'meaningful' information in randomly presented dot patterns, and although believers are more prone to make these type 1 errors, this cognitive style is also associated with higher creativity. Believers have also been shown to produce more original responses than non-believers on word association tasks, again suggesting higher creativity in believers. Shermer calls this tendency "patternicity", the tendency to find meaningful patterns in meaningless noise and he suggests that we display this behaviour as it can have survival advantages, and where it is not an advantage, it is not a disadvantage for survival. However it may be that this increased tendency for creative responses can also influence the mistaken creation of words and phrases in EVP recordings as the listener uses the priming effects of the questions they ask of the spirits, in combination with sounds that may be similar to speech phonemes present on the recordings, to manufacture an apparent response.

Schizotypy

Schizotypy is a personality type which has also been described as varying along a continuum from normal at one end of the scale to the upper end where a second continuum encompasses clinical psychosis and schizophrenia. One factor described within the schizotypy construct is Aberrant Perceptions and Beliefs, and this appears to describe anomalous experiences such as hallucinations. People who score highly on this scale, but are also mentally healthy, have been described as Healthy, or Happy Schizotypes. These Happy Schizotypes experience unusual experiences but have higher levels of health and well being than the other types.

Research has shown that Happy Schizotypes are more likely to report hallucinatory experiences and unusual cognitive and perceptual experiences than normal controls. Strong associations between belief in the paranormal and happy schizotypy have been found, so the suggestion is that Happy Schizotypes who are paranormal believers are more likely to experience unusual experiences, including auditory hallucinations.

Auditory Hallucination

In clinical schizophrenia, patients can experience functional hallucinations. These are hallucinations that occur when the patient perceives a real stimulus. For example, one patient hallucinated voices over the sound of an engine, or even over a real voice on the television. The hallucinated voices took on the characteristics of the underlying sound, so when the engine sound was present, the hallucinated voice had the characteristics of an engine sound and showed no features such as gender or accent. Obviously this is an effect found in clinical patients, not in the general public, however conditions such as schizophrenic tendencies have been described as existing on a continuum, ranging from normal cognitive processes at one end and full schizophrenia at the other, and so these hallucinations may be present in a diluted form in the general non-clinical population so, for example, a voice may be constructed from the mechanical sound of a tape recorder, but still retain some characteristics of a human voice.

Reality Testing

Reality testing describes how people use their perception and actions to define their beliefs about the world around them, and distinguish between their internal world and the external world around them. These beliefs can be amended and revised, according to new information being processed, however this process is not subjected to internal critical testing, and may result in incorrect beliefs being formed. There are a number of factors that can influence reality testing, and can therefore possibly account for interpretation of sounds as EVPs. Hallucinators are deficient in reality testing ability, and clinical patients who show both vivid auditory imagery and impaired reality testing are more likely to experience auditory hallucinations. Obviously this is not to say that everyone who hears an EVP is hallucinating, and most EVP experiencers are not in the clinical population, however, using the model described previously where everyone is on a continuum, it makes sense that even in a non-clinical population some people are more likely to tend towards hallucination. There is a link between paranormal belief and reality testing and deficits in reality testing can predict paranormal belief, which might suggest that deficient reality testing may account in part for the formation and maintenance of paranormal beliefs. There is some evidence that people who are deficient in reality testing ability and cannot discriminate between internal and external events may mistake subvocalisation as an external event and experience an auditory hallucination. Subvocalisation is the process that occurs commonly when people are reading, but can occur in any situation where language is at the front of a mental process. It is the process that occurs when you imagine the words that you are reading or thinking about, and it enables you to hear the words in your mind. The larynx and vocal cords can move as if you are actually speaking. If reality testing deficits can account partially for both hallucinatory experiences and the formation and maintenance of paranormal beliefs, it may be that people with high paranormal beliefs who experience auditory EVPs might also display these reality testing deficits.

Dissociation

Dissociation describes the process whereby mental processes that are usually integrated (thoughts, emotions, memory, identity) are separated. There is evidence of correlation between some paranormal experiences and dissociation, particularly psi experiences. Particular correlations have been found with waking clairvoyance, precognition, apparitions, psychokinesis and volitional telepathy. There is no research describing correlation between experiencing EVP and dissociation, however, it may be that a tendency to dissociation may aid the interpretation of sound recordings. Longden, Madill and Waterman describe the hearing of voices as a dissociative disorder, again on a continuum, with inner speech at one end and full hallucinatory voices at the other, so it is possible that a tendency to construct and interpret paranormal voices such as with EVP may lie on this continuum.

Fantasy Proneness

Fantasy prone individuals display a number of traits, including the tendency to fantasise a considerable amount of the time, and claim to hallucinate objects and experience what they fantasise, but they also have difficulty distinguishing between real and fantasised events. Fantasy proneness can also predict paranormal belief, and people showing a high level of dissociation also demonstrate a positive response bias in memory tasks, which is mediated by fantasy proneness. A correlation has been shown between dissociative tendencies and a number of paranormal experiences, so it may be that paranormal believers (and thereby EVP experiencers) display dissociative tendencies that are mediated by fantasy proneness, and this is causing them to think that they are hearing EVP voices.

Death Anxiety

As people who use EVP techniques describe apparent communication with the dead, both of deceased people known to them and historic figures, it would make sense that this would predict some form of afterlife belief that encompasses the continuation of the personality after death. It would seem logical that this belief in an afterlife might reduce death anxiety, as apparent proof of an afterlife would be expected to provide comfort that "death is not the end". However, research has shown that neither Paranormal Belief nor Experience of the Paranormal correlate with scores on a Death Anxiety scale. Instead, gender proved more of a predictor. It may be that people who describe communicating with spirit via EVP might show lower scores on the scale, or it may be that only people with positive EVP experiences show this trait, and people who have had negative EVP experiences might show more death anxiety.

Narcissism

Narcissism has been found to correlate significantly with some paranormal belief measure sub-scales, specifically extrasensory perception (ESP) and psychokinesis (PK) subscales. This was interpreted as a control need, possibly being satisfied by these participants by exercising a power fantasy via belief in paranormal ability via ESP and PK. This trait may also direct some individuals to believe that they are communicating with the dead via EVP, particularly if they can act as an apparent channel for communication for others.

The Big Five Personality Traits

The big five personality traits are five different dimensions of personality that are described to make up human personality. The five factors are usually described as Openness (or intellect/imagination), Conscientiousness, Extraversion, Agreeableness and Neuroticism (or emotional stability). An association has been found between Paranormal Belief and Openness, and Openness has been found to partially predict paranormal belief. It may be that certain personality types are more likely to be attracted to not just the paranormal, but EVP in particular, and maybe a certain type of personality is a predictor for both using the technique and experiencing EVPs.

Nature and Neuropsychology of 'pure' White Noise

White noise is sound that consists of every frequency in the audio bandwidth, at equal energy levels. It is perceived by the human ear as a hiss, because each octave contains twice as many discrete frequencies as the one below it and therefore seems louder – the lower octaves are masked by the higher ones thereby causing the perception of a hiss.

The usual method of recording EVPs on ghost hunts is guaranteed to introduce a level of noise that increases the likelihood of hearing sounds that could be interpreted as EVP. Most people who record EVPs use standard recording equipment, due to the prohibitively high cost of professional recording equipment.

Low frequency noise can be introduced from a number of sources such as doors, water pipes, computer fans and electrical equipment. These kinds of ambient sounds can impinge on recordings and prevent analysis of the first speech formant (there are a number of speech formants which are concentrations of acoustic energy in human speech waves, each one corresponding to a resonance in the vocal tract.) This impingement can prevent accurate computer analysis of any voice sounds heard, and can also alter the perception of sounds heard when listening to sound clips.

One point to bear in mind when recording EVPs is that tape recorders have a noise floor (the minimum level of a system). In standard recording equipment particularly (although high end equipment can have this problem if it is not used correctly), this noise floor will consist of white noise and machine sounds. If the recorder is a wired one, as opposed to a battery one, it will also have a 50Hz mains hum (in the UK, other countries may be 60Hz.) If someone plays white noise as a carrier signal, then records it on this recorder, it will be picking up the noise floor of the recorder, the white noise being played, and then the noise floor in the room. This is assuming the white noise has not also been recorded and played on another recorder. All these noise sources will combine to produce a very noisy recording, and additionally there may be a number of harmonics introduced which all means the EVP tape could have a multitude of anomalous sounds on it even before we look at the possibility of a paranormal influence. Add to this the noise produced from a radio sweeping through radio stations, and it is easy to see where misinterpretations can easily occur.

Auditory and Speech Perception

It has been suggested that the words that make up speech can be broken down into smaller units called phonemes, however, this is not universally accepted, as words can be distinguished even during speech that is so rapid that it is impossible to make out individual phonemes.

Therefore it may be that longer stretches of sound are required for word perception to occur.

When sounds are perceived as being from a single source, a number of criteria must be met for the perception to occur. In a mixture of sounds, elements are more likely to be attributed to one source if they are close in frequency. There is a phenomenon called phonemic restoration – in certain circumstances the brain can create missing portions of speech, so it appears to the listener that the missing portions are actually present. This appears to be a method employed by the brain to allow for speech perception in less than optimal conditions, and appears particularly successful in creating the illusion of continuous speech when gaps in the speech are filled with white noise. If there are elements in EVP recordings that mimic speech sounds, it may be possible that this phonemic restoration effect causes listeners to create apparent words out of the noise. If there is no actual speech present, this may explain why EVP recordings are often described as being in multiple languages – the brain is simply trying to create sense out of random noise. In laboratory tests using the phonemic restoration effect, the broadband noise must be louder than the speech sounds, again this appears to replicate the effect in EVP sound clips, where the apparent voices can be quite faint compared to the white noise, necessitating multiple attempts at listening before sense can be made. Results from more serious EVP researchers suggest that apparently anomalous voices are clearer and louder in the presence of background noise, with some correlation between the level of background noise and the amplitude of the apparent voices. This would appear to add evidence to the suggestion that EVPs are simply misperceptions of the brain.

There is great stress placed in EVP research on the importance of listening training – the more EVPs that are listened to, the easier it becomes to pick out the apparent words. However this also holds true for non-paranormal sounds. Speech intelligibility in listening tasks using interrupted speech improves with training. Also as previously described, a variety of top-down mechanisms are employed when attempting to make sense of degraded speech, including prior knowledge and expectation. This may account for the interpretations that people assign to ambiguous EVP clips.

In normal human speech, strong syllables which contain a full vowel, are usually found as the initial syllables of lexical words (ones which supply meaning to a sentence, for example "answer", "hold", "very", "yes".) Grammatical words (which relate these lexical words to each other) are defined by having a weak syllable as their initial syllable (for example "giraffe".) Weak syllables are also found in non-initial positions (for example "jumper".) When speech is ambiguous, people will insert a speech boundary before a strong syllable and delete boundaries before a weak syllable. Some examples are: inserting a word boundary before a strong syllable ('analogy' becomes 'an allergy'); inserting a boundary before a weak syllable ('effective' becomes 'effect of'); deleting a boundary before a strong syllable ('is he really' becomes 'Israeli') and deleting a boundary before a weak syllable ('my gorge is' becomes 'my gorgeous'.) This effect may have some relevance to EVP clips if sounds are misperceived, as this may cause the creation of an apparent word or sentence, depending on whether the listener has perceived a sound similar to a strong syllable or a weak syllable.

Pronunciation of words within speech can vary according to a number of different factors. Some words are not pronounced in the same way during casual speech as they are during formal speech, an example is the phrase 'this shop'. In casual speech these are frequently pronounced with a blending of the words to give a long 'S' sound. There is a process called vowel reduction in which a vowel in an unstressed syllable may be reduced to a schwa sound (this is a mid-central vowel sound, for example the 'a' in about, the 'o' in harmony - at the end of the chapter is a link to a webpage where you can hear what this sounds like.) In this process, the sound is either the full vowel sound or the reduced vowel sound, but is not a sound in-between the two, and also does not depend on the rate of speech. However, this schwa sound may be reduced or absent in certain situations such as faster speech, so a vowel may be reduced to a schwa sound, and this schwa sound may itself be reduced or absent. The effect of vowel reduction varies between languages – in Spanish reduced vowels still maintain their basic qualities, but in English the reduced vowels may be so distinctive as to become phonemes in their own right. This variability in pronunciation not only within but also between languages may affect what EVP experients report when faced with ambiguous sound clips.

Languages also differ in their expression of a number of linguistic categories, for example, whilst the schwa sound is common in the English language, it has no corresponding sound in Spanish. For multilingual speakers, this may be a further factor that confounds the perception of apparent speech within noise, for example, the listener may perceive a voice as speaking in Spanish, but then perceives a word that contains a schwa. As this is not typical of a Spanish word, the listener may then perceive a switch of language to one that does contain this sound, for example English.

Practical Auditory Tasks

As well as looking at psychological factors that may be influencing the perception of EVP, there is a need to investigate how people interpret standardised ambiguous sound clips to see if the psychological factors have any bearing on the interpretation of EVP clips. The usual methods used for these tasks are ones that utilise Signal Detection Theory – this allows the separation of whether participants can correctly distinguish the presence or absence of EVP and also their bias towards deciding whether or not an EVP is actually present. This allows researchers to account for differences in whether, for example, paranormal believers are more likely to report hearing voices in ambiguous clips than non-believers. Previous studies have shown that schizophrenic patients who have auditory hallucinations are more likely to both misperceive speech stimuli and to assign meaning to meaningless sounds.

However, a previous study concentrating on EVP has shown that whilst moderate paranormal believers were more likely to report a signal being present in ambiguous clips than non-believers, they were also more sensitive to signals. This may suggest that a moderate level of paranormal belief is actually an advantage, with strong believers reporting voices where none are present, and non-believers not reporting voices where ones actually are present.

Conclusions from the Evidence So Far

Evidence from existing studies has shown that paranormal believers show certain characteristics. They are more likely to be Happy Schizotypes who may hear voices, particularly in a dissociative state, and non-clinical high schizotypes are more likely to record false alarms in ambiguous auditory tests. There is a correlation between some apparent paranormal experiences and a dissociative state in non-clinical populations, so believers may have experiences that include the hearing of voices if they show dissociative tendencies. A high level of dissociation can cause participants to demonstrate a positive response bias in memory tasks, mediated by fantasy proneness. Both fantasy proneness and deficits in reality testing can predict paranormal belief, also openness to experience and sensation seeking partially predict paranormal belief. Narcissism is significantly correlated with some paranormal belief subscales, possibly indicating a need for control.

Form these previous studies, it can be predicted that EVP experients should be Happy Schizotypes and show dissociative tendencies (possibly mediated by fantasy proneness.) Assuming they show high levels of paranormal belief, they should also display fantasy proneness, openness to experience and sensation seeking. They should also show some level of narcissism, particularly if they use EVP as a method of passing information onto others.

Of course, it may prove that these factors have no effect on whether people are more likely to experience EVP, but research is currently underway by the author to try and find an answer. The author is also currently creating an EVP questionnaire to both describe EVP experiences, and define the concept of 'an EVPer' – someone who experiences hearing the apparent voices of spirits on recording equipment. Very preliminary results appear to show that EVPers have stronger belief in Spiritualism and Extraordinary Life Forms than non-EVPers, and they also report more anomalous/paranormal experiences and display higher self-reported anomalous/paranormal beliefs and abilities. They also have a higher tendency to display the personality variables of Agreeableness and Conscientiousness.

Work on the study is ongoing, and hopefully a full picture of the EVP experience and the psychology of the people who record EVPs will emerge very soon.

SPONTANEOUS MUSIC AND VOICES

C. R. Foley

When the editors of this book invited me to write a chapter for *Paracoustics,* I enthusiastically agreed. Despite having studied and investigated psychical research for most of my life, I am aware that our understanding of such is rudimentary at best. I learned a long time ago that in this field we learn by progression, moving like the hour hand on a timepiece. I am also aware that any contribution may assist in paving the way for future research. Each new well-attested case is a potential gold nugget, waiting to be appraised for the evidentiary value that it may contain. Callum Cooper agreed that the new cases that I shall be presenting should be told to the greater *psi* community, as well as to all who thirst for knowledge in this fascinating field.

In this chapter I shall examine the subject of paranormal music as well as cases that involve voice phenomena when there is a connection to melodious sounds. I shall also provide hypothetical models that may explain certain aspects of the phenomena. As the subject matter is extremely broad with some relevant topics having already been examined elsewhere in this volume, I have restricted my discussion accordingly. Further, due to the subjective nature of paranormal music, I have used various terms such as "volume" and "hearing" out of convenience, as the actual experience may not entail any physical properties that we commonly ascribe to sound.

***

Reports of spontaneous music and related voice phenomena are among the most complex and disturbing facets of psychism. They are complex by virtue of their nature, as well as their shared relationship with a wide range of other psychical occurrences. Further, that in contrast to the laboratory study of the faculties of *psi*; spontaneous music and voice phenomena study does not lend itself to that manner of research. The primary means of investigation is therefore the analysis of case reports, as it is not possible to replicate the manifestations under controlled scientific conditions, with Electronic Voice Phenomena (EVP) perhaps providing an exception.

In his first book, the late parapsychologist D. Scott Rogo chronicled the history of phantom music, which he culled from the annals of psychical research as well as those from his personal files. Rogo was exceptionally well versed in the history of psychical research and he was also a brilliant abstract theorist, a quality necessary when analysing psi phenomena. Rogo chose NAD as the title of this volume,[1] noting that the term is of Sanskrit origin and that it refers to the apparent paranormal production of music. NAD was the first English work devoted to the subject and Rogo's keen analysis shed much light on this enigma. Rogo also examined the theories postulated by Dr Robert Crookall to provide a working hypothetical model to account for the production of NAD when experienced under certain conditions. Rogo further noted that there was a religious element associated with some cases, and that a degree of commonality existed between those and other psychical occurrence.

NAD *Classifications*

Rogo cited five categories of NAD also noting an apparent crossover of phenomena within these classifications. In my opinion, Rogo's findings actually represent six categories of NAD to which I shall add a seventh in this chapter of *Paracoustics*.

In view of the above, paranormal music can be classified as follows:

1. *Mythological & Religious* NAD – including the pagan traditions.
2. *Spontaneous* NAD – devoid of any apparent linkage to another event.
3. *OBE & NDE* NAD – out of body and near death experiences.

[1] Sometimes spelled "Nada", see also Melton (1996, p. 907, vol. 2). I have also expressed Rogo's work *NAD* in italics, though in general reference to the subject I have elected to forego the use of italics in this chapter.

4. *Mediumistic* NAD – including use of real instruments.[2]
5. *Hauntings* NAD – in relation to specific locales.
6. *Electronic* NAD – as experienced through various electronic media.[3]
7. *Deathbed* NAD - at the deathbed of the dying.[4]

At the time of writing, I believe these seven classifications best capsule the various manifestations of the NAD experience. As previously noted, there is also much interconnectivity among these categories.

Mythological & Religious NAD

Historical references to NAD are often found within a mythological and religious context such as those noted from a Tantric perspective, or from the old pagan traditions. For example, in Vergil's epic poem *The Aeneid,* sirens were mythological creatures, said to be half woman, half bird, which lured sailors to their death by their sweet, irresistible song. Homer also made reference to sirens in the *The Odyssey,* where their music was described as "*heav'nly*" with "*charms so strong*". Many early religious and pagan traditions imbued both divinity as well as evil in the production of NAD, which was clearly described as being divine or godlike in nature. Rogo even speculated that our ancestors may have developed music after having been influenced by their NAD experiences.

In The Holy Scriptures there is a reference to Heavenly music including that produced by the Angels, even the instruments they used, such as harps as noted in Revelation 15:2. Musical references in certain biblical translations are sometimes deleted and caution therefore must be exercised when studying Scripture. For example, in reference to Satan, The King James Version states that, "The workmanship of thy tabrets [a drum or tambourine] and of thy pipes was prepared in thee in the day thou was created" (Ezekiel 28:13).

Although the Revised Standard Version makes no mention of these instruments.[5] Historical and contemporary references to NAD are often intangible, abstract events, impossible to describe let alone quantify due to the transcendental nature of the experience. If viewed as an

[2] Rogo grouped Mediumistic NAD to the Religious classification.

[3] Electronic NAD is a new category.

[4] Deathbed NAD covered elsewhere in *Paracoustics.*

[5] See *The Bible: An Owner's Manual* (*Paulist Press* New York, 1983) Robert R. Hann, for a discussion of the various editions of the Bible and the hazards associated with using various translations.

art form, then some of the music reported as NAD is a total abstraction of which the ancients would not have been capable of producing, nor modern man.

Spontaneous NAD

Perhaps of more interest to psychical researchers is the account of Pierre Jurieu, who reported numerous instances of heavenly music coming from the sky in the region of Cevennes, France. The phenomenon, which was recognised by the authorities, may have been linked to the persecution of the Huguenots, a Protestant sect that flourished in this region during the reign of Louis the XIV. The phantom music was widespread and experienced usually in the evening, sounding as if the Heavenly host had descended upon the land replete with trumpets and other musical instruments as well as the sound of a choir. The case has both spontaneous and religious attributes, and as such reflects the crossover effect noted earlier.

Rogo cited a spontaneous case, which also had an apparent religious overtone as reported by his fellow colleague and friend Raymond Bayless, the noted psychical researcher, author and painter.[6] Shortly after retiring to bed, Bayless experienced the sound of music which gradually ebbed, prior to fading away. Although fully awake, he was unable to determine the origin or location of the music in physical space, or oddly whether it was choral or instrumental. At some length he described the music as being not of this world and "*clearly superhuman*" with the ensemble sounding as though it was comprised of an enormous number of musicians. Bayless also commented that the greatest musical compositions of man would sound "*crude*" and "*inharmonious*" in comparison.[7] Finally, due to the sheer majesty and eminent nature of the sound, he believed that it was somehow connected with religion. Some thirty-six years later, Bayless wrote that the experience remained both "*powerful and unforgettable*". A discussion of the incident reviewed the subjective elements of the experience, with Rogo interpreting such within a paranormal context (see Rogo, 1970, pp. 15, 17).

---

[6] Bayless wrote a book dedicated to paranormal voices entitled, *Voices From Beyond* (*University Books* New Jersey, 1976), in which Rogo wrote the Forword.

[7] Bayless commented further on this experience, see his Foreword in Rogo (1972).

Out of Body NAD

Those who hear paranormal music often use adjectives similar to those employed by Bayless as a means to describe the unearthly quality of the sound. While conducting a content analysis of OBEs that featured NAD, Rogo discovered a peculiar effect that was common in many of the reports. In obvious reference to his musical training, Rogo applied the term *"crescendo effect"* which refers to the gradual amplification of the sound such as in the Bayless case. Further, Rogo also noted the *"decrescendo effect"* (or diminuendo effect), which was also reported by Bayless, as the music *"diminished"* prior to it fading away completely. While other categories of NAD lacked these effects, Rogo noted that they followed other patterns, which he identified through his content analysis. For example, in other accounts, the music was suddenly experienced with no crescendo effect. Rogo provided a hypothetical analysis to explain this anomaly, using a number of case histories.

In his equally impressive tome, *NAD Vol 2*, Rogo speculated that the crescendo effect may be related to the *"loosening"* of the astral body,[8] thereby extending one's sensitivity to the field containing the NAD signal, so to speak. Conversely, the decrescendo effect may occur as a result of the attenuation of the "signal" when the astral body retracts thereby lowering one's sensitivity to NAD (and perhaps to other phenomena.) An attenuation or apparent exponential decay effect has also been noted by other researchers, especially in poltergeist case studies that involve psychokinesis (PK). The reported *"decline"* effect with respect to the paranormal movement of objects was hypothetically addressed by Roll and Persinger using the above noted parameters as well as incorporating inverse square. The actual source of the NAD signal that one or multiple witnesses are tapping into is open to yet even greater conjecture.

Rogo also noted that a *"bird singing"* or a *"chirping"* sound may be heard just prior to a sudden outburst of NAD, with no ebbing as noted in other cases. The lack of crescendo was hypothetically explained by the full release of the provisionally described astral body. Rogo was of the opinion that NAD is associated with the mechanics of the OBE and it shares similarities to that experienced at the deathbed of the dying (as well as the NDE.) An intriguing analysis followed, which the reader is strongly encouraged to examine.

[8] Astral Body in theory is a spiritual duplicate of a human being, often synonymous with the etheric double, soul and other related terminology. For convenience I have used these terms interchangeably.

Mediumistic NAD

Anomalous music has also been reported at séances, which typically involved real instruments after those at the sitting encouraged the agency to play them, ostensibly by paranormal means.[9] Some of the music was described as immensely beautiful and angelic, while at other times an opposite effect was noted. In his autobiography, the great 19th century medium D. D. Home also described how his room was subject to "*impressive manifestations of music*" that increased in volume until others in the house also heard the phenomenon. The music was apparently spontaneous, however as Home was a medium he may have unwittingly enabled the phenomenon to manifest as it ceased the moment he awoke from his sleep.

Indeed, works on 19th century Spiritualism are replete with accounts of "spirits" allegedly manipulating and playing a variety of musical instruments placed in the séance room for that purpose. A general survey of séance musical phenomena was reviewed by Campbell Holms in *The Facts of Psychic Science and Philosophy* in 1925. Following Holm's survey of the phenomena, the noted linguist Dr Neville Whymant reported that a phantom flute was heard during a sitting with medium George Valiantine during the well-known Confucius communications. The music was not skillfully rendered, and faded with a decrescendo, though later an archaic chant was also heard.

One of the most curious footnotes in the history of psychical research is the mediumship of Mrs Elizabeth Blake, who was investigated by the inventor and noted magician David P. Abbott as well as Professor James H. Hyslop, an early prominent psychical researcher. Blake was a direct voice medium, a term which refers to the ability to produce manifestations of speech by presumed discarnate entities.

Despite suffering from ill health, Blake began producing single syllable fragments of speech which were followed by faint, whispery voices from a speaking trumpet that had been held in her hand then placed to her ear by investigators. Subsequently loud voices were produced including one that was audible from 100 feet away. A hissing noise was also heard emanating from the trumpet and at other times a "*clucking*" sound could be heard from her head. This noise sounds suspiciously

9 Home provided a lengthy description of an example of NAD produced at a séance in Hartford, 1851, which included the descriptor, "*immortal*" (p. 90-93), as well as a possible crescendo effect. He also described this music as "*unearthly*" (p. 262).

similar to the *"chirping"* sounds that are sometimes reported prior to a NAD experience as noted by Rogo. Clicks or clicking sounds are sometimes also regarded as a precursor to having an OBE as noted by Melton. These sounds have also been reported in both apparition and poltergeist manifestations, such as the Antrobus (reported by Mackenzie, 1987) and Epworth (reported by Price, 1945) cases. I shall have more to say about poltergeists and NAD later in this chapter.

Of particular interest, is that a magician known as E.A. Parsons had also investigated Blake and reported hearing faint piano music emanating from her speaking trumpet. Allegedly, the piano sounded as though the player was *"running arpeggios,"* based on Parson's account. Subsequently, Abbott investigated and published a selection of Parson's correspondence in his monograph, *History of a Strange Case*. Abbott also described hearing a *"melodious"* voice that seemed to emanate from above and beyond Blake's head. Though Abbott was the consummate sceptic, he concluded that the case was "shrouded in mystery" adding that he did not detect fraud. Blake was not the only medium associated with lyrical voices, as the medium Home described an apparent OBE in which a musical voice spoke to him regarding death and God.

"Sing Song" voices are also reported in connection with Unidentified Flying Object (UFO) close encounter cases. For example, a number of odd telephone conversations with a mystery caller who spoke in a *"strangely, sweet sing song"* voice are reported in *The Warminster Mystery*, authored by Shuttlewood in 1967. The apparent connection between "extraterrestrials" and the "dead", at least with respect to cases involving anomalous telephone phenomena, have recently been investigated by Callum E. Cooper and myself, the report of which we published in *Anomaly* in 2012.

I have also noted that in haunting and poltergeist cases, whistle like sounds are occasionally reported usually at the onset of voice phenomena. These sounds appear to have some relationship with the formation of speech as the agency 'learns' to vocalise. In that event, these may not be reflective of NAD, as there is no apparent attempt to produce a melody, rather they seem to be the result of fragmented speech formation. Rogo also briefly reported on this matter in the foreword of Raymond Bayless' book, *Voices From Beyond*. Bayless also experienced these whistle intonations while working with the medium Atila von Szalay.

In summary, NAD's linkage to those with mediumistic abilities as well as the unearthly nature of some medium induced music is duly noted.

Hauntings and NAD

When experienced in association with a haunting, NAD is occasionally described as superhuman or at least involving execution that would suggest perhaps an unearthly origin, dependant on the extant of the facts reported. The novelist Violet Tweedale reported such when she heard piano music while resting one afternoon. The music was "*suddenly*" heard as if being played by a "*brilliant performer*". Tweedale further described the playing as "*professional*" and "*brilliant...requiring a great amount of technique...*[and] *execution*" though it was "*soulless*". After approximately 20 minutes, the music abruptly ceased. Servants in the house had also heard the music and the piano in the house was found to be open following the incident. Tweedale was quite taken by the music and set about to determine who was responsible, though to no avail.

Although the Tweedale account suggests that the music had an unearthly quality, Rogo remarked that when experienced in connection with a haunting, the quality of NAD, however, is usually not as remarkable. In other words, that unearthly quality is often missing. This trend was also revealed in cases that I have personally investigated. As Rogo devoted much of his NAD literature to OBE and deathbed experiences, I shall further explore NAD in relation to hauntings from my personal files.

Case One

> On February 22nd, 2013, I had stopped at a coffee shop in Mississauga, Ontario (Canada), following research that I had just completed for this chapter. I recall having spent more time than usual inside the premise (as if delayed) and then I exited through the south end of the vestibule where a large group of youths were congregating. Although I realized that I had the option to safely exit via the north end of the vestibule where no one was present, I felt compelled to walk through this group to access a refuse bin! Of note is the fact that there was also an identical bin at the north end, though I chose to ignore this logical option. As soon as I exited, I overheard a male discussing an apparent NAD experience, much to the chagrin and ridicule of his friends. Quite astonished, I stopped to listen and watch the body language of all present to assess the veracity of this unsolicited account. Eventually he became aware of my presence to which I then felt obliged to identify myself as well as my interest in his experience.

Subsequently "Scott" proved to be an 18 year old with an interesting story that involved both himself and his 30 year old co-worker who were engaged in laying a new floor in a local Church. Apparently the premise was empty, and as they prepared to leave they experienced unusual difficulty in opening a door to exit. Suddenly they both heard a "creepy violin that sounded as if it were from a horror movie" play from the darkened corner of the room. Scott then made a valiant attempt to mimic the sound that they heard. The witness made it clear that there was also no crescendo or decrescendo effect, rather it was just there. The witness also confirmed that there was nothing remarkable about the playing, adding that with some practice he could probably replicate it with proper training. Therefore, there was no unearthly quality to the music – which is in agreement with Rogo's general findings with respect to hauntings. Frightened, both witnesses physically burst through the door and fled the building.

Later I reviewed this matter with a friend who is also a violinist. I was informed that this sound can best be described as a sliding scale effect caused by running a finger up and down the instrument while under one long stroke of the bow. Further, that she demonstrated such using her violin to which she replicated the sound reported, playing string "A" while working up and down the scale. Indeed, the resultant effect was easily replicated and further it matched what had been described.

The witness further stated that both parties had re-entered the premise to complete their contracting work. Both parties then heard "knocking and rapping sounds" coming from a nearby room, which ceased upon their entry. The sounds resumed in another room with the pair in pursuit. Subsequently the manifestation moved from room to room as if to avoid being in close proximity to them. The pair had only just experienced the raps on this interview date, while the violin music was heard approximately a week earlier. Curiously, I had just begun my NAD research with respect to hauntings, as well as the elusive nature of psi and its possible relationship with the new physics and the so-called 'observer effect' only hours before. As a result, I thought that I may have also experienced a case of synchronicity.

What caused the violin sound (and the raps) is of course unknown, as is the reason why they had occurred. As it appears that the premise may be haunted, it is possible that the renovations may have played a role in triggering the manifestations. While this particular NAD effect is vaguely reminiscent of the Blake arpeggio (piano) due to the playing of scales, the violin music differed, in that it would have sounded a little faster and quite fluid, based on the statement provided.

Case Two

While providing security services for the Government of Ontario in a sprawling early 19th century building in downtown Toronto (Canada), 22 year old Neline Fernando witnessed a haunting that included a NAD experience. In September 2001, at approximately 2:00 a.m., Fernando was working the night shift with her partner who was asleep at the time of the incident.

After having checked the office doors in a hallway to ensure that they were locked, Fernando proceeded to patrol another area when she heard about 4 slams of the doors just inspected. Upon looking back she observed 3 locked doors suddenly open inwards about one foot then slam shut. This activity took place in consecutive order. Fernando panicked and ran down a flight of stairs to a command office, which was dimly lit by light spilling in from a nearby room. Fernando was breathing heavily from her sprint as she attempted to collect her thoughts and recover from the experience. Suddenly she heard a melodic female voice that sounded "tinny", "metallic" and "high pitched", singing an unknown melody (which lacked lyrics). The sound was heard to originate from a corner near the ceiling. There was no musical accompaniment, just a lone singer producing a melody that she did not recognise. There was no crescendo effect as it suddenly "was just there". Fernando also did not report an unearthly quality with respect to the rendition of the melody, however, she described it as "not happy" adding that it "wanted to make you cry". Fernando also reported that the singing sounded, "acoustically correct" for the room.

The melody perhaps shared a vague similarity with plainsong, an archaic form of religious chant (which Fernando acknowledged when I played her an example). Rather than sounding contemplative, however, she described the singing like it was "from a horror movie". Further, the unaccompanied voice displayed more of a portamento effect; much like the sound one may obtain using a tremolo bar on a guitar, the eerie 'glide' effect of a Theremin, or a singing saw. Regardless, Fernando was of the opinion that the experience was meant to frighten her, rather than to charge her emotions with religion.

Fernando bolted from the command office having listened to the singing for about 5 – 10 seconds, reporting that the music was not heard outside the room as if her exit terminated the manifestation. After about 20 seconds she re-entered the office, and within 5 seconds heard the same eerie singing coming from the same darkened corner of the ceiling. Fernando fled again after listening to the sound for about 2 seconds. No other paranormal markers were noted in association with the music such as unnatural cold, unusual odours, or any electromagnetic effects, for example. Regardless, Fernando was not sure why she re-entered the office or for that matter why she even entered this darkened room at all, following her experience with the slamming doors. Fernando believed that the door incident was also connected to the singing due to their having occurred in consecutive order. On a speculative note, such may have provided the impetus for her to run into the darkened room where the singing occurred. In other words, she may have been led there to experience the singing.

Fernando reported that there were no speakers, radios, or windows in the room, nor any rational explanation to account for the sound. Fernando also reported that aside from her sleeping colleague, no one else was in the building at the time of the incident. Following this experience Fernando's superior granted her request that she be removed from this posting. I have personally known the witness for several years and I have found her to be a responsible and reliable individual.

Theoretical Analysis of Cases 1 and 2

Interesting similarities exist between the phantom violin and the Fernando case, as in both accounts the music emanated from a dark space that was also a corner. A theory in psychical research is that light can inhibit the production of some phenomena (as well as physical mediumship.) Further, that should the music have been acoustic in nature and not telepathically perceived the point of origin is consistent with the production of efficient acoustics due to the angular nature of the space from which the music originated. Sound emanating from a corner would have more focus as well as volume, as the angled surface of the walls act as an efficient reflector of sound. As NAD can be both objective as well as subjective in nature, we must also explore other theoretical concepts in our search for answers.

Both parties reported experiencing other paranormal phenomena, which they associated with a haunting. In the Fernando case, it appears that her presence was required to trigger the music, as it was not heard once outside the room, though the phenomenon was re-activated upon her return. This localisation phenomenon is often associated with hauntings as well as psychometry, which posit that an object may hold certain memory attachments that a sensitive individual can perceive. Haunting phenomena therefore usually occurs in close proximity to the observer due to an apparent spatial relationship that exists with the locale and the agency responsible – as suggested by Price and Dilley. In that event, one's etheric double (or astral body) is required to experience the phenomena with perhaps the mind to provide interpretation. The phantom singer appeared to have been locked to a specific area, with it only being perceived when the etheric brain of the witness interpenetrated the haunted space. This form of NAD perception would appear to agree with Price's comments on psychic ether and how the mechanics of some hauntings may occur.

Of particular interest is that those interviewed were of the opinion that the purpose of these events was to frighten them. Indeed, both parties described the phantom music as though it was from a *"horror movie"*. As an overlapping of mind and matter may occur in such scenarios, it is possible that certain emotions may actually favour psychic communications. Conversely, sad, wailing voices may actually be more reflective of the mechanics of the event. At least one researcher, the Reverend Charles Tweedale associated *"wailing...sad...pathetic"* tones with the successful production of the direct voice, rather than the actual emotion. If correct, the effects reported, especially in the Fernando case, may actually be reflective of a characteristic associated with the production of the manifestation, rather than the intent to frighten.

On a final note, both cases revealed relatively un-remarkable examples of NAD insofar as that heard was certainly not superhuman or angelic in composition. Rogo argued that any loosening of one's presumed astral body may create a condition that favours a NAD experience especially as the surrounding psychic ether may be impacted. This may facilitate an interaction with the psychic realm causing it to interpenetrate our world. By extrapolation, Fernando's etheric essence may have been just loose enough to have allowed her to perceive the slamming doors. The resultant shock may have further loosened her etheric matter to facilitate her subsequent NAD experience. In that event, the NAD may not have been acoustic, and there remains the possibility that the two incidents are not even related. Fernando may have just been in a receptive state to experience psychism in a location that was loaded with potential 'hot spots,' so to speak. The fact that Fernando entered the darkened room twice for no apparent reason, however, may also be reflective of the agency having 'prepped' her in some way to experience the NAD, if we presume that an intelligence was involved.

As hauntings often display a curious blend of objective and subjective elements, one cannot conclude whether the singing was acoustic or otherwise, let alone the rationale behind the phenomenon. With respect to the slamming doors, there is not enough information to state whether they physically opened or whether such was a hallucination induced by whatever generated the event. Both the agency responsible and the purpose of the manifestations are not clear. These observations also apply to the violin case, thus the nature and purpose of that event is also unclear.

Case Three

> Old Fort Henry was built by the British between 1832 and 1837, and served to guard the town of Kingston, Ontario (Canada). On October 10, 2009 at approximately midnight, I was with a group which in total consisted of two males and four females, crossing the Equipoise Bridge which links the Lower and Upper Fort by traversing a dry ditch. Suddenly the two trailing females, Melanie Turner and Jennifer Sheehan, suddenly heard what they both described as the sound of a music box playing. There was melody to the notes, though the tune was not recognised nor was it described as unearthly. An immediate search of the area revealed nothing to account for the phenomenon. Four of those present (including myself) did not experience the music, though all were in close proximity to one another. The music seemed to come from behind the witnesses and to their left, which is in the vicinity of the Officer's Guard Room. This area is decorated with period furnishings (though no music box was observed). The NAD was probably not acoustic, as it was not collectively heard. A number of other paranormal events also occurred that evening.

Electronic NAD

In this new classification, I shall report on the production of NAD as experienced through electronic devices. My primary case involves NAD and anomalous telephone phenomena, though in 1976 I received a case that involved a traditional haunting in the Ontario village of Brougham that occurred in the mid 1950s. One of the oddest occurrences involved the sudden playing of music from an old, unplugged radio. As the witness could recall, the radio was disconnected, as it was not even functional. Unfortunately, due to the passage of time no further details were recalled, or what type of music was heard.

In *Phone Calls from the Dead*, Rogo and Bayless provided an odd case, which involved Zoe Richmond, Honorary Associate of the Society for Psychical Research (London), and her husband and psychical researcher Kenneth Richmond. While playing the gramophone, they listened to a familiar song by a solo male singer. Suddenly he was joined by a female voice which sang in a "*most beautiful soprano*". Quite surprised, they re-played the record but the accompanying female voice was not heard again. Enquiries were conducted with Sir Oliver Lodge as well as the recording company, but to no avail. The authors then provided two other cases that involved odd music as well as voices that emanated from vintage gramophone devices.

Case Four

The following is an extremely bizarre account from a highly credible witness I have known for 55 years. It is indeed fortuitous to obtain such a case from a trusted source especially as this individual works in law enforcement. Further, that this case also represents a new classification of NAD as it was experienced over the telephone, and as such extends the phenomena clearly to the electronic domain.

On 1 May 2000, at approximately 9:00 p.m., Eva called her friend Robert, who lived in Toronto, on her cell phone while at home in Cobourg, Ontario (Canada). While she did not recall hearing any ring tone she suddenly heard "eerie" female singing on the line which she listened to for about one minute before hanging up. Puzzled, she used the re-dial button to place the call again and to confirm that she had called the correct number. Unbeknownst to her, Robert did hear Eva during the first call, but only faintly.

Robert answered the second call, which was also made on Eva's cell, and both parties could faintly hear one another, as well as the mysterious singing which was still present, though perhaps with more volume. Eva then resorted to trying her land line within a couple of minutes and dialled Robert's number a third time. She stated that, if it rang at all, it was only once and Robert picked up. The creepy singing was also still there and both individuals were now hearing it "crystal clear". Robert stated that it was "weird" and also "really eerie". Eva recalled that he hung up and she called back in a fourth attempt to shake the voice.

The fourth call was also made on her landline and, as before, the eerie singing persisted, which was clearly heard by Robert and Eva. They described the voice as female which sang in a "shrilly, high pitched, musical" tone. Initially Eva thought there was a "happy" edge to it, but quickly determined otherwise as she recounted that it both frightened and terrified her as she described it repeatedly as sounding "eerie, creepy and chilling" as well as "abnormal", "bizarre" and "really strange" with a "vibrato" effect (compare this to cases 1 & 2.) Eva further stated in exasperation that "nobody in the world sings like that", adding that it sounded as if it were in an auditorium and that it was also "a little boomy (sic) with some echo effect". As Eva is no stranger to music, I asked what was actually sung, to which she replied, "almost opera but like nothing I've ever heard". Eva added that there was no recognisable melody, song structure or lyrics, just this impossible voice hitting the highest as well as the lowest notes, "up and down all over" adding that it "didn't tell a story". The best description she could provide was that it sounded like "baleful wailing".

While this sombre display persisted, Eva and Robert noted that the volume of the voice was increasing, (Rogo's crescendo effect), which she interpreted as "an interruption". As discussed, this curious artifact was probably the result of the mechanics that produced the call, rather than such providing evidence of intentional interference.

Eventually both parties were yelling at each other to be heard, but to no avail. They mutually agreed to end their call as it was difficult to hear each other over the singing. Of particular interest is Eva's comment that she felt "connected" with it, though upon repeated questioning she was unable to state how, or to even provide an explanation to account for such a statement. At the time this frustrated me as it seemed absurd, however, the reader will recall how Bayless was unable to state whether the music he heard was choral or vocal or where it was located in physical space. Bayless also described his music as sounding "superhuman" (Rogo, 1970, p. 15), which clearly fits Eva's case. While this form of NAD is impossible to describe, the witness is keenly aware that certain elements of the manifestation defy description.

Both individuals were shaken by the experience and Robert suggested it best that she not come over for a visit. Robert advised that this was his first such experience, adding that he was the only one in the house and that he did not have a party line nor a dial up modem. Further, that no electronics were turned on. Subsequently Eva contacted the telephone company who immediately ran a check on the system while she waited, who then reported no problems adding that no party line was detected.

During the call Eva, who lives alone, thought she recognised the voice, though Robert claimed that he was unaware of the singer's identity. Robert was a physician as well as a noted specialist with at least one text book to his credit. He was also an atheist who had no belief in survival after death. Though clearly disturbed by the voice, Robert refused to discuss the matter afterwards even though Eva thought she knew who the caller was. While the pair had feelings for one another, she advised that these were never explored as Robert was an older man who had been married until about 2–3 years prior, when his wife suddenly passed away. Afterwards he divided his time between his practice and his family.

Approximately 3 months after the experience, Eva confronted Robert regarding the identity of the caller. Eva contended that the phantom was actually his dead wife Ruth to which Robert agreed, stating that he had recognised her voice as well, adding that it "scared" and "frightened" him. At that point he made it clear that he never wanted to talk about it again. Sadly, due to his reticence I was never able to interview Robert, though Eva had reported the incident to me a day after it had occurred. Despite the absence of lyrics in the singing, I asked Eva her thoughts were on the purpose of the call, to which she wryly stated, "don't fool around with my husband". Further, she confirmed that Robert's wife had been an avid fan of opera when alive and that she had met her on a couple of occasions. Eva described her voice then as sounding "squeaky" and "high pitched," adding that one "couldn't miss it". That same quality persisted in the eerie singing though it sounded "out of this world" to which she added that no living person could sing like that. Curiously, Robert's wife had suddenly passed away after having attended a live operatic performance.

As in the Bayless case, which continued to impact his life thirty-six years later, Eva found herself in a similar situation with one difference. The Bayless experience was a positive one, ostensibly connected with religion, though the opera singing was doom laden with the apparent intent to frighten. I have brought this matter up over the years with Eva, and her response always remains the same. Some thirteen years after this harrowing incident I re-interviewed her for this chapter of *Paracoustics*, and one can watch the colour drain from her face as she solemnly swears that she would never wish this experience on anyone. Clearly frightened by the manifestation, the account still chills her to the bone with the resultant anger for my causing her to re-live it. Both Bayless and Eva found their experiences *"powerful and unforgettable"* though they remain in sharp contrast to one another. Bayless pursued a life-long career of investigating psychical research in an attempt to find answers. Eva wishes to forget.

Elements of NAD Related to Anomalous Telephone Phenomena

Eva and Robert's NAD experience is odd as it is also what I classify as a 'dead call case' because it occurred over the telephone. The subject of anomalous telephone calls was investigated by Rogo and Bayless who co-authored the first work on the subject entitled, *Phone Calls from the Dead.* Cooper then followed this up and revised the research with *Telephone Calls from the Dead.* Briefly, Rogo and Bayless reported that some individuals have received phone calls from the dead which revealed a number of repeating patterns. The agency responsible somehow uses direct psychokinesis action on the telephone to complete the call. In that sense, the phone could be thought of as being "haunted" for the duration of the event. Although Rogo and Bayless posited that the dead were responsible for most of this phenomenon, they noted that witnesses may also unconsciously create some of the calls as well. I addressed this seemingly absurd matter in my review of the Rogo and Bayless work in the *Canadian Ufologist* in 1996, as well as other common attributes found in such cases. Later in this chapter I shall examine this matter in thorough detail.

Most absurd, as well as disturbing, was that in the majority of accounts the agency is coy with respect to its true identity, especially if the witness is aware that the caller is deceased. That knowledge seems to change the dynamics of the call. As an example, both Eva and Robert knew who the singer was and that she was no longer alive. In agreement with Rogo and Bayless, the agency remained aloof with respect to providing its identity, which ironically was never in doubt. This is an absurd anomaly in a NAD case as it was illogical for the singer not to have provided verbal identification. It is also an example of an electronic NAD case involving the telephone, which provides further oddities within the dead call case spectrum. For example, it is unclear as to whether the agency contacted Eva when she picked up the phone or whether it was 'hiding out' at Robert's end (most likely). There were also two witnesses. Regardless, Eva's call was placed to Robert, with "Ruth" apparently cutting in. It is also odd that the singing persisted through four phone call attempts, as anomalous telephone phenomena with those known to be deceased is usually brief and lacking repeat performances, especially in rapid succession. This appears to be what I call an example of an "interception" or "interloper" choral based NAD call that involved several telephones.

Eva and Robert's experience is reflective of another dead call case that I investigated which concerned "Norma", a widow who received 35-40 telephone calls from her deceased husband "Jack" between 1990 and 1991. Most curious was the first call in which she immediately recognised her dead husband's voice, though she asked for the caller's identity. In response the male voice cryptically replied "*You know who I am*," after which the call abruptly ended. The voice would never identify itself and the conversations were always one-way. Most attempts by Norma to ask questions or get involved in the call resulted in the immediate termination of the event. Of note is that Jack was described as being a "*placid, introvert*" who was also a "*nice guy*" and "*quite kind*" when alive. The pair had been married 25 years and had children, with the husband having tragically drowned in 1986. Death seems to have brought about a change in "Jack's" personality though.

Although not a NAD experience, the Norma case exhibit features consistent with the opera singing occurrence, as well as being in agreement with the analysis of Rogo and Bayless for dead call cases. The coy nature exhibited by both entities further demonstrates connectivity between NAD and anomalous telephone phenomena. Norma also reported that haunting phenomena occurred in her home, apparently linking the dead calls with those manifestations. Although Norma reported that she received most of her calls when depressed, she asserted the reality of all anomalous telephone calls received.

Both entities refused to identify themselves, despite the fact that all witnesses recognised their voices. The presumed opera singer also 'chose' a rather dramatic way to become involved in the lives of the two witnesses – by singing. Indeed, the connection between opera and tragedy seems to imbue that case with exotic symbolism, though why the charade? Had the opera singer spoken her name and stated that she was jealous and perhaps capable of striking out from the grave, she would have more logically put her point across. The means of communication, however, appear to have redoubled her effort to both impress and frighten the witnesses. While neither scenario would be a pleasant experience, the lurid anonymity, which the entity stubbornly clung to, had in effect removed much of the "human" element from the communication. In that sense, knowing who the communicator is, while they play cruel mind games with you, adds an additional element of terror to the experience. Taken at face value, this is a frightening scenario, however, it may provide evidence of an alternative explanation, which we shall explore in the following sections.

NAD Recorded, EVP, & Ufology

Although NAD phone cases would appear to be rare, EVP researcher Sarah Estep reported in *Roads to Eternity* that she had received a recorded phone message on her answering machine in 1998, which featured 'unidentified music'. Also heard was a female entity that spoke in a "*monotone*". Estep believed that both the music and the voice were not of this world, though no additional details were provided.[10] Estep included a CD recording with this published work that featured several examples of musical EVP voices as well as a lengthy recording of EVP music.[11]

---

[10] See also, Cooper's *Telephone Calls from The Dead* (Tricorn, 2012, p.81) for his Miscellaneous Accounts classification which includes 'Voicemail Messages'.

[11] The CD was titled "Voices From Beyond". Track #42 featured the lengthy instrumental NAD recording.

Musical EVP voices have also been reported by other researchers including Raymond Bayless and Konstantin Raudive, the noted EVP researcher. The "*sing song*" telephone voice noted earlier in connection with *The Warminster Mystery* (a UFO case), would seem to imply that a relationship exists between Ufology, NAD and *psi*, as Cooper and myself noted in our article on the matter in 2012.

General Theory and Discussion

Psychic Ether

Many researchers contend that a realm exists beyond the reach of our five senses, though a connection may be established when certain conditions are present. An individual, who is experiencing death or an OBE for example, may by default have extended the range of their sensitivity, thus enabling an interaction with this other environment. Rogo speculated that our material world is partitioned from one or more such environs by a field that has ideoplastic properties which are sensitive to thought and matter. While Rogo was not the first to postulate the existence of the so-called psychic ether theory, he applied it to account for certain aspects of NAD experiences.

Variations in witness narratives are to be expected as the experience is often dependent upon one's degree of connectivity with the psychic ether where the event is either stored (or occurring.) If a connection is not established, there may be no phenomena, a curious attribute noted in many hauntings. Indeed, the presence of a living agent is sometimes required to trigger manifestations. Further, that it may also account for those cases in which the haunt lies dormant during a particular tenancy. Reasoned speculation posits that some locations such as buildings have the ability to record certain events and maintain them in a latent state, thereby enabling future interactivity with a sensitive individual. Similarly, in certain NAD cases while multiple witnesses may be present, the experience is not always collective, as in the Bayless account (see Rogo, 1972, p. 99.) Indeed, I can personally attest to such, having experienced this curious aspect of NAD during the haunting investigation noted at Fort Henry. This would seem to apply regardless as to whether the 'signal' was latent, as in the case of a so-called residual haunting or in the case of a more dynamic (or intelligent) manifestation.

Theoretically should man survive bodily death, it would appear that what remains was fashioned to exist in this other world, if only for a limited time. Indeed the composition of such a body may very well share properties consistent with or identical to the presumed psychic ether, hence an etheric double. A change in our consciousness during an OBE, NDE, or after death, would take place as the released etheric double is designed to exist in the psychic realm. Indeed, while the furtive nature of psychic phenomena is partially reflective of our inability to pierce the psychic veil from our three dimensional world, the theory of the etheric double provides a hypothetical explanation to account for the mechanics of the OBE. Indeed, such may also account for the 'personality' changes noted in the alleged communications of both "Ruth" and "Jack". Presumably, they must undergo certain psychological changes to exist in their new world. Rogo further added that such could account for all *psi* phenomena, noting that the presumed existence of an ideoplastic environment is also consistent with the theory of Parallel Universes posited by the new physics.

Admittedly, Rogo's analyses concerning NAD and OBEs are indeed speculative, however they do not fall into the realm of sheer speculation. Rogo contended that *"all psychical phenomena are composite in nature"* and he provided a compelling argument for such after identifying patterns in NAD cases. The interaction of witnesses in presumed haunted locales tentatively support his theories concerning psychic ether as well as their ability to perceive NAD. Psychic ether may be thought of as providing the 'carrier wave' containing NAD (or other *psi* effects), with the witness acting as the receiver.

Theoretical Analysis: The Observer Effect and Secondary Personalities

In his fascinating work *The Holographic Universe*, Michael Talbot examined theories contemplated by the new physics and neuroscience to explain how the mind and universe may operate. Talbot also made reference to the observer effect, noting how electrons, for example, can be affected by the act of observation. Talbot noted how this curious enigma may demonstrate the interconnectivity between mind and matter.

The furtive nature of *psi* also implies that the active participation of a witness interferes with the propagation of phenomena. This form of observer effect is so widely noted in psychical research that it is seldom reflected on, rather that researchers have indeed come to expect *psi* phenomena to display a fugitive nature. Rogo reported a NAD case that involved the observer effect when the medium Attila von Szalay attempted to record the sound of a phantom flute during his historic sessions with Raymond Bayless in 1956. While in bed he heard a distinctive flute sound manifest approximately one foot from his face. The medium reported that any movement would disrupt the NAD and that he was wary that his interaction may inhibit the phenomenon. When von Szalay reached for his tape recorder the sound then diminished and faded away. Perhaps most curious is that another medium who von Szalay and Bayless met the next day elsewhere for breakfast, also reported hearing the same flute like music the night before.

It is possible that contact with "Ruth" or "Jack" may have immediately ceased had either agency attempted to reveal their identity. Indeed, Norma could not even engage Jack in conversation without the loss of contact. Unless it is a dictatorship on the other side, it appears that these agencies are only partially reflective of what was once human, with connectivity being extremely sensitive and easily disrupted. Indeed, Eva thought she was "*connected*" with whatever was on the phone. The agency may have realised that verbal identification would have somehow terminated contact or that it was simply unable to communicate further.

Ostensibly our opera singer was displeased at the prospect of her surviving husband finding someone else. "Ruth" was able to voice her displeasure to both Eva and Robert, though she was unable to reveal her identity without collapsing whatever was supporting the communication. As a result, Ruth was compelled to hide her identity lest destroy the mechanics of the call while she imparted her message. Oddly, no lyrics were present in her NAD, though the vocal harmony was imbued with tragedy, an apparent symbolic artefact linked with her passion for opera when alive. Indeed, she passed away immediately after having attended an operatic performance. Perhaps her surviving intellect was most reflective of what she loved and in particular what she was last engaged in prior to death? Sadly, such cases may also reflect a decline in personality after death, as well as other attributes that make one 'human,' thus reducing an individual to their baser instincts when they communicate as a discarnate entity.

Perhaps we should stop thinking in terms of these entities as being our deceased loved ones, though I cannot exclude the possibility that the dead pass through various transitional stages, much like a moth exiting a cocoon. That may explain the less than 'human' attributes exhibited by the 'dead' as noted in these and similar cases. I also cannot exclude the possibility that "Ruth" was a psychic artefact created unconsciously by one of the witnesses in response to an unresolved inner conflict. Therefore, "Ruth" may have provided them with a means of externalising their anxiety. Hypothetically, one of the parties may have experienced guilt at the thought of expressing their feelings to the other. The manifestation of "Ruth" may have resolved this dilemma by permitting one or both parties to subliminally shift responsibility from making a decision concerning their relationship as "Ruth" made it for them. Rogo and Bayless briefly addressed this matter in connection with UFO witness related cases where anomalous telephone phenomena were also reported.

Regardless, the lack of lyrics in her song is perhaps indicative of a diminished intellect due to the transition of death or of the self-limiting aspects displayed by a secondary personality created by one (or both) of the witnesses. Both possibilities must seriously be considered as hypothetical explanations. With that in mind, a parallel appears to exist with poltergeist phenomena, where reasoned speculation also links the unconscious production of various *psi* phenomena with a living person or 'agent'.

As certain poltergeists display an anthropomorphic nature (as well as voice phenomena), why not the production of music, especially vocal? Indeed the infamous Bell Witch was reported to have driven Lucy Bell to tears when the entity sang for her. The unearthly singing was described as "*beautiful*", and that:

> [No] rhythmical sound or melody ever fell upon the ear with sweeter pathos...like...symphony from a bursting heart...while friends would turn away to hide repressed weeping. (Ingram, 1894, p. 157)

Although the poltergeist also sang hymns, it also engaged in "*derisive songs*" following the death of John Bell Sr.

"Gef" (pronounced Jeff) was another alleged talking and singing poltergeist that was investigated by psychical researchers Harry Price and R.S. Lambert in the 1930s and reported in their book *The Haunting of Cashen's Gap*. Gef's voice was said to possess a vague unearthly quality as it sounded much higher in pitch than a human's. It was also said to be "*very shrill*" and "*whistling*" with a "*clear, sweet tone*". The NAD bordered on becoming "*a nuisance*" due to its prolific nature which included the Tonic Sol-fa scale. As in von Szalay's phantom flute sound, Gef's voice would sometimes be heard a foot from one's head, though usually it was not possible to determine its location. Similarly, Bayless was also unable to determine the source of his NAD in physical space.

As linkage exists between NAD and poltergeists, such would further involve the theories that apply to both manifestations, in particular that relating to the production of secondary personalities.

In 1993, the late Gerhard D. Wassermann, who held a PhD in Quantum Mechanics, had his intriguing work *Shadow Matter & Psychic Phenomena* published. Briefly, Wassermann re-worked in extreme detail the concept of the etheric double, which he called the Shadow Matter Body, and applied it to theoretically account for a variety of *psi* phenomena.[12] A prominent feature of his thesis postulated that the etheric double may act as a "*template*" in which an additional model can be replicated. The copy may produce additional replicates, thus resulting in a "*reciprocal templating mechanism*". Enormous numbers of these replicates may occur and move freely about in space while hosting *psi* information, though some may only represent partial constructs of the host template. Wassermann contended that such would apply to both animate as well as inanimate objects.[13]

Further, Wassermann speculated that with respect to OBEs, when ejection of the etheric double occurs, sometimes only part of the etheric brain splits off (thus meshing with Rogo's crescendo related effect). From an OBE perspective, Wassermann theorised that the released etheric brain would be able to act independently and amass new information (memories) outside the earthly body. Detached replicates may also become bound to the walls and structure of a building for example, and exist beyond the material life of the human creator. Those experiencing haunting phenomena may unconsciously be interacting with these replicates using their own etheric sensory mechanisms. Wassermann also addressed the spatial proximity issue with respect to haunting phenomena, noting that an attenuation effect would appear to be present, in part due to the binding of the replicates within the structure.

Aside from updating the etheric double theory, Wassermann's views on haunting further refined the concept of trace memories by providing a more substantive hypothetical model to work with. The concept

[12] Arguably Wassermann's work also updated, in part, F.W.H. Myers theory of "*psychorrhagic diathesis*", as noted in his monumental *Human Personality and its Survival of Bodily Death,* (1903), vol. 1, pp. 263- 265. The term Myers coined was derived from the Greek that translates as "*to let the soul break loose*".

[13] Myers "*phantasmogentic centre*" theory also accommodated inanimate objects (Myers, 1903, vol. 1 p. 265).

of "residual" versus "intelligent" hauntings also appear to have been impacted as it remains possible that separation of them may only relate to the degree of replication achieved as well as how many new memories the copy has been able to acquire, if any. In short, perhaps a residual haunting may eventually be classified as intelligent should the replicate continue to evolve.

Perhaps in support of such is that Rogo and Bayless reported on an anomalous telephone case where a long deceased cleric responded to a switchboard call and provided current information with respect to the whereabouts of the abbot. The entity displayed an awareness of the present, as it knew where the abbot was now located and what new extension he could be reached at. Wassermann's replicate theory may tentatively address why our phantom cleric was in possession of new information, which he could only have received in his post mortem state. Of further note is that he did not report that he was dead. These are yet further examples of absurd anomalies associated with a dead call case.

"Ruth" therefore may have been an incomplete replicate that had attached itself to her former dwelling place. The restrictive latitude "she" demonstrated during her communication may have simply revealed the limitations of the incomplete source material that she was created with. Indeed, there may have been no powers of speech, though what intellect was imbued within the replicate merely enabled "her" to sing and possibly voice her displeasure as the agency still retained powers of limited consciousness. Some of Wassermann's replicates are therefore akin to a "*psychic lobotomy*,"[14] as key powers of reasoning and intellect may not be present in all etheric copies. Indeed, with respect to hauntings, EVP work, and medium communications, for example, such disassociate personalities manifest routinely. Further, I still believe that there are a number of inhibition factors that also impact not only NAD but *psi* in general. The distance maintained by the rapping phenomenon that Scott and his colleague pursued is an example. Reduced intellect or another inhibition factor perhaps akin to a form of the observer effect may also be operating with respect to those agencies that refused to provide their names or answer questions concerning their identities.

The annals of psychical research contain intriguing data to support the contention that human beings are capable of producing secondary

[14] The term "*Psychic Lobotomy*" was first used by Nandor Fodor in *Haunted People* (1951, p. 168).

personalities that can manifest in our three dimensional world. Perhaps the most noteworthy of such is the so-called Philip Experiment in which members of the Toronto Society for Psychical Research conducted a series of experiments to determine whether they could create an "artificial ghost". The group drafted a fictional male character which they later made attempts to communicate with in a mock séance setting. Subsequently, they made contact with "Philip" who communicated via a series of raps and other phenomena. At one point the entity "*beat time to various tunes*" as reported by researcher Iris Owen in the *New Horizons* journal in 1977. As previously reported by Cooper and myself in 2012:

> Had the group's fictional character been an ET, it is reasonable to surmise that it would have also worked with the script provided, and masquerade itself as an alien. The author's research suggests that the mechanism responsible for the creation of Philip may also be responsible for some anomalous telephone experiences.

The Philip experiment clearly implicates a connection between some manifestations and the collective thoughts of witnesses. Perhaps "Ruth" was Eve and Robert's "Philip", so to speak. If they are not unconsciously responsible for her creation, then "Ruth" may very well have been an example of a replicate that was bound to Robert's phone, if one applies the theory of Wassermann.

With respect to the actual music itself, the unearthly aspect of some NAD is probably caused by the 'sound' having been modified by the environment that produced it. This process would be akin to the difference we would experience when hearing sound in the air as opposed to that traveling through water, for example. Bone conduction as opposed to direct ear canal sound wave travel creates further differences. Should NAD be telepathically received, then further anomalous effects would almost certainly be expected and therefore the concept of psychic ether and its ideoplastic properties are sensitive to our thought processes. This would present additional variables, perhaps distorting communications where their intonation is interpreted incorrectly as posited by Tweedale. Perhaps the voice of "Ruth" underwent a similar change in order to manifest?

While space did not permit me to properly examine accounts of instrumental, NDE or deathbed NAD, Rogo speculated that any weakness in the psychic ether may permit a witness to perceive "*properties*" of this other world which may include more complex NAD. The Parallel Universe theory lays the foundation for the existence of at least one realm that could accommodate the psychic ether theory as well as a dimension for various entities to dwell. Intrusions by our etheric bodies may tear or damage the psychic ether, thereby allowing fragments of whatever sounds or experiences that may occur in that environ to be temporarily perceived by us. What of course may exist in that environ is open to debate and may very well belong to a higher order.

Final Thoughts

In this brief study, I have examined the diversity and interconnectivity of NAD in its various guises while revealing that the phenomena are also operative within the greater *psi* spectrum. While much of this chapter dealt with applying hypothetical working models to theoretically account for some of the phenomena within a psychical research perspective, clearly much investigative work remains. I have little doubt that NAD occurs, though I am unsure as to the cause due to the interconnectivity of the manifestations as well as the inherent investigative issues previously noted. The dead are indeed clearly implicated in many cases as are secondary personalities which may involve Wassermann's replicates.

I do not believe that "Ruth" or "Jack" represented spiritual agencies at least in the classical sense. They appear to have been personality fragments bound to their former residences. Of note is that both entities apparently contacted our witnesses from their former dwelling place, which supports my contention that both haunters were probably bound to their specific locales. This supports Rogo's contention that in such cases the telephone is haunted at least for the duration of the event. I only ponder whether "Ruth" and "Jack" were created before or after the death of their host. Both "Philip" and Wassermann's replicates are both a form of secondary personalities, which if produced in numbers may also explain the apparent mutually exclusive nature of *psi* noted in some hauntings. Indeed, the concept of Parallel Universes may theoretically allow replicates to operate within a specific environ independent of other such Shadow Matter copies. This would provide answers to other anomalies noted in haunting phenomena.

One of the most curious matters I ever read concerned the alleged communications from the deceased mystery writer Edgar Wallace in

1932. Noted psychical researcher Nandor Fodor reported on a sitting that he organised with a trance medium in an attempt to communicate with the decedent. Fodor wrote in 1959 that the Wallace sitting was one of the few cases he investigated where survival was strongly implied. Most interesting was the comment made by "Wallace" that his fictional "*characters*" did not tag along with him to the afterlife, as was the case with other writers. The parallel with the "Philip" matter is obvious, with the additional claim that these apparent thought creations were said to persist even after the death of their creator.

This remark is astonishingly reflective of Wassermann's Shadow Matter brain replicates as well as our fictional ghost, "Philip". The concept that our coy telephone personalities are actually abandoned thought forms capable of rudimentary, independent thought and action, while cut off from their living or deceased creators is currently the 'best fit' in which to begin addressing some of these matters. I realise that such speculation may sound crazy, however, the claims made by the witnesses are no less fantastic. Unless witnesses are proven to be delusional or compulsive liars, then phenomena is occurring which defies conventional explanation and is also capable of dodging current scientific scrutiny. My research supports Rogo's contention that *psi* phenomena are composite in nature and that spontaneous music and voices are subsets of that system.

Due to our limited knowledge of paranormal music, it would be illogical to deem any data as being irrelevant until more is learned of the subject matter. Despite formidable investigative obstacles, these cases demand our scrutiny to satisfy both our innate scientific curiosity as well as to search for an explanation for those who have experienced such phenomena. While we presently remain unable to thoroughly investigate these occurrences, it would be intellectually dishonest to ignore them.

MUSIC AND DEATH

Melvyn Willin

"Music is associated with death and around the time of death in a whole lot of fascinating ways, and to bring those perspectives into the picture ... might be really interesting and enriching"

(Clarke, 2009)

It has the power to generate transformations and can influence the electro-conductivity of the body whereby acting as a bridge between the "real and the unreal", the "conscious and the unconscious" – as stated by Alvin in 1975. These viewpoints have been repeated by a large number of people, not only from the academic disciplines of music and thanatology, but also from the general public. Throughout recorded history, composers have chosen death as a source of inspiration for their works, including *Death and the Maiden* by Franz Schubert, *Death and Transfiguration* by Richard Strauss, and *The Isle of the Dead* by Sergei Rachmaninoff. *The Dream of Gerontius* by Edward Elgar deserves a special mention since the text by the Roman Catholic Cardinal John Newman focused on the story of a man's death and soul's journey into the next world. Elgar believed that much of the music came about by instinct and not conscious work. The origins of composers' inspiration have been discussed elsewhere at length but they have consistently believed in, at the very least, an altered state being accessed for their creative moments and the near-death experience (NDE) is possibly the ultimate such altered state. The realm of music is broadened further when such concepts as 'The Music of the Spheres' (discussed by D. Scott Rogo) are embraced, with its implication of transcendental manifestation beyond one's natural understanding. Occultists such as Agrippa, Macrobius, Boethius and Ficino firmly believed in music's exceptional importance within the psyche and its connection with the soul (cited by Tomlinson in 1993). Before leaving this brief skimming of the surface of the hidden depths of music, perhaps one needs to remember that many of the 'great and the good' have shared a belief in music's special place in the human psyche. These include Einstein:

> If I were not a physicist, I would probably be a musician. I often think in music. I live my daydreams in music. I see my life in terms of music. (cited in Williams, 2008)

And Jung:

> Deeply listening to music opens up new avenues of research I'd never even dreamed of. I feel from now on music should be an essential part of every analysis. (ibid.)

Because of the lack of available space, it is not my intention to present in any detail the arguments for and against the veracity of the NDE as an actual glimpse into what lies beyond the grave. The philosopher Michael Grosso has suggested that the very concept of death has undergone radical changes, originally from a magical interpretation followed by religious definitions, and most recently death is treated as the purely physical extinction of the brain and surrounding body. The NDE has been expounded upon at length by many authors including Blackmore, Moody, Sabom, Corazza, and Holden, Greyson and James. Kenneth Ring provides further information about various overviews of the available literature. The sceptics believe that ketamines, the release of endorphins, temporal lobe seizures, a lack of oxygen, increased carbon dioxide, false memories, or the absence of an actual experience of death, causes the hallucinations. The believers retaliate with the anomaly of 'Peak in Darien Experiences' whereby the dying patient is allegedly visited by dead people who they believed to be alive at the time of their NDE. People who have undergone what might be called a 'real' NDE, as opposed to a drug-induced experience, seem to have changed lives after the event. This has been studied at length in cases of cardiac arrest patients.

The much quoted 'composite' case formed of the most common experiences of the NDE includes a feeling of euphoria, out of body experiences (OOBEs), entering a tunnel with bright, guiding light, meeting either divine beings or deceased friends or family. It does not usually include music in its list of core experiences. One reason for this might be that questionnaires often do not ask whether it has been experienced.[1] The 'Greyson Scale', a sixteen-point questionnaire, similarly omits music, but he did draw attention to auditory phenomena, claiming that 80% of NDErs witnessed positive auditory sensations. *The Tibetan Book of the Dead* (*Bardo Thödol*) highlights life's successive stages of consciousness with birth's 'incarnation' and death's 'disincarnation' and a literal translation of *Bardo Thödol* is 'hearing on the after-death plane'. It is said (ibid. xxviii) that sounds are heard at death and up to fifteen hours after and a study was undertaken by one Dr Collingues in 1862. Better-known studies that have discovered musical phenomena surrounding the NDE have included Bozzano, Rogo, Greyson and Stevenson, Gallup and Proctor, and Sir William Barrett, as well as numerous examples in the magazine *Light*. The Gallup poll, taken over an eighteen month period in the USA, stated that 17% of interviewees mentioned auditory phenomena, but not specifically music in every case. Similarly the Greyson and Stevenson study does not differentiate but stipulates a 57% hit rate, albeit from a relatively small sample of seventy eight cases. Other cases can be found scattered around the literature but they are more difficult to uncover and research. For instance, a few can be found in unpublished literature compiled by Peter and Elizabeth Fenwick housed in the Alister Hardy Trust at the University of Wales, Lampeter.

Historical Cases

It is not possible here to mention every case even when they have been published. Furthermore, some important works have not been translated into English, which presents further difficulties, especially when the original language used is also somewhat archaic. Therefore, a useful starting point for "the numerous cases in which music is heard at the time of death" is the 'Eton College Case', originally recorded in *Phantasms of the Living* (1886, vol. II, p. 639.) A memorandum was sent to Gurney in February 1884 that was written soon after the death of a Mr L.'s (a master of Eton College) mother which occurred at about 2

[1] For instance: Osis, (1961); Moody, (1978)

a.m. on July 28, 1881. He stated that immediately after her death music was heard by several people present. These included a matron, the doctor in attendance, a friend, and two other people. Curiously, Mr L. did not hear the music. It was variously described as "low, soft music, exceedingly sweet, as of three girls' voices" and as "very low, sweet singing". The outside area was checked but no one was seen or heard. Unless the people present were mistaken, or there were indeed singers outside who were neither seen nor heard on immediate investigation, then it would appear that the music emanated from an unknown natural source.

Another case from Barrett's excellent chapter on the subject is taken from the SPR's 1885 *Proceedings,* in Volume 3, page 92. A well-known Irish gentleman (Colonel Z.), who wished to remain anonymous, recounted that at the time of his wife's death she claimed to not only hear angelic voices singing but also the specific voice of a professional singer friend (of a friend) whom they both believed to be alive and well. The Colonel's wife also claimed to be able to see her although he experienced nothing. After her death, he found out that the singer had indeed died eleven days before his wife and that she continued to sing during that time. He confirmed that there was no way of knowing about her circumstances during this time. Was this purely a coincidence or an example of the 'Peak in Darien Experiences'?

One cannot leave the historical cases without mentioning the many examples that are given in the journal *Light* which provides details of music being heard at the death of Louis XVII in the French Revolution; the author Johann Wolfgang von Goethe and the mystic Jakob Böhme among many others. The problem that arises from these cases is the lack of specific information concerning the music. Expressions such as "mysterious music", "divine music", "beautiful music", "heavenly music", etc., abound notably in the Spiritualist literature. However, it is not just this type of writing where such descriptions exist, as Heim also wrote about "heavenly music" being heard at the time of life threatening climbing accidents. The musicologist Joscelyn Godwin presented many examples from historical sources of angels singing, but there is a dearth of information concerning exactly what and how they were singing. Cultural elements within the society of the times and places seem to dictate the content on the rare occasions that specifics were provided. Therefore, the strength of religious beliefs in pre-modern Europe, further enhanced by the visual arts, no doubt influenced the number of harp-playing angels that were encountered. To break away from this stereotypical concept it was therefore necessary to look at more modern cases where such concepts may not be so prevalent.

Modern Cases

For more recent cases I relied on the literature once more, but I also made direct contact with people who claimed to have heard music in a NDE. A debt of gratitude must be made to D. Scott Rogo whose works provided an impressive starting point for the discovery of many examples. He believed that the relative scarcity of accounts of such experiences might be due to the lack of intimacy in modern hospitalised death situations which could be contradictory to psychic functioning and that they may not be reported because researchers did not seek them out. He favoured the term 'transcendental' and cited several examples where he believed such music was experienced from the researches of Robert Crookall in the 1960s and Raymond Moody in the 1970s. Rogo took the subject further by providing examples that he uncovered himself. For instance, his 'Case no. 34' (cited in the 1970 book *NAD*) from 1966, recounted a death bed scene where "the room was suddenly filled with the sound of an organ playing and voices singing a hymn". A follow up to this event from a witness wrote that the hospital matron denied services were held in the Chapel there by nurses and that "the music was so powerful it vibrated through the floor and up through the walls of the large waiting room and *gradually faded out*" (ibid. p. 54.) A further example of music heard at a NDE from 1968 came from the brother of a deceased man who spoke of the joy his brother felt at hearing music during an unconscious period just prior to his death (ibid. p. 136-7.)

Important though Rogo's work is, he is not the only person to have discovered examples of music during the NDE. Margot Grey found in a UK study that 11% of NDErs heard the "music of the spheres" and extensive examples are quoted on the internet by Kevin Williams. Although these examples are not explored in depth, they nevertheless describe a wide range of different experiences. He summarises his correspondents' experiences in words that remind one of the imprecise language used in the past cases, but perhaps words are not able to convey the immensity of the experience. These include 'transcendental', 'unearthly harmonic beauty', 'sublimely beautiful', 'exquisite harmonies', 'heavenly', 'a celestial choir of angels', 'joyous and beat-less melody', 'an orchestra of voices', the 'Music of the Spheres', 'mystical tones', 'music that transcends all thought', 'bells and wind chimes', 'celestial symphony', 'complicated rhythms with unearthly tones', 'music that is experienced from within'. Furthermore, he says, music and light/colour are synthesised together (ibid.).

A few people have expressed their NDEs of music in more depth and have spent time analysing the occurrence. Gilles Bèdard spent five months in hospital "on the brink of death" with Crohn's disease in 1973. During this time he heard powerful music that was to change his life as he sought to reproduce it. He found the nearest he could get to it was a combination of Tangerine Dream's 'Mysterious Semblance at the Strand of Nightmares' from the album 'Phaedra' and Steve Roach's 'Structures from Silence'. He claims that Steve Roach told him that he had an NDE and had tried to recreate the sounds he heard when he was "in the light", but it has not been possible to verify this statement.

Another interesting case is that of Tony Cicoria which has been written about by Oliver Sachs. Briefly, this New York surgeon was struck by lightning in 1994 which led to an insatiable desire to play piano music which came to him in dreams. He evidently had no interest prior to this. This case is different to others since the music is widely available (Cicoria), but it does not follow in the 'angelic' tradition sounding quite firmly from the Romantic nineteenth-century Western piano tradition of Chopin and Liszt. Far better known than Cicoria is the composer Arnold Schönberg (1874-1951) who suffered a cardiac arrest in 1946 and was considered clinically dead for an uncertain period of time. While he was still in hospital he began work on a String Trio (op. 45) which may have been an attempt to reproduce the various stages of his journey in the afterlife. However, it needs mentioning that he had already been commissioned to write the work before his collapse and had made some tentative plans for the music. Despite Schönberg having described the piece as a "humorous representation of my sickness", many people have interpreted the work as a musical NDE with sections representing the NDE itself followed by the return to life. Corazza and Terreni take this further with an implication of peace and calmness; dialogue and meeting with others; and other transcendental experiences. Another example is Marcey Hamm's music which was composed as a result of her suffering an NDE during a road traffic accident in 1985. She spoke of being "engulfed" in music and colour after a period of recovery and that, having made the music public, she was approached by a man who "told me that he had open heart surgery seven years prior and was pronounced dead for sixteen minutes. He told me that during the time he was dead, this music he heard [i.e. Marcey Hamm's music] was the same music he heard while he was dead" (Hamm, n.d.). The music is synthesised and consists of concordant, homophonic choral effects that are slow and sustained and dwell on distinct bass and treble pitches. She maintains that the music, which has a duration of one hour and twelve minutes, could be used for meditation or path-working (visualised meditation) of a "suitable" nature.

Of the greatest interest to me was the prospect of finding cases that I could research directly through conversation and correspondence with surviving NDErs. In this respect I suffered some disappointments, since I was not allowed details from hospital staff of patients who may (or may not) have had NDEs. Conversations with Bruce Greyson, Penny Sartori, Sam Parnia, and other researchers in the field were helpful, but similarly did not lead to new unpublished cases. There were nevertheless some successes in finding new cases and one in particular since it came about as a result of a somewhat bizarre coincidence.

Whilst attending a rehearsal in 2008 for a public performance of the Rodrigo Guitar Concerto by one of my students, I happened to chat to a musician (David Ditchfield) who was a stranger to me and who's first classical work was evidently going to be performed in the same concert. He explained it was composed as the result of a dramatic NDE. I later heard the work and interviewed him about the experience (8th May, 2009.) He revealed that his coat was trapped in the door of a departing train and that he was dragged under the train for some distance. His injuries were substantial and life threatening. He subsequently decided to record the experience by a sketch that developed into a canvas painting and then he began receiving messages from his subconscious (or spirits – he was unclear about which) to put these ideas into music. Although he had some experience of pop music, he had never attempted anything on such a grand scale himself. The ideas "seemed to come from elsewhere and easily" and even finding performers seemed to "fall into place" which was no mean feat considering the work required an orchestra and soloist. The work *The Divine Light* is harmonically concordant, slow and sustained. Similarities can be found in the chamber works of Ralph Vaughan Williams. He believes his life has been changed in a positive way because of this experience and that he must now embrace a new musical direction from his previous world of pop music.

Soon after this interview, a number of other cases came to my attention not related to my connection with David. I was approached to participate in a BBC Radio 4 documentary, first broadcast on 14th July 2009. During the programme, the violinist Paul Robertson mentioned his own fairly recent NDE when he heard what he described as "ragas". As a result of this programme I was also invited to attend the first public performance on 6th July, 2009 in Winchester Cathedral of John Tavener's *Towards Silence* – a work composed to "explore the nature of consciousness and the process of dying" after Tavener's own close brush with death. It consists of a meditation on the four states of Hindu Atma namely, the waking, dreaming, deep sleep and that which is beyond ('Turiya'). The work for four string quartets and Tibetan bowl was performed as a meditation and the audience was encouraged to close their eyes and let go of their normal waking consciousness. A deep feeling of peace prevailed.

I was also contacted via email by people who were willing to share their NDEs because of my particular emphasis of music phenomena. Ann spoke of a heart attack in 2009 when she explained with difficulty: "The music isn't heard but lived. You hear it, see it, taste it, FEEL it. It isn't heard but experienced". She found words were inadequate to explain it. Another correspondent (Sharon) told me that after a minor operation in 1997 she entered a trance and heard what she described as the "the music of the spheres ... disjointed set of musical chords came together to sound like the world's biggest and most angelic orchestra". In 1981, another contact (Mike) experienced "massed waves of sound" which his friends couldn't hear. He specified that it was a different sensation to that which he experienced when smoking marijuana but had some similarities after too much psilocybin mushroom wine. These people were unanimous in believing that their experiences were genuine and not part of a drug-fuelled hallucination.

Further Discussion

Examples from historical and recent sources have been presented which, at the very least, it is hoped allow further scrutiny by interested readers. In much the same way as different researchers place different interpretations on visual material, the same can be maintained of musical phenomena. As previously mentioned, William Barrett believed that at least some of the cases might be hallucinatory, but Scott Rogo importantly drew implications of survival from his finds. These can be categorised as follows:

- The music heard is felt to be beyond the percipient's "imagination and creative aptitude, and to be caused by some external agent". (In private conversation, John Tavener told me he believed his own "inspiration" came from an "external force".)
- During a NDE "the music was heard most vividly as human voices and seemed to issue from the 'other world' ".
- The dying have heard "celestial" music and have also seen apparitions.

He felt that this might come about by a "rupture in the ether" and if these interpretations are correct then one is forced to reconsider not only the nature of music but the whole issue of survival. The avant-garde composer John Cage used to quote a Native American Indian belief that music sounded permanently in much the same way as looking or not looking at a landscape doesn't mean it's not still there.[2] A continuation to this idea might be explored in the minimalist music of Terry Riley that allegedly produces the sensation of a loss of time awareness as one becomes one with the music.

So where does this leave us? It would appear that from the cases presented, and the very many more that were not discussed here from the people who have claimed to have had a NDE, about 11% experience music during the occurrence. The music is often of a type that would not be listened to by the percipients in their normal healthy lives and it is often described as "divine" and beyond verbal description. Precision as to instrumentation, tonality, rhythm, etc., is usually absent from the recollections since the sensations are more of a feeling rather than simply *hearing* music. Before the modern period, the source of the music was believed to come from God or angelic beings, but this idea has diminished somewhat in arguably more enlightened times, although not entirely. Try as we might to pin down the actual significance and origin of the NDE, and the effect that music has upon the psyche within this experience, or indeed outside of it, intangibility would still seem to be the dominate factor in its understanding. This will probably remain the case until more research is undertaken to what must ultimately be the most important factor in our brief lives, namely what happens, if anything, after physical death.

(Note: This chapter was originally published as an article in the *Paranormal Review* of the Society for Psychical Research, April 2011, no. 58.)

[2] cited in Dickinson (2001, p. 4)

MUSIC IN SHAMANISM AND SPIRIT POSSESSION

Jack Hunter

A connection between ritual music and communication with the spirit world through altered states of consciousness has long been recognised in the anthropological literature. This chapter will explore these apparent connections through presenting a sample of the ethnographic and theoretical literature as it pertains to the role of music in the induction of altered states of consciousness, frequently referred to as trance states. In particular, this chapter will focus on the practices broadly known as shamanism and spirit possession, and the role that music plays within them.

What is Trance?

The term 'trance' is often bandied around quite freely without much worry as to what precisely it refers. Before embarking on our discussion of the role played by music in the induction of trance states, therefore, it will be necessary to define a little more precisely what trance states actually are. Etymologically the term's roots go back to the Latin word *transire* meaning to 'cross over,' and the Old French word *transe*, meaning 'to die' or 'pass on.' So the word 'trance' has usually been associated with liminal states of consciousness, and particularly with the threshold between life and death. From this perspective, then, to be in a trance state is to be somehow between the worlds of the living and the dead.

Trance is an altered state of consciousness (ASC). Broadly speaking altered states of consciousness can be defined as phases of consciousness that differ from our everyday waking state of consciousness - our baseline state, as discussed Professor Charles Tart. There are many different states of consciousness, including waking consciousness, sleep, meditative states, psychedelic states, and hypnosis, amongst others, each with distinctive neurophysiological correlates.

In popular parlance there are many different states of consciousness, as well as certain unusual sensory experiences, that are categorised as trance states. Judith Becker's definition of trance is intentionally broad, so as to include a wide variety of different experiences and bodily states. Trance, she writes, is:

> ...a state of mind characterised by intense focus, the loss of the strong sense of self and access to types of knowledge and experience that are inaccessible in non-trance states. (Becker 1994, p. 41)

Becker's definition encompasses a wide variety of states of consciousness including meditative states, possession trance, shamanic trance, communal trance, aesthetic trance and other moments of transcendence. Similarly, Brian Inglis, in his book *Trance: A Natural History of Altered States of Mind*, also lays out a broad spectrum of experiences and states of consciousness encompassed by the term:

> At one extreme it is applied to what can loosely be described as possession, in which the individual's normal self seems to be displaced, leaving him rapt, or paralysed, or hysterical, or psychotic, or taken over by another personality. At the other extreme is sleep. Between the two are conditions in which consciousness is maintained, but the subliminal mind makes itself felt, as in light hypnosis or the kind of reverie in which fancy, or fantasy, breaks loose. (Inglis 1989, p.267)

Inglis' spectrum of trance states runs from the extremity of dissociative states of consciousness, whereby the individual feels that their consciousness is displaced from the body to reveries and flights of fancy. The term 'trance,' therefore, is often applied to conditions in which consciousness is seemingly restricted, as in dissociation, as well as conditions in which consciousness appears to be expanded, as in reveries and flights of fancy.

In his 1986 article 'Trance States: A Theoretical Model and Cross-Cultural Analysis,' Michael Winkelman presents a psychophysiological model of trance states, arguing that although there are differences in terms of trance experiences and methods for inducing trance states, there are key psychophysiological similarities between specific states, in particular a 'parasympathetic dominance in which the frontal cortex is dominated by slow wave patterns originating in the limbic system and related projections into the frontal parts of the brain' (p.174). Winkelman asserts, therefore, that there is a 'common set of psychophysiological changes underlying a variety of trance induction techniques' (p. 175). So while there may be a variety of trance experiences, the physiological activity in the brain appears to be similar in nature.[1]

As it stands, then, trance is still a fairly general term applied to a wide spectrum of unusual experiences. The following sections will deal with social phenomena that employ specific states of consciousness usually classified as trance states: shamanism and spirit possession. These two, again broadly defined, social phenomena appear to represent both sides of the spectrum of trance states suggested by Inglis. Shamanism, at the one extreme, whereby the shaman retains awareness in interacting with the spirit world while on soul excursions, and spirit possession at the other extreme, whereby conscious awareness is lost and the sense of self temporarily displaced.

Ethnographic Examples

Shamanism and the Spirit World

The writings of the Romanian historian of religion Mircea Eliade (1907-1986) are frequently taken as the starting point in explorations of shamanism, and this brief discussion will do just the same. Eliade's primary interest was in the forms of shamanism practiced in Siberian and Central Asian cultures, exemplified by the Tungus (from whom we get the word Shaman, from the Tungusic word Šaman), which he held to be the 'purest,' most 'archaic,' forms of shamanic practice. Indeed, quite controversially, Eliade held the ecstatic techniques of the Siberian shamans to be superior to those of other regions, often regarding the use of psychoactive substances, for example, as a 'crude,'

[1] For a comprehensive overview of neurophysiological research into trance states see Krippner & Friedman (2010).

'mechanical' and 'corrupt' method of inducing the shamanic experience. Regardless of his apparent ethnocentric bias against psychoactive plant use, however, Eliade's comments on other techniques for altering consciousness, and in particular what he called 'magico-religious music,' are worth considering. In his classic text *Shamanism: Archaic Techniques of Ecstasy*, Eliade goes to great lengths in describing the central importance of the shaman's drum in many, predominantly Siberian, shamanic traditions. The drum, he writes, 'has a role of the first importance in shamanic ceremonies'. He goes on to describe several of the main uses of drumming in shamanic cultures:

> [The drum] is indispensable in conducting the shamanic seance, whether it carries the shaman to the "Center of the World," or enables him to fly through the air, or summons and "imprisons" the spirits, or, finally...enables the shaman to concentrate and regain contact with the spiritual world through which he is preparing to travel. (1989, p. 168)

For Eliade, then, music represents the *sin qua non* shamanic technique of ecstasy, arguing that 'there is always some instrument that, in one way or another, is able to establish contact with the 'world of the spirits'.

Writing more recently, psychologist and parapsychologist Stanley Krippner has further expanded on Eliade's use of the term 'techniques of ecstasy' in his discussion of 'shamanic technologies.' Krippner defines shamanism as comprising 'a group of techniques by which practitioners deliberately alter or heighten their conscious awareness to enter the so-called "spirit world," accessing material that they use to help and to heal members of the social group'. Krippner highlights the fact that 'rarely is one procedure used in isolation,' and emphasises the frequent combining of different techniques. He describes, for example, the traditional healing procedures of the Native American Ojibway, for whom it was customary for the *wabeno* (shamans) to 'heal by means of drumming, rattling, chanting, dancing erotically (while naked), and handling hot coals' (see Krippner, 2000, p. 102). Music, drumming, chanting and dancing, therefore, might all be employed in combination, or alongside other techniques for the induction of shamanic states of consciousness, including, for example: sensory deprivation, sensory stimulation, dietary restrictions, sleep deprivation, hyperventilation, and consumption of psychoactive substances, amongst others.

It is clear, however, that in spite of the many different techniques for the induction of contact with the spirit world, music is the most cross-culturally prevalent. Indeed music often serves to 'enhance the experience's profundity' – as Krippner has also stated – performing an important role in shamanic rituals employing other modes of consciousness alteration. Marlene Dobkin de Rios and Fred Katz, for example, describe how amongst certain Amazonian Peruvian populations, whistling incantations during periods of ritualised psychoactive intoxication 'served as a vital link in bridging separate realities induced by the ingestion of a plant hallucinogen' (1975, p. 65). They suggest that the rhythmic structure inherent in many musical forms serves to create a 'jungle gym' for consciousness during the altered state 'providing a series of pathways and banisters through which the drug user negotiates his way' (1975, p. 68). This structuring of the altered state experience is necessary, so Dobkin de Rios and Katz argue, in order to give the experience meaning and to allow the shaman to achieve culturally important goals, such as communication with spirit ancestors and healing.

Uwe Maas and Süster Strubelt have suggested that the polyrhythmic music that accompanies the ritualised use of the psychoactive drug *Iboga* during initiation rituals in Gabon, Central Africa, actually, "[I]ncreases the effect of the drug...so that patients may need smaller amounts...of this potentially harmful drug." (Maas & Strubelt, 2003, p. 1-2)

Maas and Strubelt describe the *Iboga* initiation ceremony of the Mitsogo as a 'controlled near-death experience', the experience of which features many phenomenological commonalities with those documented in the traditional near-death experience literature.

In addition to the role played by music in initiating contact with the spirit world, Michael Winkelman, drawing on experimental studies into music's physiological effects on the body (including its capacity to counteract stress related biological change, reduce muscle tension, heart rate, blood pressure, and alter mood and attitude, amongst others), has highlighted the significant therapeutic role of music in many shamanic traditions. Similarly, neurologist Oliver Sacks has highlighted the positive influence of both rhythm and melody in the therapeutic treatment of various neurological conditions. He writes:

> Patients with Parkinsonism, in whom movements tend to be incontinently fast or slow or sometimes frozen, may overcome these disorders of timing when they are exposed to the regular tempo and rhythm of music. (Sacks, 2006, p. 2528)

Anette Kjellgren and Anders Eriksson conducted a study in which twenty-two individuals participated in a twenty minute shamanic-like drumming session. After the drumming, participants were asked to produce written accounts of their experiences during the session. Amongst the reports of the participants were numerous experiences considered to be classically shamanic in nature, including entry into holes and tunnels, moving through different levels, visual imagery, bodily transformations, inner sounds, encounters with animals, plants and insects, visionary landscapes and insights.

It is clear then that music is a multi-purpose shamanic technology: it provides access to spiritual realms, helps to structure altered state experiences for attaining culturally significant goals, and serves the therapeutic needs of the social group, as well as (of course) providing entertainment (which in itself may perform an essential cohesive social function.)

Spirit Possession

Music also plays a central role in many spirit possession traditions. Spirit possession differs from shamanism in a number of key respects, most importantly: during spirit possession performances, the possessed/medium claims to surrender control of their body to an external spirit or deity, while the shaman always remains in control; following the spirit possession performance, the possessed/medium is unable to recall the events that took place during their trance, while for the shaman, recollection of the events that take place during his/her excursion to the spirit-world is an essential component of their socio-cultural role. Despite these apparent differences, however, it is clear that shamanism and spirit possession practices often overlap with one another in a number of ways, with the use of musical trance induction techniques being just one of them.

In many Afro-Brazilian traditions, including Candomble, Umbanda and Batuque, rhythm in particular plays a very important role. During Candomble trance performances, spirit mediums must dance according to very specific rhythms, employing very specific bodily postures, in order for the individual *Orixa* to express itself. Each *Orixa* in the Yoruba pantheon has its own characteristic rhythm and dance movements by which it is recognised. Oshala, the *Orixa* of creation, for example, dances slowly and ponderously to a steady drum rhythm, while Oya, *Orixa* of the wind, whirls gracefully to a quick polyrhythmic beat. During Candomble possession rituals, if the possessed person does not dance the correct dance to the correct rhythms, the possession is not deemed to be authentic.

Erlmann describes the use of music in the *boori* spirit possession cult of the West African Hausa. Music plays a particularly important role in *boori* possession ceremonies. Musicians perform specific songs, known as *taakee*, for each of the four hundred plus spirits usually incorporated by cult members, who become 'mares' (*goo'dilyaa*) upon which the spirits ride. The music is performed on gourd rattles, calabashes and single-stringed lutes called *googee*.

My own field-research with a Spiritualist home-circle in the UK, also found music to have a central role in contemporary trance and physical mediumship séances. In this context, however, the music is generally popular music from the past twenty years. The music used to help the medium return from his/her trance state at the end of the séance, for example, is a short instrumental piece by the American rock band REM. It would seem, therefore, that any kind of music can be used for the induction and modulation of altered states of consciousness, which would support the notion that trance is not necessarily an automatic response to particular musical forms, but rather is a learned response.

Music, the Brain, and Altered States of Consciousness

There is a great deal of debate about the actual effect of music on the psycho-physiological functioning of the brain, especially as it relates to the induction of altered states of consciousness and anomalous experiences, as frequently reported by those who practice forms of spirit possession and shamanism. The debate can broadly be split into two camps, those who argue that music has a direct physiological effect on the brain, essentially *causing* or *inducing* the trance state, and those who suggest that trance is a learned response to particular culturally significant musical forms.

The theory of 'auditory driving' was first put forward in the 1960s by psychologist Andrew Neher to describe the observation that EEG readings from subjects exposed to repetitive rhythms appear to show a synchronisation of brain wave frequencies to the frequency of the drum beat. Neher further expanded on this research by investigating the use of percussion in shamanic cultures. Winkelman suggests that auditory driving is a universal feature of shamanic healing practices, particularly as a result of drumming, singing and chanting, arguing that the work of Neher suggests that 'the cortex is easily set into oscillation at the alpha frequency or slower and that singing, chanting and percussion procedures produce or enhance this state of dominance of slow-wave frequencies' (see Winkelman, 2000, p. 149). The phenomenon of auditory driving would appear to suggest that specific percussive frequencies can produce specific alterations of consciousness.

Drawing on fieldwork in Venda spirit possession rituals in the 1950s, Blacking argues that there is no 'direct causal relationship between the sounds of music and human responses to them.' He offers instead that 'if organised sounds are to affect people's feelings and actions, people must not only be predisposed to listen to them, they must also have acquired certain habits of assimilating sensory experience' (1985, p. 64). In other words, Blacking suggests that spirit possession is a learned response to what he terms 'musical symbols,' rather than a direct response to the musical sounds themselves. It is not the music that creates the trance, but rather the music serves to give structure to the trance experience. Arguing along similar lines, Fachner suggests that: '*Music creates conditions* that favour the onset of trance, that regulate form and development, and make them more predictable and easier to control' (2007, p.176), but does not create the trance state itself.

Concluding Remarks

While it is clear that music, and indeed sound more generally, plays an important role in the trance induction techniques of many different cultural and sub-cultural groups, the question of whether music has the capacity to *create* alterations of consciousness, or whether it simply aids in the *control* and *modulation* of altered states is still up for debate. Regardless of the outcome of this debate, however, music's role in spirit possession and shamanic rituals is undeniable, indeed ethnomusicologist Ruth Herbert has argued that 'dissociation from self, surroundings, or activity in conjunction with music, is a common occurrence in everyday life,' thus suggesting that music's capacity to induce and/or modulate ASCs is a universal, cross-cultural, human phenomenon that is not restricted to specific ritual settings.

THE ACOUSTIC PROPERTIES OF UNEXPLAINED RAPPING SOUNDS

Barrie G. Colvin

Rapping sounds emanating from an unknown source have been widely described in the literature, particularly with respect to investigations of apparent recurrent spontaneous psychokinesis (RSPK) and Spiritualist-type sitter groups (Roll, 1976 and Pearsall, 1972). The phenomenon has been described in cases covering many hundreds of years and varies from slight rapping sounds, scratchings, a "sawing" sound, to thunderous banging sounds. RSPK studies, often referred to as poltergeist activity, indicate that as many as 50% of all cases include the production of rapping sounds, often accompanied by other phenomena such as object movements, luminous effects, cold breezes and disturbed bedclothes (Gauld & Cornell, 1979). The quality and frequency of rapping sounds vary enormously from isolated single raps to series of raps occurring on a very regular basis. In a small minority of cases a rapping intelligence has been capable of communicating via a code and answer simple questions put to it by those present. Probably the most well-known case of this type is that of the Fox sisters, dating from 1848. This case had a profound effect upon the wider public and led to the rise in modern Spiritualism (Gauld, 1968). Other similar cases are those of Cideville (Lang, 1904) and Karin (Wijk, 1905). In more recent times, the Andover case of 1974 consisted of messages being clearly rapped out on a wall and on a bed-head, all in the presence of investigators (Colvin, 2008). The rapping sounds in this case varied from light knocks to very heavy bangs, sufficient to cause the walls of the house to vibrate. Of particular importance, the position of the raps could be determined and the localised vibrations felt by the principal investigators. Furthermore, the quality of the messages was good in that there was no ambiguity with regard to specific letters being rapped out using a coded format. From a personal perspective, I confess that I was unable to find a satisfactory explanation for the coherent, unmistakable rapping sounds produced at Andover. In particular, the episode involving raps to the bed-head was rather perplexing. As I stood closer than a metre to the bed-head in good daylight conditions, listened to the sounds and asked that they be made at a very specific part of the bed-head, I could clearly hear the sounds and feel the vibrations within the wooden structure. My subjective feeling at that point was that the raps were not produced by normal means, and most definitely not produced by anything hitting the bed. The observation that no apparent means of percussive action appeared to be relevant to the production of these unusual raps led me to consider whether the sounds were acoustically different in any way from similar sounding raps produced by conventional percussive methods.

General Acoustics

In order to determine whether inexplicable raps are in any way different to normal rapping sounds, it was necessary to fingerprint the rapping sounds using generally accepted methods of acoustic analysis.

Sound can be regarded as the vibration of matter, as perceived by the sense of hearing. Physically, sound is vibrational mechanical energy that propagates through matter as a wave. The waves are characterised by the generic properties of waves, namely frequency, wavelength, period, amplitude, intensity, speed and direction. Sound can be transmitted through gases (including air), plasma, liquids and solids. The matter that supports the sound is called the medium. When passing through air, sound waves are transmitted as longitudinal waves, also called compression waves. The type of medium they pass through or are reflected from will influence the properties of the waves.

Two important properties of sound are the amplitude and the frequency. Broadly speaking, these properties relate to the loudness of the sound and its pitch. The amplitude is often measured in terms of sound pressure level, which is defined as the difference between the actual pressure in the medium at a particular point and time, and the average pressure of the medium at that same point. As the human ear can detect sounds with a very wide range of amplitudes, sound pressure is often measured as a level on a logarithmic decibel scale. The amplitude of any sound, including a very simple sound such as a rap, varies with time. The amplitude/time graph is known as the acoustic waveform and is a pictorial view of how the amplitude or strength of the sound varies with time. Clearly, when an object is struck, such as a hammer hitting a bell, the amplitude immediately rises to a maximum and then decays with time. In the case of a bell, the decay period may be many seconds. In the case of a knuckle being used to hit a solid wooden desktop, the amplitude will again reach its maximum very quickly but the decay period will be very short due to the dampening effect of the solid wooden structure.

The pitch of the sound is expressed in terms of frequency, that is the number of wave vibrations occurring in a second. The higher the number of waves occurring within one second (cycles) the higher the pitch of the sound.

Modern techniques allow the waveform to be modified, having firstly converted it into a digital format. For example, background noise can be eliminated or certain frequency bands can be either excluded or included in the analysis of a sound. In this way, a waveform can be generated in which, for example, only lower frequencies are included. Furthermore, amplitude, frequency and time can all be presented as a composite graph, known as the Fast Fourier Transform. This is particularly useful and has become an integral part of acoustics procedures. It is essentially a mathematical method for transforming a function of time into a function of frequency. It is based on Fourier theory, which states that any waveform consists of an infinite sum of sine and cosine functions allowing both frequency and amplitude to be quickly and easily measured. It is often used for filtering and for frequency analysis procedures.

Normal Rapping Sounds

In order to allow the comparison between unexplained and normal rapping sounds, I have included waveforms and frequency graphs of both types of raps. These visual representations were obtained using

Adobe Audition software. Normal raps are clearly produced by tapping a hard object against another hard object. This striking action causes a localised increase in air pressure that is transmitted to the ear-drum, causes a vibration, and is heard as a sound. The waveform shown in Fig.1 represents the amplitude-time graph of a rap produced by tapping on a wall using the knuckle of the middle finger. The horizontal axis represents time, in this case covering a period of about half a second, the vertical axis representing the volume of the sound, expressed as amplitude.

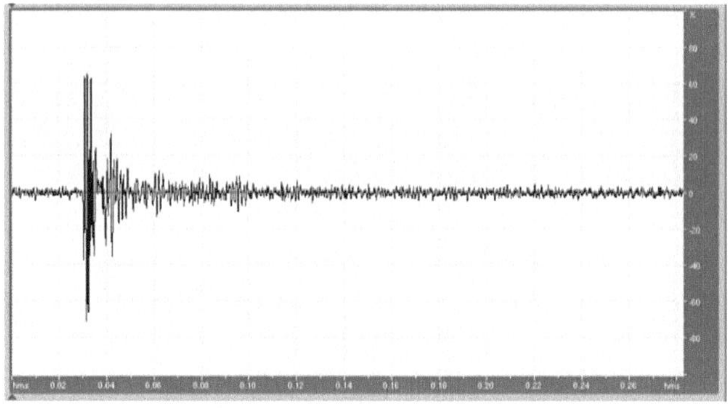

Fig.1 Waveform of Knuckle on Wall

It is evident that the amplitude increases instantaneously the moment that the knuckle makes contact with the wall. The impact causes a localised vibration of molecules within the wall, although the vibrations last only a fraction of a second as seen by the rather fast decay of the amplitude, something which is very common in a highly damped situation. At least part of the waveform during the decay period results from sounds recorded after having been reflected from walls or other solid surfaces.

Digital Evaluation of Inexplicable Rapping Sounds

Recordings of inexplicable rapping effects were obtained from several sources involving RSPK cases in several countries, covering the forty-year period from 1960 to 2000. The objective was to use modern techniques of analysis, based on the idea of converting the recorded analogue sounds to digital format followed by analytical techniques aimed at deriving maximum information about the waveforms and frequency distributions.

Each of the recordings was played back on appropriate equipment and the output fed into the "Line In" socket of a Lenovo computer, operating under Windows XP software. The recordings were digitised by saving them as wav files, using Adobe Audition as the recording and analysing software. This software is a powerful tool used extensively in the music industry and capable of accurately monitoring the details of acoustic subjects. It is also capable of modifying and enhancing the waveforms, allowing one to reduce hiss and noise as well as evaluating the frequency characteristics. The versatility of this software allows a detailed analysis of sounds to be easily made.

Evaluation of Rapping Sounds

The same digital evaluation techniques as described above (using Adobe Audition software) were used to analyse the various rapping sounds described previously. Taken in chronological order, the various waveforms are described below.

Sauchie (1960)

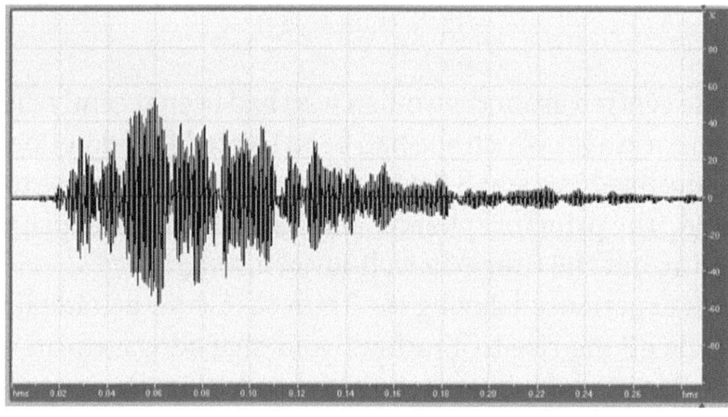

Fig. 2 Sauchie (1960)

The Sauchie case involved typical poltergeist activity in the vicinity of an eleven year old girl, Virginia Campbell. The case was investigated at the time by a local priest, Rev. T. W. Lund and two physicians, Dr W. H. Nisbet and Dr William Logan. Other witnesses to some of the events were Sheila Logan (Dr Logan's wife) and Virginia's teacher, Miss

Margaret Stewart. The details of the case (Owen, 1964) show that the main phenomena witnessed by the above can be summarised as both soft and loud knockings and the movement of various objects including a large linen chest, a pillow, and a school desk.

This rapping sound, which contained relatively high levels of noise, does show a rather slow increase to maximum amplitude followed by an even slower decrease. The overall pattern of the waveform is quite unlike those produced by normal means and could be described as "working up to a maximum".

Thun (1967)

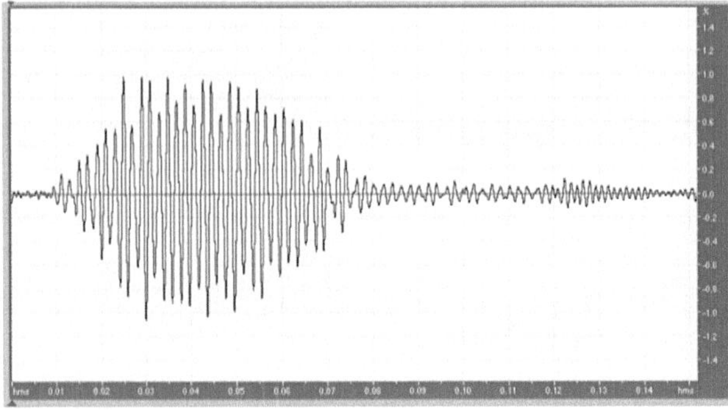

Fig. 3 Thun (1967)

This case centred around a woman who had been recently discharged from a sanatorium in which she had been treated for addiction and depression. She lived in a small flat in Thun, a small town close to Bern in Switzerland. The principal phenomenon was that of unexplained raps, often beating out the tune of a well-known song.

The raps experienced during the Thun case show a gradual increase in amplitude giving rise to a rather ovoid-shaped waveform resulting from a similar gradual decrease in amplitude (Fig. 3).

Schleswig (1968)

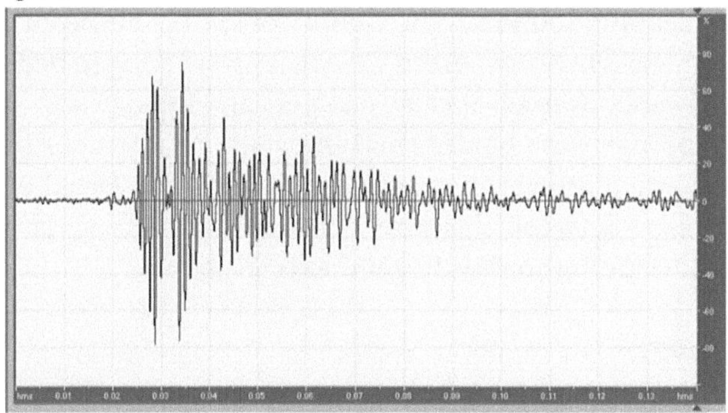

Fig. 4 Schleswig (1968)

This Swiss case mainly involved rapping phenomena, centred around a 13 year old boy. The boy had lived with elderly foster parents since the age of five. There were also some examples of inexplicable object movements, including a cushion that rose vertically and then moved slowly through the air towards the kitchen door. There were several witnesses to the events who recorded that on occasions the knocking sounds were so intense that the couch and the floor vibrated as though a pneumatic drill was being used in the vicinity. Rather similar in form to the Sauchie case, Schleswig shows the gradual, although faster, increase in amplitude. There are at least six relatively small but progressively increasing vibrations prior to the point of maximum amplitude (Fig. 4).

Pursruck (1971)

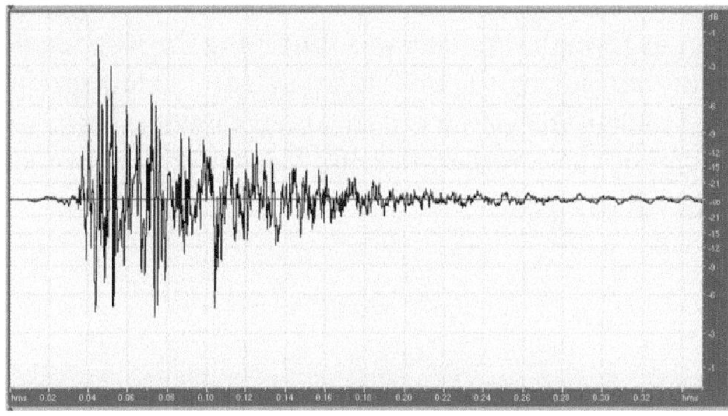

Fig. 5 Pursruck (1971)

This case, researched by Hans Bender, involved the production of significant rapping sounds in the vicinity of two sisters, aged 11 and 13. The phenomena usually occurred when they were lying in bed together. The effects were observed at close quarters and Bender was convinced that the rappings were paranormal in origin. Many recordings were made of the phenomena themselves as well as the verbal exchanges that took place between the sisters. The overall pattern is typical of unexplained rapping sounds in general (Fig. 5).

Ipiranga (1973)

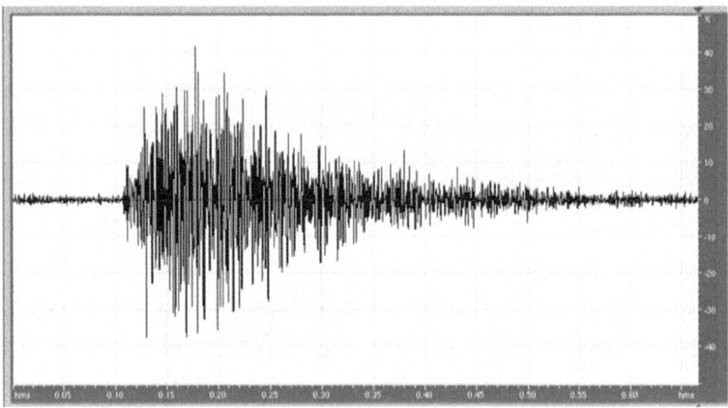

Fig. 6 Ipiranga (1973)

Mr Guy Playfair, an experienced investigator of alleged poltergeist activity, experienced very loud banging sounds just as he was falling asleep (Playfair, 1975). Managing to switch on his tape-recorder in time, he obtained good quality recordings of events including eleven deafening bangs as though someone was thumping the wooden floor with a broom handle. During the investigation, Mr Playfair produced several normal raps in the vicinity of the unexplained rapping sounds by hitting the floor with a broom-handle. A trace of this normal rapping sound is shown in Fig.7.

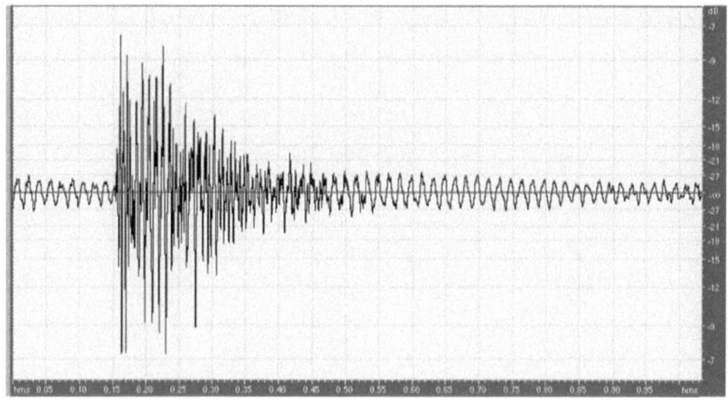

Fig. 7 Normal Rap at Ipiranga (1973)

Again, although there is clear evidence of noise, probably due to the recording equipment, the instantaneous amplitude increase is typical of a normal rapping sound.

La Machine (1973)

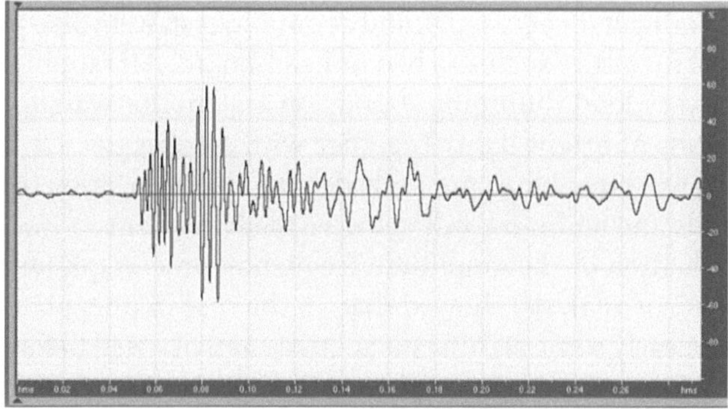

Fig. 8 La Machine (1973)

The events surrounded an 11-year old boy who often directed questions to the rapping entity. However, various police agents also performed this task and received meaningful messages in the form of a rapping code. It is recorded that the raps ranged from very slight to extremely loud. On at least one occasion the walls were felt to vibrate and the chandelier would swing from the ceiling.

Andover (1974)

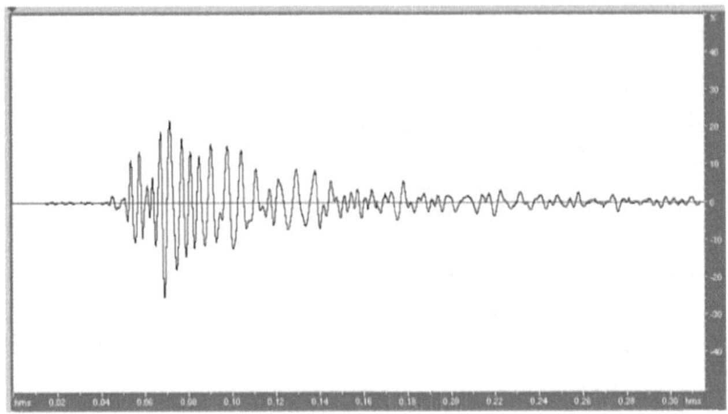

Fig. 9 Andover (1974)

I investigated this case (Colvin, 2008) and recorded rapping sounds in the bedroom of a young girl, Theresa Andrews. Unusually, the rapping sounds spelled out messages in reply to questions posed by the family and by myself. The rapping sounds were often produced on a bedroom wall but on occasions, and at our request, were also produced on items of furniture such as a bed or head-board. All rapping sounds, including very loud thumping sounds on an exterior wall, took place in conditions of bright light. Together with a colleague, Dr Reinhart Schiffauer, we were able to precisely determine the location of the rapping sounds and audio recordings were made of them.

An evaluation of the amplitude/frequency/time graph (using Fourier Transform analysis) showed that, in the case of unexplained raps, there was clearly some significant acoustic activity well before the occurrence of the maximum amplitude. It was also found that the frequency at maximum amplitude was relatively low, at about 150 Hz. In fact, all of the acoustic activity in the unexplained rap occurred below 1000Hz, something that appears to be typical for unexplained raps. By contrast, normal raps exhibited frequencies up to about 10kHz. It was also clear that in the case of normal raps, the maximum amplitude occurred much sooner in the development of the rapping sound.

Enfield (1977)

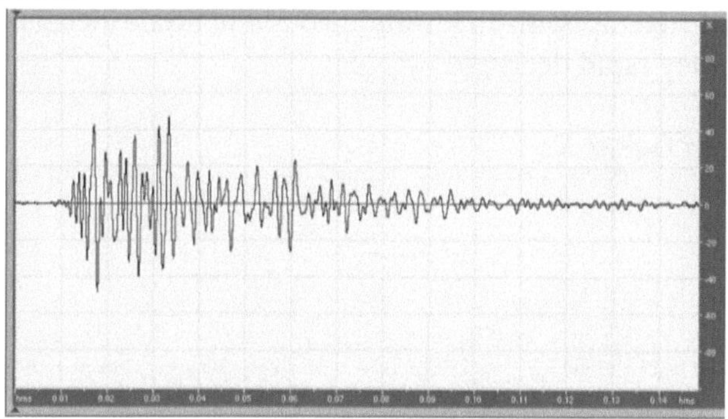

Fig. 10 Enfield (1977)

This case has been reported in detail (Playfair, 1980) and has been the subject of a number of television documentaries. It took place in a north London council house which was rented by a single mother, Peggy Hodgson, and her four children. Rapping sounds were heard on a bedroom wall and it was reported that toys were thrown around by an unseen force. In addition, a police officer witnessed a chair being moved, again by an unknown force. The case was investigated on behalf of the SPR by Maurice Grosse and Guy Lyon Playfair, both of whom were convinced of the paranormal interpretation of events following their 13 month investigation. I obtained access to the original recordings, made on a reel-to-reel recorder by Maurice Grosse.

On the evening of 23rd October 1977, one of the investigators rapped by normal means on the bedroom floor. The acoustic envelope of the sound is shown in Fig. 11.

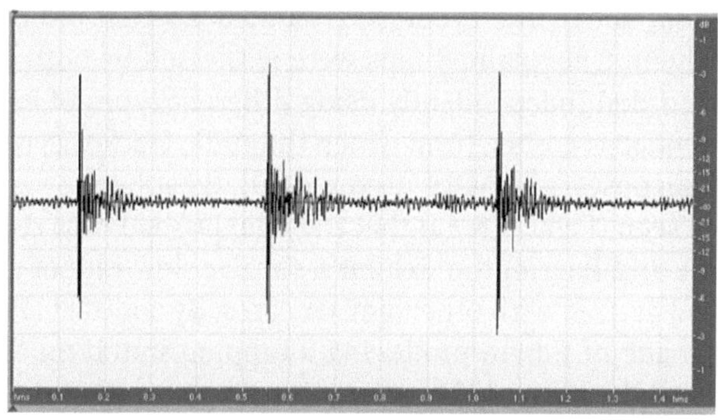

Fig. 11 Normal Raps at Enfield (1977)

The three consecutive raps show the typical form expected of a normally-produced rap, with an instantaneous amplitude increase followed by a relatively rapid decrease.

Santa Rosa (1988)

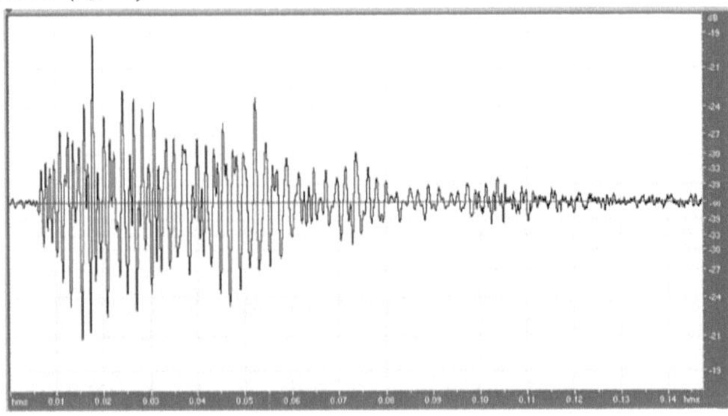

Fig. 12 Santa Rosa (1988): Taken from TV Recording

This case was televised and the rapping sounds were taken from the audio track of the programme. Again, the same type of waveform is seen, as shown in Fig. 12.

Very little is known about this case other than what appeared on a Brazilian television programme.

Euston Square (2000)

This case was investigated by Maurice Grosse (MG) and Mary Rose Barrington (MRB), using both video and audio recording methods to help in the examination of events at an apartment in London (Grosse & Barrington, 2001). The events surrounded a 7-year old boy by the name of Edwin. Unexplained raps were witnessed by both investigators and recorded independently using different types of equipment. MG used a video recorder, from which the audio track was isolated for analytical purposes, and MRB used a small dictaphone.

It can be seen (Figs. 13 & 14) that the unexplained raps recorded by both Grosse and Barrington exhibit a similar slow rate of amplitude development as seen with other similar cases. By contrast (Fig. 15), the recording made of Edwin producing a rapping sound on the side of his bed has all the normal characteristics of a naturally-produced rap.

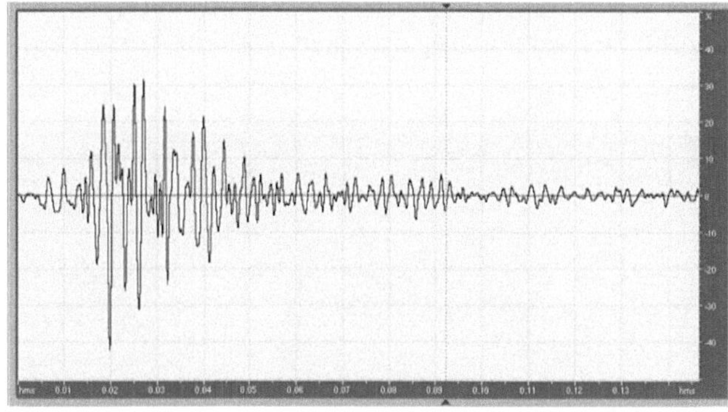

Fig. 13 Euston Square (2000) : M. Grosse Recording

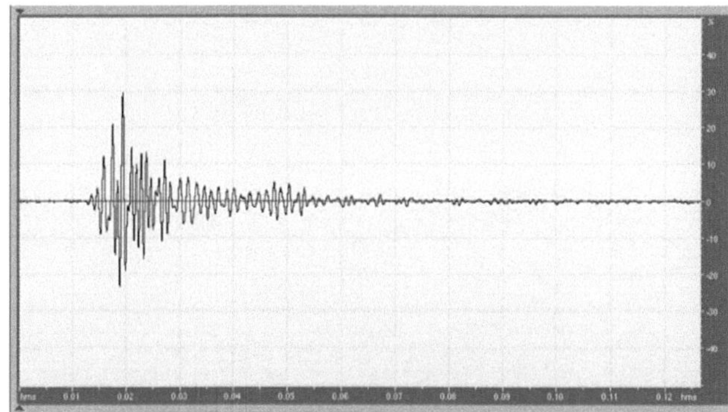

Fig. 14 Euston Square (2000) : M. R. Barrington Recording

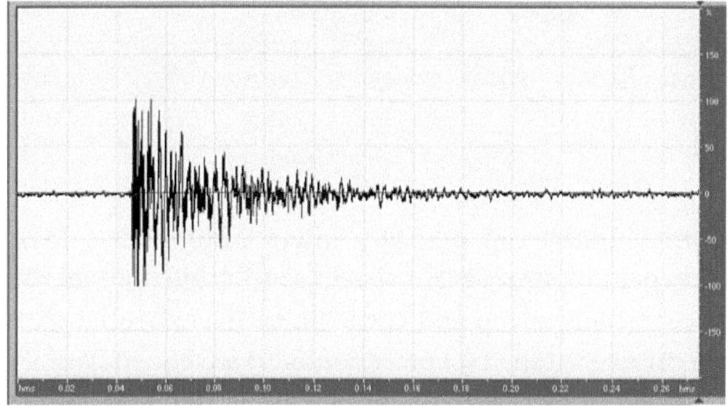

Fig. 15 Euston Square (2000) : Normal Rap (Edwin)

This effect is even more pronounced when one compares Figs.16 and 17, showing the FFT versions, again taken from the Euston Square case.

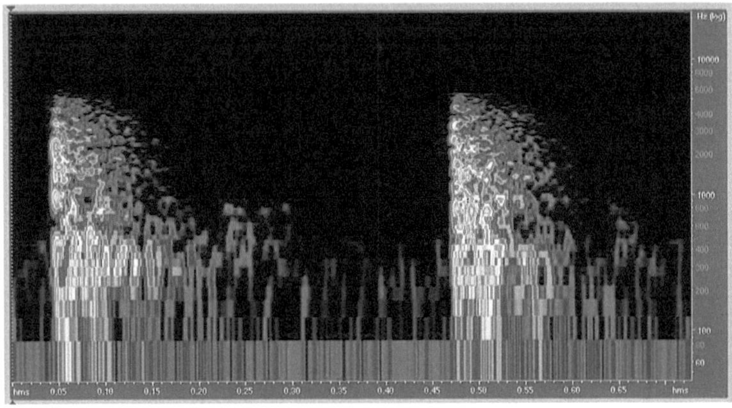

Fig. 16 Edwin's normal double rap

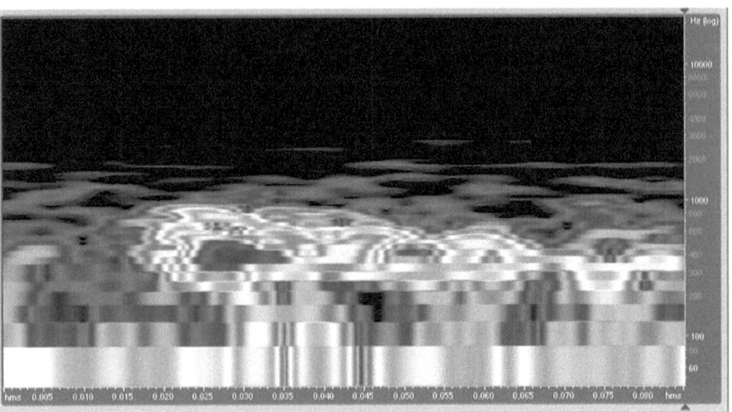

Fig. 17 Unexplained rap

The normal, double rap, made by Edwin tapping the side of his bed, shows the expected, immediate rise in amplitude (Fig. 16). The wavefronts are extremely sharp and conform to the expected pattern. The area of maximum intensity, corresponds to a frequency of about 400 Hz, although significant activity takes place at frequencies up to 8kHz. By contrast, the unexplained rap (Fig. 17) lacks both the abrupt amplitude escalation and any significant activity at frequencies above 1000Hz.

Summary of Results

Preliminary findings based on the work described above indicate that there is a fundamental difference between normally produced rapping sounds and those obtained from recordings made during poltergeist investigations. To summarise the differences between the two types of audio waveforms:

1. **Normal raps:** a very rapid, almost instantaneous, increase in amplitude followed by a steadily decreasing amplitude to zero, the length of which is determined by the dampening behaviour of the vibrating object(s). The waveform is usually, but not exclusively, symmetrical about the x (time) axis.

2. **Unexplained raps:** a relatively gradual increase in amplitude, sometimes exhibiting several wave cycles before reaching a maximum. The waveform is generally symmetrical about the x (time) axis.

Other Evidence

Other researchers have undertaken analyses of rapping sounds and have found similar results. A particularly interesting example involves a rapping sound recorded at Borley Church in the early 1970s by Geoffrey Croom-Hollingsworth and Denny Densham (Fig. 18).

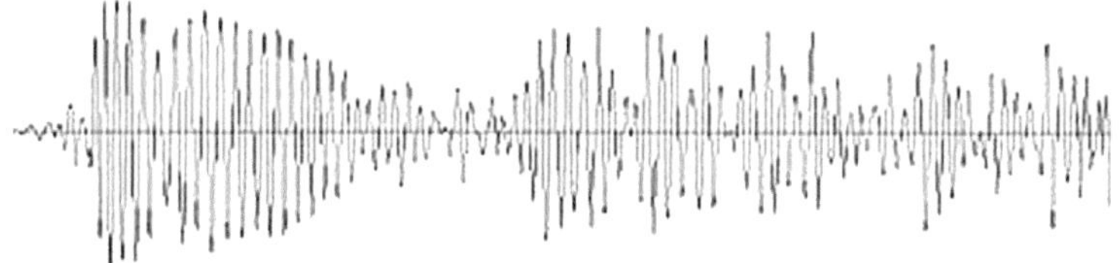

Fig.18 Borley Church waveform

A further example from Borley church, recorded by a Mr Butcher in 1974, is shown in Fig. 19. The original recording, which was digitised as a wave file, shows the relatively slow amplitude increase at the beginning of the waveform.

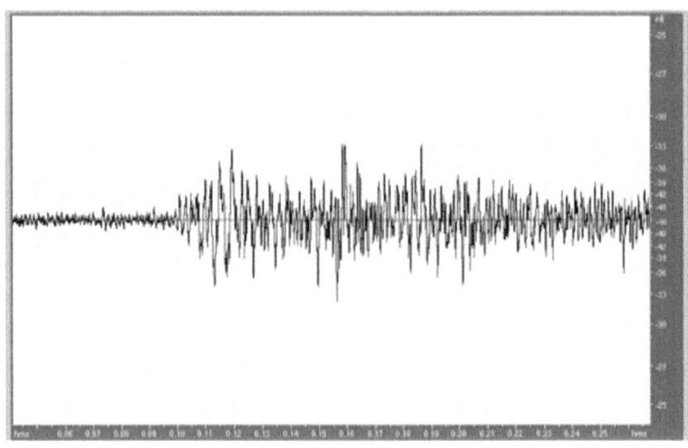

Fig.19 Borley Church (Butcher)

One might wonder how the unexplained raps described above are produced. The waveform patterns tend to indicate that they are not produced by percussive means but they do show similarities to some natural phenomena. In particular, they strongly resemble waveforms associated with earthquakes where a period of vibration, caused by a build-up of stress, is followed by a loud bang and then a decay period as the amplitude decreases over a period of time. An example of this effect is shown below.

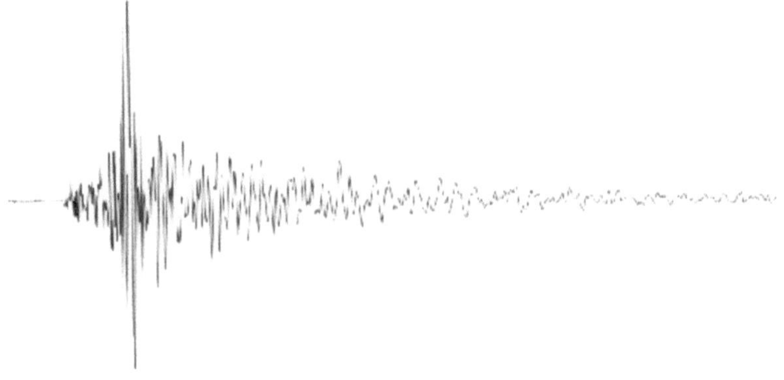

Fig. 20 Folkestone Earthquake Waveform, 2009

Furthermore, during the experimental Philip Group sittings (Owen & Sparrow, 1976), in which unexplained rapping sounds were recorded emanating from a wooden table, it was noted by the participants that "the initial raps in a sitting are not usually heard but *felt*, as a kind of vibration within the table top. As the sittings continue, the raps become loud enough to hear. Perhaps each individual rap builds up from a small vibration into a loud noise. Possibly each rap starts with the movement or vibration of molecules within the table-top until the disturbance is strong enough to produce noise".

Similar ideas have been expressed as a result of experiments carried out by the SORRAT group in 1961 (Richards, 1982). It was recorded that: "We all agreed that the vibrations seemed to come from within the wood itself. As Dr Neihardt said 'It is almost a molecular or sub-molecular vibration, as though the components of the wood fibres are straining against one another'." Elsewhere in the same publication it was noted that "Whatever caused the raps, it did not seem to be a solid object striking the surface of the floor or other resonating areas. The sounds seemed to come from within the wood itself".

These speculations do seem to support the notion that the rapping sounds are fundamentally different to sounds generated by percussive methods. They appear to develop from within the molecular structure of the substrate, go through a vibrational phase, and then emit an audible sound as the resultant stress is released.

An alternative explanation derives from attempts to produce unusual waveforms using conventional methods. There has been some limited success, brought about by two different approaches.

Firstly, it is possible to obtain a loud crack, with a resultant unusual audio waveform, by producing thermal stress within either epoxy or high-modulus polyurethane blocks. These polymers are thermoset materials that develop heat during the curing process. Under certain circumstances it is possible to obtain a sufficiently high exotherm to cause a significant thermal stress within the block. This can lead to internal cracking and the release of stress, accompanied by a loud sound. This cracking sound exhibits the unusual waveform, similar in many ways to that produced on a much larger scale by an earthquake.

Secondly, it is possible to establish an unusual waveform by allowing a percussive rap to reflect from a series of strategically placed surfaces. These surfaces might, for example, be walls within a building. In this scenario, the first part of the recorded sound would derive directly from the source of the sound. However, after a very short time (several milliseconds) reflected sounds from nearby walls can reach the recording microphone. If several reflected audio waves arrive "in sync", a higher than expected amplitude can result, giving rise to the unusual waveform described above.

By their very nature, the unusual waveforms obtained during apparent poltergeist activity have not been examined under strict experimental conditions. However, it is felt that the principal reason for describing the effects in such detail, and putting forward a very tentative theory of a localised explosive/stress-relieving system, is in order to ensure that future investigators take account of this possible mechanism when carrying out their own scientific analysis of similar cases. In addition to recording rapping sounds using conventional acoustic measures (including the use of infrasonics and ultrasonics), it would be useful to introduce vibrational analysis using both conventional techniques and other methods. These would include laser interferometry, a technique that is capable of analysing, and visually portraying, the patterns of vibrating surfaces.

ENDWORD

It is clear that sound and hearing are one of our major sensory systems and therefore it comes as no surprise to have discovered that sound has played such an important role in many paranormal experiences. Sound affects us profoundly, sometimes in ways that we are mostly unaware of. Sound triggers emotions, it evokes memories, and it can fill us with fear and awe. Sound can confuse and create false impressions. Sound can simulate or perhaps even stimulate paranormal experiences. It is little surprise therefore to discover that so many people who are engaged in studying the paranormal find themselves studying sound.

Sound will always be significant to paranormal investigators, be they psychologists in the lab, or ghost hunters in haunted houses. Much of the past and current research has focused upon sounds that we can hear, defined by the frequency and amplitude of the sound energy. Increasingly however, researchers are considering sound energy that lies outside this range of 20 Hz to 20,000 Hz. Over countless millennia, our sense of hearing has developed to deal with just a small part of the enormous frequency spectrum of acoustic energy and we have evolved a complex sensory mechanism that we call hearing to deal with it. But our hearing is just one way in which we are able to perceive sound; our bodies perceive sound through mechanisms such as bone conduction or the vibrations that impinge upon our bodies and their component parts. Such perceptions may be perceived by way of the other senses or by way of mere feelings and vague sensations that we find to attribute to a cause or source.

We have discussed infrasound but what about ultrasound? That region of sound frequency, which lies above our normal hearing range. There are acoustic devices such as the Mosquito and the LRAD (Long Range Acoustic Device) which exploit our sensitivities to very high frequencies and the uncomfortable even disturbing effects they can have upon humans, sometimes without there being a conscious awareness of any actual sound source. Does the sound even have to be of a frequency that our ears cannot hear? The audio spectrum is full of sound waves that lie within the range of hearing and yet are simply too quiet to be normally perceived. Could these 'unheard' sounds also affect us in ways that we cannot yet fully comprehend? There is no such place as one that is totally quiet – we might believe that to be the case, for that is what our hearing is telling us, but in reality if one measures the sound you will soon discover it is present.

If some component or aspect of the human survives death then how would it communicate? Speech? How could that take place without vocal cords to move the air molecules? Yet ghosts are reported to moan, wail, and speak. Is it easier for the discarnate and deceased to knock and rap and by what mechanism and means that they undertake this? Perhaps as some claim, they make use of electronic means, using their 'energies' to impart voices onto our electronic devices and recordings or maybe they direct this energy into the knocks raps and sounds of the séance room or of the poltergeist.

So many questions but few answers. Some things we can be more certain of; sounds, be they heard or unheard can affect us in ways that we do not always expect and these sounds might then be interpreted as being of a paranormal origin. We can also be certain that people hear voices on recordings and telephone calls and that seemingly intelligent responses via a series of raps are given at séances or in response to questions called out during ghost hunts. Those are sureties; machines have objectively recorded them. It is because they are sureties that we must study them, try to understand them, and seek answers to the many questions that remain to be answered.

— S.T.P.

Section 3
APPENDICES

APPENDIX 1

THE GHOST IN THE MACHINE

by VIC TANDY and TONY R. LAWRENCE

ABSTRACT

In this paper we outline an as yet undocumented natural cause for some cases of ostensible haunting. Using the first author's own experience as an example, we show how a 19 Hz standing air wave may under certain conditions create sensory phenomena suggestive of a ghost. The mechanics and physiology of this 'ghost in the machine' effect are outlined. Spontaneous case researchers are encouraged to rule out this potential natural explanation for paranormal experience in future cases of the haunting or poltergeist type.

INTRODUCTION

When investigating a haunted building it is good practice to attempt to exclude as many possible normal causes for the 'haunting' as possible. The ways in which normal earthly events might conspire to convey an impression that a house is haunted (or even beset by poltergeist behaviour, see Eastham, 1988) are numerous. Thus, all of the following may well be the more mundane cause of an ostensible haunt: water hammer in pipes and radiators (noises), electrical faults (fires, phone calls, video problems), structural faults (draughts, cold spots, damp spots, noises), seismic activity (object movement/destruction, noises), electromagnetic anomalies (hallucinations), and exotic organic phenomena (rats scratching, beetles ticking). The exclusion of these counter-explanations, when potentially relevant, must be the first priority of the spontaneous cases investigator. To this end, we feel the 'virtual paranormal experience' reported and explained in this paper might be of interest to the spontaneous case research community.

Though many of the above counter-explanations for ghost-like phenomena may be quite easy to discount in any one case, at least some normal causes of seemingly paranormal phenomena may in fact be quite subtle, and not at all easy to discern for the untrained observer, as we hope to show in this paper.

THE CASE OF THE GHOST IN THE MACHINE

The first author's background is as an engineering designer and at the time of the incident he was working for a company that manufactured medical equipment. Three people worked in a laboratory made from two garages back-to-back and about 10 ft wide by 30 ft in length. One end was closed off by doors normally kept closed and the other end had a window, the other side of which was a cleaning bay. As an example of creativity with corrugated iron, this structure was home for anyone with a passion for playing with jets of water and foam.

The company's business was in the design of anaesthetic or intensive-care, life support equipment so there was always some piece of equipment wheezing away in a corner. When V.T. heard suggestions that the lab was haunted this was the first thing he thought could be behind it and paid little attention. One morning, however, none of the equipment was turned on and V.T. arrived just as the cleaner was leaving, obviously distressed that she had seen something. As a hard-nosed engineer V.T. put it down to the wild cats, wild other furry things, moving pressure hoses (as the pressure fluctuates, flexible hoses sometimes move) or some sort of lighting effect.

As time went on V.T. noticed one or two other odd events. There was a feeling of depression, occasionally a cold shiver, and on one occasion a colleague sitting at the desk turned to say something to V.T. thinking he was by his side. The colleague was surprised when V.T. was found to be at the other end of the room. There was a growing level of discomfort but the workers were all busy and paid it little attention. That is, until V.T. was working on his own one night after everyone else had left. As he sat at the desk writing he began to feel increasingly uncomfortable. He was sweating but cold and the feeling of depression was noticeable. The cats were moving around and the groans and creaks from what was now a deserted factory were 'spooky', but there was also something else. It was as though something was in the room with V.T. There was no way into the lab without walking past the desk where V.T. was working. He looked around and even checked the gas bottles to be sure there was not a leak into the room. There were oxygen and carbon dioxide bottles and occasionally the staff would work with anaesthetic agents, all of which could cause all sorts of problems if handled inappropriately. All of these checked out fine so V.T. went to get a cup of coffee and returned to the desk. As he was writing he became aware that he was being watched, and a figure slowly emerged to his left. It was indistinct and on the periphery of his vision but it moved as V.T. would expect a person to. The apparition was grey and made no sound. The hair was standing up on V.T.'s neck and there was a distinct chill in the room. As V.T. recalls, "It would not be unreasonable to suggest I was terrified". V.T. was unable to see any detail and finally built up the courage to turn and face the thing. As he turned the apparition faded and disappeared. There was absolutely no evidence to support what he had seen so he decided he must be cracking up and went home.

The following day V.T. was entering a fencing competition and needed to cut a thread onto the tang of a spare foil blade so that he could attach the handle. He had all the tools necessary but it was so much easier to use the engineer's bench vice in the lab to hold the blade that he went in early to cut the thread. It was only a five-minute job, so he put the blade in the vice and went in search of a drop of oil to help things along. As he returned, the free end of the blade was frantically vibrating up and down. Combining this with his experience from the previous night, he once again felt an immediate twinge of fright. However, vibrating pieces of metal were more familiar to him than apparitions so he decided to experiment. If the foil blade was being vibrated it was receiving energy which must have been varying in intensity at a rate equal to the resonant frequency of the blade. Energy of the type just described is usually referred to as sound. There was a lot of background noise but there could also be low-frequency sound or infrasound which V.T. could not hear. As it happens sound behaves fairly predictably in long thin tubes such as organ pipes and ex-garages joined end to end so V.T. started his experiment. He placed the foil blade in a drill vice and slid it along the floor. Interestingly the vibration got bigger until the blade was level with the desk (half way down the room); after the desk it reduced in amplitude, stopping altogether at the far end of the lab.

V.T. and his colleagues were sharing their lab with a low frequency standing wave! The energy in the wave peaked in the centre of the room indicating that there was half a complete cycle. It is important to understand that what we call sound is caused by variation in the pressure of the air around us. It is represented graphically as a wave. If someone were to shout at you the sound wave will travel from them to you transmitted by the air between you both, i.e. it is a travelling wave. However the wave sharing our lab was of just the right frequency to be completely reflected back by the walls at each end, so it was not going anywhere, hence it was a standing wave. In effect the wave was folded back on itself reinforcing the peak energy in the centre of the room. Once V.T. knew this he calculated the frequency of the standing sound wave as follows:–

$f = v/\lambda$
where $\lambda = 2 \times l$
f = frequency of sound
v = velocity of sound (1,139 ft/sec)
λ = wavelength ($l \times 2$ = 60ft)
l = length of room = 30ft
so we have $f = 1{,}139/60 = 18.98$ Hz (cycles per second)

We should not be impressed by the apparent accuracy of the frequency, because V.T.'s measurements were 'quick and dirty'. For example, the speed of sound can also vary depending on temperature and pressure so, overall, plus or minus 10% on the above figure would be a reasonable estimate.

There are now two questions. The first is where is the energy coming from? The second is what does a 19Hz standing wave do to people? The first was answered very quickly when V.T. discussed the problem with the works foreman, who told him that they had installed a new fan in the extraction system for the cleaning room at the end of the lab. We switched off the fan and the standing wave went away. The second question required a bit more research. A book by Tempest (1976) was consulted and a couple of interesting case studies were found (pp.81–82):–

> Noise consultants were asked to examine one of a group of bays in a factory where workers reported feeling uneasy. The bay had an oppressive feel not present in the adjacent areas although the noise level appeared the same. Management, workers and consultants were all aware of the unusual atmosphere and on investigation it was found that low-frequency sound was present at a slightly higher level than in other bays. However the actual frequency of the offending noise was not obvious. The cause of the noise was a fan in the air conditioning system.
>
> Workers in a university radiochemistry building experienced the same oppressive feeling together with dizziness when the fan in a fume cupboard was switched on. Conventional sound proofing had reduced the audible sound to the point where there was hardly any difference in the noise with the fan on as off. The situation affected some people so much that they refused to work in the lab. It was concluded that the low-frequency component of the sound was responsible.

On page 107 the book lists symptoms caused by frequencies in the range 15–20 Hz. V.T. had no idea of the amount of energy (spl) the infrasound had because we had nothing to measure it with. These effects are quoted by Tempest at an spl range of 125–137.5 dB, which would be very damaging to hearing if the frequency were in the audible range. It is a considerable amount of power but is not thought of as unreasonable by those V.T. has talked to, considering that the energy was originated by a one-metre-diameter extractor fan driven by something like a 1 kW electric motor. In any case, the symptoms listed by Temple (1976) for low-frequency sound waves are: severe middle ear pain (not experienced), persistent eye watering, and respiratory difficulties, sensations of fear including excessive perspiration and shivering.

Table IV on page 212 of this book shows frequencies causing disturbance to the eyes and vision to be within the band 12 to 27 Hz. A more recent book by Kroemer (1994) describes the effects of low frequency vibration as follows:–

> Vibration of the body mostly affects the principal input ports, the eyes, and principal output means, hands and mouth. [p. 287]
>
> Exposure to vibration often results in short-lived changes in various physiological parameters such as heart rate . . . At the onset of vibration exposure, increased muscle tension and initial hyperventilation have been observed. [p.280]

Tables 5–12 of Kroemer (1994), on p. 288, indicate that the resonant frequencies of body parts are: Head (2–20 Hz causing general discomfort); Eyeballs (1–100 Hz, mostly above 8 Hz and strongly 20–70 Hz effect difficulty in seeing). However, different sources give different resonant frequencies for the eye itself. The resonant frequency is the natural frequency of an object, the one at which it needs the minimum input of energy to vibrate. As you can see from above, any frequency above 8 Hz will have an effect and some sources quote 40 Hz. Most interestingly, a NASA technical report mentions a resonant frequency for the eye as 18 Hz (NASA Technical Report 19770013810). If this were the case then the eyeball would be vibrating which would cause a serious 'smearing' of vision. It would not seem unreasonable to see dark shadowy forms caused by something as innocent as the corner of V.T.'s spectacles. V.T. would not normally be aware of this but its size would be much greater if the image was spread over a larger part of his retina.

Another NASA report (NASA Technical Report 19870046176) mentions hyperventilation as a symptom of whole body vibration. Hyperventilation is characterized by quick shallow breathing and reduces the amount of carbon dioxide retained in the lungs. Note that Tempest (1976) also mentions respiratory difficulties caused by frequencies in our range. Hyperventilation can have profound physiological effects. For example, Flenley (1990) describes the symptoms of hyperventilation as "breathlessness usually at rest, often accompanied by lightheadedness, muscle cramps, fear of sudden death and a feeling of difficulty in breathing in". Fried (1987) describes a panic attack as "a synergistic interaction between hyperventilation and anxiety" and suggests that as the carbon dioxide is expired physiological changes cause the body to respond by feeling fear. This feeling of fear activates the sympathetic nervous system which increases the respiration rate making the hyperventilation worse. The panic attack will therefore feed itself and increase in intensity. This would seem consistent with V.T.'s experience of fear and panic when the 'ghost' appeared. V.T. knows from the experiment with the foil blade that the peak energy, known as an anti-node, was in line with the centre of the desk. As V.T. sat up and turned to look at the object he moved from this zone of peak energy to a zone of slightly lesser energy and the ghost disappeared!

EXORCISING THE STANDING-WAVE GHOST

Once the problem was recognised a modification was made to the mounting of the extractor fan and our ghost left with the standing wave. Low-frequency sound is not easy to detect without the proper equipment. It was sheer luck that the foil blade happened to be the right length and material to react and reveal the presence of the standing wave (although 19Hz might just be heard on its own, it is in fact unlikely to exist alone so other sounds would drown it out). V.T. has since heard of a similar experience to this which happened in a corridor in a building that had a wind tunnel in the basement. The wind tunnel was on at the time of the sighting but V.T. was unable to do any measurements. Long tubes such as corridors are ideal places for standing waves especially if they are closed at both ends. The resonant frequency of one person's body parts would also be different from another's, so standing-wave resonances may affect one individual but not another. Our advice for researchers in the future is to be very wary of ghosts reported to haunt long, windy corridors!

School of International Studies and Law VIC TANDY
Coventry University
Priory Street
Coventry CV1 5FB

School of Health and Social Sciences TONY R. LAWRENCE
Coventry University
Priory Street
Coventry CV1 5FB

REFERENCES

Eastham, P. (1988). Ticking off a poltergeist. *JSPR 55,* 80–83.

Everest, F. A. (1994) *The Master Handbook of Acoustics, 3rd edition.* Blue Ridge Summit, PA: TAB Books.

Flenley, D. C. (1990) *Respiratory Medicine (2nd edition).* London: Bailliere Tindal.

Fried, R. (1987) *The Hyperventilation Syndrome, Research and Clinical Treatment.* London: Johns Hopkins University Press.

Kroemer, K. H. E. (1994) *Ergonomics: How to Design for Ease and Efficiency.* London: Prentice Hall.

NASA Technical Report 19770013810.

NASA Technical Report 19870046176.

Smith, A. P. and Jones, D. M. (eds.) (1992) *Handbook of Human Performance, Vol.1.* London: Academic Press.

Tempest, W. (ed.) (1976) *Infrasound and Low-Frequency Vibration.* London: Academic Press.

APPENDIX 2

Something in the Cellar

Published in Journal of the Society for Psychical Research, Vol. 64.3, No 860

Vic Tandy

School of International Studies and Law

Coventry University

Priory Street

Coventry

CV1 5FB.

Abstract

An investigation into the link between infrasound and the perception of apparitions was performed in the 14th Century cellar beneath the Tourist Information Centre in Coventry. Based on the effect described in The Ghost in the Machine (Tandy and Lawrence 1998) details of individuals experiences were recorded and an analysis performed to test for any infrasound present in the cellar. Infrasound was found to be present at the point at which individuals had reported apparitional experiences at exactly the same frequency as that predicted in the original paper.

Introduction

This paper describes an investigation into the phenomena described in the Ghost in the Machine (Tandy and Lawrence 1998) which proposes that low frequency sound can cause individuals to experience what may appear to be an apparition. In the original paper, a frequency of 18.9 Hz was found to be present in a laboratory where several people experienced what could reasonably be described as an encounter with an apparition. While measuring low frequency sound is not technically difficult, it does require specialist equipment that is expensive. An opportunity arose recently to explore a 14th Century cellar where hauntings had been reported. Situated near to Coventry University, the cellar is very conveniently placed and has electrical power available to drive the instrumentation. The expectation was that a correlation would be found between infrasound and the experiences of individuals who had visited the site. While it had been found that 18.9 Hz was responsible for one apparent haunting

(Tandy and Lawrence 1998) it was thought that a range of frequencies in this area might well give the same results. The actual measurements were so astonishing that they were repeated several times by the members of the research team, Vic Tandy and Sam Maunder of the School of International Studies and Law and Bill Dunn of the School of Engineering at Coventry University.

The 14th Century Cellar

The cellar is adjacent to Coventry University beneath the Tourist Information Centre, which is built on the site of a 14th century house, 38/39 Bayley Lane. The house was originally owned by the Benedictine Priory that stood opposite, where Coventry Cathedral now stands. A plan of the cellar is included in appendix1 to this paper. Initially an undercroft it would have been open to the road on one side, however, as the area developed it was buried completely leaving access only available from the house above. At the time the cellar was built, Coventry was a centre for the wool and cloth trade and it would most likely have been used to store merchandise (Tourist Information Centre 2000). Niches in the walls would have contained valuable goods such as spices and would have had lockable doors attached. The cellar is built of local red sandstone and is of such quality that it has survived many new houses being built above it. The final house was destroyed, along with the Cathedral, during the Coventry Blitz of 1940. This blocked the cellar's remaining entrance and its presence was forgotten for a time. Rediscovered during the excavation for the foundations of the Tourist Information Centre, the cellar now serves this new building. Accessed by well-lit modern steps and underground passageway it is open to the public and has a steady flow of visitors.

Apparitions

It is the strange experiences of some visitors to the cellar that prompted this investigation. A number of stories began to emerge form several witnesses as follows. In 1997 Coventry Tourguide, Colin Cook accompanied a Canadian journalist touring Britain into the cellar, he noticed that the journalist gave the appearance of being taken ill as he crossed the threshold of the room. "The gentleman was frozen to the spot and the colour drained from his face, the hairs on his arms rose up and goose pimples formed". Concerned for the man's health, Mr Cook asked him if he could be of assistance. The journalist described a feeling as if a balloon was being pushed between his shoulder blades and an intense feeling of a presence. Eventually he reported that the face of a woman seemed to be peering over his right shoulder. Mr Cook was unable to feel or see anything but the visitor had become "ashen" and looked very unwell. Mr Cook became seriously concerned for the health of his visitor and suggested they return to the Information Centre. The journalist recounted his experience to staff in the centre and exhibited the physical symptoms for some time before recovering. Mr Cook also gave details of a Latvian Gentleman who experienced a strange feeling upon entering the room, he described feeling a presence, a cold chill, as if there was a ghost in the room but there was no physical manifestation. A husband and wife visiting from the USA were also accompanied by Mr Cook and entered the cellar together but the woman suddenly stopped on the threshold of the room, she claimed to be experiencing a very strong feeling of presence and described it as barring her way. Neither her husband nor Mr Cook experienced any phenomena at all. However the woman became pale and refused to enter the cellar however much her husband encouraged her. On returning to the

Information Centre, staff noted the very pale complexion of the woman. However they did make the point that they had not seen her prior to the experience, so although she struck them as unusually pale it was not known whether this was her natural complexion. Staff at the Information Centre were interviewed and confirmed that a significant number of visitors do report a presence in the cellar but generally give few details, some are just noticed to leave rather hastily. Staff did however remember two white witches visiting the cellar to "make contact". They announced that there was the spirit of a woman in the cellar but it was friendly and there was no need for any concern. Another white witch also visited, according to Carole Jung, assistant manager of the centre at the time. However, she was greeted with less charity by the presence and "frightened to death" by the experience, left rather rapidly. Mrs Jung, who also acted as a tour guide, had first hand experience of the apparition, she said she hated going down into the cellar, "there was a very strong sense of presence as if she were intruding, disturbing something, there was a strange chill to the atmosphere." While no physical apparitions appeared to her the presence felt so strong that she said she found herself talking to it. A fluent German speaker, Mrs Jung often accompanied German visitors into the cellar, who also remarked on the feeling of intruding. It is particularly interesting that so many foreign visitors have experienced the apparition, because they would be less likely to know of the cellar's growing reputation.

Infrasound

In The Ghost in the Machine (Tandy & Lawrence 1998) apparitional experiences of several people were traced to a low frequency standing wave within the building. The wave was detected accidentally by its effect on a foil blade (fencing weapon), which the author was attempting to cut a screw thread on, in preparation for fitting a new handle. This five-minute job resulted in several hours of research when the blade began to vibrate. The blade was clearly receiving energy and calculations showed that a standing wave of approximately 18.9 Hz was present in the laboratory. The equipment was not available to measure amplitude but to excite the foil blade in the way described it must have been substantial. There are a number of recorded events in which infrasound has been shown to affect humans in strange ways, the original paper cites work by which describes workers feeling uneasy or dizzy as a result of exposure to infrasound. A French research team under the direction of Dr Gavreau also experienced strange results from exposure to infrasound in 1957(Vassilatos,G). A disconcerting feeling of nausea mystified Dr Gavreau and his team and frequently caused them substantial discomfort. Originally, put down to airborne toxins no trace was found of any agents that could cause the symptoms. Scientist brought in to investigate also experienced the phenomena. Finally, a researcher found that the sickness ceased when certain laboratory windows were closed. The nausea was caused by a low frequency sound wave which resonated with the structure of the laboratory, closing the windows altered the resonant frequency and made the situation for the occupants either better or worse. This discovery lead to experiments in infrasound weapons that continue in several countries (Dunning 1968) (Lewer 1997).

The Test

The cellar was a prime opportunity to test the theory that infrasound could cause humans to experience hallucinations suggestive of an apparition. Located next door to

Coventry University it was easy to move measuring equipment in and even had a mains voltage power supply. A Bruel & Kjaer precision sound level meter Type 2209 fitted with a microphone sensitive to frequencies down to 1Hz was attached to a Zonic AND Type 3525 Dual Channel FFT analyser. The microphone was placed in the centre of the cellar and connected to the analyser in the corridor leading in. The hypothesis was that the structure might have the potential to support resonance in the infrasound area. The longest dimension of the cellar was 7.7m which, if treated as a simple mathematical model, would resonate at about 22Hz by the calculation below.

$f = v / \lambda$

where $\lambda = 2 \times l$

$f =$ frequency of sound

$v =$ velocity of sound (343 m/second at 20 degrees Celsius)

$\lambda =$ wavelength ($l \times 2 = 15.4$m)

$l =$ length of room = (7.7m)

so we have $f = 343 / 15.4 = 22.27$ Hz

While it is theoretically possible to treat the cellar as a collection of boxes that would resonate in any plane, reference to the layout of the cellar as shown in appendix 1 gives an idea of the complexity, which this would involve. It would be extremely difficult to create a theoretical model of all the possible interactions of the various steps, corridors and shafts attached to the room, which itself has complex shapes in the roof and walls The instrumentation enables us to analyse the resonances directly using a simple stamp test. This is a fairly straightforward experiment where someone stamps his or her foot causing a loud bang. Impacts produce a wide spectrum of sound that will interact with any resonances in the structure and enables them to be seen as peaks on the spectrum analyser. Another approach, often used by audio engineers is to burst a balloon, however in the absence of such sophistication a stamp test was considered adequate. Prior to the "stamp" it is normal practice to take a background reading and it was during this that an astonishing result was recorded.

The experimenters withdrew from the cellar and left the instrumentation to sample and average any ambient sounds present for 20 seconds. A Fast Fourier Transform (see appendix 2) was then performed providing a spectrum of the sounds present in the cellar. The trace was printed out and can be seen as figure1.

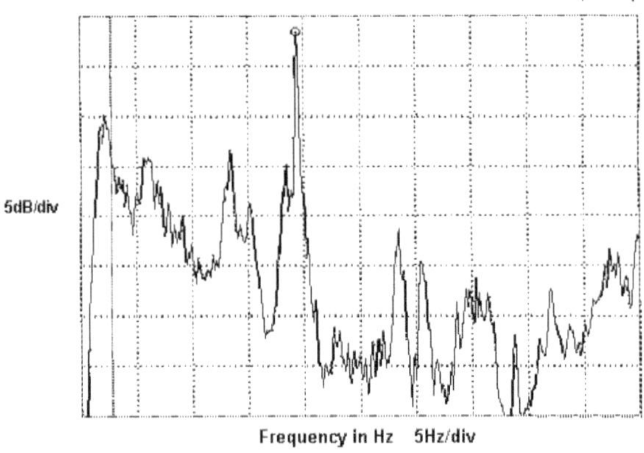

fig 1. **FFT analysis of ambient noise level in cellar dB scale**

Each division along the horizontal (X) axis represents 5Hz. The vertical (Y) axis provides a measure of amplitude, each division representing 5dB. The trace therefore provides a picture of the frequencies present and their amplitude. Appendix 2 has a very brief introduction to the use of these units for the uninitiated.

There is a clear peak at 19 Hz, exactly the frequency predicted in The Ghost in the Machine paper. The amplitude of the signal is about 38dB and is substantially above any of the other background noise. Decibels are a logarithmic scale used to make the measurement of the ratios of one sound to another practical because there is often to big a difference between levels to plot successfully. However this can sometimes mask the true scale of a signal and it is useful to view our infrasound on a linear scale just to place it in context, see figure2.

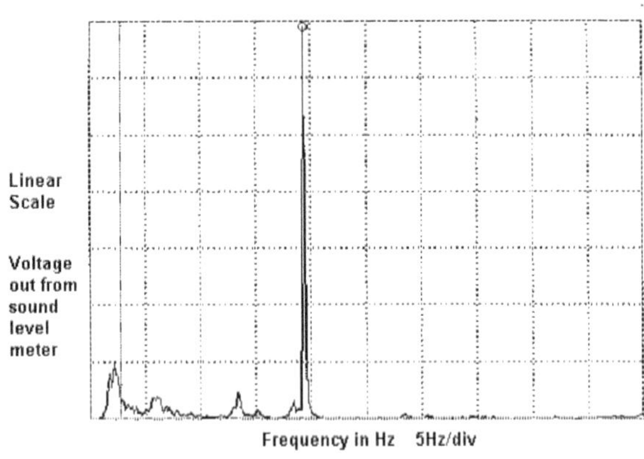

fig 2. **FFT analysis of ambient noise level in cellar linear scale**

The amplitude measurement is simply the voltage output of the sound level meter and is only valid for this comparison. The amplitude of the 19Hz signal and the background noise is now very apparent. This test for background level was repeated several times over a period of three hours and no measurable difference was observed. For the signal level to be so consistent was in itself, rather surprising and the instrumentation was used to isolate the actual signal, which was almost sinusoidal, see figure 3.

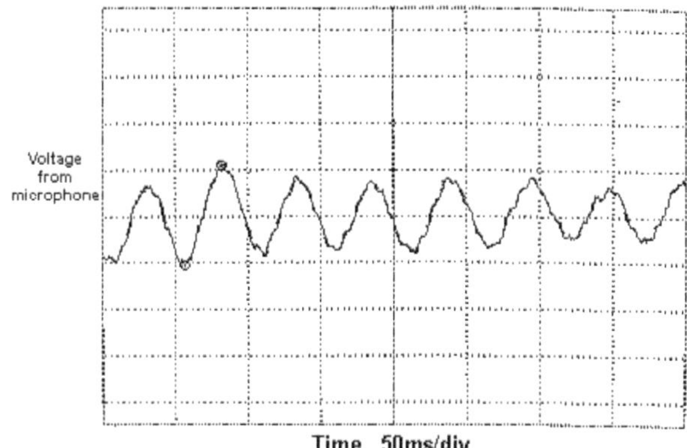

***fig 3.* 19Hz signal present in the cellar (X axis = 50mS/div)**

It can be seen that the level of the signal varies in amplitude during the measurement and it was suspected that the sound might be modulated (appendix 2). Therefore, another trace was made over a longer period with results shown in figure 4.

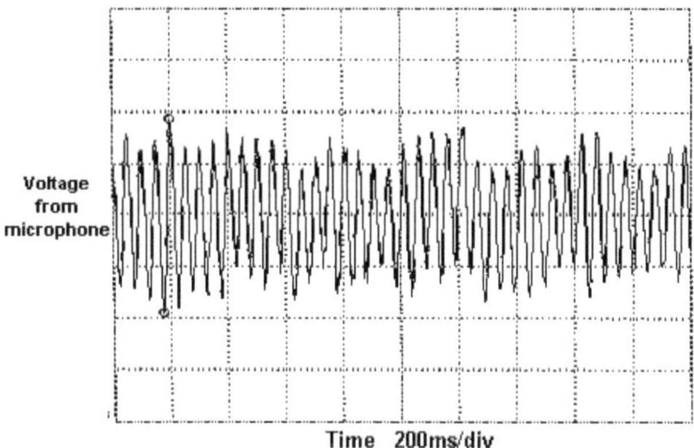

***fig 4.* 19Hz signal modulated by 2-3Hz signal present in the cellar (X axis = 200mS/div)**

It is clear from this trace that the signal is, indeed, modulated by another frequency, which itself is complex in nature, estimated to be varying between 2 to 4Hz. This is consistent with the spectrum shown in figure 1, where closer inspection shows a peak at 3-4 Hz. It is most probable that this signal is influencing the 19 Hz signal. The results of the stamp test, which we eventually got around to doing, are also supportive of this assertion. Inspection of figure 5 does show a peak at 2 to 3 Hz and another has now appeared at about 23Hz (23Hz is the resonance of the cellar about its length). The unmarked peak at around 50Hz is the resonance about the cellar's width, which is probably too high a frequency to influence the current findings significantly. The level of the 19Hz signal is enhanced by about 3dB (see appendix 2) which, in linear terms, corresponds to an increase of 1.41 in its sound pressure level and points to the conclusion that it is not just a passing sound but a local resonance, a standing wave. Further investigation found that the corridor leading to the cellar is 10.95m in length, which would resonate at about 16.3 Hz following the calculation above. However, the corridor is not straight and it is suggested that the door opening would reduce this effective length in the same way that a finger hole in a wind instrument would behave. When this is taken into account the effective length is more like 9.5 m, which would resonate at 18 Hz. The relationship is not simple but at the moment, this looks to be the most likely resonator. The witnesses also refer to the feeling of presence being strongest at the threshold of the cellar, which would be consistent with this explanation.

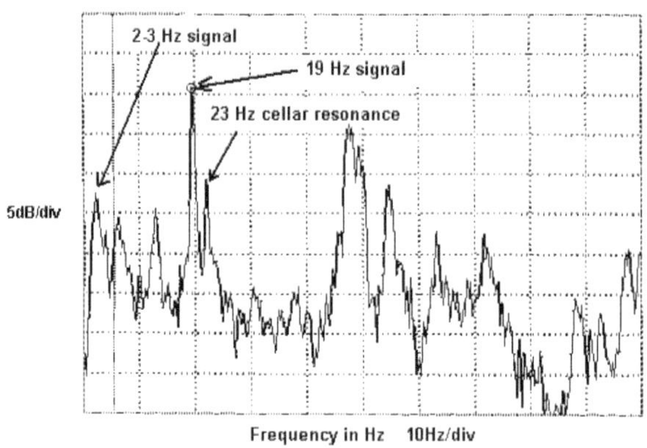

***fig 5.* 19Hz Stamp test showing resonances in the cellar complex**

The other peaks on the trace, figure 5, represent other resonances in the cellar complex.

Discussion

There are two significant points, which come from these results. The first is to question the low amplitude of the signal present and the second is the effect of the modulation. There is no proof as to the exact amplitude of the infrasound wave at the time of the apparitional experiences. Of course, there is no absolute proof that it was there at all at the time. However, the fact that the corridor has the correct physical proportions to resonate at 19Hz combined with the fact that the experimenters measured it doing so, consistently for several hours, seems sufficient circumstantial evidence to pursue. If the signal were present at around 38dB, it would be completely inaudible. Sources such as Tempest (1976) describe physiological responses to infrasound at levels well above the threshold of hearing. However, Mr Cook (tour guide) reported that he was not aware of any sound during the incidents he described. Experiments reported in the New Scientist (Brown1973) suggest lower levels may have effects. The experiments described found that a frequency of 12 Hz at levels as low as 85dB could cause "sudden and violent nausea". This is still substantially higher than the level measured in the cellar but the effect is also rather less spectacular.

A paper by Green J, (1968) suggests a more subtle connection between infrasound and human behaviour. It draws a correlation between naturally occurring infrasound and selected human behaviour. A test was carried out to see what effect natural infrasound from a storm some 1,500 miles away would have on the population of an area enjoying "innocuous local weather conditions". Infrasound can travel enormous distances without appreciable attenuation so the only evidence of the storm was inaudible infrasound monitored by instrumentation. The results of the test show an increase in automobile accident rate and a higher rate of absenteeism among school children when the storm infrasound was present, compared to the normal state. It may be that the effects of infrasound at low level are underestimated and may only affect a small part of the population. The whole area of infrasound and its effects has seen little experimentation over the past 10-20 years and it would seem these findings could well justify more work in the area.

Modulation of the infrasonic signal is considered, by those engaged in the design of infrasound weapons as an important property if the weapon is to be effective. An article in the New Scientist (1999) suggests that experiments in the use of pure, airborne infrasound as a weapon have been ineffective whereas direct coupling of the energy in the form of vibration has been shown to cause physiological effects. The problem is the coupling of the energy to the body. It will come as no surprise that little is written about this area of research. However, Dr Kalus-Dieter Thiel of the Fraunhofer Instiut für Chemische Technologie (ICT), a colleague working in this area, has stated that current research into infrasound weapons places emphasis on the use of modulation to enhance their effectiveness. In his recent book, Future War, Colonel John Alexander (2000) refers to experiments with Pulsed Periodic Stimuli (PPS) an extreme form of modulation.

> "The technique.. [PPS] .. can be applied to situations where it is desirable to cause perceptual disorientation in targeted individuals. This is important, as it is the first acoustic weapon that does not rely on high intensity to cause the desired effects. Rather low-intensity, pulsed, acoustic energy can induce fairly strong effects in humans."
> (Alexander 2000)

The weapon designers are, of course looking for something which will reliably disable its target whereas the effects considered in this paper clearly only effect a small part of the population and, even then in a very subtle way. Dr David Swanson (1999) makes the point that a small part of the population is "hypersensitive" to the effects of infrasound. These individuals have been known to become physically ill living near the seashore (a source of natural infrasound) or near airports. It would seem reasonable to suggest that sensitivity combined with a "spooky" atmosphere are significant components in the apparitional experience and that in other surroundings different interpretations might be made.

The source of energy to create the standing wave remains a mystery. Most visitors come to the centre in the summer and the events described by Mr Cook took place in pleasant weather conditions. The heating system at the Tourist Centre was eliminated as a potential source by simply being shut off at the request of the investigators. Coventry is still a centre for industry and there are industrial plants all over the City.

Vehicle noise is possible but it is unlikely to be so consistent. It is hoped that further trials will be carried out with the permission of the owners and more clues to the source will be gained.

Conclusion

The findings of this investigation would seem to support the effects described in the Ghost in the Machine (Tandy and Lawrence 1998). To find exactly the predicted frequency was astonishing and the experiment was repeated several times to ensure that it was not an anomaly of the equipment. While reluctant to rule out other frequencies in the infrasound band, clearly 19 Hz must be of particular interest. The dimensions of the corridor leading to the cellar fit well with the assertion that it is resonating at this frequency and contains a standing wave.

Acknowledgements

I would like to thank the staff at the Tourist Information Centre for their patience and help in providing access to the cellar.
The following colleagues from Coventry University. Bill Dunn of the School of Engineering both for his help with the technical aspects and for carrying out the actual measurements. Graeme Vanner of the School of Art and Design, Martin Simons of the School of the Built Environment, Ian Baker, Sam Maunder of the School of International Studies and Law and all the technical staff who have given so freely of their time to discuss and support the research.

References

Tandy.V and Lawrence T. R. (April 1998), The Ghost in the Machine, Journal of the Society for Psychical Research Vol.62, No 851
http://home.edu.coventry.ac.uk/cyberclass/vicweb/parapsychology.htm

Tempest, W. (Ed.) (1976). Infrasound and low frequency vibration. Academic press: London.

Vassilatos. G.(1998) The Sonic Weapon of Vladimir Gavreau
http://borderlands.com/newstuff/research/gavreaus.htm

Dunning, J, (1968), The Silent Sound that Kills, Science and Mechanics, January p30-33 +p75

Lewer N & Schofield S(1997), Non-lethal Weapons: A Fatal Attraction? Zed Books, London,

Brown, New Scientist (8 November 1973), New worries about unheard sound. p414

Green J,E, & Dunn F(1968), Correlation of Naturally Occurring Infrasonics and Selected Human Behaviour. The journal of the Acoustical Society of America. Vol 44, No5,

Hecht J (20March 1999), New Scientist, Infrasound Weapons,

Swanson .David, (1999), Penn State University, Non-lethal Acoustic Weapons: Facts, Fictions and the future. Paper for the Non-Lethal Technology and Academic Research (NTAR) Symposium1999

http://www.unh.edu/orps/nonlethality/pub/presentations/1999/swanson/swanson.html

Coventry Information Centre, (2000). Information sheet for visitors on the 14th Century Cellar.

Alexander, Col J B, (2000) Future War , Non-lethal weapons in Twenty-First-Century Warfare, Thomas Dunne Books.

Bibliography

Speaks, Charles E,(1992) Introduction to sound acoustics for the hearing and speech sciences. Chapman & Hall

Mackenzie A.(1982) Hauntings and Apparitions, an investigation of the evidence. Paladin

Green C and McCreery C,(1975) Apparitions, Hamish and Hamilton

Appendix 1

Plan of the 14th Century Cellar

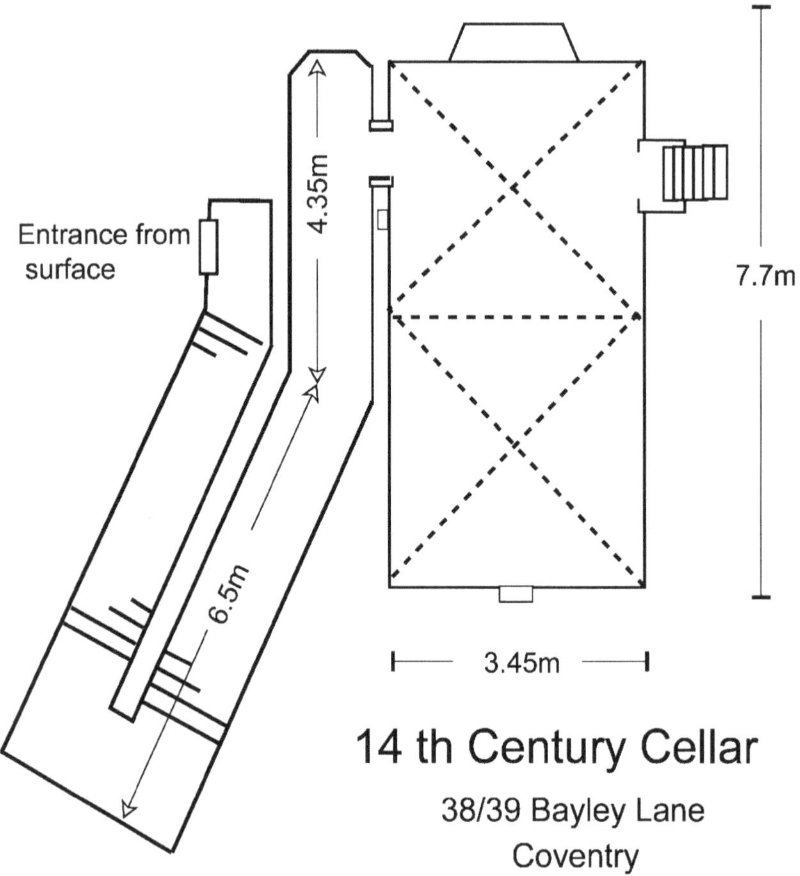

Appendix 2

Frequency, Amplitude, FFT and Modulation Explained

The purpose of this paper is to communicate with as wide an audience as possible so it was felt that this quick explanation of some of the technical concepts introduced might be appropriate.

Sound has two major parameters, frequency (pitch) and amplitude (humans perceive this as loudness). The frequency is the number of cycles per second in the sound signal and is measured in Hertz (Hz) so 20 cycles per second is the same as 20Hz. The piano keyboard has low frequencies at the left-hand end and high frequencies at the right. If the piano keyboard were extended to the left, it could include the infrasound frequencies referred to in this paper. Clearly, it would be hard to find a market for such an instrument because the audience would simply not hear it unless it was made very loud. Some church organs do produce these frequencies and their effect is to modulate the audible sound rather than stand as notes in their own right.

Pressure waves of particular frequencies in the atmosphere create a sensation which humans describe as sound. Our ears and the microphone in the monitoring equipment are sensitive to the level of this sound pressure. We would describe a low sound pressure as quiet and a high one as loud. The ratio of the quietest sound a human can hear to the loudest sound, which can be heard without immediate damage to the ear, is a ratio of ten million to one (10^7) in pressure terms. However, human hearing is non-linear. For a human to perceive a slight change in loudness the actual sound pressure level will have increased by a factor of up to around two times its original level. There is a very good reason for this property of our hearing. Early survival depended on our ability to detect predators so, at one end of the scale, the further away we could hear the foot falls of a hunting sabre tooth tiger the greater the chance of escape. At the other end of the scale, the same ears have to cope with a clap of thunder, with sound pressure level of anything up to a ten million times higher, without permanent damage.

When measurement of sound was in its infancy there was a clear need for a logarithmic unit of measurement that had similar properties to the way we hear. The decibel (dB) was already in use by electronic engineers and was adopted to simplify the representation of the massively variable signal levels. An example of the use of decibels is well illustrated in the early stages of this paper. A linear scale is used in figure 2 to show the peak at 19Hz but the other information, in the lower level signals, has been lost. Figure 1 shows exactly the same signal on a logarithmic scale measured in dB. It may take a while to become comfortable with this, but it is important for us to retain the other signals for comparison.

Without a logarithmic scale, plotting signal levels can become impractical. As an extreme example, if we were to draw a linear bar graph that represented the sound pressure level of the quietest noise a human ear can detect as a bar1meter high. Then tried to plot the thunderstorm on the same scale, the bar representing the sound pressure level of that signal would need to be ten million meters high, the piece of graph paper would be a hazard to space satellites!

While it is possible to quote the formula for conversion of linear changes in amplitude to dB, in practice the following examples are easier to remember and may help interpret actual results. A rise or fall of 6dB in sound pressure level represents a linear doubling or halving of the signal amplitude. A rise or fall of 20 dB represents a multiplication or division of 10 times the signal amplitude. So a rise of 40dB would be 10x10 = 100 times increase in signal amplitude. We need to remember this when we discuss two signals that only vary in sound pressure level by 6dB, in linear terms, one is actually twice the size of the other.

Fast Fourier Transform

Most sound that we are familiar with is complex, a single note on a pipe organ can produce a reasonably pure tone and if viewed on an oscilloscope it could well look like a sine wave. However, humans rarely encounter simple sinusoidal waves in the wild. A French mathematician by the name of Joseph Fourier stated that the complexity of a complex sound wave depended on the number and specific dimensional values (amplitude, frequency and phase) of it's sinusoidal components. The Fast Fourier Transform Analyser is a device that breaks a complex wave into component parts, which enables us to see the frequencies that give rise to it. The graphs shown in figure 1, figure 2 and figure 5 of this paper therefore represent the spectrum of frequencies present in the cellar. Frequency is plotted on the horizontal, X axis while amplitude, either as a linear or logarithmic scale, is on the vertical, Y axis.

Modulation

In the case of the signal in figure 4 the amplitude of the signal is being influenced by another signal of much lower frequency. This is described as amplitude modulation. In this case the signal of lower frequency is not simple itself and represents a complex interaction of several frequencies. As a result, we do not see a smoothly varying signal but a pattern that repeats with time. We know from this that it is the influence of another waveform and the FFT analysis in figure 5 provides us with possible culprits in the region of 2-3 Hz.

APPENDIX 3

A LITMUS TEST FOR INFRASOUND

by VIC TANDY

ABSTRACT

A significant barrier to extending research into the link between infrasound and apparitional experiences is the high cost of monitoring equipment. This paper is offered in response to requests from researchers looking for a method of measuring infrasound within a reasonable budget. It provides the construction details for a filter-set, which can be used in combination with a commercially available sound level meter. The latter is operated slightly outside its intended parameters to produce what is described as the equivalent of a litmus test for infrasound. Operating thus is clearly a risk and no absolute guarantee of success can be given. However, using this meter saves so much time and money that it was felt warranted. As part of the development process three units were built and four meters tested. Their performance compares very well with devices costing up to twenty times that invested and they are now entering use in the field. Some prior experience of electronic circuit construction is assumed.

INFRASOUND METER

In previous papers (Tandy & Lawrence, 1998; Tandy, 2000) the author has discussed the potential link between infrasound and individuals believing they have seen an apparition or felt a presence. A major drawback to exploring this phenomenon further is the expense of the monitoring equipment required. A sound level meter capable of measuring infrasound will cost around £1,000, and a spectrum analyser with associated microphone and calibration equipment would cost at least £3,000, while for very high quality equipment another zero could easily be added in both cases. This paper is offered in response to requests from groups of investigators for a low-cost infrasound meter which would enable them to experiment in their own areas of interest. A conventional sound level meter gives an immediate measurement of the amplitude of sound being measured. If a low-pass filter is added it will only show sound levels for frequencies below the cut-off frequency of the filter. However, it will not provide details of the specific frequencies present in that band. A spectrum analyser is required for that level of detail. None the less, a simple measure of intensity across a range of infrasound frequencies is valuable for eliminating infrasound as the cause in a potential case of haunting.

Working with paranormal investigators, it was decided that an experimental meter be built and the design shared among interested parties. The result is what could be described as a 'litmus test' for infrasound rather than a reference instrument. It uses equipment which is pushed beyond the manufacturer's specification and consequently involves risk. Clearly no absolute guarantee of success can be given. However, the results obtained with the particular combination of devices used during development consistently exceeded expectation and compared very well with those provided by reference instruments.

Compromises

The design parameters for this project were challenging and inevitably led to compromises. The idea was to build a device that could provide a reading of the sound pressure level for frequencies lower than 35 Hz, 25 Hz and 15 Hz, the value to be selectable by switch. The reading should to be in decibels, following the convention of 0 dB equalling the notional threshold of human hearing, with a maximum reading range selectable from 30 to 120 dB. The device also had to be capable of being constructed by someone with hobby-level knowledge of electronics but with no sound calibration equipment, and costing less than £50.

It has not been possible in practice to escape completely the need for calibration to a known standard. The designers of professional equipment know the performance parameters, and low frequency response can be inferred by using graphs. As a result, most professional equipment is calibrated using audible sound via a device called a calibrater, often at around 1 kHz and then extrapolated. Calibraters are expensive, so using one of these would defeat the objective of keeping costs low. It is possible to provide an adequate but less accurate means of calibration simply by generating an audible tone of known amplitude via the sound card on a computer. Unfortunately, the low-cost meter used here has not been primarily designed for low frequency use, so it is not possible to be completely confident about extrapolated results. However, we can be confident that the meter will not read high, so employing this rough method of calibration should not produce false positives. Two levels of calibration are proposed, the first being a coarse audio frequency calibration and the second being calibration against a reasonable, known infrasound standard. For the coarse calibration and test, a webpage with an audio frequency tone and instructions has been created. For calibration against a known standard, a low-cost calibrator has been designed which Frank Smith, Technical Consultant to Parasearch, has built and tested. In addition to providing tremendous help during the development process, FS has also generously offered to help calibrate meters for anyone who has constructed the device. He has limited resources but may also be able to build a meter completely for readers who lack the facilities (contact details are provided at the end of this paper).

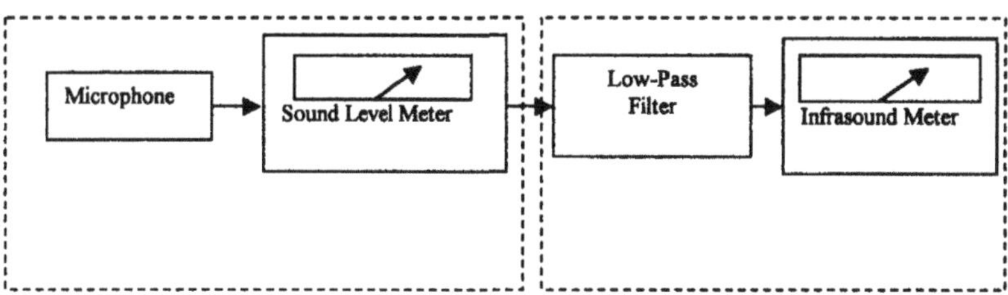

Radio Shack/Tandy Sound Level Meter **Low-Pass Filter Set**

The Details

There are essentially two component parts to this project: A RadioShack/Tandy (no relation to the author) sound level meter, Cat. No. 33–2050 (purchased by the author for £15 but it might be necessary to shop around), and the filter-set with its own meter which can be built from the information given here.

The sound level meter contains a microphone, some attenuators to set the sensitivity and a meter calibrated in decibels. This meter will be pushed beyond the manufacturer's performance figures and one cannot expect compensation if things do not work as well as hoped. However, the four meters tested by the author all performed well and compare favourably when considering the cost.

Just as our ears vary in their sensitivity to different frequencies, so do electronic circuits and microphones. The specification provided with this meter shows it to have a flat frequency response down to 20 Hz when set to C-Weighting. In practice, however, the performance of the four meters tested exceeded the manufacturer's parameters, so a 15 Hz filter setting has been included in the design. Frequencies below 10 Hz will almost certainly be subject to significant attenuation, but may still be seen as pulses of the meter needle. The sound level meter has two settings that are referred to as weightings, labelled A and C. The A-weighting actually adds another filter to the circuit which makes the meter perform with a similar sensitivity to the human ear. This will effectively remove the infrasound before it reaches the new device, which will then read zero. In practice this has been the most common error during testing, so caution is advised. It is vital that the weighting switch is set to the C position. The author has not come across any calibrated sound level meter cheaper than the RadioShack/Tandy model and, before deciding to attempt the design, four meters were checked with calibraters used to calibrate professional equipment. The worst was found to be within 1 dB of the correct setting, which is excellent considering their cost. The sound level meter also has an output via a phono-socket on the side, which is used to connect it to the filter-set.

The circuit for the filter-set is built around the Maxim 8th-order, low-pass, elliptic, switched-capacitor filter MAX293. A low-pass filter is an electronic device that filters out frequencies above a pre-set level, in the same way that a tea strainer filters out tea leaves above a given size. As a result, the filter-set circuit will only 'pass' low frequencies, the level of which can then be read from its built-in meter.

There is no formal definition of infrasound; meteorologists for example would call one hundredth of a Hertz infrasound, so for the purposes of this device, infrasound is defined as frequencies between 1 Hz and 35 Hz.

Circuit Description

Please refer to the circuit diagram (next page) as you read the following.

An audio signal is available from a phono-socket marked OUTPUT on the left-hand side of the sound level meter and this is fed to the input shown on the diagram, the centre pin being wired to capacitor C4. There is a DC component to this signal, which is decoupled by C4 before being fed to an uncommitted Op-Amp on board the second integrated circuit (IC2). The output impedance of the sound level meter is relatively high, so the input impedance of the Op-Amp and value of C4 are also rather high to ensure that low frequencies are not significantly affected. VR1 is used to adjust the gain of this Op-Amp, thus providing a calibration facility. It would be sensible to mount this on the circuit

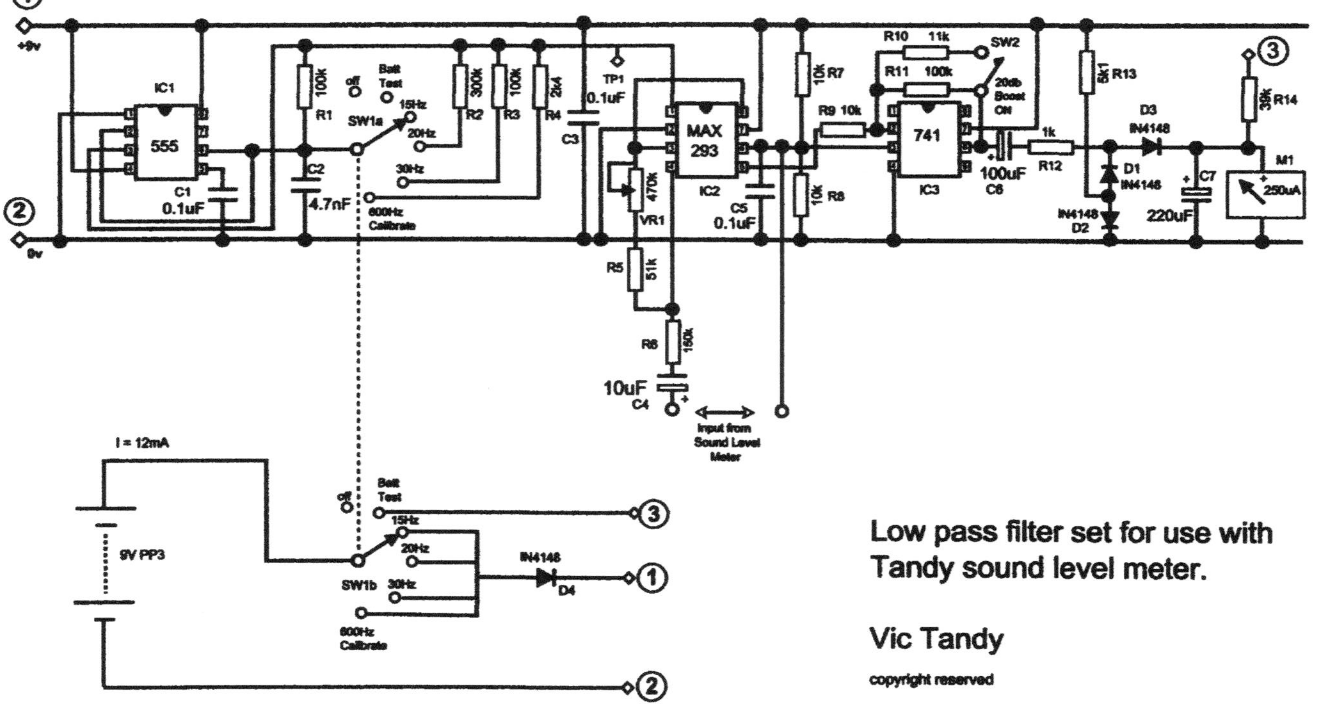
Low pass filter set for use with
Tandy sound level meter.
Vic Tandy
copyright reserved
Input from Sound Level Meter
I = 12mA
9V PP3

board so that it can be easily adjusted during calibration. Output from the Op-Amp in IC2 (pin3) is connected to the input of the switched-capacitor filter, also in IC2, via pin 8.

The frequency at which the filter cuts off is referred to as the corner-frequency and is set by the frequency of clock pulses provided by IC1, which is a 555 timer chip designed to supply a 1:1 mark/space ratio clock-pulse of frequency determined by C2 in conjunction with R1, R2, R3 and R4 (C1, C3 and C5 are simply decoupling capacitors for stability). All resistors are 1% tolerance, so accuracy of the clock frequency and therefore corner-frequency depends predominantly on C2, which can be a polystyrene, polyester layer or polyester film and foil capacitor, whichever offers the best tolerance. If you have an oscilloscope, or even better, a frequency counter, the frequency can be checked at TP1; note this so that you can quote the accuracy of your meter. During development FS replaced R2, R3 and R4 with variable resistors that could be adjusted to compensate for the capacitor tolerance but this is only valuable if you have the equipment mentioned above for calibration.

As the corner frequency of the filter is the frequency of the clock divided by 100, the frequencies at TP1 should be 1.5 kHz, 2.5 kHz, 3.5 kHz and 60 kHz. The latter setting will allow all sound at frequencies below 600 Hz to pass and can be used for rough calibration with an audible signal. If you cannot get access to instrumentation, you should note the tolerance of C2. For example, if it has a 20% tolerance at 25 Hz the actual corner-frequency could be between 20 Hz (–20%) and 30 Hz (+20%). Experience suggests that it is very unusual to get a capacitor at the extreme of its notional tolerance, so it is unlikely to be that bad. The author's capacitor has a tolerance of 20% but is actually within about 1% of its stated value. Exercise caution when wiring the resistors to switch SW1 to ensure that the switch does not read 25 Hz with the oscillator connected to the resistor for 35 Hz or, worse, 600 Hz. The clock input on IC2 is pin 1.

IC2 and IC3 require a split power supply, so to avoid the cost of a regulator and extra batteries this is provided by the potential divider R7/R8; C5 is decoupling (you can never have too much decoupling). The filtered output from IC2 (pin 5) is fed to the input of IC3 (pin 2) via R9. IC3 is a conventional 741 Op-Amp, the gain of which is set by R10 and R11, so that with switch SW2 closed, the gain is unity and this setting should be used during calibration. By opening SW2, the gain is increased to ten, which corresponds to an increase in low frequency sensitivity of 20 dB. The Tandy sound level meter reads down to 50 dB, and by opening SW2 this can be reduced to 30 dB for the low frequency component. During construction, the wires to this switch should be as short as possible to avoid instability.

The filtered sound is taken from IC3 at pin 6 and isolated from the metering circuit by C6. This capacitor may slightly decrease the accuracy of the reading if an audible frequency is used for calibration, but the discrepancy is so small in practice that it can be ignored. D3 rectifies the filtered signal, but unfortunately silicon diodes drop up to 0.7 volts when forward-biased, which would lose most of our signal, so R13, D1 and D2 provide an offset voltage to compensate. C7 smoothes the signal and effectively damps transients, making the meter easier to read. The value of this capacitor can be increased, within reason, to increase damping if required. R14 simply limits current to provide a battery test facility. The circuit is fairly resilient to variation in battery voltage, but will produce unpredictable results if the battery begins to fail. D4 is simply a protection against accidentally connecting the battery backwards with the device switched on. Without this, there is a danger of complete destruction, so it is worth the extra few pence. M1 is the meter and as supplied needs to have a new scale fitted. The scale should follow the same format as the sound level meter and can be printed off as suggested below.

Construction

Three units have been constructed and tested. All perform well and no particular problems have been experienced. The building of the author's device within a small box actually made construction physically more demanding and allowance for more room is recommended. As noted above, the wires connecting to SW2 should be as short as possible to avoid any instability. In general, the circuit has been well behaved, and as the sound level meter itself has no electromagnetic shielding there is little point in shielding the filter. In normal conditions no anomalous results have been experienced.

The meter M1 will need to have its scale replaced, which can be derived from the version provided here or copied from the website. Note that photocopiers are rarely linear so a copy may not be dimensionally accurate. The front of the meter is held on by sticky tape and the mechanism is very vulnerable to damage once the front is removed. Trying to remove the existing scale will cause damage, so stick the new one on top, being careful to align it as precisely as possible.

Calibration

Rough calibration can be carried out by logging onto the website given at the end of this paper and following the instructions. Alternatively, set the filter to Calibrate and find a constant source of sound below 600 Hz (200 Hz is ideal). Adjust VR1 so that the meter on the filter reads the same as the meter on the sound level meter. For final calibration please contact Frank Smith of Para-search, who has generously offered to help. His contact details are given at the end of this paper and any updated information will be on the webpage.

Use

Measuring low frequency sound requires a slightly different technique to conventional audible signals. If one listens to a constant tone at about 1 kHz, moving the head a few inches from side to side will cause a variation in amplitude, perceived as the sound getting louder and quieter, and caused by standing waves in the listening venue. The distance needed to move for this effect varies with the wavelength of the sound, which is dependent on frequency. Wavelength is around 35 cm at 1 kHz, but becomes tens of meters below 20 Hz. It is suggested that this is why haunting effects are location-specific, even down to particular areas of a room. For most purposes it is suggested that a battery check on the filter and sound level meter is done at the start and end of a session to ensure the level did not fall during measurements. Set the weighting to C on the sound level meter and the scale to 60 dB.

Those particularly interested in effects at around 19 Hz should switch to the 25 Hz range on the filter which will pass signals below that frequency. Then, if a signal is read which disappears when the filter is switched to 15 Hz, the predominant infrasound frequency must be between 15 Hz and 25 Hz.

It is theoretically possible to build a mathematical model of the behaviour of sound in a room, but there are often unexpected properties in real rooms that cause unpredictable results. Therefore attempts to prejudge a room, except to suggest paying particular attention to alcoves and doorways, should be resisted. It might help to divide the room into a grid pattern and note measurements on a grid. Infrasound is not present everywhere so it is quite possible to read nothing. It is not clear what level of infrasound might cause an effect with a particular individual, so a 20 dB boost is available and should be used if there is no reading at 60 dB. With the boost switched on, the scale on the filter becomes 20 dB more sensitive than the sound level meter, so the 0 on the filter meter now represents 40 dB rather than 60 dB.

Any plosive utterance, or coughing, will cause the meter on the filter to kick. This is because a sudden shock produces broadband noise, and although human speech contains no infrasound component, anything that causes a sudden expulsion of air, such as saying the word 'plosive', will cause transient pressure waves which will be detected. Also, while an ideal reading would have the meter relatively stable at a constant sound pressure level, at frequencies below 10 Hz the response seen will be a regularly pulsed movement of the meter needle.

It is not suggested that all apparitional experiences are associated with infrasound, so users are referred to the original research for guidance on the type of phenomena which might warrant investigation in this regard.

Component List

All components can be purchased from Maplin Electronics Ltd unless otherwise stated. (http://www.maplin.co.uk/)

R1–R14 are 1% tolerance 0.6 Watt Metal Film (Maplin).

C1, C3 and C5 are Decoupling Ceramic Disc 16v.

C2 can be polystyrene, polyester layer or polyester film and foil.

The timing and hence the accuracy of the roll-off frequency is dependent on how close this capacitor is to the stated value, so tolerance is more important than type.

C4, C6 and C7 are standard electrolytic capacitors; radial types were used in the prototype.

D1-D4 are IN4148 signal diodes.

IC1 is a standard 555-timer chip.

IC2 is a MAX293 8th-order, low-pass, elliptic, switched-capacitor filter (Maxim).

Buy on line (http://www.maxim-ic.com/) or phone Maxim UK Distribution 0800-585-048 (a data sheet is also available).

IC3 is a standard 741 Operational Amplifier.

M1 is a 250 µA FSD Signal strength meter (Maplin order code LB80B).

SW1a/b is a 2-pole 6-way rotary switch.

APPENDIX 4

ACOUSTIC RESEARCH INFRASOUND DETECTOR (ARID)[1]

STEVEN T. PARSONS and CIARÁN J. O'KEEFFE

INTRODUCTION

Infrasound, which is normally defined as audio frequency energy, lies below the range of normal human perception, typically 20 Hz, (Leventhall, Pelmear & Benton, 2003). It has captured the attention of paranormal investigators following research that indicates possible psycho-physiological effects as a result of exposure to such audio frequencies (Persinger, 1974). Other studies have postulated a causal link between infrasound energy and the appearance of apparitions (e.g. Tandy & Lawrence, 1998). Measuring infrasound is not technically difficult but it can involve the use of specialist and expensive equipment. For this reason little effective research has, to date, been carried out examining the potential of infrasound as a causal factor at many locations that are described as being 'haunted'.

Tandy (2002), following earlier papers merely postulating the link between infrasound and haunting experiences, provided construction details for a filter-set which could be used in combination with a commercially available sound level meter. There are a number of problems with this set-up which are readily acknowledged by Tandy (2002). These include using equipment that "is pushed beyond the manufacturer's specification and consequently involves risk. Clearly no absolute guarantee of success can be given," (Tandy, 2002, p167). In addition, the effectiveness of the system falls short when the entire infrasound frequency range is taken into account. Indeed, Tandy (2002, p173) states "while an ideal reading would have the meter relatively stable at a constant sound pressure level, at frequencies below 10Hz the response seen will be a regularly pulsed movement of the meter needle." Nevertheless, the Tandy (2002) system was solely intended as a 'litmus test' and not as a reference instrument. The current authors respectively acknowledge Tandy's (2002) motivation however, and subsequently adopt the underlying purpose of making infrasound research accessible to paranormal investigators. The following paper, therefore, tackles all aforementioned issues and presents a technical description of a highly efficient 'reference instrument', a workable infrasound detection and measurement system.

The principle

It *is* possible to build a perfectly efficient and capable infrasound detector for a reasonable cost. This is achieved by using a large loudspeaker as an infrasound microphone. This method permits a detector to be constructed that is capable of being used to measure a continuous range of audio frequencies from 1Hz to 100Hz, covering both the IF (Infrasound) and LF (Low Frequency) sound regions.

It is not crucial to provide a detailed description of the operating principles of microphones and loudspeakers as this information is considered elsewhere in a

[1] The name 'Acoustic Research Infrasound Detector' and its abbreviation, ARID, are copyright © 2006 Parsons & O'Keeffe.

number of publications (e.g. Talbot-Smith, 1994). A basic introduction to their respective operating principles, however, is provided here.

A microphone simply converts sound waves into electrical signals. The most basic form of microphone makes use of a thin diaphragm which is attached to a coil of very fine wire. The diaphragm and coil are mounted within a fixed permanent magnetic field. This type is known as a dynamic microphone. Sound waves cause the diaphragm to vibrate. As this happens the motion of the coil within the fixed magnetic field causes a voltage to generate within the coil. The voltage is extremely small - typically less than 1 millivolt - but the amplitude and frequency of the output voltage is directly proportional to the diaphragm's movements and hence the sound waves which strike it. The very low output voltage normally requires further amplification before it can be used effectively.

Most microphones are normally designed to record audio frequencies within the range of typical human hearing i.e. 20Hz~20kHz although they are often optimised for a specific range of frequencies depending upon their designed uses. Outside this optimised frequency range the microphone's response diminishes quickly. The small physical size of the microphone diaphragm also limits the range of effective frequencies the device is sensitive to.

A loudspeaker uses the same operating principle as a dynamic microphone, though reversed, to produce sound. An amplified voltage from an audio frequency source such as a music player is fed into the coil of wire. This creates a fluctuating magnetic field surrounding the coil. The fluctuating electromagnetic field reacts with the fixed magnetic field of the permanent magnet producing a series of attractions and repulsions. This series of movements is transferred to the diaphragm or speaker cone, which is then thrust back and forth synchronous with the applied audio frequency signal. The movements of the speaker cone exert a force onto the surrounding air generating sound waves.

A loudspeaker, therefore, can be readily used as a microphone with movement of the speaker coil generating a small current within the attached coil as it moves within a permanent magnetic field. Ambient sound waves create resonant vibrations in the cone thus moving the coil and generating an electrical signal that corresponds directly to the sound waves. In effect the loudspeaker has become a dynamic microphone. Some commercial devices such as baby monitors and intercoms make use of this principle to allow the same component to function both as a microphone and a loudspeaker.

ARID

The initial requirement was to produce a pair of identical infrasound microphones to permit two nearby locations to be measured simultaneously or to allow better Omni directional acoustic information to be obtained by positioning the units at 180 degrees to one another and combining their outputs into a single display channel of the spectrum analyser. Therefore this experimental design uses a matched pair of 12" diameter sub-woofer type loudspeakers. Matched loudspeaker pairs are available to order from most manufacturers. Sub-woofer designs are optimised for the handling of low frequency sound waves and therefore it was felt would produce a more linear output. 12" diameter models were selected to be an effective compromise between sensitivity to the desired frequency range of interest, portability and overall ease of use in the field.

Components & Construction

An identical pair of custom-built boxes (cabinets) was commissioned from a small (P.A.) Public Address speaker builder. Each was designed to house a single 12" loudspeaker and its associated electronic components. The cabinets, built from 25mm MDF with screwed and glue joints to ensure rigidity are in the form of a trapezoidal box, lined with a 25mm thick acoustic absorbing rubber compound. The shape and the construction elements of the cabinets are an important consideration of the ARID design and minimise any very low frequency resonance[2] of the cabinet that could have potentially affected the final measurements. The exterior of each cabinet is covered in a high quality loudspeaker carpet to further control resonance and also to provide physical protection. Prior to installation of the loudspeaker the resonant frequency of each cabinet was tested by the manufacturer and was found to be above 500Hz and thus cabinet resonance could safely be excluded as a factor in the resulting measurements. The overall cabinet dimensions are 44cm wide, 36cm high, 32cm base depth, 22cm top depth and having an internal volume (prior to fitting of the speaker and other components) of 28 cubic litres[3].

The output voltage of the resulting loudspeaker / microphones is extremely small and it was necessary to use a suitable microphone pre-amplifier in order to boost the output voltage to suitable levels. In order to be able to achieve this it was necessary to provide some form of impedance matching[4] between the low impedance output of the voice coil and the high impedance microphone input of the microphone pre-amplifier. This was simply achieved using a pair of suitable audio frequency transformers (Jaycar Electronics, cat no. MM2530). This transformer model has an input impedance of 8 Ohms and an output impedance of 1K Ohms which closely

[2] Resonance: Air within the loudspeaker / microphone enclosure and also the enclosure itself is caused to oscillate due to exposure to sounds and vibrations. Depending upon the physical size of the enclosure and the materials used, the system will have natural frequencies at which the microphone diaphragm movement will be either inhibited or amplified, this is known as resonance. Tuning the enclosure ensures that the natural frequencies of the enclosure and the air contained within it minimally interfere with the movement of the microphone diaphragm.

[3] It is worth noting that the actual loudspeaker model used is not critical and it is possible to substitute almost any convenient and similarly sized loudspeaker units. As no power will be applied to the loudspeakers, specifications relating to power handling can be ignored. However, the loudspeaker (microphone) units should be identical and selected with regard to the resonant frequency. For most 12" units this will typically be within the region of 21Hz-25Hz.

[4] Impedance, simply stated, is the ratio of voltage to current within the different components of the system circuitry. In order to obtain the maximum transmission of the signal voltage between the microphone and the amplifier it is necessary to ensure that components are adjusted to give equality of impedance. A typical method of achieving maximum signal voltage transfer between the source (microphone) and the load (amplifier) is by use of a matching transformer. Transformers are regarded as ideal solutions for such applications as voltage losses are negligible.

matches the impedance requirements of both the loudspeaker and the microphone pre-amplifier input.

The transformer input was connected directly to the speaker terminals using a 10cm length of 20 SWG twin-core copper wire. The transformer was then physically attached to inside of the cabinet using epoxy glue and self-tapping screws and positioned well away from the permanent magnet on the loudspeaker. This was done to minimise any unwanted electromagnetic fields being created within the transformer as a result of movements within the loudspeaker/microphone voice coil. The output voltage of the loudspeaker/microphone prior to amplification is very low and thus any such interference could potentially affect the final voltage output and the resulting measurements.

ARID was initially designed to provide an optimum level of response from 1Hz to 100Hz. In order to reduce unwanted higher frequency responses (i.e. those above 80Hz) from the loudspeaker/microphone being passed to the microphone pre-amplifier that may interfere with the measurement accuracy, it was necessary to use some form of low-pass filter which electronically restricts the high frequency signal. The ARID uses a studio-grade sound mixer unit (Phonic MU-1002); this has a built-in microphone pre-amplifier and includes a high quality low-pass filter network. The microphone pre-amplifier has a lower operating frequency limit of 0.1Hz, the low-pass filter reducing all frequencies above 80Hz by – 60dB. This did slightly lower the working frequency range of the detector from the original 100Hz but was felt to be an acceptable compromise as we were mainly interested in the measurement of those frequencies below 50Hz.

The transformer output wires are attached internally to an electrically balanced 3-pin (known as an 'XLR' type) terminal mounted through the cabinet wall. Balanced wiring requires 3 conductors: two carry the signal and one is for an earth connection. This arrangement ensures that if there is a nearby source of electrical interference, the interfering voltages generated within the signal wires will be equal and therefore tend to be cancelled out. This design allows the use of off-the-shelf shielded microphone cables of various lengths depending upon the desired placement of the microphone and the observer's position thus avoiding the need to coil overly long cable lengths. This step further helps to minimise induced electrical and radio frequency interference (i.e. the cable needs to be long enough to allow placement of the loudspeaker/microphone at a convenient distance away from the measurement position but overly long lengths should be avoided whenever possible to minimise electrical interference). Use of properly shielded microphone cables further reduces unwanted interference from any nearby electrical noise sources such as electrical supply cables.

Most sound measurement meters are designed to measure sounds within the range of 20Hz-20kHz. In order to achieve a criterion of equal loudness it is normally the case that some form of compensation for the variable sensitivity of the human ear to different frequencies is made. This takes the form of compensation weighting that is applied to the microphone output. Several standards exist for such weightings, i.e. 'A weighting' and 'C weighting' (Rushforth, Styles & Moorhouse, 2000). There is currently no definitive standard for the measurement of very low frequency sound or infrasound and it was felt that using an un-weighted measurement would allow us to produce more acceptable results. Such un-weighted measurements are often termed Z or Zero weighting or referred to by the term 'LIN' measurements by many manufacturers of sound measuring equipment (e.g. Bruel & Kjaer). In fact some research has suggested that use of un-weighted measurements of low frequency sound may produce more acceptable results in some instances than use of either A or C weighting (Bullen, Hede & Job, 1991). The ARID design allows the electrical output from the microphone to be measured directly as a voltage for use with a variety of signal handling systems and devices. The lack of any single definitive weighting for low frequency sound measurement leads to this decision. Depending upon future requirements it is possible to apply any current weighting standard to the signal either directly at the point of measurement or retrospectively to the previously captured raw signal data by use of adjustments within the software.

Use of the combined pre-amplifier/mixer unit permits several different signal applications to be used either independently or in combination as desired. For example, it is possible to send the output directly to a laptop PC that is running any suitable FFT (Fast Fourier Transform) frequency analysis programme such as Sigview[5] and/or simultaneously to an uncompressed broadcast wave file digital audio recorder (e.g., Tascam HDP-2) This permits real-time observation and measurement of the sound level to be made within the spectrum analyser software whilst direct recordings of the microphones output can also be made permitting further signal analysis to be done at a later stage and to enable constant archiving of the measurement data.

An additional and useful option permits an auxiliary output to be taken to a pair of headphones allowing the user to monitor the microphone output directly (depending upon the frequency handling of the headphones – some models will work effectively at frequencies as low as 10Hz). This facility provides an excellent method of quickly assessing the amount of infrasound and low frequency sound that is present.

Throughout all stages of construction, care has been taken to ensure that all the components used are closely matched to ensure that direct comparisons may be made between the measurements from both microphones. Using the first authors' previously constructed infrasound generator – ARIA[6] a series of measurements were obtained to check that the resulting output from each separate microphone unit was balanced. The final output of each microphone was found to be within +/- 0.1dB over a frequency range of 5Hz – 100Hz. (the output frequency limits of the ARIA generator).

In Use

ARID comprises three main component parts for use in field detection: the 2 microphone units; the mixer / pre-amplifier; and a laptop PC. Housing the laptop PC and the mixer / pre-amplifier in a flight case gives ease of transport and a good degree of ruggedness important for field use. A set of commercially available

[5] There are several suitable software programmes available commercially or as shareware or freeware

[6] ARIA – Acoustic Research Infrasound Array. The authors intend to include details of this generating system in a future paper.

height-adjustable P.A. speaker stands is used to raise the microphones 1.5metres off the floor to reduce the effects of structure-born vibrations to an acceptable amount.

After positioning the microphone in the desired position it is then a simple matter of connecting each microphone cable to it's respective mixer / pre-amplifier input and taking the output from the mixer to the stereo line input of the external 24bit analogue to digital converter (A/D) linked to a laptop PC using an IEE1394 (Firewire) cable. Care is taken to avoid placing any cables in close proximity to any electricity supply cables or the power supply transformers of the mixer and the laptop (this is done to reduce any electrical noise to a minimum). The laptop and any other desired auxiliary equipment can then be located in a convenient position within the location, although it is best to choose a position a good distance away from the microphone to avoid any sounds of the recorder or laptop being picked up.

ARID is capable of being used to simultaneously display and measure the frequency and amplitude outputs of the two microphones. The software permits selectable data sampling rates to be chosen. For any resultant data to be considered meaningful (regardless of the number of microphones) it must be capable of being calibrated against some existing standard. This was done using a Bruel & Kjaer type 2009 sound impulse meter fitted with a type 1613 filter network. As discussed previously several weighting standards for the measurement of sound pressure levels and loudness exist although most are optimised for the measurement of higher frequencies. Calibration of ARID was undertaken against the B&K meter using the non weighted LIN setting. The Sigview software currently being used with ARID allows the selection of most existing weighting scales and also can be tailored to allow matching of future weighting scales. As such the ARID design offers the potential to conduct rigorous infrasound and low frequency research at a reasonable cost for amateur investigators. It can be used to readily demonstrate the presence and frequency of infrasound at almost any location.

The ARID system design and low unit cost permits a number of microphones - the current mixer / pre-amplifier has 6 available microphone inputs and therefore permits up to 6 microphone units to be used simultaneously. This allows more microphones to be connected to the system thus allowing simultaneous measurements to be made from several areas within the same location providing even greater accuracy to future measurements.

It is planned to develop both the hardware and software applications further in conjunction with assistance from acoustic specialists, such as the National Physics Laboratory, in order to obtain the best data calibration methods possible. A discussion of these improved capabilities and the results of a substantial series of field measurements, which are now underway, will form a follow-up paper. The series of field measurements are being conducted to determine if any Infrasound levels are present at a range of geographically, and architecturally, diverse haunted and associated co-located control ('non-haunted') locations and in order to obtain baseline information of ambient Infrasound levels present at a range of locations. This series of field measurements is being partially funded by a generous grant from the SPR.

STEVEN T. PARSONS

Liverpool Hope University

CIARÁN J. O'KEEFFE

Université de Toulouse
CLLE-LTC (CNRS, UTM, EPHE),
Maison de la recherche
5 allées A. Machado
31058 Toulouse Cedex 9
France

Email: enquiries@theparapsychologist.com

References

Bullen, R.B., Hede, A.J., & Job, R.F.S. (1991). Community reaction to noise from an artillery range. *Noise control Engineering Journal, 37*, 115-128.

Leventhall, G., Pelmear, P., & Benton, S. (2003). *A review of published research on low frequency noise and its effects.* London: DEFRA Publications.

Persinger, M. A. (1974). *The paranormal: Part II Mechanisms and Models.* New York: MSS Information Corporation.

Rushforth, L., Styles, P., & Moorhouse, A. (2000). Industrially induced Low-Frequency Noise & Vibration in Residential Buildings. *Proceedings of Acoustics 2000, University of Liverpool, April, 2000.*

Talbot-Smith, M., (1994). *Audio Recording & Reproduction, Practical Measures for Audio Enthusiasts*. London: Newnes Publishing.

Tandy, V. (2000). Something in the cellar. *Journal of Society for Psychical Research, 64*,129-140.

Tandy, V. (2002). A litmus test for infrasound. *Journal of Society for Psychical Research, 66*, 167-174.

Tandy, V., & Lawrence, T. R. (1998). The ghost in the machine. *Journal of the Society for Psychical Research, 62,* 360-364.

APPENDIX 5

INFRASOUND AND THE PARANORMAL

by Steven T. Parsons

ABSTRACT

Infrasound has become established within paranormal research as a causal factor in the production of subjective experiences that may be interpreted by the percipient as having a paranormal origin. This paper introduces infrasound and describes the nature of sound and infrasound, its production and measurement and interactions with structures. Human hearing and the perception of low-frequency sounds and the psycho-physiological interactions between infrasound and human percipients are discussed. This paper will consider infrasound measuring techniques and choice of a suitable sound filter weighting scale, together with a description of equipment designed by the author to permit infrasound monitoring and measuring to be undertaken at selected locations throughout the UK and Eire. The historical links between low-frequency sound and infrasound and the development of the case for infrasound in the production of anomalous experiences are examined. Following the hypothesis that a frequency of close to 19Hz was key in the production of anomalous experiences (Tandy & Lawrence, 1998), the focus of parapsychology has been towards testing this hypothesis. Studies such as 'The Haunt Project' (French et al., 2009) and pilot studies by the author have focused on this range of infrasound frequencies. This paper will argue that the original hypothesis failed to understand fully the manner in which the frequencies of infrasound standing waves are determined and will examine critically the results of The Haunt Project, suggesting that the failure of the experimenters to understand all the problems of infrasound measurement and propagation may have led to an unreliable conclusion. Finally, the paper will discuss the question of an infrasound role in the production of anomalous experiences.

Introduction

Infrasound is generally considered to be audio-frequency energy that lies below the range of normal human hearing, typically 20Hz (Leventhall, Pelmear & Benton, 2003). Ambient infrasound within the environment is produced by both natural and man-made sources. Natural sources include weather-related effects (e.g. wind and storms) surf and wave action, volcanic eruptions and upper atmospheric phenomena (e.g. the jet stream and meteors —cf. von Gierke & Parker, 1976; Gossard & Hooke, 1975). Man-made infrasound is associated with vehicles and aircraft, machinery and the interactions of weather with buildings and other structures (Blazier, 1981; Stubbs, 2005). Ambient infrasound levels from natural and man-made causes are variable in intensity and there have to date been a limited number of measurements of ambient environmental infrasound (e.g. Bruel & Olesen, 1973). From these few studies, however, and the author's own unpublished survey of ambient infrasound levels at more than 30 locations in the UK, it is clear that ambient infrasound is often to be found at levels of 50–80dBS in rural locations, and frequently in excess of 90 or 100dBS in suburban areas and close to industry and major transport routes. Bruel and Olesen showed that the amount of infrasound rose markedly as a result of increased weather (particularly wind) interactions with structures, a finding that the author also noted in his own measurements. Because of its low frequencies and long wavelengths, infrasound is capable of travelling long distances with little attenuation. Consequently, much of the infrasound energy, even from sources which produce sound energy across the entire sound-frequency spectrum, will be apparent at considerable distances. The infrasound shockwave or sonic boom from Concorde travelling between London and New York has been measured at up to 75dBS in the North of Sweden (Berglund et al., 1996). The infrasound from volcanic and other seismic events can be recorded as it travels around the Earth numerous times, losing only a small percentage of its total energy on each circuit (Backteman et al., 1983). It is therefore clear that infrasound is not only present almost everywhere but it is also present at considerable amplitudes, although it is largely undetectable by normal hearing and unmeasurable by the majority of available sound-level measuring equipment. Westin (1975) noted in a review paper dealing with the effects of infrasound on man that the amounts of natural and man-made infrasound that man is subjected to are larger than is generally realised, and commented that few studies have concerned themselves with the physiological effects of moderate-to-high levels of infrasound exposure.

In the past decade, infrasound has captured the attention of investigators of the paranormal. This interest follows studies that have postulated a causal link between infrasound energy and the appearance of apparitions (e.g. Tandy & Lawrence, 1998). Although not the first to link infrasound with paranormal experiences, Tandy proposed that exposure to infrasound close to 19Hz was instrumental in the production of psycho-physiological experiences that were subjectively reported as being paranormal in their origin (Tandy & Lawrence, 1998). As a result of Tandy's research, paranormal investigators have taken a keen interest in infrasound. Tandy's suggestion was based upon existing studies carried out on behalf of the United States space programme and military weapons research (Altmann, 1999). These research programmes were set up to study the physiological and psychological effects of infrasound exposure on astronauts and military personnel. Experiments used high infrasound exposure levels (150dBS–170dBS)—much higher than would be expected to be found in homes, industry or from environmental sources.

The secrecy surrounding lethal and non-lethal acoustic weapons development and a lack of information detailing the effects of high levels of infrasound exposure have resulted in periodic dramatic and even alarmist claims being made within the media about infrasound and its effects ("The Silent Sound Menaces Drivers", *The Daily Mirror*, 19th October 1969, p.18; "Brain Tumours 'caused by noise'", *The Times*, 29th September 1973, p.7; "The Silent Killer All Around Us", *London Evening News*, 25th May 1974, p.11). As a result of these distorted claims, infrasound began to develop a popular mythology and was blamed for many ailments and misfortunes for which no other explanation could be forthcoming. These have included brain tumours, cot death and road accidents (Tempest, 1971). In 1973, Lyall Watson published *Supernature: A Natural History of the Supernatural,* in which he repeated a series of claims originally made by French weapons scientist Vladimir Gavreau, including: "that in an experiment with infrasonic generators, all the windows were broken within a half mile of the test site", later adding that "two infrasonic generators focused on a point five miles away produce a resonance that can knock a building down as effectively as a major earthquake" (Watson, 1973). Gavreau's original claims (Gavreau, 1966) have never been substantiated and they have been disputed by many subsequent researchers. However, these sometimes extraordinary and frequently misleading claims about the physical and physiological effects of infrasound, combined with a general lack of research into the effects of exposure both to naturally occurring and to man-made infrasound have permitted some to popularise the idea that infrasound is the cause of many paranormal experiences (Fielding & O'Keeffe, 2006).

Many field researchers have developed their own theories and explanations of a relationship between infrasound and the paranormal. Some of these, however, appear to be the work of a creative rather than a logical mind. On their internet site an established and well-known paranormal group claim that "infrasound is caused by ghosts and spirits as they use electromagnetic energy to move things or materialise, just as lightning which is moving energy creates thunder which is infrasound, this can be recorded and used to prove that spirits are present." Another respected team of investigators claim to have recorded many infrasonic EVPs (electronic voice phenomena) using handheld digital dictation recorders, which are completely incapable of recording or measuring such infrasound. There seems to be a generally poor understanding of the original work by Tandy, and of the technical constraints in making infrasound measurements, and this has led to misunderstanding of any actual relationship between infrasound and paranormal experiences and accounts.

Therefore this paper will examine some of the physical properties of low-frequency sound and consider some of the techniques to detect and measure infrasound. Furthermore, it will consider the perception of infrasound and the psycho-physiological effects of infrasound exposure, and examine links to reports of anomalous and paranormal experiences.

The Physics of Sound

Our most common experience of sound is in air, but sound is able to travel through any solid, liquid or gaseous medium. Sound is normally produced by anything that is vibrating and causing the surrounding molecules to vibrate in sympathy with the source. These vibrations travel in the form of a wave which can be defined as a travelling disturbance consisting of coordinated vibrations that transmit energy with no net movement of matter (Ostdiek & Bord, 2000). Sound waves take the form of alternating compression and rarefaction; this is known as a longitudinal wave. In air, sound waves travelling past a fixed point cause the atmospheric pressure to vary slightly above and below the steady barometric pressure.

Wavelength, Frequency and Velocity

The distance between any two corresponding points on successive waves is termed the wavelength. Frequency refers to the number of successive waves that are emitted from the source in one second. Frequency is stated in units of Hertz (Hz), i.e. 100 wavelengths per second are expressed as 100Hz. In air, under normal conditions, sound waves travel at about 342 metres per second (m/s). In air the velocity of sound varies slightly with the air temperature (Talbot-Smith, 1994). In materials that have a higher molecular density, sound waves will have a higher velocity. For example:–

Air (at 18°C)	342.04 m/s
Water	1480 m/s
Glass	5200 m/s
Steel	5000–5900 m/s; depending on the composition of the metal
Helium Gas	965 m/s

Wavelength, velocity and frequency are linked by a simple mathematical formula:–

$$\text{wavelength} = \frac{\text{velocity}}{\text{frequency}}$$

Using this formula we are able to determine the wavelength for any given frequency. For example, in air, for a frequency of 20Hz and a temperature of 18°C, the wavelength would be 342.04 ÷ 20 = 17.10 metres. The same formula allows the calculation of frequency, as velocity divided by wavelength, which in this case gives 342.04 ÷ 17.10 = 20Hz.

Units of Measurement Used for Sound

Sound waves are oscillations in atmospheric pressure and their amplitudes are proportional to the change in pressure during one oscillation. There are several ways of expressing the amplitude or intensity of sound waves. However, it is commonly expressed as sound pressure. In scientific terms this is defined as the force acting on a unit of area. Thus sound pressure waves are normally given as Newtons per square metre (N/m^2). More recently it has become the official practice to refer to the N/m^2 as the Pascal (Pa). The sound pressure variations that are detectable by a typical human ear are immense. For example, the quietest sound that can be detected has a Sound Pressure Level (SPL) of 0.00002 Pascal (Pa) and the loudest sound has an SPL of around 200Pa. In order to simplify the expression of sound pressure levels the decibel (dB) is more commonly used. This is a unit of comparison and so must be stated against a reference value to be meaningful. Formally expressed, the number of dB represents a ratio of two powers using the formula dB = 10 log(power ratio). An SPL of 0.00002Pa is referred to as 0dB, and this is the reference value against which all comparisons of SPL are expressed.

This standard allows any sound pressure to be quoted as (x)dB above that pressure and is expressed as dB(SPL) or more often simply dBS. Thus a sound that is 10 times more powerful than the reference SPL is expressed as 10dBS, a sound 100 times more powerful is 20dBS, a sound 1,000 times more powerful is 30dBS, etc. An SPL of 140dB (200Pa), which is 100,000,000,000,000 more powerful than the reference, will cause rapid ear damage and aural pain.

Sound Waves and Structures

Sound waves are absorbed, reflected or diffracted by obstacles in their path. Absorption or reflection of a sound wave reduces the amount of energy it is able to transmit. This will reduce the loudness of subsequent sounds and will also cause an attenuation of the distance that the sound waves can travel. For reflection of the sound waves to occur, the wavelength must be smaller than the dimensions of the reflecting object. For example, if the side of a building is 10 m high and 20 m long, these dimensions of the building will have an appreciable effect upon the reflection of sounds with wavelengths of less than 10 m. This corresponds to frequencies of around 34 Hz. Sounds above that frequency will be more easily reflected. If sound waves with a lower frequency and correspondingly longer wavelength encounter the same obstacle they will not be reflected but will instead bend around the obstacle, a process called diffraction. If the wavelength is much greater than the obstacle size then there will be marked bending around the obstacle. At infrasonic frequencies the wavelengths are considerable, and therefore very little of the infrasound wave energy is reflected. Absorption of the infrasound wave may also be significantly lower than for audible sounds. Therefore infrasound waves are able to travel greater distances from the source without significant attenuation; in air infrasound may be detectable over tens or even hundreds of kilometres and even further through liquid or solid media (Mihan House, 2005).

Acoustic pressure waves reflected and refracted by the structure of a building from infrasound sources such as machinery and vehicles, both surrounding and within it, may combine with naturally produced infrasound from wind and weather interactions upon the structure, thus creating regions within the building that have significantly higher and lower levels of infrasound. Such regions may be highly localised and dependent upon the actual acoustic wave/structural interactions. Factors that will affect the local levels of infrasound and must be considered include the dimensions, shape and construction materials of a building together with the frequency and amplitude of the infrasound. If the infrasound is produced by weather and other natural sources of infrasound these too must be acknowledged. Local infrasound levels will vary over time because of variations in the ambient infrasound sources, natural or man-made, and the resultant change in their structural interactions.

When measuring infrasound within any location, a single measuring point will rarely produce an accurate overall result for that location. When measuring human infrasonic exposure, the measurements should be made as close as possible to the position of the percipient, as a difference of just a few feet can create a significant difference of the SPL in the local infrasound levels (Para.Science, 2007).

Hearing and the Perception of Low-Frequency Sound

The human ear has a generally quoted frequency range from about 20 Hz to around 20,000 Hz. However, it has been demonstrated that acoustic stimuli with frequencies as low as 1Hz can not only be heard, but can also be described in terms of loudness (Yeowart et al., 1967).

The actual mechanisms of infrasound detection are not fully understood but it has been suggested that at very low frequencies detection does not occur through hearing in the normal sense. Rather, detection results from nonlinearities of conduction within the middle and inner ear, created as the vibrations pass through body tissues of different densities such as bone and soft tissue, which have different sound conduction properties. This generates harmonic distortion in the higher, more easily audible, frequency range (von Gierke & Nixon, 1976). Infrasound waves may also be detected through skeletal bones, bones within the ear, resonance within organs and body cavities, and tactile senses (Job, 1993). The inability of most people to 'hear' infrasound means that its effects upon a person are largely unexpected and therefore more likely to be attributed to other causes, and in some instances where the percipient is in a haunted location or involved in the pursuit of ghost-hunting such effects are frequently blamed upon a paranormal agent or cause.

Low-Frequency Hearing Thresholds

Although infrasound is normally defined as audio-frequency energy that lies below the range of normal hearing, a number of studies have been conducted for the purpose of determining the lowest sound levels which are audible to the average person with normal hearing (Corso, 1958; Lydolf & Moller, 1997; Moller & Andresen, 1984; Watanabe & Moller, 1990). From these studies the average low-frequency thresholds can be established. Thus, referring to Figure 1, it can be seen that an average person might be expected to hear a sound with a frequency of 16 Hz when the sound pressure exceeds 120 dB (SPL) and a sound of 4 Hz at a sound pressure exceeding 130 dB (SPL). Simply stated, it is perfectly possible for an average person to hear infrasound provided that the amplitude is sufficiently high.

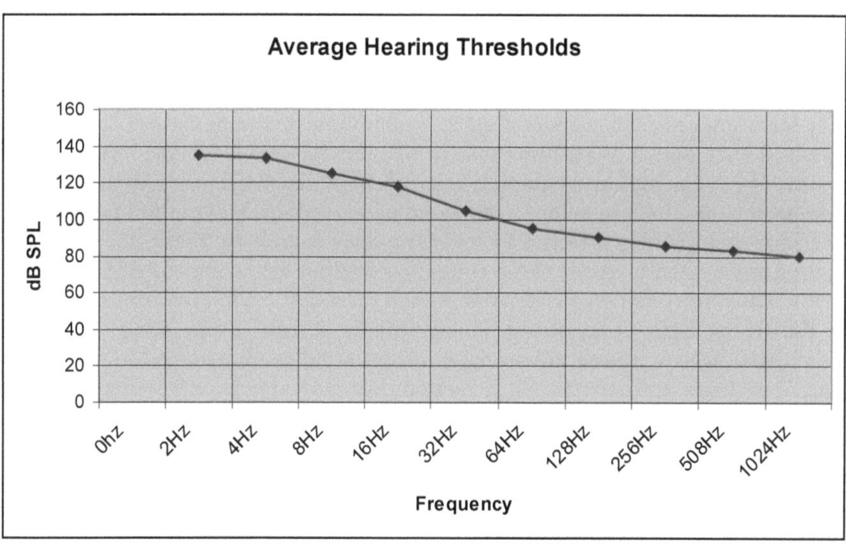

Figure 1. Low-frequency hearing thresholds.

Individual Hearing Thresholds

The threshold levels described are an average over groups of people. An individual's threshold may vary considerably from these values. Frost (1987) compared two subjects over a range of frequencies from 20 Hz to 120 Hz. At 40 Hz one individual was 15 dB more sensitive that the second. Yamada

(1980) reported female thresholds to be around 3dB more sensitive than male thresholds except at the lowest frequencies, below 16Hz. It was also found that individual differences could be large. In one case, a male subject had a hearing threshold which was 15dB more sensitive than the average. Thus an individual's ability to hear sound, including infrasound, will be dependent upon his or her actual hearing threshold.

Perception of Low-Frequency Sound and Infrasound

The function of the auditory system is to perceive objects and events through the sounds they make (Masterton, 1992). The physical dimensions of sound are usually expressed in experiments using perceptual terms; the amplitude, frequency and complexity of the sound vibrations are perceived as loudness, pitch and timbre respectively.

The relationship between the acoustic signals and perception has been tested although the research has concentrated on speech and language (e.g. Lisker & Abramson, 1970). Studies looking at low frequency and infrasound have mainly been concerned with predicting loudness or annoyance and for the establishment of safe exposure limits (Challis et al., 1978; Fields, 2001). The research so far has concentrated on using very high sound pressure levels to establish safe exposure limits (e.g. Jerger et al., 1966). There is currently no comparable research that has provided data for normal exposures. Data to indicate the infrasonic sound pressure levels that might normally be expected to be found in the general environment are also unavailable.

In psychophysical terms, the perceived loudness of a pure tone grows as a power function with sound pressure (Stevens, 1975). Goldstein (1994) showed that for a low-frequency tone of 20Hz a doubling in the perceived loudness is achieved with only a 4–5dB increase in SPL for the low-frequency tone, whereas the SPL of a higher-frequency tone of 1,000Hz (1kHz) would need to be increased by 9–10dB to achieve the same perceived doubling in loudness. Pitch discrimination is also affected by low-frequency sound. At 25Hz, the ability to discriminate pitch is about three times worse than for sounds at 63Hz (Usher, 1977). The ability to determine from which direction a sound is coming, known as the 'Haas Effect', is also seriously impaired. Low frequencies can travel great distances without substantial attenuation and can easily penetrate many buildings and structures. Directionality may also be affected by the way low-frequency 'hearing' involves multiple structures within the body rather than just the ears.

The ability of an individual to perceive infrasound is also affected by the presence of other ambient sound within the audible-frequency range, i.e. above 20Hz, the audible sounds having a tendency to mask or reduce the threshold of perception of infrasound by between 6 and 12dB (Yasunao et al., 2009).

Psychological and Physiological Effects of Infrasound

A number of studies have been conducted to study the psychological and physiological effects of infrasound on individuals (e.g. Chen & Hanmin, 2004; Moller, 1984). Such studies have used a range of pure infrasound tones at high sound-pressure levels to examine the effects of infrasound exposure upon subjects. Individuals subjected to infrasound at high SPLs reported ear pressure, headaches and tiredness, and feeling uncomfortable or 'troubled' (Moller, 1984). Karpova and colleagues (1970) reported effects on the cardiovascular and respiratory systems, including changes in heart rate, blood pressure and respiratory rate. Although the effects of infrasound exposure have been objectively demonstrated, the results obtained from these experiments have shown highly variable effects, with different individuals experiencing different responses to the infrasound exposure (Chen & Hanmin, 2004). Infrasound exposure has also been reported to include effects on the inner ear, leading to vertigo and imbalance; intolerable sensations, incapacitation, disorientation, nausea and vomiting (Hansen, 2007). Subjects exposed to infrasound at 5Hz and 10Hz with levels of 100dB–135dB reported feelings of fatigue, apathy and depression, pressure in the ears, a loss of concentration, drowsiness and vibrations of the internal organs (Karpova et al., 1970). In a study of airline pilots, Lidstrom (1978) found that long-term exposure to infrasound of 14Hz–16Hz at levels around 125dB caused decreased alertness, a faster decrease in the electrical resistance of the skin and an alteration in time perception. Other researchers have reported that infrasound exposure produced sensations of apprehension, visual effects, nausea and dizziness (Stephens, 1969), depression, fatigue and headaches (Gavreau, 1968). Gavreau (1968) further observed that ordinary man-made sources of infrasound such as fans and defective air conditioners may produce similar effects.

Anecdotally, many people report adverse physiological and psychological effects which they claim result from exposure to man-made infrasound. In response to a series of articles about the possible dangers of low-frequency noise (Anon., 1977a, 1977b), *The Sunday Mirror* received over 700 letters from readers describing a wide range of adverse health and psychological effects they attributed to low-frequency sounds, including severe headaches, nausea, palpitations, dizziness, extreme fatigue, visual hallucinations, disturbed sleep, nightmares and suicidal thoughts.

From the various studies of the biological effects it would appear that the effects of exposure to infrasound may be variable. Studies carried out using animals have also reported adverse effects from exposure to infrasound.

Measuring Low-Frequency Sound and Infrasound

A number of techniques are available to detect and measure low-frequency sound and infrasound. At the lowest frequencies (i.e. below 1.5Hz) seismometers are normally used for measuring infrasound in the form of structural vibration from tectonic sources such as earthquakes and volcanoes (Garces et al., 1998) and man-made mining explosions (Hegarty et al., 1999). Micro-barometers are preferred for the detection and measurement of infrasound transmitted through the air. These devices are highly accurate and were originally developed for the detection of infrasound generated by atomic bomb tests. They have also been used for the study of meteors, thunderstorms and weather-related phenomena, mainly in the range 0.1–5Hz (McKisic, 1997).

For higher infrasound frequencies (typically those above 5Hz) microphone-based measuring systems are commonly employed, such as the Bruel and Kjaer Type 2209 sound-level meter. This meter employs a microphone that is sensitive to 1Hz and can be connected to a Fast Fourier Transform (FFT) analyser such as the Zonic AND Type 3525 to allow spectrum analysis measurements to be made. Many of these systems have been developed to allow environmental noise measurement to be made, and the measurements are weighted using electronic filtering in order to replicate as closely as possible normal thresholds of human hearing. This has led to the development of a series of filters optimised to cover a range of different environmental and acoustic conditions. The most commonly used is the 'A' filter, which is designed for general environmental monitoring. However, a major drawback of the 'A' weighting scale is that it underestimates the importance of frequencies below 100 Hz (Berglund et al., 1996). Alternative weighting filters have been developed for specialist measurement of sounds having a significant low-frequency component, these include the 'C' filter, which is recommended for artillery noise (Schomer, 1981), and the 'D' filter, which is used for aircraft noise measurement. Both of these commonly used filters are based on hand-extrapolations into the lower frequencies and are not based upon empirical low-frequency data (Goldstein, 1994). The best noise weighting for infrasound remains to be settled but Bullen, Hede and Job (1991) found that equal energy units, sometimes called Zero or 'Z' weighting, has often provided the most effective predictor for community reaction to infrasound. Such environmental monitoring systems are expensive. Additionally, there is as yet no single standard for the measurement of environmental low-frequency sound and infrasound, which can result in difficulties when trying to make comparisons between existing studies.

Acoustic Research Infrasound Detector

With the advent of powerful personal computers it is now possible to perform measurement and analysis of these low-frequency sounds using a laptop computer and suitable software. Microphones that can operate effectively down to as low as 1 Hz remain almost prohibitively expensive but it has been possible to adapt existing loudspeaker technology to construct a microphone that will respond accurately at very low frequencies. This concept has been the basis for the author's infrasound measuring system known as the Acoustic Research Infrasound Detector (ARID; Parsons & O'Keeffe, 2008). ARID used the principle that a loudspeaker is in effect a microphone operating in reverse. A pair of large-diameter loudspeakers can be modified so that they can be used as large microphones sensitive to frequencies below 1 Hz. Signal processing is then carried out using a laptop PC with adapted available FFT spectrum analysis software.

Early trials with ARID proved that the concept worked well in practice, although the first system was bulky to transport and was occasionally prone to picking up structural vibrations via the stands. The biggest drawback with the ARID system, however, was a lack of any accepted calibration standard, and whilst we had great confidence in the resultant data, it was felt that an improved system could be developed. Continued work has resulted in a new system, referred to as ARID2. This new system replaces the earlier 'loudspeaker' microphones with a pair of one-inch-diameter dual-diaphragm air-pressure transducers housed in modified microphone cases, together with an improved Analogue to Digital (D/A) converter and modified software.

The use of microphone cases means that commercial anti-vibration mounts for the transducers can be used, thus reducing structural vibration noise affecting the measurements. Improvements to the D/A converter, fully balanced and shielded cables, and the improved software have resulted in lower instrument noise levels and therefore improved data sampling and quality. Data sampling can be obtained continuously or at any user-selected interval from 1 s to 23 h 59 m. The biggest advantage the new system offers is that it has been possible to calibrate the data to current ANSI (1) sound measurement standards.

Environmental sound-measuring equipment is normally designed to measure the peak sound pressure level (Lpeak) or an equalised value (Leq) over a selected period of time. Sudden (impulse) high acoustic pressure sounds; for example, the sudden closing of a door, footsteps and wind gusts, may cause erroneously high infrasound measurements. Measurement errors can also be caused by short-duration and transient events, such as passing vehicles or the operation of machinery. In order to minimise any measuring errors resulting from such sounds, measurement of low-frequency sound should be made over a period of several minutes or more (DIN: 4560, 1997). ARID measurements are obtained over a 15-minute period, which gives an Leq result that should remove measurement errors caused by impulse and transient events.

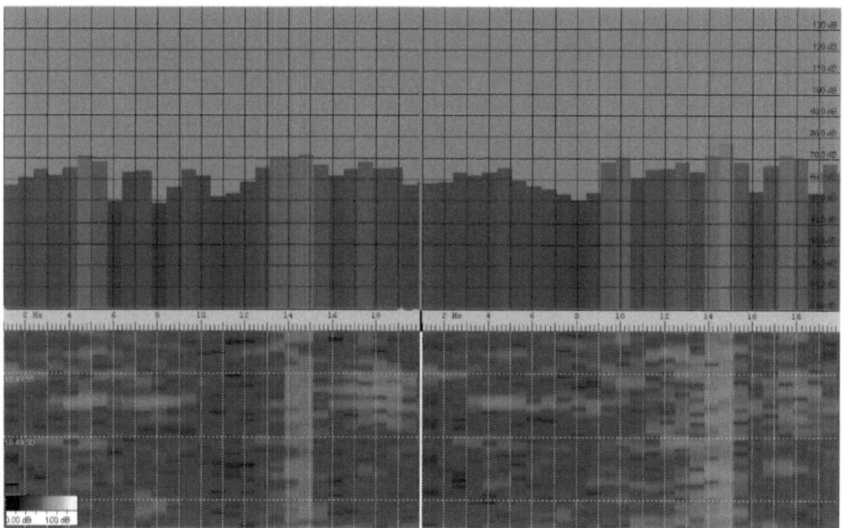

Figure 2. Typical ARID infrasound data screenshot: 0.1 Hz–20 Hz, 0 dBS–130 dBS.

Infrasound and the paranormal

Historical Links

Early investigators of the paranormal recognised that vibrations were a component in some reported haunt and poltergeist cases. Harry Price, for example, included a bowl of mercury in his personal ghost-hunting kit for the detection of tremors in a room or passage (Price, 1974, p.31). Price was also aware of the ability of certain notes and sounds to cause a sympathetic vibration in other objects. For example, he observed that in one case a particular pealing of nearby church bells caused the wires of a piano in a haunted house to vibrate in sympathy, leading to the residents reporting that ghostly music was at times being played by unseen hands (Price, 1974, p. 38).

Earlier researchers of psychical reports also noted that sound vibrations played a mysterious part in the production of psychic phenomena (Fodor & Lodge, 1933). None of the early investigators directly mention infrasound, as the concept of low-frequency sounds that exist below the normal human hearing range did not gain general scientific recognition until the 1940s. Later research shows greater familiarity with infrasound. In an experiment that was set up to examine vibrations and jolts associated with poltergeist activity, Gauld and Cornell (1979) used a powerful mechanical vibrator attached to a group of abandoned houses that were scheduled for demolition. This created powerful vibrations throughout the structure of the building and could be set to vibrate at frequencies between 45Hz and 120Hz. The aim of the experiments was to test the claim that geophysical forces might be responsible for some aspects of poltergeist activity. The experiment would also have produced large amounts of infrasound within the building as the various structures were vibrated by the powerful machinery. The investigators did not report any anomalous physiological or psychological experiences during any of these experiments and confined their reporting of results to observed physical effects upon the structure.

The first direct claim of a possible causal link between infrasound exposure and reported anomalous experiences was made by Persinger (1974). He stated that:–

> Infrasound, however, is an excellent candidate for at least some types of precognitive experiences. Weak infrasound energy from ambient sources could evoke vague responses and lead to reports of feelings of foreboding, depression or impending doom ahead of natural phenomena such as earthquakes or storms.

The exploration of any potential link between infrasound and paranormal experiences was not undertaken for many years, possibly because of the perceived technical difficulties in properly measuring infrasound energy within a haunt location and the lack of data relating to levels of ambient infrasound within the environment.

The Development of a Case for Infrasound and the Paranormal

Increased paranormal interest followed the publication by Tandy and Lawrence (1998) of their infrasound hypothesis. They suggested a causal role for infrasound in some instances of haunt phenomena and apparitions. The initial suggestion was based upon the observed effects on a metal sword blade and the anecdotal reports of paranormal experiences within the same location. The source of the infrasound was traced by trial and error to a defective fan within the haunted workplace. The actual frequency and amplitude of the infrasound were never directly measured but they were estimated from the authors' personal experiences, mathematical calculations and the observation of the effects (Tandy & Lawrence, 1998). The authors also noted similarities in psycho-physiological effects reported by workers exposed to low-frequency fan noise originally reported by Tempest (1976). A key suggestion of this research was that infrasound at a specific frequency range (around 19Hz) was causing eyeball vibration and leading to visual effects that might be interpreted as apparitional encounters. Tandy later conducted a series of infrasound measurements in a 14th-century cellar beneath a tourist information centre in Coventry (Tandy, 2000). In this experiment objective measurements of the ambient infrasound were made using contemporary environmental monitoring equipment. He observed that a frequency of 19 Hz was present within the location, confirming his earlier observation. Tandy's infrasound hypothesis was quickly picked up by the media and the paranormal community, and seems to have been the catalyst for the claims now being made for infrasound involvement in paranormal cases.

Without exception, infrasound exposure studies carried out other than by paranormal investigators have been for the purposes of trying to establish whether there are any adverse human health or performance implications in people who are exposed to infrasound in the workplace. These studies have predominantly used pure-tone infrasound at high or very high amplitudes or long exposure periods in their experimental design. The use of pure tones in many of the infrasound exposure studies may severely restrict the applicability of their findings to real-world situations, since ambient infrasound from both natural and man-made sources is almost without exception in the form of broadband noise consisting of fundamental notes, harmonics and resonant frequencies. The findings from these studies were reviewed earlier in this paper and describe feelings of anxiety or dread, nausea, sickness and sudden onset of headaches, effects that are similar to those reported in spontaneous paranormal cases. Initially, this similarity of experience may seem impressive and should certainly not be dismissed, but a number of problems remain to be addressed. For example, Kawano, Yamaguchi and Funasaka (1991) found that long-distance truck drivers who were exposed to infrasound at around 115 dB showed no statistically significant incidence of fatigue, subdued sensations or cardiovascular changes.

Should Paranormal Research be Interested in 19 Hz?

Studies by those interested in the possible links between reported paranormal experiences and infrasound exposure have so far tended to focus most of their experiments on infrasound frequencies of close to 19 Hz. Interest in this frequency range comes as a direct result of the papers produced by Tandy and Lawrence (1998), and Tandy (2000). The frequency was identified by a mathematical calculation (Tandy & Lawrence, 1998):–

> The following day V.T. was entering a fencing competition and needed to cut a thread onto the tang of a spare foil blade so that he could attach the handle. He had all the tools necessary but it was so much easier to use the engineer's bench vice in the lab to hold the blade that he went in early to cut the thread. It was only a five-minute job, so he put the blade in the vice and went in search of a drop of oil to help things along. As he returned, the free end of the blade was frantically vibrating up and down. Combining this with his experience from the previous night, he once again felt an immediate twinge of fright. However, vibrating pieces of metal were more familiar to him than apparitions so he decided to experiment. If the foil blade was being vibrated it was receiving energy which must have been varying in intensity at a rate equal to the resonant frequency of the blade. Energy of the type just described is usually referred to as sound. There was a lot of background noise but there could also be low-

> frequency sound or infrasound which V.T. could not hear. As it happens sound behaves fairly predictably in long thin tubes such as organ pipes and ex-garages joined end to end so V.T. started his experiment. He placed the foil blade in a drill vice and slid it along the floor. Interestingly the vibration got bigger until the blade was level with the desk (half way down the room); after the desk it reduced in amplitude, stopping altogether at the far end of the lab. V.T. and his colleagues were sharing their lab with a low frequency standing wave! The energy in the wave peaked in the centre of the room indicating that there was half a complete cycle. . . . Once V.T. knew this he calculated the frequency of the standing sound wave.

The mathematical calculation of the standing wave within the lab is based solely upon a single room dimension, specifically its length, given as 30ft, and a wavelength of twice the length of the room, i.e. 60ft.

Tandy used the formula given earlier to compute frequency as the velocity of sound (1139ft/sec) divided by wavelength (60ft), which equals 18.89Hz. Apparently no account was taken of the height or width of the room, the dimensions of which are not provided. In order to determine the acoustic properties of any space and accurately calculate the frequency of standing waves within the space, calculations involving all three dimensions of the space must be used.

Broadly speaking, three types of standing wave will exist inside any space (see Figures 4–6, taken from Bruel & Kjaer, 1982). The most powerful of these are Axial waves, which involve any two parallel surfaces, such as walls, or floor and ceiling. With Axial waves there are always sound-pressure maxima at the walls. In addition Tangential waves involve any two sets of parallel surfaces—all four walls, or two walls and the ceiling and floor. These are about half as strong as the Axial modes, and also give maxima at the walls. Oblique waves involve all six surfaces (four walls, the ceiling and the floor) and are about one quarter as strong as the Axial modes, and half as strong as the Tangential modes. Oblique modes, which are rarely of much relevance, also give sound pressure maxima at the walls.

It is noteworthy that with all three types of standing wave within a room or space there is always a pressure maximum at the walls—something which seems to be contrary to the observation made by Tandy: "interestingly, the vibration got bigger until the blade was level with the desk (half way down the

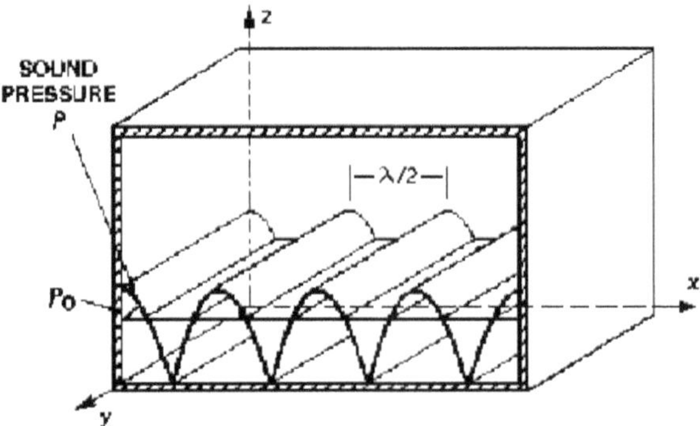

Figure 4. Axial room waves.

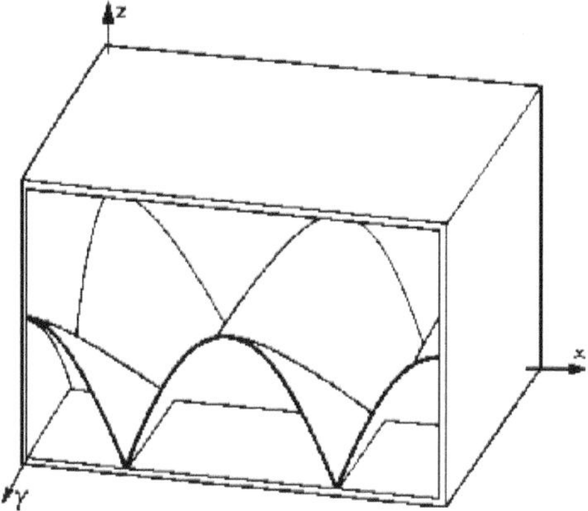

Figure 5. Tangential room waves.

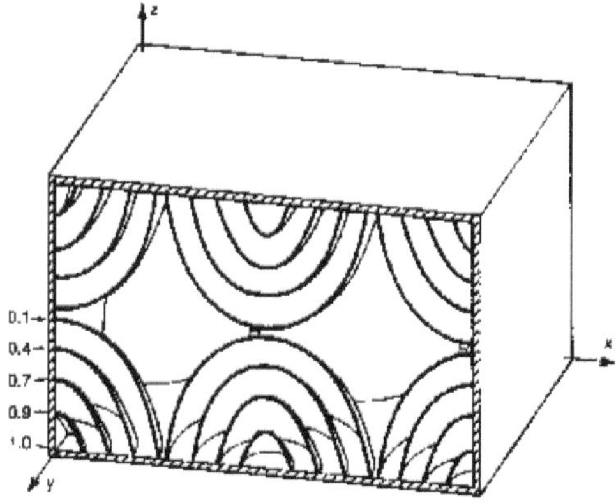

Figure 6. Oblique room waves.

room); after the desk it reduced in amplitude, stopping altogether at the far end of the lab." (Tandy & Lawrence, 1998). To calculate the frequencies of the axial, oblique and tangential modes, the following formula may be used:–

$$f = \frac{c}{2}\sqrt{\left(\frac{n_x}{L}\right)^2 + \left(\frac{n_y}{B}\right)^2 + \left(\frac{n_z}{H}\right)^2}$$

f = Frequency of the standing wave in Hz
c = Speed of sound (1139 ft/sec. at 20°C)
n_x = Order of the standing wave for room length
n_y = Order of the standing wave for room width
n_z = Order of the standing wave for room height
L, B, H = Length, width, and height of the room

Using the above formula and assuming the stated length of 30 ft and estimating a reasonable width of 12 ft and a height of 10 ft we are presented with a range of fundamental (first order) low-frequency standing waves present inside the lab room:–

18.8 Hz (x axial wave)	50.7 Hz (x-y tangential wave)	75.9 Hz (x-y-z oblique wave)
47.1 Hz (y axial wave)	59.6 Hz (x-z tangential wave)	
56.5 Hz (z axial wave)	73.5 Hz (y-z tangential wave)	

As can be seen, there is not one standing wave existing inside the lab room but several, all of which to a greater or lesser degree may have affected the sword blade. Furthermore, the authors do not provide any information regarding the dimensions, i.e. the length, width and thickness, of the blade that was seen to be vibrating; thus it is impossible for us to calculate the resonant frequency of the blade itself and to know which standing wave(s) might therefore have been responsible for producing the observed vibrations within it.

Without extensive measurements being undertaken it will be practically impossible to predict all the various effects that acoustic vibrations might produce within structural systems (Broch, 1980). Tandy's mathematical modelling of the standing wave within the lab also assumes that the source of the standing infrasound was a new fan fitted to the lab's extraction system. Turning off the fan caused the sword blade to cease vibrating and the untoward experiences also ceased, which might indicate that the fan was indeed the source of a standing wave. However, this could equally indicate that an infrasound standing wave of unknown frequency/ies had been formed by the interactions of the fan noise with an external infrasound source. We have seen that infrasound has been shown to be capable of travelling large distances without significant attenuation, and as no infrasound measurements were made within the lab, both with and without the fan, it is not possible to know which is the case here. Taking the above into consideration, it could be argued that the case for a 19 Hz standing wave effect is not as strong as it first appeared. This is further borne out by the pilot study in Edinburgh and the concert applications of infrasound, neither of which produced the visual hallucinations or the apparitional experiences that Tandy suggested were caused by a 19 Hz infrasound exposure.

Is Infrasound Being Measured Properly by Paranormal Researchers?

Tandy (2000) reports finding an infrasound standing wave at 19 Hz with amplitude of 38 dB in the haunted cellar. Unfortunately, he does not specify what weighting filter (if any) was applied to this measurement. As has already been described, the use of a filter weighting scale (i.e. A, B, C, or D) when obtaining infrasound measurements of the ambient levels of infrasound within the environment may result in the erroneous under-reporting of the actual levels present. Given the type of equipment used by Tandy (a Bruel & Kjaer Type 2209 sound-level meter), if one of the standard weighting filters was applied to the data, either the 'C' or more likely the 'A' weighting, its use could lead to a serious underestimate of the infrasound pressure levels. Broner (1978) describes a case in a London home where infrasound which was causing annoyance to the wife but not the husband was measured to be only 32 dB using 'A' weighting, but the SPL was actually measured at 63 dB.

In September 2006, immediately before its closure, the author was able to undertake a series of infrasound measurements at the haunted cellar in Coventry, using ARID to repeat the experiment carried out by Tandy. Replicating Tandy's placement, the microphone was positioned in the centre of the cellar with infrasound measurements being made automatically at one-minute intervals in the empty cellar. These previously unpublished measurements did not support his claim of finding a 19Hz standing wave within the cellar, although infrasound was found to be present at a broad range of frequencies, exceeding 30dBS between 20Hz and 2Hz, with a peak at 44dBS at 5.7Hz.

It is difficult to make any further comparisons between the two infrasound surveys because of the variability of location of infrasound production on account of changes in the ambient sources; plus not knowing the filter weighting that Tandy used for his measurements, and the lack of proper calibration for the prototype ARID system at that time.

Tandy (2000) acknowledges that his measured value of 38dB within the cellar is substantially lower than those previously reported to have effects on people, but suggests that as the effects are rather less spectacular this may simply be the result of the lower amplitudes found. Braithwaite and Townsend (2006) also make the point that there are no published studies that have found any implications for cognition or experience of infrasound as weak as this. In fact, as already noted, the actual levels of infrasound present may have been substantially higher and therefore much closer to those demonstrated to have produced effects. This difference in measuring and quoting infrasound levels between field and laboratory studies may also provide an explanation for the results of other experiments where low-amplitude infrasound has been suggested to have effects (Brown, 1973; Green & Dunn, 1968).

Another difficulty in determining infrasound amounts from field measurements is the sampling period used. In his experiments within the haunted cellar Tandy (2000) reports using a sample time of just 20 seconds. Although we are informed that the measurements were repeated a number of times it is not made clear whether the resultant data came from one sample period or were the average of a number. A short sampling period of 20 seconds will inevitably involve the overall measured infrasound values being affected by transient high-energy events; for example, a passing bus or other vehicle or the slamming of a nearby door. Weather effects and weather interactions with the structure of the location being measured such as a wind gust might also generate infrasound during the sampling period. Using a longer sampling period would permit such transients to be taken in account and would allow a more realistic assessment of the true ambient infrasound levels to be made. The author's own measurements at the haunted cellar showed that there were indeed short-duration infrasound events caused by passing vehicles, including buses and delivery vehicles. It was also discovered that the presence of people within the cellar contributed significantly to the production of infrasound. Increases in the measured infrasound levels of between approximately 15 and 30dBS were recorded as members of the experimental team moved and walked about within the cellar. Tandy records that he vacated the cellar prior to his measurements being carried out. However, the original incidents took the form of visitors' personal anomalous experiences during tours of the historic cellar, suggesting that vacating the cellar may not have provided an accurate reflection of the prevailing conditions at the time of the original incident(s).

Following the death of Tandy there had been little effective research into the possible involvement of infrasound in the production of paranormal experiences. However, since 2006, the author has undertaken a series of broadband infrasound measurements using ARID at a number of locations around the UK, and has conducted a number of experiments to study the link between infrasound exposure and reports of anomalous and paranormal experiences. A pilot study was carried out at a former shipyard on Merseyside during 2006 (Para.Science, 2007). The location had a reputation among staff of being haunted, and paranormal investigators reported physiological and psychological effects that might be associated with infrasound exposure. Results of the pilot study suggested a strong link between high ambient levels of infrasound (up to 80dBS) at frequencies between 7Hz and 15Hz and reports of anomalous experiences in the percipients. The source of the powerful ambient infrasound was traced to the engines and associated equipment of ships berthed in an adjacent dock. A psychic medium also reported changes within the 'psychic energies' at the location that closely corresponded to the objectively measured regions of high levels of ambient man-made infrasound.

Infrasound Exposure Pilot Study

During 2007, the author was part of a team that conducted a pilot study at the Real Mary Kings Close tourist attraction in Edinburgh as part of their annual *GhostFest* event. A controlled level of infrasound was produced using the author-designed infrasound generator, Acoustic Research Infrasound Array (ARIA). Throughout the study period ambient levels of infrasound were measured using ARID2. Hourly tour groups to Mary Kings Close were unknowingly subjected to either only the ambient infrasound that is normally present or the ambient infrasound plus experimenter-produced high-level (>100dBS) infrasound at a frequency of 18.9Hz. The route of the tours and the commentary of the tour guides were observed and remained consistent for all the tour groups. The physical conditions such as lighting and temperature within the location were constant throughout the period of the study. Upon completion of the tour the subjective anomalous experiences of 439 individuals were surveyed. The results obtained strongly indicated that infrasound exposure played a significant role in the production of subjective paranormal experiences for around one-third of the total survey. However, the study failed to demonstrate any of the visual disturbances and resulting apparitional experiences that Tandy had suggested would be created by exposure to the frequency range around 18Hz (Para.Science, 2008).

ARIA has also been used in two public performances (Silent Sound, 2006, 2010) in which a frequency of 18.9Hz was produced at an SPL exceeding 90dBS. Anecdotal accounts from participants and audience members did indicate a significant number of psycho-physiological effects, such as feeling ill at ease, anxiousness and physical discomfort, being experienced when ARIA was in use. For example, during the first performance with ARIA at the 2006 Silent Sound performance held in Liverpool St George's Hall a number of the musicians within the auditorium reported feeling unwell and nauseous and were unable to play their instruments, ultimately abandoning the room during a rehearsal session as the output level of ARIA was being set. During this set-up test infrasound levels of more than 90dBS were measured at 10m from the infrasound generator. Following the ARIA test, the author also discovered that on the ground level, three floors below the auditorium, a security guard had also reported feeling suddenly unwell and had left the building. None of these unfortunate side-effects of the infrasound exposure lasted more than a few minutes and they ceased once the infrasound generator was switched off. For the actual performance infrasound levels of 60dBS were used (measured at 10m from the infrasound generator). Following the performance audience members and several musicians anecdotally reported unexpected sensations, including vertigo, pressure in the ears and the sensation of 'having something pressed tightly over the head'. Similar experiences were reported during the 2010 concert held in Middlesbrough. At neither performance were any visual or apparitional experiences reported.

The 'Haunt' Project

Tandy's hypothesis that infrasound may be responsible for inducing anomalous sensations was tested by French, Haque, Bunton-Stasyshyn and Davis (2009) in the 'Haunt' Project, which used infrasound to investigate the possibility of creating an artificially 'haunted' room. Specifically, they investigated whether exposure to infrasound, complex electromagnetic fields, or both in combination, would lead to an increased reporting of anomalous sensations in participants, compared with a baseline condition. The room was a circular chamber of wood, fabric and canvas built inside an empty room approximately 4m × 4m (based upon the plans of the experimental area). A pair of electromagnetic coils were hidden outside the chamber along with a single infrasound speaker positioned outside the chamber in a corner of the main room. The infrasound was generated by "combining two sine waves at 18.9Hz and 22.3Hz" output via a "purpose-built cabinet" These frequencies were chosen to be representative of the infrasound recorded by Tandy in the Coventry cellar. Participants each spent 50 minutes in the chamber and recorded on a floor plan a brief description of any anomalous sensations that they experienced, also noting their position within the chamber and the time the sensation was experienced. The participants were randomly allocated to experimental conditions according to the presence or absence of infrasound and electromagnetic field.

Many of the participants reported having anomalous sensations, a number of which have previously been linked to infrasound exposure: dizzy or odd feelings (79.7%), spinning around (49.4%), tingling sensations (32.9%) and pleasant vibrations through their bodies (31.6%). Other sensations linked to infrasound exposure were also reported, including the sense of presence (22.8%), terror (8.9%) and sexual arousal (5.1%). Sensations that may be associated to infrasound were additionally reported such as hearing a 'ticking sound' (25.3%). This may have been the result of changes within the air pressure caused by the infrasound acting on the ear or acting upon some structural component within the room or chamber and causing resonance. Sensations were reported that have no association with infrasound exposure, such as the participants feeling they were somewhere else (32.9%), feeling detached from their bodies (22.8%), sadness (11.4%) and odd smells (10.1%).

The researchers reported that they had failed to find any support for a link between the presence of infrasound and the experiencing of anomalous sensations, suggesting that "the case for infrasound inducing haunt-type experiences now appears to be extremely weak". However, this experiment fails to address properly a number of issues relating to the physics of infrasound, so this conclusion seems unsound. In order to establish undetectable levels of infrasound within the chamber a series of pilot trials were carried out, participants being asked to indicate when they became aware of the infrasound stimulus at a range of frequencies: 15Hz, 17Hz, 19Hz, 21Hz, 23Hz and 25Hz. During this pilot it was determined that "no participant was able to perceive infrasound at a level below 75dB". It is not stated what equipment or method was used to obtain these sound-level data or what (if any) weighting was applied to the measurements. As previously discussed, it is perfectly possible that significantly higher amplitudes of low-frequency ambient sound and infrasound may have been present throughout the entire experiment without being measured by the experimenters. Moreover, the use of two combined sine waves (18.9Hz and 22.3Hz) will result in the production of secondary frequencies as a result of inter-modulation between the two primary signals. These secondary tones (harmonics) are equal to the sum and difference of the two primary frequencies, i.e. $f_1 \pm f_2$ (3.4Hz and 41.2Hz). Other harmonic frequencies well within the region of normal human hearing might also be expected to be present. The experiment also did not consider interactions of the infrasound within the room itself caused by reflected and refracted sound waves bouncing off the walls, floor and ceiling and the possible effects upon the participants as they walked through what might have been large variations in both the sound frequencies presented, although interestingly the experimenters noted in relation to the electromagnetic field that "the nature of the field itself can vary infinitely and the participants' movements through the field will add an extra level of complexity to the field as experienced". Measurements that were made are stated to be "50dB with all the equipment turned off, 65dB with the air-conditioning switched on and 75dB" when the infrasound was switched on. No information was provided about the sound-measuring equipment that was used or any indication whether any frequency weighting was applied to the measurements. Without this crucial information about the ambient infrasound levels present, the experimenters' argument against the role of infrasound as a causal factor in the production of anomalous sensations reported by the participants must be questioned.

Should Paranormal Researchers be Interested in Infrasound at all?

The work by Tandy and Lawrence (1998) and Tandy (2000) remains the only real basis for the assumption of an infrasonic involvement in personal experiences at haunt locations. Inevitably, such primary studies are flawed because there is little or no preceding data for the authors to make use of when developing their arguments. However, there are clear similarities between the reported experiences and sensations of those people who have experienced infrasound and those reporting paranormal experiences and sensations. The author's preliminary studies in the former shipyard and in Mary Kings Close, together with the anecdotal reports from the infrasound concerts, also strongly suggest that infrasound is a component in the production or enhancing of reported paranormal experiences. The suggestion of a link between infrasound and reported paranormal experiences was also tested in 2003 in a series of 'Soundless Music' concerts that took place in Liverpool and London (Arenda & Thackara, 2003). Questionnaires handed to the audience elicited a range of reported experiences. Many unusual experiences were reported during the concerts, ranging from the emotional (e.g. 'sense of sorrow'), 'brief moment of anxiety' and 'excited' to the physiological (e.g. 'increased heart-rate'), 'headache', 'tingling in neck and shoulders', 'nausea', 'sense of coldness' (Infrasonic, 2003). The 'Soundless Music' concerts used an infrasound frequency of 17 Hz but from their own spectral measurements of the infrasound we can readily see that infrasound is present at all frequencies below 20 Hz at considerable intensity.

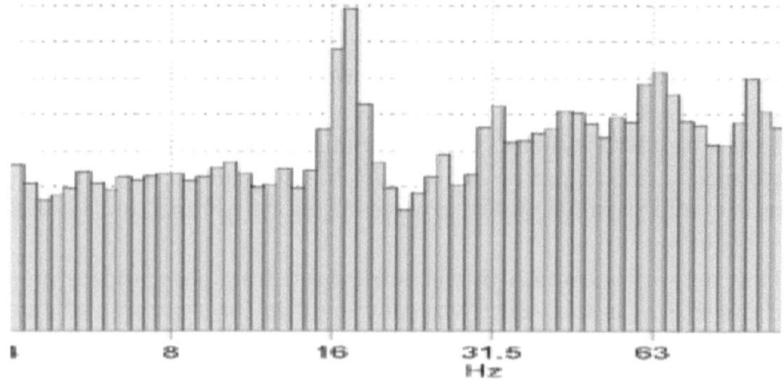

Figure 7. Spectral plot from Silent Sound concert (Infrasonic, 2003).

Susceptibility to psycho-physiological effects of infrasound exposure seems to be linked to both exposure duration and overall sound-pressure level (Kitamura & Yamada, 2002). Prolonged exposure to low infrasound pressure levels has been suggested as a likely cause of adverse psycho-physiological effects (Benton, 1997). Although the limited research does not directly indicate it, it might be fair to assume that short-duration exposure to high infrasound pressure levels may cause similar effects. Existing research does indicate that exposure to high levels of low-frequency sound at concerts or in some industry explosions does cause aural pain and other physical effects; such effects may be temporary or permanent (Fearn, 1973).

A key problem lies with the lack of information about levels of ambient infrasound at haunt locations. Such studies that are available have been made either following noise complaints or for the establishment of safe exposure limits and thresholds within high noise environments. This lack of baseline data is a crucial problem for paranormal researchers seeking to test or develop the case for an infrasound involvement and must be addressed urgently if meaningful research is to continue. The ongoing survey also measures the infrasound at similar or co-located control (non-haunt) sites in order to ascertain whether there are any significant differences in the ambient infrasound frequencies and amplitudes at haunt locations compared with the control sites. The survey also undertakes measurements of the ambient infrasound at a wide range of locations regardless of any paranormal association or reports, in order to establish a set of baseline ambient infrasound data to support future infrasound studies. The need for such baseline data was also highlighted by Braithwaite and Townsend (2006).

From the limited studies conducted to date and the knowledge that infrasound is produced by so many natural and man-made sources, it now seems highly likely that infrasound is just one of many factors that may lead to the reporting of anomalous or paranormal experiences by some individuals. A number of other possibilities are indicated:–

(i) Infrasound alone does not produce anomalous and paranormal experiences.

(ii) The frequency range around 18Hz does not produce the apparitional experiences as suggested by Tandy and Lawrence.

(iii) That infrasound presented at a range of frequencies is more likely to produce reports of anomalous and paranormal experiences than single-frequency infrasound.

(iv) That a rapid variation in the infrasound frequency and/or amplitude i.e. > 1Hz per second or 3dB per second is more likely to contribute to the reporting of anomalous and paranormal experiences than infrasound that is constant or is slowly changing.

(v) That a small variation in the infrasound frequency and/or amplitude, i.e. ±2Hz or ±3dB, is more likely to contribute to the reporting of anomalous and paranormal experiences than greater variations.

A series of studies are under way or are being planned to test the indicated possibilities. Further developments of both ARID and ARIA are planned which will permit better measurements of the ambient infrasound to be made and to support further studies of infrasound exposure experiences.

7 Ashdale Lane
Llangwn, Haverfordwest SA62 4NU parascience@btinternet.com

REFERENCES

Altmann, J. (1999) *Acoustic Weapons, A Perspective Assessment: Sources, Propagation and effects of Strong Sound.* Occasional Paper #22, Cornell University Peace Studies Program. New York.

Anon. (1977a) Hounded by this nagging noise. *The Sunday Mirror (26th June).*

Anon. (1977b) Hum—that mystery noise that drives sobbing wife out of the house. *The Sunday Mirror (3rd July).*

Arenda, B. and Thackara, D. (2003) *Experiment: Conversations in Art and Science.* The Wellcome Trust.

Backteman, O., Kohler, J. and Sjoberg, L. (1983) Infrasound: tutorial review, Part 2. *Journal of Low-Frequency Noise and Vibration 2,* 176–210.

Berglund, B., Hassmen, P. and Job, R. F. (1996) Sources and effects of low-frequency noise. *Journal of the Acoustical Society of America 99 (5),* 2985–3002.

Blazier, W. E. (1981) Revised noise criteria for application in the acoustical design and rating of HVAC systems. *Journal of Noise Control Engineering 16,* 64–73.

Braithwaite, J. and Townsend, M. (2006) Good vibrations: the case for a specific effect of infrasound in instances of anomalous experience has yet to be empirically demonstrated. *JSPR 70,* 211–224.

Broner, N. (1978) The effects of low-frequency noise on people. *Journal of Sound Vibration 58,* 483–500.

Brown. (1973) New worries about unheard sound. *New Scientist,* 414 (*8th November).*

Brüel and Kjaer (1982) Sound Intensity. Part 1: Theory. *Technical Review 1982 (3).*

Bruel, P. V. and Olesen, H. P. (1973) Infrasonic measurements. *Paper Presented at the Inter-Noise Conference, Copenhagen, 1973.*

Bullen, R. B., Hede, A. J. and Job, R. F. S. (1991) Community reaction to noise from an artillery range. *Noise Control Engineering Journal 37,* 115–128.

Challis. L. A. (1978) Low-frequency noise problems from gas turbine stations. *Proceedings Internoise 78,* 475–480.

Chen, Y. H. Q. and Hanmin, S. (2004) An investigation on the physiological and psychological effects of infrasound on persons. *Journal of Low-Frequency Noise Vibration and Active Control 23 (1),* 71–76.

Corso, J. F. (1958) Absolute thresholds for tones of low frequency. *American Journal of Psychology 71,* 367–374.

DIN: 4560 (1997) *Measurement and Evaluation of Low-Frequency Environmental Noise.*

Fearn, R. (1973) Pop music and hearing damage. *Journal of Sound and Vibration 29,* 396–397.

Feynman, R. P., Leighton, R. and Sands, M. (1963) *The Feynman Lectures on Physics, Vol.1,* ch.49. New York: Addison-Wesley.

Fielding, Y. and O'Keeffe, C. (2006) *Ghost Hunters: A Guide to Investigating the Paranormal.* London: Hodder & Stoughton.

Fields, J. M. (2001) *An Updated Catalog of 521 Social Surveys of Resident's Reaction to Environmental Noise.* NASA Report, NASA/CR-2001-211257.

Fodor, N. and Lodge, O. (1933) *Encyclopedia of Psychic Science.* London: Arthurs Press.

French, C. C., Haque, U., Bunton-Stasyshyn, R. and Davis, R. (2009) The 'Haunt' Project: an attempt to build a 'haunted' room by manipulating complex electromagnetic fields and infrasound. *Cortex 45 (5),* 619–629.

Frost, G. P. (1987) An investigation into the microstructure of the auditory threshold and of the loudness function in the near threshold region. *Journal of Low-Frequency Noise Vibration 6,* 34–39.

Gamberale, F., Goldstein, M., Kjellberg, A., Liszka, L., and Lofstedt, P. (1982) *Perceived Loudness and Annoyance of Low-Frequency Noise.* Stockholm: Arbete & Halsa.

Garces, M., Hegarty, M. and Schwartz, S. (1998) Magma acoustics and the time-varying melt properties at Arenal volcano, Costa Rica. *Geophysical Research Letters 25 (13),* 2239–2296.

Gauld, A. and Cornell, A. D. (1979) *Poltergeists.* London: Routledge & Kegan Paul.

Gavreau, V. (1966) Infra Sons: Générateurs, Détecteurs, Propriétés physiques, Effets biologiques. *Acustica 17 (1),* 1–10.

Gavreau V. (1968) Infrasound. *Science Journal 4,* 33–37.

Goldstein, M. (1994) *Low-Frequency Components in Complex Noise and their Perceived Loudness and Annoyance.* Unpublished PhD dissertation, Stockholm University.

Gossard, E. E. and Hooke, W. H. (1975) *Waves in the Atmosphere.* Elsevier Science Publishers, USA.

Green, J. F. and Dunn, F. (1968) Correlation of naturally occurring infrasonics and selected human behavior. *The Journal of the Acoustical Society of America 44 (5),* 1456–1457.

Hansen, C. H. (2007) *The Effects of Low-Frequency Noise and Vibration on People.* Essex: Multi-Science Publishing.

Harris, C. S., Sommer, H. C. and Johnson, D. L. (1976) Review of the effects of infrasound on man. *Aviation and Space Environmental Medicine 47,* 582–586.

Hegarty, M., Kim, W. and Martysevich, P. (1999) Characteristics of infrasound produced by large mining explosions in Kazakstan. *Proceedings of the 21st Annual Seismic Research Symposium: Technologies for Monitoring the Comprehensive Nuclear Test-Ban Treaty, Las Vegas, USA, 1999.*

Infrasonic. (2003) Infrasonic—Summary of results 31st May, 2003, Purcell Room, London. http://www.spacedog.biz/extras/Infrasonic/infrasonicResults.htm [Accessed 1st December 2011]

Jerger, J., Alford, B., Coats, A. and French, B. (1966) Effects of very low frequency tones on auditory thresholds. *Journal of Speech and Hearing Research 9,* 150–160.

Job, R. F. S. (1993) Psychological factors of community reaction to noise. In Vallet, M. (ed.) *Noise as a Public Health Problem, Vol. 3,* 48–70. France: INRETS.

Karpova, N. I., Alekseev, S. V., Erohkin, V., Kayskina, E. N. and Reutov, R. P. (1970) Early response of the organism to low-frequency acoustic oscillations. *Noise and Vibration Bulletin 11,* 100–103.

Kawano, A., Yamaguchi, H. and Funasaka, S. (1991) Effects of infrasound on humans: a questionnaire survey of 145 drivers of long-distance transport trucks. *Practical Ortology 84,* 1324–1325.

Kitamura, T. and Yamada, S. (2002) Psychological analysis of sufferers of low-frequency noise and relation between brain structure and psychological response. *Proceedings of the 10th International Meeting on Low-Frequency Noise and Vibration and its Control, York, UK, 2002.*

Leventhall, G., Pelmear, P. and Benton, S. (2003) *A Review of Published Research on Low-Frequency Noise and its Effects,* 7. London: DEFRA Publications.

Lidstrom, I. M. (1978) The effects of infrasound on humans. *Investigation Report (UMEA) 33,* 1–42.

Lisker, L. and Abramson, A. (1970) The voicing dimension: some experiments in comparative phonetics. *Proceedings of the 6th International Congress of Phonetic Sciences, 1967. Prague:* Academia.

Lydolf, M. and Moller, H. (1997) New measurements of the threshold of hearing and equal loudness contours at low frequencies. *Proceedings of the 8th International Meeting on Low-Frequency Noise and Vibration, Gothenburg, 1997,* 76–84.

Masterton, R. B. (1992) Role of the central auditory system in hearing: the new direction. *Trends in Neurosciences 15,* 280–285.

McKisic, J. M. (1997) Infrasound and the infrasonic monitoring of atmospheric nuclear explosions. *USAF Technical report, PL-TR-97-2123, Phillips Labaratory, Hanscom AFB.* USA: US Dept of Defense.

Mihan House, S. (2005) *Infrasonic Wave Propagation Over Near Regional and Tele-Infrasonic Distances.* Ann Arbour: ProQuest Information & Learning.

Moller, H. (1984) Physiological and psychological effects of infrasound on humans. *Journal of Low-Frequency Noise Vibration 3 (1),* 1–17.

Moller, H. and Andresen, J. (1984) Loudness of pure tones at low and infrasonic frequencies. *Journal of Low-Frequency Noise Vibration 3 (1),* 78–87.

Nishimura, K., Kudoda, M. and Yoshida, Y. (1987) The pituitary adenocorticol response in rats and human subjects exposed to infrasound. *Journal of Low-Frequency Noise Vibration 6,* 18–28.

Ostdiek, V. and Bord, D. (2000) *Inquiry into Physics.* USA: Brooks/Cole.

Para.Science (2007) Cammell Laird Shipyard, Birkenhead. http://www.parascience.org.UK/investigations/laird/laird.htm [accessed 1st December, 2011]

Para.Science (2008) Mary Kings Ghost Fest, 2007 — Preliminary results. http://www.parascience.org.uk/mkgfr.htm [accessed 1st December 2011]

Parsons, S. and O'Keeffe, C. (2008) Acoustic Research Infrasound Detector. *JSPR 72,* 51–57.

Persinger, M. A. (1974) *The Paranormal: Part II. Mechanisms and Models.* New York: MSS Information Corporation.

Pichon, A. L., Guilbert, J., Vega, A., Garces, M. and Brachet, N. (2002) Ground-coupled air waves and diffracted infrasound from the Arequipa earthquake of June 23, 2001. *Geophysical Research Letters 29 (18),* 331–334.

Price, H. (1974) *Confessions of a Ghost Hunter (Causeway Edition).* New York: Causeway Books.

Schomer, P. D. (1981) Community reaction to impulse noise: initial Army survey. *US Army Construction Engineering Research Laboratory, Technical Report N-100.* Champaign Il.

Silent Sound. (2006 and 2010) http://www.silentsound.info/sound_silentsound.html [accessed 1st May 2010]

Stephens, R. W. B. (1969) Infrasonics. *Ultrasonics (January),* 30–35.

Stevens, S. S. (1975) *Psychophysics: Introduction to its Perceptual, Neural and Social Prospects.* New York: Willey.

Stubbs, C. (2005) Tactical infrasound. *JASON, JSR-03-520.* Virginia: The MITRE Corporation.

StudioSixDigital http://www.studiosixdigital.com www.apple.com/itunes/

Svidovyl, V. I. and Kuklina, O. I. (1985) State of the 3-hemolymph circulatory bed of the conjunctiva as affected by infrasound. *Noise and Vibration Bulletin,* 153–154.

Talbot-Smith, M. (1994) *Audio Recording and Reproduction: Practical Measures for Audio Enthusiasts.* London: Newnes.

Tandy, V. (2000) Something in the cellar. *JSPR 64,* 129–140.

Tandy, V. (2002) A litmus test for infrasound. *JSPR 66,* 167–174.

Tandy, V. and Lawrence, T. R. (1998) The ghost in the machine. *JSPR 62,* 360–364.

Tempest, W. (1971) Noise makes drivers drunk. *The Observer (28th November).*

Tempest, W. (1976) *Infrasound and Low-Frequency Vibration.* London: Academic Press.

Usher, N. (1977) Pitch discrimination at low frequencies. *Acoustics Letters 1,* 36–37.

von Gierke, H. E. and Parker D. E. (1976) Infrasound. In Keidel, W. D. and Neff, W. D. (eds.) *The Handbook of Sensory Physiology Vol. 3,* 585–624. Berlin: Springer-Verlag.

von Gierke, H. E. and Nixon, C. W. (1976) Effects of intense infrasound on man. In Tempest, W. (ed.) *Infrasound and Low-Frequency Vibration,* 115–150. London: Academic Press.

Watanabe, T. and Moller, H. (1990) Low-frequency hearing thresholds in pressure field and free field. *Journal of Low-Frequency Noise Vibration 9,* 106–115.

Watson, L. (1973) *Supernature: The Natural History of the Supernatural,* 91–96. London: Hodder & Stoughton.

Westin, J. B. (1975) Infrasound: a short review of effects on man. *Aviation Space Environmental Medicine 46,* 1135–1140.

Yamada, S. (1980) Hearing of low-frequency sound and influence on the body. *Proceedings of the Conference on Low-Frequency Noise and Hearing, Aalborg, Denmark,* 95–102.

Yasunao, M., Yukio, T., Setsuo, M., Hiroki, Y., Kazuhiro, Y. and Jishnu, K. S. (2009) *An Investigation of the Perception Thresholds of Band-Limited Low-Frequency Noises: Influence of Bandwidth.* Essex: Multi-Science Publishing.

Yeowart, N. S., Bryan, M. and Tempest, W. (1967) The monaural MAP threshold of hearing at frequencies from 1.5 c/s to 100c/s. *Journal of Sound Vibrations 6,* 335–342.

Appendix: A Rough and Ready Test for Ambient Infrasound

Whilst techniques for measuring infrasound frequency and amplitude can be prohibitive both in terms of the equipment and cost, it is possible to undertake a simple test that will act as a rough guide to the presence or otherwise of significant levels of infrasound at a location. Tandy (2002) provides construction details for modifying a standard sound-level meter by the addition of a DIY low-pass filter network. This required a considerable expertise in electronics and integrated circuit construction techniques but did provide the user with a general indication of the amplitude of sound at frequencies below about 35 Hz. There is, however, a much simpler method for quickly determining if low-frequency sound and infrasound are present at significant levels.

This simple method exploits the filter weighting already built into most sound-level meters. Suitable meters can be readily obtained from a number of sources including online retailers for less than £25. The method can even be employed by use of a sound-level meter App for the iPhone (3GS, 4, 4S), Ipad 2 and Ipod Touch (4th Gen.) such as 'SPL' (StudioSix-Digital), but with a reduced degree of accuracy. In order to carry out this simple test the sound-level meter must have both 'A' and 'C' weighting filters. Two consecutive measurements of the ambient SPL are taken: the first measurement is made using the 'A' filter, noting the SPL value; a second measurement using the 'C' filter is carried out, again noting the SPL value. If the SPL value of 'C' is greater than 'A' this indicates that there are increased levels of low-frequency sound present. The greater the difference between the 'C' value and the 'A' value, the higher the level of low-frequency sound at the measurement location. If the SPL value of 'C' is significantly higher than 'A', i.e. 10dBS or more, then it is likely that appreciable levels of infrasound are likely to be present. The technique exploits the difference in weighting between the 'A' and 'C' filters in the low-frequency sound region (Figure 8)

Although no direct information about either the frequency or amplitude is provided by this technique, it does permit the user to make a judgement about the level of low-frequency sound and infrasound. The overall accuracy of this technique can be improved by making a series of consecutive measurements over a period of time and/or taking measurements using the time average (Leq) function that some meters provide.

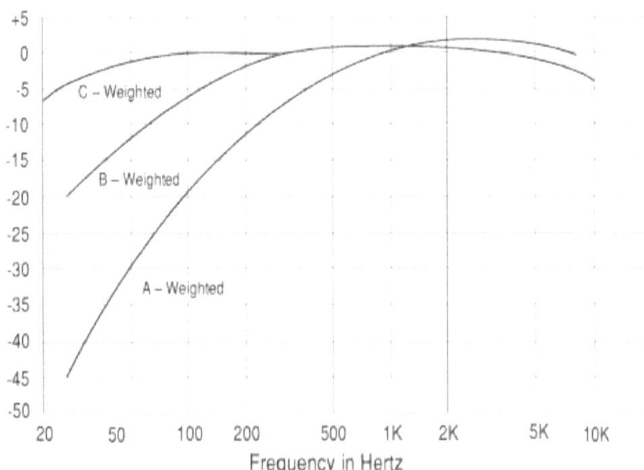

Figure 8. Comparison of sound-measurement weighting filters.

APPENDIX 6

A ROUGH & READY TEST FOR AMBIENT INFRASOUND

Steven Parsons

Whilst techniques for measuring infrasound frequency and amplitude can be prohibitive both in terms of the equipment and cost, it is possible to undertake a simple test that will act as a rough guide to the presence, or otherwise, of significant levels of infrasound at a location. Vic Tandy provided construction details for modifying a standard sound level meter by the addition of a DIY low-pass filter network in his 2002 paper *A Litmus Test for Infrasound*. This required a considerable degree of expertise in electronics construction techniques but did provide the user with a general indication of the amplitude of sound at frequencies below about 35Hz. There is, however, a much simpler method for quickly determining if low frequency sounds and infrasound is present within a location at significant levels.

This simple method exploits the filter weighting already built into most sound level meters. Suitable meters can be readily obtained inexpensively from a number of sources including online retailers. The method can even be employed by use of a suitable sound level meter 'App' for a number of smartphones and similar devices, but with a reduced degree of accuracy. In order to carry out this simple test, the sound level meter or app must have both 'A' & 'C' weighting filter options.

Two consecutive measurements of the ambient sound are taken: The first measurement is made using the 'A' filter, noting the numeric sound level value. It is better to make such a measurement over a period of at least a minute and note the highest value observed, some meters and apps permit peak measurement values to be stored which simplifies this process. Next, a second measurement using the 'C' filter is carried out, again noting the sound level value using the same method as before.

If the overall value of the 'C' weighted value is greater than the 'A' weighted value, this usually indicates that there are increased levels of low frequency sound present. The greater the difference between the 'C' value & the 'A' value, the higher the potential level of low frequency sound at the measurement location.

If the value of 'C' is significantly higher than 'A' i.e. 10dBS or more, then it is likely that appreciable levels of infrasound are also likely to be present.

This technique exploits the difference in the function of the filter weighting between the 'A' and 'C' filters in the low frequency sound region. It is important to note that although no direct information about either the frequency or amplitude is provided by this technique, it does permit the user to make a judgement about the amount of low frequency sound and infrasound likely to be present. The overall accuracy of this technique can be improved by making a series of consecutive measurements over a longer period of time and/or taking measurements using the time average (Leq) function that some meters provide.

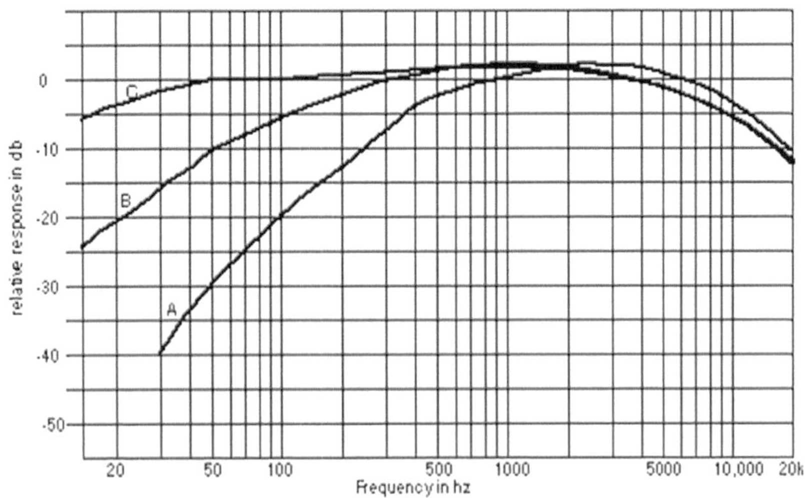

Comparison of the filter weighting at low and very low frequencies

APPENDIX 7

SOME PRACTICAL CONSIDERATIONS WHEN RECORDING SOUND DURING A LOCATION INVESTIGATION AND AFTERWARDS

Steven Parsons

Recording

The widespread use of easily portable and affordable sound recording equipment means that almost every investigator owns or carries at least one sound recorder when they conduct their investigations. Digital recording techniques and the Internet have resulted in many of the subsequent recordings being placed online. Some recordings are mislabelled as being Electronic Voice Phenomena (EVP) when in actual fact they are merely sound recordings of actual acoustic events. Whilst there are still some investigators who make use of tape-based analogue recording equipment, the majority these days use some form of digital recording equipment. But regardless of the technology that is employed, it seems surprising that so many of these recordings of claimed paranormal events and sounds are of relatively poor quality. Such recordings have little, if any, usefulness as evidence to support the claims that are being made. However, when one examines the techniques and methods that are used for location sound recording it may not be that much of a surprise to discover why so many poor quality recordings are made. In this digital era, many investigators pay little attention to the selection of the recorder, the choice of microphone, and the placement of their equipment. Sound recorders tend to be either carried or placed around with little apparent thought to the technical requirements of making a successful recording. Extraneous sounds, often made by the investigators themselves, can mask or override the apparently paranormal sounds. The overuse of domestic grade sound editing software in the name of analysis frequently leads to alterations and distortions of the recording that at best leave the recording liable to serious questioning and are more often worthless as proof of anything except a noisy sound being recorded.

Sound recording is an important asset to the ghost investigator in the search for information and objective verification of a witnesses' experience. It is only with due care and attention to the selection, use and placement of the equipment together with equal care being given to the post investigation handling and interpretation of the recordings, that sound recording will be a useful and helpful asset to the investigator.

The Recorder

Two different methods exist for the recording of sounds, analogue and digital. Both are merely a means of capturing a sound and storing a representation of the various amplitudes and the range of frequencies that make up that sound. As already discussed in more detail in **The Physics of Sound**, both methods have advantages and disadvantages that need to be considered by anyone who is seeking to record sound as part of the overall process of investigation. However, as the majority of recording is now carried out using some form of digital recorder, the following considerations will focus on that recording method.

The type and model of recorder chosen is often dictated by the budget. It may be tempting to get several less expensive models rather than fewer more costly machines but this is, I believe, a mistake. There is an old saying 'you get what you pay for' and it's generally good advice. More expensive recorders normally offer a better range of options for adjusting the recorder to suit the particular requirements of different locations and circumstances. For instance, a less expensive recorder designed for dictation and audio note taking may not be the best choice for trying to record the sound in a larger room due to limitations with the gain controls and possibly an inability to connect an external microphone. Cheaper machines are likely to be less well built, and make use of cheaper components. As a result, they tend to be less reliable and produce more electronic noise on the subsequent recording. There are some recorders that are advertised and sold on the basis that they are optimised for paranormal use and, in some instances, particular models of recorder have become highly sought after (and expensive) because of their perceived reputation as being better than other machines for recording 'paranormal' sounds. Such claims and reputations are entirely false and misleading. A sound recorder is just that, a device for recording sound, and the methods and means by which they achieve this are well understood. I have examined several of these so called 'optimised for paranormal use' recorders and, without exception, they are either entirely standard or have had some amateur modifications carried out – such modifications often involving turning the microphone amplification up to levels whereby the electrical signal from the microphone is distorted and the recording becomes overloaded with noise.

How you plan to use your subsequent recordings is an important consideration when selecting a recorder, it will also affect the way that it needs to be set-up. For instance, if you plan to do nothing more than listen to the recorded audio, there is nothing to be gained by setting a very high sample rate and bit depth. The standard for CD audio, i.e., a sample rate of 44.1 kHz and 16 bit will more than suffice for any listening only task. If you are planning to use the recording for some form of measurement or post recording analysis, then higher sampling rates and a greater bit depth may be advantageous. It is worth mentioning that in a recorder that makes use of a fixed amount of memory, then higher settings for the sample rate and/or bit-depth will inevitably result in a lot more data being written to the memory and this will decrease the available recording time. Of course, if the recorder uses removable memory in the form of a memory card or disc, then this consideration does not apply.

When selecting your recorder, it is wise to select models that offer the ability to use one of the uncompressed recording formats rather than a format that uses compression. Uncompressed recording formats include the .wav file format and there are several others. Compressed recording formats such as the universal adopted .mp3 may be perfectly adequate for general listening, but information from the original sound is irretrievably lost in the compression process. Our ears may not notice this loss too much but, if you wish to make any form of post recording analysis or measurement, this is a significant issue. Fortunately, the advent of affordable, portable, high quality recorders aimed at the musician or broadcaster, means that high quality recordings can be obtained. These machines permit adjustments to the recording parameters to be made that are specific to the particular requirements of an investigation or location. Most of these recorders will also offer additional and very useful features such as the ability to attach external microphones. Also, consider the means and methods of powering the recorder when making your selection. Internal batteries may be preferable in some circumstances but they will limit the time that the device is capable of operating. Mains power will allow extended recording periods limited only by the capacity of the storage media.

The majority of recorders have an automatic gain, which sets the overall level of the electrical signal coming from the microphone to what the manufacturer considers to be an optimum setting for general use. Gain is also called 'recording level'. Automatic gain (rec level) may be a user selected option on more expensive recorders but cheaper machines often lack any form of manual gain control and are completely reliant upon the automatic gain circuit within the recorder. Automatic gain is almost certainly a disadvantage when trying to use the recorder in an investigation scenario. In quiet locations or when there is very little sound, the recorder will increase the gain and if louder sounds are encountered the amount of amplification is reduced to lower the signal level from the microphone. Such systems have an inherent flaw, they need time to respond. Even with the best recorders this will result in some sound being misrepresented on the recording. In a quiet environment, any sudden loud transient sound such as a bang or thump may sound much louder on the subsequent recording than it actually was. Conversely, in a noisy environment, quieter sounds may not be recorded at all. It is always better to be able to set the recording level manually. A professional soundman on a film or TV shoot or the sound engineer in a studio would never use automatic gain.

Ultimately, the recorder is there to capture the signal coming from the microphone. The microphone is undoubtedly the most important individual component of any recording set-up. Many people consider that all microphones are pretty much the same, but there are substantial differences between a microphone bought for a few pounds and one costing several thousands of pounds. Those differences will directly affect the quality of the recorded audio. There are few circumstances where spending thousands of pounds on a microphone will be advantageous, but there are many circumstances where spending just a few pounds on a microphone are extremely disadvantageous. As a general guide, the cost of the microphone should at least equal the cost of the recorder. Microphones are normally optimised for a range of frequencies specifically chosen by the manufacturer for its intended use. Some microphones are designed primarily for human speech, others for musical instruments or industrial applications such as the measurement of noise levels around airports. Reputable microphone manufacturers provide information about their products in the form of a frequency and amplitude response graph for their different models and this information should be considered when making your selection. Microphones can also be designed to be more responsive to directional sound. Note, these designs do not amplify the sound coming from a particular direction, rather they are designed to reduce the amount of sound that is picked up from unwanted directions. Microphones may be highly directional or they may be omni-directional, responding to sound from all directions more or less equally. Although most microphones are mono, meaning a separate microphone is normally required for both left and right stereo channels of a recorder, there are some designs which are stereo and have two microphone capsules one for each of the stereo tracks in a single microphone body.

It is not just the microphone that needs to be considered, some thought needs to be given to how the signal is carried from the microphone to the recorder. The signal coming from a microphone is tiny, often just a few millivolts and this needs to be amplified by the recorder in order to drive the recording circuits effectively. One method that electrical noise can interfere with a recording is when it is picked up through the cable and connectors. Professional systems use a three-wire connection which eliminates some of this electromagnetic noise from nearby electrical systems such as faulty power blocks, machines and motors. This is achieved by sending the signal down two of the wires, each wire carrying the same signal voltage but phase reversed with respect to the other, therefore acting to cancel out much of the electromagnetic interference. The third wire is a shield and is normally connected to a foil or braided metal shield that surrounds the inner wires. This is internally connected to an earth or ground inside the recorder. These methods are generally referred to as 'balanced' whereas a standard domestic two-wire microphone and connection is known as 'unbalanced' and is much more prone to any induced electromagnetic interference being picked up through the cables and connectors. Some microphone types such as condensers require power to be supplied to the microphone capsule, this may be in the form of an internal battery within the microphone body or as 'phantom power' with the power coming from an external source such as the recorder via the microphone cable.

Whichever recorder you are using, analogue, digital, professional or domestic grade, wherever possible avoid handholding any sound recording device in order to minimise handling noise picked up through the body of the device itself. This step is especially important when using a recorder that is using a built-in microphone. If the recorder has the facility, it is always preferable to use an external microphone for recordings as it reduces the likelihood of internal recorder noise, such as from motors or electrical circuits or handling noise being picked up by the recording device. An external microphone will also generally be of better quality, assuming careful selection and appropriate choice is made, than a built-in microphone. If you are using an external microphone, ensure that it is always used with a suitable microphone stand to avoid handling noise but remain aware that vibrations may still be transmitted through the stand to the microphone and be picked up. Vibration reducing microphone stands are available which will reduce, but not totally eliminate vibration pick-up in this manner by the microphone. If you are using a small handheld portable recorder such as a portable cassette or digital recorder with only a built-in microphone, a simple technique to reduce handling noise and other vibrations from being picked-up is to simply place the recorder on a piece of sponge or foam rubber (a simple bath sponge is perfect and very cheap to acquire). This will also work when placed beneath microphone stands that lack a suitable vibration reducing microphone mount.

It is not just vibration that needs to be considered, but the actual placement of the microphone itself is important to the final quality of the recording. From observation, it appears that many people simply place the recorder or microphone down with little regard to how placement or the type of microphone they are using will affect their recording. A position close to a wall or in the corner of a room will greatly increase the amount of reverberation and echo that will be picked up, particularly if the microphone they are using is an omni-directional design. Reverberation will add additional acoustic noise to the recording and may make the sounds less distinct and intelligible. Omni-directional microphones would best when placed toward the centre of a space away from surfaces and obstructions to the sound path. If the recording is to be made in a long space such as a corridor, then a directional design is preferred, again such a choice minimises reverberation and echo. Due to the way in which acoustic standing waves may also form in such places, it is also sometimes better to position the microphone around a third of the way from the end wall of such a space.

The worst possible scenario for making a good quality recording is to just place the recorder or microphone onto a floor, table, or hard surface.

Listening

Assuming you have discovered something of interest on your recording, perhaps a recognisable sound or merely an interesting noise, is there anything that you can do with it to help your investigation? The recording may be unclear, noisy, or simply downright confusing. It is important to remember that it does represent a record of an actual acoustic event, regardless of any problems, technical, or otherwise, that the recording may have. As such, it is objective information about the event and needs to be considered as potentially vital to the overall investigation and treated accordingly.

The first step is obviously to listen to the sound recording, but try to avoid the temptation of listening to it straight away during the investigation, except perhaps to briefly check that the event was actually recorded. Playing back during the investigation may cause you or others hearing the playback to make assumptions that could affect the remainder of the visit. Listening should ideally be done using the original recording device to reduce any effects caused by the playback machine or by the transfer process. One useful method for trying to understand what the recording might contain is to play it to several people. Ideally, these should not be people who have been on the investigation or have any knowledge of the location. Friends and family members with little or no interest in the paranormal often make good candidates, as they are somewhat less likely to subjectively bias their impressions of the recording. Most people have a very low tolerance whilst listening to typical investigation recordings, so it is wise to avoid playing your listeners overly long recordings. The recording might need to be shortened, or parts that are not of interest edited out. If you need to do this, make sure you leave a sufficient amount of lead-in and lead-out on the recording in order to give the listener some time to adjust to the volume and sound of the recording, at least 10 seconds run-in before the point of interest and a similar amount of run-out is a good general guide. It might also be a good idea to make a 30 – 60 second recording of a 'control' section that contains nothing of interest to play to your listeners beforehand to allow their ears to tune-in or acclimatise to the general sound of the recording.

It is crucial that you provide no information to the listener about the content of the recording and avoid statements such as **"Listen to the voice in this recording"** or **"Can you hear the footsteps in this bit?"** Such statements and comments will inevitably lead to the listener becoming unduly fixated by the recording and will affect how they subsequently perceive it.

Conduct each individual's listening session separately and avoid group listening sessions or opportunities for listeners to exchange their views or opinions with each other at any time during the listening session.

Immediately after the listening session ends, ask the listener to write down their comments and thoughts. Do not wait, even for a few minutes, as the human memory for sound is notoriously short and unreliable. Ensure that the listeners don't discuss the recording between themselves until they have all listened and written down their comments.

The same due care should be employed when dealing with recordings that you consider to be examples of electronic voice phenomenon (EVP) but with the additional caveat that you should make no reference to your own consideration or belief that it is some unheard (at the time of recording) sound. It is also crucial that you provide the listener with no clue about what they may be listening to or what you are interested in obtaining. A common but simple error is to commence the listening session with a leading statement such as **"Have a listen to this EVP and tell me what you think it is saying"**.

To Analyse or Not?

Audio analysis is a highly specialised skill that requires extensive training in order to be properly undertaken, it is not simply a matter of playing around with the sound using home audio software such as Audacity, Cool Edit, or your computer's media player, although there are many paranormal investigators who use such techniques and call what they do analysis. It is of course possible to use such software, but it must be used with care and practice. It should NOT be used to analyse the sounds, but to assist and to help the investigation process. Careful reading of the software instructions and help files, and a good knowledge of what the software is capable of doing are also necessary.

Often a recording will be indistinct, noisy or difficult to understand. Software can be used to help the process of understanding. Remember that, whilst any software changes applied to the recording may aid the process of understanding, it will alter the recording and may change the way that it is interpreted. If you do decide to use software to help you, it is essential that every change is documented and recorded. Start by making a duplicate copy of the original recording, this is now your working copy. Each and every time you make a single change to any of the recording's parameters, gain, filters, in fact any changes at all, save the change with a new and meaningful file name. A handy tip is to use the file name followed by a sequential number e.g., sound.gain.1, sound.gain.2, sound.filter.1, sound.filter.2, etc. For each and every subsequent change, save the changed file using a new meaningful file name. This will build up an archive of the stages you have gone through.

Document Every Change and Step

In addition to the sound files sequential labelling, use a notebook and ensure you document each step of the analysis process, linking your notes to the appropriate sound file. Note the action taken to each particular file such as "sound.gain.1 – gain increased by 5%" "sound.gain.2 – gain increased by 2%, etc. Also, don't overlook noting the software that you are using including the version and any tools/plug-ins that you use. This technique is how forensic audio analysts work and this technique will ensure that your recording will have the highest possible value in supporting your investigation results and conclusions.

Sound analysis requires specialised knowledge of sound, the software, and the effects of any changes that are made. Software can be complicated to use and often difficult to understand. Software can be used to objectively measure some parameters of the recording such as amplitude and frequency of the component sounds. This information can be used to make direct comparisons with known sounds and may prove helpful.

Ultimately however, the final interpretation of the recording will most often be a subjective one based upon the operators knowledge and experience, information about the recording, and a range of other factors including the recording equipment, it's use, and the techniques used.

So you have completed the listening tests and any analysis and you are still sure that you have recorded something unusual, perhaps truly anomalous. So what do you do with it? Many will be tempted to simply write a brief account of how amazingly evidential their recording is and stick it onto their website, or they will also post it onto their YouTube channel. But before you do anything at all, consider what the value of the recording is? It might reasonably be argued that a recording on its own is of little evidential value, after all, a recording of a sound is just that, a recording of a sound! It proves nothing except that an acoustic event took place and that it was recorded. This at least confirms that a witness who also heard and reported the sound didn't imagine it. The debate over the validity of sound recordings made during paranormal investigations remains on-going but, at least by the proper application of the right equipment and correct post recording treatment of your recordings, you may at least be able to demonstrate that you are aware of some of the issues and have acted to address them.

APPENDIX 8

EVP METHODS

Steven Parsons

Early encounters with spirit voices tended to be almost accidental, as was the case with Jürgenson and Carrington. The voices appeared spontaneously, often seemingly interacting with, or trying to respond to the conversations of the living. Researchers quickly discovered that they, often cryptically, could obtain responses to questions they asked and were frequently reliant upon the researcher's own interpretation of the responses. The simplest technique involved setting up a microphone and a recorder and then asking for the spirit voices to respond to the questioning researcher. Normally, replies were only discovered when the recording was played back although in some instances, as at the Wigmore Hall séances, the voices apparently responded in real-time. Raudive was perhaps the first to make a deliberate use of noise to aid the voice communications. That is not to say that before Raudive the recordings were noise-free, the technology available inherently produced noise, whether from within the equipment or in the form of ambient noise from the surroundings. Raudive appreciated that this noise seemed to be needed by the voices in order for them to be produce better responses. He used a radio that was de-tuned to frequencies between the broadcasting stations and observed the static hiss produced aided the production of the voices, but left room for critics to claim that, in reality he was simply recording snatches of real radio broadcasts as the radio tuning frequency wandered slightly or picked up harmonic frequencies (multiples or divisions of frequencies) from the original transmission.

To counter such criticism, he experimented using a Germanium diode connected directly to the microphone input of the tape recorder, replacing the microphone and the radio receiver. The diode was a simple device that acted as a primitive radio frequency receiver capable only of picking up a broad spectrum of radio frequency energy and passing it as a wide audio frequency hiss, usually referred to as White Noise. This resulted in a dramatic improvement in the quality of recorded voices. Other researchers continued to pursue methods that used artificial or natural noise sources. Some continued using de-tuned and modified radios or specially constructed white-noise generators, whilst others used wind or water, from real life or from recordings, to provide the noise source to help the voices manifest. To ensure that the voices were not simply the product of radio and other interference applied, researchers used increasingly stricter controls and radio and sound engineers, together with physicists, were brought in to assist. Regardless, the voices continued to be recorded and led to many of the critics and specialists becoming converted to the idea that the voices had a supernormal origin. Thousands and tens of thousands of recordings were amassed by the various researchers using a variety of methods, mostly derived from the work of the Raudive group.

Basic Methods

The simplest method for conducting EVP experiments is to simply set up a microphone and a recorder. Experimenters recommend and favour an external microphone rather than using any built-in microphone. The recorder is started and the experimenter asks aloud a series of questions with pauses of suitable length in-between for any responses to be recorded. At the end of the experimental session, the recording is played back and any responses can be examined. Experimental sessions are normally short, typically 5-15 minutes. Many experimenters discovered that results were rarely forthcoming at first, but repeated sessions over a period of many weeks or even months would eventually produce voice responses to their questioning. Other researchers added a simple de-tuned radio or white noise generator to the set-up, the output of which was broadcast via a loudspeaker to be recorded along with the experimenter's questions using a microphone. Again, it was observed that it typically took many sessions before voices began to appear on the recordings.

Some EVP researchers also make recordings at sites of reported hauntings or other paranormal activity. These should not be confused with straightforward audio recordings made during an investigation which may also contain seemingly paranormal voices, for example, those made during the Enfield Poltergeist case which apparently came directly from one of the children involved.

Many ghost hunters also use EVP recording as part of their investigation. They have developed a less stringent method using simple handheld cassette or digital recorders, which are either just placed or held whilst any questions are asked. Keen to explore these voice communications further, researchers have developed new technologies and approaches which has led to the introduction of specialist EVP apparatus. The diode device used by Raudive has already been mentioned, but one of the most influential early devices for EVP use was the Spiricom series. There are also a number of software Spiricom emulator programmes available via the Internet.

Simple DIY EVP Experiments

Recording the voices seems to be remarkably easy and does not require any special equipment or costly and supposedly purpose built EVP/ITC devices. The following list should suffice for anyone interested in investigating this interesting phenomenon:

- Cassette tape recorder - full size cassettes are preferred to ensure best quality.
- A digital audio recorder that records uncompressed sound files such as .wmv is a good alternative, try to avoid mp.3 audio as it is compressed and may lose detail.
- A reasonable quality external microphone, the built-in microphone of many recorders is prone to picking up machine noise from the recorder.
- If you are using a cassette recorder, then ensure only new tapes are used.

And that's all you really need, except a great deal of patience. Many EVP researchers claim that it requires weeks and even months of regular sessions before any voices are heard and many more before good quality voices are regularly recorded. The initial sessions should be regular, i.e., the same time every week or day and last for around 30 minutes. Limit the questions to around 10 per session, and leave 30-second intervals between each question to permit any response to be made. Questions really should be simple at the start, for example: "Is there anyone who wishes to communicate?" "Will you tell us who you are?", etc.

The recording can be played back following the session and any responses noted.

You may wish to add some form of ambient noise, this could be in the form of a radio that is tuned in-between stations and considered to be producing white noise, the typical inter-station hiss on AM is a good source. Computer programmes are also available that can generate white noise which may be played aloud using the computer's speakers.

For those who wish to experiment using the Germanium Diode method that Raudive claimed was highly effective, it is becoming more difficult to find these components, but they are still available from some suppliers and an internet search should readily locate several sources. You will also need a suitable cable to attach it to the microphone input of your recorder, the easiest way is to buy a really cheap microphone with the correct sized jack plug for your recorder - typically 1/8 or 1/4 inch mono. Cut the microphone off so that you have a microphone jack plug attached to a length of wire. Strip back the cut end and reveal the inner conductors and, using solder, join the inner conductors of the wire to the wire 'tails' of the diode, one to each. It doesn't matter which way round you do it.

Plug the completed assembly into your recorders microphone socket and you have a fully functioning Raudive Diode (assuming you can of course solder - which if you can't, then simply join the conductors and the diode tails by twisting them together tightly). Using the diode, means you won't be able to record your own questions as the diode cannot pick up normal sounds, so either use a notebook to record your questions and the point in recording when they were asked or, by using a suitable splitter adaptor or audio input mixer, it should be possible to plug in your normal microphone.

The Voices

EVP researchers have recognised certain characteristics of the voices that differentiate genuine EVP voices from standard radio broadcasts. These characteristics have been observed by experimenters from the earliest days of EVP study right through to the present day and are consistently reported regardless of the geographical location of the experimental recording. Raudive, writing in 'Breakthrough' observed:

I will summarise briefly the characteristics [of the voices] I have mentioned:

1. The voice-entities speak very rapidly, in a mixture of languages, sometimes as many as five or six in one sentence.
2. They speak in a definite rhythm, which seems to be forced upon them by means of communication they employ.
3. The rhythmic mode of speech imposes a shortened, telegram-style phrase or sentence.
4. Presumably arising from these restrictions, grammatical rules are frequently abandoned and neologisms abound.

These characteristic features of the language of the voices and their speech content are the outstanding paranormal aspects of the phenomenon and the guide-lines to further research, and in my opinion this is, at least for the time being, the best approach to our endeavours to get closer to its essence.

Over recent years, there has been a number of devices launched onto the market that claim to be able to obtain real-time direct communications with discarnate entities and are now routinely included in many ghost investigator's kits. Direct and real-time two-way communications with the realm of the deceased and the discarnate has been the desire of mankind for millennia and was, for the most part, the domain of oracles and mediums. Many of the current devices claim to provide this capability to the modern investigator regardless of, or in some cases, with the contrivance of some degree of mediumistic ability. Many investigators claim that this is the case and that using such devices does indeed provide a communication channel to the deceased or otherworldly intelligences. Most of the devices are simple adaptions of well-understood radio technology. Others appear initially more complex, but ultimately, when examined closely, are little more than the aforementioned simply adapted radio. Such devices include the Frank's Box, The Ghost Box, The Shack-Hack and others, too numerous to mention. The use and usefulness of these devices appears to be driven more by broadcast and social media than any properly constructed experimentation. Those who wish to conduct their own EVP experiments are encouraged to do so in the full knowledge that they are entering into research where results will be constantly questioned, and methods will be questioned, criticised and, in all likelihood, dismissed almost out of hand.

SUGGESTED FURTHER READING AND REFERENCES BY CHAPTER

Editorial Note: A number of the books suggested below are long out of print and the original editions therefore are hard to come by. Various publishers have re-printed some over the years and in several instances, the books are now available as downloadable free eBooks in various formats. Wherever possible, we have provided links to these downloadable books. Over time, some of these links may be changed by the provider and cease to work, in which case, using an internet search based upon the book title and author should normally suffice. Some of the dialogue from certain chapters may have been originally produced as a correspondence [letters to the editor] to research journals, and access to most of those journals is still regularly available, especially through the Society for Psychical Research. In some of the chapter listings below, they are referenced separately from books and journal articles, and are written in the Harvard referencing format due to their substantial use within those chapters, thus making them easier to source for the reader and interested scholar.

1. The Physics of Sound:

The Physics of Sound 3rd Edition (2004) by R. Berg & D. Stork. Boston: Addison Wesley. ISBN 978 0131457898.

The Theory of Sound, 2nd Edition (1998) by Lord Rayleigh. New York: Dover Publications. ISBN 978 0486602929.

Anatomy and Physiology for Speech, Language, and Hearing, 3rd Edition (2009) by A. Seikel. Boston: Delmar. ISBN 978 1401825812.

Measuring Sound (1984) by Bruel & Kjaer. Bruel & Kjaer. Denmark: Company Publication. Original edition sometimes available.

Sound Engineering Explained, 2nd Edition (2001) by M. Talbot-Smith. London: Focal Press. ISBN 978 0240516677.

Basic Microphones (2000) by P. White. London Sanctuary Publishing. ISBN 978 1860742653.

2. The Psychology of Sound:

Healing Sounds: The Power of Harmonics (2002) by J. Goldman. Vermont: Healing Arts Press. ISBN: 978 0892819935

"The power of sound" (2005) by A. Haddow. *Christian Parapsychologist, 16* (8), 240-245.

"Psi and internal attention states: Information retrieval in the ganzfeld" (1978) by C. Honorton. In B. Shapin, & L. Coly (Eds.) *Psi and States of Awareness*. New York: Parapsychology Foundation.

"The Scammell device" (2012) by C.E. Cooper, & S.T. Parsons. *Paranormal Review*, 64, 15-21.

Sound (1881) by A.M. Mayer. London: Macmillan & Co.

The Psychology of Music (2008) by H.P. Rao. K. Delhi: Low Price Publications.

Auditory Perception: A New Synthesis (1982) by R.M. Warren. New York: Pergamon Press. ISBN: 008025957X

The Psychology of Sound (1917) by H.J. Watt. Cambridge: Cambridge University Press.

Acoustics (1953) by T.M. Yarwood. London: MacMillan & Co.

3. Some Noisy Ghosts:

Sadiucismus Triumphatus (1681) by J. Glanvill. eBook available as free download in various formats - https://archive.org/details/saducismustriumpooglan

Memoirs of Extraordinary Popular Delusions and the Madness of Crowds (1841) by C. MacKay. eBook available as free download in various formats - http://www.gutenberg.org/ebooks/24518

Cock lane and Common-Sense (1894) by A. Lang. eBook available as free download in various formats - http://www.gutenberg.org/ebooks/12674

Deutsche Mythologie (1835) by J. Grimm. eBook available as free download in various formats - https://archive.org/details/deutschemytholo07grimgoog

Poltergeist Over England: Three Centuries of Mischievous Ghosts (1945) by H. Price. Country Life Publishing. Original edition still sometimes available. Later editions and re-prints including eBook readily available online.

Of Ghostes and Spirites Walking by Nyght (1572) by L. Lavater. Kessinger Publishing. ISBN 978 0766179615

Ghosts Vivisected (1957) by A.M.W. Stirling. London: R.Hale Publishing.

The Alleged Haunting of B- House (1898) by A. Goodrich-Freer, John, Marquess of Bute. eBook available as free download in various formats - http://www.gutenberg.org/files/16538/16538-h/16538-h.htm

This House is Haunted (1980) by G. L. Playfair. Souvenir Press. Original edition still sometimes available. Reprinted (2011) Guildford: White Crow Books. ISBN 978 1907661785

4. Some Noisy Spirits:

Sermons, Soap and Television, 2nd Edition (1990) by J. L. Baird. London: Royal Television Society.

The Enigma of the Poltergeist (1967) by R. Bayless. New York: Parker. ASIN: B001C3EA64

"On a series of drop in communicators" (1971) by A. Gauld. *Proceedings of the Society for Psychical Research*, 55, 273-340.

"Poltergeists" (1991) by M. Grosse. *Light*, 111, 5-11.

Phantasms of the Living, 2 Volumes (1886) by E. Gurney, F.W.H. Myers, & F. Podmore. London: Trübner. [Abridged in 1918 and available on Kindle and modern reprint]

Strange Experiences (1955) by L. Henderson. London: Psychic Book Club.

"Telephonic communication with the next world" (1921) by F.R. Melton. *Light, August 20*, 534-537.

Parapsychology: A Century of Enquiry (1975) by D.S. Rogo. New York: Taplinger. ISBN: 978 0800862367 [Reference to the Fox Sisters]

5. Infrasound and the Paranormal:

"Infrasound and the paranormal" (2012) by S. T. Parsons. *Journal of the Society for Psychical Research, 76.3*, 150-174. (see Appendix for full paper & references)

The Effects of Low-Frequency Noise and Vibration on People (2007) edited by C. Hansen. Essex: Multi-Science Publishing. ISBN 978 0906522455.

6. A Brief History of EVP Research:

Carry on Talking: How Dead are the Voices? (1972) by P. Bander. Gerrards Cross: Colin Smythe. [USA Edition, *Voices from the Tapes.* New York: Drake]. ISBN: 978 0900675669

There is No Death and There are No Dead, 4th printing (2008) by T. Butler, & L. Butler. Reno, Nevada: AA-EVP Publishing. ISBN: 978 0972749305

Electronic Voices: Contact with Another Dimension. (2010) by A. Cardoso. Ropley, Hants: O-Books. ISBN: 978 1846943638

The Mediumship of the Tape Recorder (1978) by D.J. Ellis. Pulborough: D.J. Ellis. ISBN: 978 0950602400

Voice from Eternity (1988) by S. Estep. New York: Ballantine Books. ISBN: 978 0449134245

The Ghost of 29 Megacycles (1985) by J.G. Fuller. London: Souvenir Press. ISBN: 978 0285626911

Rösterna från Rymden (1964) by F. Jürgenson. Stockholm: Faxon & Lindström.

Sprechfunk mit Verstorbenen (1967) by F. Jürgenson. Freiburg i.Br.: Hermann Bauer.

Breakthrough: An Amazing Experiment in Electronic Communication with the Dead. (1971) by K. Raudive. Gerrards Cross: Colin Smythe. ISBN: 978 0800809652

NAD: A Study of Some Unusual "Other-World" Experiences (1970) by D.S. Rogo. New York: University Books. [Republished by Anomalist Books] ISBN: 978 0821601259

NAD (vol. 2): A Psychic Study of the "Music of the Spheres" (1972) by D.S. Rogo. New York: University Books. [Republished by Anomalist Books] ISBN: 978 0821601402

In Search of the Unknown: The Odyssey of a Psychical Investigator (1976) by D.S. Rogo. New York: Taplinger. [Republished by Anomalist Books] ISBN: 978 0800841942

"Paranormal tape-recorded voices: A paraphysical breakthrough" (1977) by D. S. Rogo. In J. White, & S. Krippner (Eds.) *Future science: Life energies and the physics of paranormal phenomena* (pp. 451-464). New York: Anchor Books. ISNB: 978 0385112031

Hints on Receiving the Voice Phenomenon (1973) by R.K. Sheargold. Gerrards Cross: Colin Smythe. [Pamphlet obtainable from Colin Smythe Ltd.]

The Dead are Alive: They Can and Do Communicate with You (1981) by H. Sherman. New York: Ballantine Books. ISBN: 9780 449131589 [Free Kindle Download Available on Amazon]

Voices of the Dead? (1977) by S. Smith. New York: A Signet Book. ISBN: Not Stated.

The Vertical Plane (1989) by K. Webster. London: Crafton Books. ISBN: 978 0586204764

Talks with the Dead (1975) by W.A. Welch. New York: Pinnacle Books. ISBN: 978 0523005805

Journal Articles, Reports, Correspondence and Theses

Bayless, R. (1959). Correspondence. *Journal of the American Society for Psychical Research*, 53, 35-39.

Bayless, R. (1976). Tape-recording of paranormally generated acoustical raps. *New Horizons, 2 (2)*, 12-17.

Bayless, R. (1977). Tape-recorded, low-amplitude psychokinesis. *New Horizons*, 2 (3), 22-26.

Bayless, R. (1979). Low-amplitude, acoustical, tape-recorded PK with target objects: Experiments conducted by Wesley Frank and Raymond Bayless.

Journal of the Southern California Society for Psychical Research, 1, 1-17.

Bender, H. (2011). On the analysis of exceptional voice phenomena on tapes: Pilot studies on the 'recordings' of Friedrich Jürgenson. *ITC Journal*, 40, 61-78.

Blackmore, S. (1979). The mediumship of the tape recorder by D.J. Ellis [Book Review]. *Journal of Parapsychology*, 43, 70-72.

Cassirer, M. (1973). Correspondence. *Journal of the Society for Psychical Research*, 47, 208-209.

Clancy, P.M. (1980). *An Investigation of Apparent Paranormal Sounds Occurring on Electronic Recording Equipment.* Unpublished master's thesis, The University of Humanistic Studies, San Diego, California.

Ellis, D.J. (1995, August). *Some further thoughts regarding the mediumship of the tape recorder.* Unpublished report.

Friday, R. (2013). *I Hear Dead People: Individual Differences in the Perception of Anomalous Voices in Ambiguous Electronic Audio Recordings.* Unpublished bachelor thesis, University of Greenwich, London.

Gaythorpe, S.N. (1972). Correspondence. *Light*, 92, 153-155.

Riley, F.J. (1977). Production of 'electronic voices' by a group practised in psychokinesis. *New Horizons*, 2, 16-21.

Rogo, D.S. (1969). Report on two preliminary sittings for 'direct voice' phenomena with Atilla von Sealey. *Journal of Paraphysics*, 3, 126-129.

Rogo, D.S. (1970). A report on two controlled sittings with Atillia von Sealey. *Journal of Paraphysics*, 4, 13-15.

Sheargold, R.K. (1973). Correspondence. *Journal of the Society for Psychical Research*, 47, 210-212.

Sheargold, R.K. (1975). Correspondence. *Journal of the Society for Psychical Research*, 48, 128-129.

Smith, E.L. (1972). The Raudive voices – objective or subjective? A discussion. *Journal of the Society for Psychical Research*, 46, 192-200.

Smith, E.L. (1973). Correspondence. *Journal of the Society for Psychical Research*, 47, 209.

Tart, C.T. (1974). Correspondence. *Journal of the Society for Psychical Research*, 47, 531-532.

Vaughan, A. (1972). Correspondence. *Light*, 92, 153-155.

Winsper, A (2010). *The Effects of Paranormal Belief and Positive Schizotypy on Response Bias in an Auditory Electronic Voice Phenomenon Task.* Paper presented at the 34th International Conference of the Society for Psychical Research, University of Sheffield, Sheffield, UK.

7. Telephone Anomalies:

Hidden Memories: Voices and Visions from Within (1992) by R.A. Baker. New York: Prometheus Books. ISBN: 978 1573920940

Telephone Calls from the Dead: A Revised Look at the Phenomenon Thirty Years On (2012) by C.E. Cooper. Old Portsmouth: Tricorn Books. ISNB: 978 0597107410

Vozes do Além pelo Telefone (1925) by O. D'Argonnel. Rio de Janeiro: Pap. Typ. Marques, Araújo & C.

The Case for Life After Death: Parapsychologists Look at the Evidence (1981) by E.E. McAdams, & R. Bayless. Chicago: Nelson Hall Publishers. ISBN: 978 0882295923

Breakthrough: An Amazing Experiment in Electronic Communication with the Dead (1971) by K. Raudive. Gerrards Cross: Colin Smythe. ISBN: 978 0800809652

Life After Death: The Case for Survival of Bodily Death (1986) by D.S. Rogo. London: Guild Publishing. ISBN: 978 0850305043

Phone Calls from the Dead: The Results of a Two-Year Investigation into an Incredible Phenomenon (1979) by D.S. Rogo, & R. Bayless. Englewood Cliffs, NJ: Prentice-Hall. ISNB: 978 0136643340

Journal Articles, Reports, Correspondence and Theses

Anderson, R. (1981). Phone calls from the dead by Raymond Bayless and D. Scott Rogo [Book Review]. *Journal of Religion and Psychical Research*, 4, 66-74.

Barrett, D. (1991-92). Through a glass darkly: Images of the dead in dreams. *Omega: Journal of Death and Dying*, 24, 97-108.

Biondi, M. (1984). Le telefonate dall'Aldila': Una nuova fenomenologia paranoramle? *Quaderni di Parapsicologia*, 15 (1), 60-67.

Biondi, M. (1996). Periscopio. *Luce e Ombra*, 96, 199-206.

"Borderland" (1897). Did the ghost use the telephone? [Letter to editor]. *Borderland*, 4, 314.

Cooper, C.E. (2010a). Phone calls from the dead. *Anomaly: Journal of Research into the Paranormal, 44,* 3-21.

Cooper, C.E. (2010b). Spontaneous cases concerning telephone calls and text messages. *Australian Journal of Parapsychology, 10,* 178-193.

Cooper, C.E. (2014). An analysis of exceptional experiences involving telecommunication technology. *Journal of Parapsychology, 78,* 209-222.

Klemperer, F. (1992). Ghosts, visions, and voices: Sometimes simply perceptual mistakes. *British Medical Journal, 305,* 1518-1519.

Lescarboura, A.C. (1920). Edison's views on life and death. *Scientific American, 123,* 444-460.

Presi, P. (2001). The paranormal in the laboratory: A comparison of psychophonic voices, telephonic voices and direct voices. *ITC Journal, 5,* 67-77.

Price, H. (1932). *Personal correspondence to F.R. Melton, 19 May.*

Randall, J.L. (2011). *Personal correspondence, 27 January.*

Rees, W.D. (1971). The hallucinations of widowhood. *British Medical Journal, 4,* 37-41.

Rogo, D.S. (1981). Author responds to book review [Letter to Editor]. *Journal of Religion and Psychical Research,* 4, 75-80.

Roll, W. G. (1980). The catch 22 of survival research. *Journal of the Academy of Religion and Psychical Research, 3,* 23-24.

Wright, S.H. (1998). Experiences of spontaneous psychokinesis after bereavement. *Journal of the Society for Psychical Research,* 62, 385-395.

Wright, S.H. (2006). Lights, radios and telephones that misbehave. In A. Cardoso, & D. Fontana (Eds.) *Proceedings of the Second International Conference on Current Research into Survival of Physical Death with Special Reference to Instrumental Transcommunication* (pp.283-294). Vigo, Spain: ITC Journal Productions.

8. The Psychology of Electronic Voice Phenomena:
A Dictionary of Hallucinations. (2010) by J.D. Blom. Springer: New York. ISBN: 978 1441912220 [Available on Kindle]

Electronic Voices: Contact with Another Dimension. (2010) by A. Cardoso. Ropley, Hants: O-Books. ISBN: 978 1846943638

Speaking to the Dead with Radios. (2012) by M.H. Edwards. Publisher: Self Published. ISBN: 978 1479325955 [Available on Kindle]

The Psychology of Paranormal Belief. (2009) by H.J. Irwin. Hertforshire: University of Hertfordshire Press. ISBN: 978 1902806938 [Available on Kindle]

The Audio Recording Handbook. (2001) by A. Kefauver. Wisconsin, USA: A-R Editions, Inc.

An Introduction to the Psychology of Hearing. (2008) by B.C.J. Moore. Bingley, UK: Emerald. ISBN: 978 9004252424 *Breakthrough: An Amazing Experiment in Electronic Communication with the Dead.* (1971) by K. Raudive. Gerrards Cross: Colin Smythe. ISBN: 978 0800809652

The Believing Brain. (2012) by M. Shermer. New York: St Martin's Press. ISBN: 978 1780335292 [Available on Kindle and Audio book]

Journals, Books Chapters and Conference Papers
Barušs, I. (2001). Failure to replicate electronic voice phenomenon. *Journal of Scientific Exploration, 15,* 355-367.

Beischel, J. (2007). Contemporary methods used in laboratory-based mediumship research. *Journal of Parapsychology,* 71, 37-68.

Benard, M.R. & Baskent, D. (2013). Perceptual learning of interrupted speech. PLOS ONE, 8 (3): e58149. doi:10.1371/journal.pone.0058149

Benard, M.R., Mensink, J.S. & Baskent, D. (2014). Individual differences in top-down restoration of interrupted speech: Links to linguistic and cognitive abilities. *Journal of the Acoustical Society of America Express Letters 88, 135* (2). http://dx.doi.org/10.1121/1.4862879

Bentall, R.P. (1990). The illusion of reality: A review and integration of psychological research on hallucinations. *Psychological Bulletin, 107,* 82-95.

Bentall, R.P. & Slade, P.D. (1985). Reality testing and auditory hallucinations: A signal detection analysis. *British Journal of Clinical Psychology,* 24, 159-160.

Blackmore, S. & Moore, R. (1994). Seeing things: Visual recognition and belief in the paranormal. *European Journal of Parapsychology, 10,* 91-103.

Brugger, P. (2001). From haunted brain to haunted science: A cognitive neuroscience view of paranormal and pseudoscientific thought. In Houran, J. & Lange, R. (Eds.) *Hauntings and Poltergeists: Multidisciplinary Perspectives* (pp 195-213). Jefferson, NC: MacFarland & Co.

Cardoso, A. (2012). A two-year investigation of the allegedly anomalous electronic voices or EVP. *Neuroquantology,* 10, 492-514

Carter, D.M. & Cutler, A. (1987). The predominance of strong initial syllables in the English vocabulary. *Computer Speech and Language, 2,* 133-142.

Cutler, A. & Butterfield, S. (1992). Rhythmic cues to speech segmentation: Evidence from juncture misperception. *Journal of Memory and Language, 31,* 218-236.

Fisher, J.E., Mohanty, A., Herrington, J.D., Koven, N.S., Miller, G.A. & Heller, W. (2004). Neuropsychological evidence for dimensional schizotypy: Implications for creativity and psychopathology. *Journal of Research in Personality, 38,* 24-31.

French, C.C., & Wilson, K. (2007). Cognitive factors underlying paranormal beliefs and experiences. In Sala, S.D. [ed.] Tall Tales About the Mind and Brain: Separating Fact From Fiction (pp 3-22). Oxford: Oxford University Press.

Gianotti, L.R.R., Mohr, C., Pizzagalli, D., Lehmann, D. & Brugger, P. (2001). Associative processing and paranormal belief. *Psychiatry and Clinical Neurosciences,* 55, 595-603.

Goulding, A. (2005). Healthy schizotypy in a population of paranormal believers and experients. *Personality and Individual Differences, 38,* 1069-1083.

Hanique, I., Emestus, M. & Schuppler, B. (2013). Informal speech processes can be categorical in nature, even if they affect many words. *Journal of the Acoustical Society of America, 133,* 1644-1655.

Hergovich, A., Schott, R. & Arendasy, M. (2008). On the relationship between paranormal belief and schizotypy among adolescents. *Personality and Individual Differences, 45,* 119-125.

Hines, T. (1999). A demonstration of auditory top-down processing. *Behavior Research Methods, Instruments, & Computers, 31,* 55-56.

Holt, N.J., Simmonds-Moore, C.A. & Moore, S.L. (2008). Benign schizotypy: Investigating differences between clusters of schizotypy on paranormal belief, creativity, intelligence and mental health. The Parapsychological Association 51st Annual Convention , Proceedings of Presented Papers (pp.82-96), August 13-17, 2008. University of Winchester, UK.

Houran, J. (1997). Preliminary study of death anxiety of believers versus percipients of the paranormal. *Psychological Reports, 80,* 345-346.

Hunter, M.D., & Woodruff, W.R. (2004). Characteristics of functional auditory hallucinations [Letter to the editor]. *The American Journal of Psychiatry, 161,* 923.

Irwin, H.J. (1993). Belief in the paranormal: A review of the empirical literature. *Journal of the American Society for Psychical Research, 87,* 1-40.

Irwin, H.J. (2003). Paranormal beliefs and the maintenance of assumptive world views. *Journal of the Society for Psychical Research, 67.1,* 18-25.

Irwin, H.J. (2004). Reality testing and the formation of paranormal beliefs: A constructive replication. *Journal of the Society for Psychical Research, 68.3,* 143-152.

Johnson, J.L. & Hathaway, W. (2009). Personality contributions to belief in paranormal phenomena. *Individual Differences Research, 7,* 85-96.

Kashino, M. (2006). Phonemic restoration: The brain creates missing speech sounds. *Acoustical Science & Technology, 27,* 318-321.

Keil, J. (1980). The voice on tape phenomena: Limitations and possibilities. *European Journal of Psychology, 3,* 287-296.

Lacabex, E.G., Lecumberri, M.L.G, & Cooke, M. (2007). Perception of English Vowel Reduction by Trained Spanish Learners. New Sounds 2007: Proceedings of the Fifth International Symposium on the Acquisition of Second Language Speech, Florianópolis, Brasil. Retrieved from http://laslab.org/upload/perception_of_english_vowel_reduction_by_trained_spanish_learners.pdf

Longden, E., Madill, A. & Waterman, M.G. (2012). Dissociation, trauma, and the role of lived experience: Toward a new conceptualization of voice hearing. *Psychological Bulletin, 138,* 28-76.

MacDonald, D.A. (2000). Spirituality: Description, measurement, and relation to the five factor model of personality. *Journal of Personality, 68,* 153-197.

MacRae, A. (2004). A means of producing the electronic voice phenomenon based on electro-dermal activity. *Journal of the Society for Psychical Research, 68,* 35-50.

McCreery, C. & Claridge, G. (1995). Out-of-the-body experiences and personality. *Journal of the Society for Psychical Research, 60,* 129-148.

McCreery, C. & Claridge, G. (2002). Healthy schizotypy: the case of out-of-the-body experiences. *Personality and Individual Differences, 32,* 141-154.

McCue, P.A. (2002). Theories of haunting: A critical overview. *Journal of the Society for Psychical Research,* 66. 1-21.

Merckelbach, H., Muris, P., Horselenberg, R. & Stougie, S. (2000). Dissociative experiences, response bias, and fantasy proneness in college students. *Personality and Individual Differences, 28,* 49-58.

Miklousic, I., Mlacic, B. & Milas, G. (2012). Paranormal beliefs and personality traits in Croatia. *Journal of General Social Issues, 1,* 181-201.

Mintz, S. & Alpert, M. (1972). Imagery vividness, reality testing, and schizophrenic hallucinations. *Journal of Abnormal Psychology, 79,* 310-316.

Padgett, J. & Tabain, M. (2005). Adaptive dispersion theory and phonological vowel reduction in Russian. Phonetica, 62, 14-54.

Plichta, B. (2002). Best practices in acquisition, processing and analysis of acoustic speech signals. Retrieved from http://flint.matrix.msu.edu/extras/Audio-technology.pdf

Remez, R.E., Rubin, P.E., Berns, S.M., Pardo, J.S. & Lang, J.M. (1994). On the perceptual organization of speech. *Psychological Review, 101,* 129-156.

Rhue, J.W. & Lynn, S.J. (1987). Fantasy proneness: Developmental antecedents. *Journal of Personality, 55,* 121-137.

Richards, D.G. (1991). A study of the correlations between subjective psychic experiences and dissociative experiences. *Dissociation, 4,* 83-91.

Roe, C.A., & Morgan, C.L. (2002). Narcissism and belief in the paranormal. *Psychological Reports, 90,* 405-411.

Smith, C.L., Johnson, J.L. & Hathaway, W. (2009). Personality contributions to belief in paranormal phenomena. *Individual Differences Research, 7,* 85-96.

Spiegel, D. & Cardena, E. (1991). Disintegrated experience: The dissociative disorders revisited. *Journal of Abnormal Psychology, 100,* 366-378.

Tsakanikos, E. & Reed, P. (2005). Seeing words that are not there: Detection biases in schizotypy. *British Journal of Clinical Psychology, 44,* 295-299.

Vercammen, A., de Haan, E.H.F. & Aleman, A. (2008). Hearing a voice in the noise: Auditory hallucinations and speech perception. *Psychological Medicine, 38,* 1177-1184.

Winsper, A.R. (2010). *The effect of paranormal belief and positive schizotypy on response bias on an auditory Electronic Voice Phenomenon task.* Paper presented at the 34th International Conference of the Society for Psychical Research, Sheffield, UK.

Wiseman, R., Greening, E. & Smith, M. (2003). Belief in the paranormal and suggestion in the séance room. *British Journal of Psychology, 94,* 285-297.

Recommended Websites:

http://www.mrc-cbu.cam.ac.uk/people/matt-davis/personal/sine-wave-speech/

http://www.newyorker.com/science/maria-konnikova/science-misheard-lyrics-mondegreens

http://www.parascience.org.uk/

http://atransc.org/

9. Spontaneous Music and Voices:

The History of a Strange Case (1908) by D.P. Abbott. Chicago: The Open Court.

Voices from Beyond (1976) by R. Bayless. New Jersey: University Books. ISBN: 978 0821602522

Haunted People (1951) by H. Carrington, & N. Fodor. New York: E.P. Dutton & Co.

Telephone Calls from the Dead (2012) by C.E. Cooper. Old Portsmouth: Tricorn Books. ISNB: 978 0597107410

"Did E.T. phone home, or was it the dead?" (2012) by C.E. Cooper, & C.R. Foley. *Anomaly: Journal of Research into the Paranormal, 46,* 128-143.

Roads to Eternity (2005) by S.W. Estep. Lakeville, Minnesota: Galde Press. ISBN: 978 1931942232

The Haunted Mind (1959) by N. Fodor. New York: Helix Press.

"Phone calls from the dead by D. Scott Rogo and Raymond Bayless" [Book Review]. (1996) by C.R. Foley. *The Canadian Ufologist*, 3.3, 15-18.

Facts of Psychic Science and Philosophy (1925) by A.C. Holms. London: Kegan Paul, Trench, Trubner & Co.

Incidents in My Life (1863) by D.D. Home. New York: Carleton Publisher.

The Odyssey (2002) by Homer [translated by G. Chapman]. Hertfordshire: Wordsworth. ISBN: 978 0410449112

Hauntings and Poltergeists (2001) edited by J. Houran, & R. Lange. London: McFarland . ISBN: 978 0786432493 [Availble on Kindle]

The Authenticated History of the Bell Witch (1894) by M.V. Ingram. Clarksville Tennessee: Wm. P. Titus. [Available in Modern Kindle and Print Format]

The Seen and Unseen (1987) by A. MacKenzie. London: Weidenfeld and Nicolson. ISBN: 978 0297790457

Encyclopedia of Occultism & Parapsychology (1996) edited by J.G. Melton. Detroit: Gale Research. ISBN: 978 0810301962

Human Personality and its Survival of Bodily Death, 2 Volumes (1903) by F.W.H. Myers. London: Longmans & Co. [Available in Modern Reprints]

"Philip's fourth year" (1977) by I. Owen. *New Horizons, 2* (3), 11-15.

Poltergeist over England (1945) by H. Price. London: Country Life Ltd.

Haunting of Cashen's Gap (1936) by H. Price, & R.S. Lambert. London: Methuen.

Philosophical Interactions with Parapsychology (1995) edited by H.H. Price, & F.B. Dilley. New York: St. Martin's Press. ISBN: 978 0333598382

Breakthrough (1971) by K. Raudive. Buckinghamshire: Colin Smythe. ISBN: 978 0800809652

NAD: A Study of Some Unusual "Other-World" Experiences (1970) by D.S. Rogo. New York: University Books. [Republished by Anomalist Books] ISBN: 978 0821601259

NAD (vol. 2): A Psychic Study of the "Music of the Spheres" (1972) by D.S. Rogo. New York: University Books. [Republished by Anomalist Books] ISBN: 978 0821601402

Miracles (1982) by D.S. Rogo. New York: The Dial Press. [Republished by Anomalist Books] ISBN: 978 1933665092

Phone calls from the Dead (1979) by D.S. Rogo, & R. Bayless. Englewood Cliffs, N.J.: Prentice Hall. ISNB: 978 0136643340

The Warminster Mystery (1967) by A. Shuttlewood. London: Neville Spearman. ISBN: 978 0426127307

The Holographic Universe (1992) by M. Talbot. New York: Harper Perrenial. ISBN: 978 0586091715

Man's Survival After Death (1925) by C.L. Tweedale. London: Grant Richards Ltd. [Available on Amazon with Reprinting Services]

Ghosts I have Seen (1919) by V. Tweedale. New York: Frederick A. Stokes. [Amazon Free Kindle Download]

Aeneid (1961) by Vergil [translated by P. Dickson]. New York: Mentor-New American Library. [Available in Paperback and Kindle]

Shadow Matter & Psychic Phenomena (1993) by G.D. Wassermann. Oxford: Mandrake of Oxford. ISBN: 978 1869928322

Psychic Adventures in New York (1931) by N. Wymant. Boston: May & Company. ISBN: 978 1908733412 [Available on Kindle]

10. Music and Death:

Talks with Great Composers (1955) by A. Abell. London: The Psychic Book Club. ISBN: 978 0806515656

Music Therapy, 85 (1975) by J. Alvin. London: Hutchinson.

Death-Bed Visions (1986) by W. Barrett. Northants: Aquarian Press. [Reprint Available from White Crow Books]

Dying to Live (1993) by S. Blackmore. London: Grafton. ISBN: 978 0879758707

Musica Trascendentale (1943) by E. Bozzano. Verona: L' Albero.

Notes from an "Accidental" Pianist (2008) by A. Cicoria. New York: Cicoria Home. [Audio CD available]

Near-Death Experiences (2008) by O. Corazza. Abingdon: Routledge. ISBN: 978 0415455206 [Available on Kindle]

Music and the Earth Spirit (2001) by B. Dickinson. Berkshire: CapallBann.

"Transcendental music" (1945) by J. Doughty. *Light*, LXV, 3305, 242-47.

The Tibetan Book of the Dead (1927) edited by W.Y. Evans-Wentz. Oxford: OUP.

Adventures in Immortality: A look Beyond the Threshold of Death (1982) by G. Gallup, & W. Proctor. New York: McGraw-Hill. ISBN: 978 0070227545

Music, Mysticism and Magic (1987) by J. Godwin. London: Arkana. ISBN: 978 0140190403

Return from Death: An Exploration of the Near-Death Experience (1985) by M. Grey. Boston: Arkana. ISBN: 978 1850630197

"Auditory hallucinations following near-death experiences" (2004) by B. Greyson, & M. Liester. *Journal of Humanistic Psychology*, 44, 320-36.

"The phenomenology of near-death experiences" (1980) by B. Greyson, & I. Stevenson. *American Journal of Psychiatry*, 137, 1193-96.

The Human Encounter with Death (1977) by S. Grof, & J. Halifax. London: Souvenir. ISBN: 978 0525474920

"Toward an explanation of near-death phenomena" (1981) by M. Grosso. *Journal of the American Society for Psychical Research*, 75, 37-60.

Phantasms of the Living, 2 Volumes (1886) by E. Gurney, F.W.H. Myers, & F. Podmore. London: Trübner. [Abridged in 1918 and Available on Kindle and Modern Reprint]

Advertisement for Inward Harmony (no date) by M. Hamm. Texas: Music by Marcy.

"Notizen über den Tod durch Absturz" [Remarks on fatal falls] (1892) by A. Heim. *Jahrbuch der Schweitzerischen Alpclub* [Yearbook of the Swiss Alpine Club], 21, 327-37.

The Handbook of Near Death Experiences (2009) edited by J.M. Holden, B. Greyson, & D. James. California: ABC-CLIO, LLC. ISBN: 978 0313358647 [Available on Kindle]

The Mysticism of Sound and Music (1996) by H.I. Khan. Boston: Shambhala. ISBN: 978 1570622311 [Available on Kindle]

Life after Life (1976) by R. Moody. New York: Bantam. ISBN: 978 07126030 [Available as an Audio Book]

Reflections on 'Life after Life' (1978) by R. Moody. London: Corgi. ISBN: 978 0552108140

Deathbed Observations by Physicians and Nurses (1961) by K. Osis. New York: Parapsychology Foundation. [Monograph]

Heading Towards Omega (1984) by K. Ring. New York: Morrow. ISBN: 978 0688062682 [Available on Kindle]

NAD: A Study of Some Unusual "Other-World" Experiences (1970) by D.S. Rogo. New York: University Books. [Republished by Anomalist Books] ISBN: 978 0821601259

NAD (vol. 2): A Psychic Study of the "Music of the Spheres" (1972) by D.S. Rogo. New York: University Books. [Republished by Anomalist Books] ISBN: 978 0821601402

The Return from Silence (1989) by D.S Rogo. Northants: Aquarian Press. ISBN: 978 0850307368

Recollections of Death (1982) by M. Saborn. New York: Harper. ISBN: 978 0060148959

Musicophilia (2007) by O. Sachs. London: Picador. ISBN: 978 0330523592 [Available on Kindle and Audio Book]

"To assess the frequency of NDEs in cardiac arrest in Barnes-Jewish Hospital, St Louis from April 1991 to February 1994" (2002) by J. Schwaninger, et al. *Journal of Near-Death Studies,* 20, 4.

"Programme note to String Trio op. 45, Schönberg, A" (2005) by F. Sherry. Naxos: 8.557529.

"Bodies of sound and landscapes" (2000) by H. Stobart. In P. Gouk, (ed.) *Musical healing in cultural contexts,* 35. Aldershot: Ashgate.

Towards Silence (2009) by J. Tavener. Programme note. Art and Mind Festival, Winchester. ISBN: 978 1847725868

Music in Renaissance Magic (1993) by G. Tomlinson. Chicago: University of Chicago. ISBN: 978 0226807928

"Near Death Experience in Survivors of Cardiac Arrest: A Prospective Study in the Netherlands" (2002) by P. Van Lommel, et al. *The Lancet* 358, 2039-45.

Music, Witchcraft and the Paranormal (2005) by M. Willin. Ely: Melrose Press. ISBN: 978 1905226184 [Available on Kindle]

Web links, Specific Journal References, and Correspondence

Bèdard, G. (2009). www.globalideasbank.org/ LA/LA-12.html.

Clarke, E. (2009). Heather Professor of Music, Oxford. Private correspondence.

Corazza, O. & Terreni, M. F. (2005). NDE in music: an aesthetic-musical analysis of String Trio by Arnold Schönberg in Cariglia, F. *Life after Life*, 1975-2005: 30 years of NDE, IX International Symposium of the Near-Death Experience (NDE), 47-51.

Light (1881) October 29; (1884) April 26; (1905) October 28.

Light (1921). April 16; April 30; May 14; June 11; September 24.

Williams, K. (2008) http://www.near-death.com/experiences/research.

11. Music in Shamanism and Spirit Possession:

"Music and trance" (1994) by J. Becker. *Leonardo Music Journal*, 4, 41-51.

"The context of Venda possession music: Reflections on the effectiveness of symbols" (1985) by J. Blacking. *Yearbook for Traditional Music*, *17*, 64-87.

"Some relationships between music and hallucinogenic ritual: The "Jungle Gym" in consciousness" (1975) by M. Dobkin de Rios, & F. Katz. *Ethos*, *3*, 64-76.

Shamanism: Archaic techniques of Ecstasy (1989 [1964]) by M. Eliade. London: Arkana. ISBN: 978 0691119427

"Trance and music in the hausa Boori spirit possession cult in Niger" (1982) V. Erlmann. *Ethnomusicology*, 26, 49-58.

"Wanderer between worlds: Anthropological perspectives of healing rituals and music" (2007) by J. Fachner. *Music Therapy Today*, *8*, 166-195.

Mediumship and Survival: A Century of Investigations (1982) by A. Gauld. London: Paladin Books. ISBN: 978 0586084298 [Available on Kindle]

"Music and dissociation: Experiences without valence? Observing self and absent self" (2013) by R. Herbet. *Proceedings of the 3rd International*

Conference on Music and Emotion, Jyvaskyla, Finland, 11th-15th June 2013.

Talking with Spirits: Personhood, Performance and Altered Consciousness in a Contemporary Spiritualist Home-Circle (2012) by J. Hunter. Unpublished M.Litt dissertation, University of Bristol, Bristol, UK.

Trance: A Natural History of Altered States of Mind (1989) by B. Inglis. London: Grafton Books. ISBN: 978 0246133038

"Music, spirit possession and the in-between: Ethnomusicological inquiry and the challenge of trance" (2007) by R.C. Jankowsky. *Ethnomusicology Forum, 16*, 185-208.

Altered States of Consciousness and Psi: An Historical Survey and Research Prospectus (2009) by E.F. Kelly, & R.G. Locke. New York: Parapsychology Foundation. [Monograph]

"Altered states during shamanic drumming: A phenomenological study" (2010) by A. Kjellgren, & A. Eriksson. *International Journal of Transpersonal Studies*, 29, 1-10.

"The epistemology and technologies of shamanic states of consciousness" (2000) by S. Krippner. *Journal of Consciousness Studies*, 7, 93-118.

Mysterious Minds: The Neurobiology of Psychics, Mediums, and Other Extraordinary People (2010) by S. Krippner, & H.L. Friedman. Santa Barbara: ABC-CLIO. ISBN: 978 0313358661 [Available on Kindle]

"Music in the Iboga initiation ceremony in Gabon: Polyrhythms supporting a pharmacotherapy" (2003) by U. Mass, & S. Strubelt. *Music Therapy Today*, 4, 1-37.

"Auditory driving observed with scalp electrodes in normal subjects" (1961) by A. Neher. *Electroenceph. Clin. Neurophysiol. 13*, 449-451.

"A physiological explanation of unusual behavior in ceremonies involving drums" (1962) by A. Neher. *Human Biology*, 34 , 151-160.

"Towards an experiential analysis of shamanism" (1980) by L.G. Peters, & D. Price-Williams. *American Ethnologist*, 7, 197-418.

Demystifying Shamans and Their World: An Interdisciplinary Study (2011) by A.J. Rock, & S. Krippner. Exeter: Imprint Academic. ISBN: 978 1845402228 [Available on Kindle]

Music and Trance: A Theory of the Relations Between Music and Possession (1985) by G. Rouget. Chicago: University of Chicago Press. ISBN: 978 0226730066

"The power of music" (2006) by O. Sacks. *Brain: A Journal of Neurology*, 129, 2528-2532.

Altered States of Consciousness (1972) by C. Tart. Oxford: Doubleday. ISBN: 978 0062508577

On the Edge of the Bush: Anthropology as Experience (1985) by V. Turner, & E. Turner. Tucson: University of Arizona Press. ISBN: 978 0816509492

"Trance states: A theoretical model and cross-cultural analysis" (1986) by M. Winkelman. Ethos, 14, 174-203.

Shamanism: The Neural Ecology of Consciousness (2000) by M. Winkelman. London: Bergin & Garvey. ISBN: 978 0897897044 [Available on Kindle]

12. The Acoustic Properties of Unexplained Rapping Sounds:

"The Andover case: A responsive rapping poltergeist" (2008) by B.G. Colvin. *Journal of the Society for Psychical Research, 72*, 1-20.

The Founders of Psychical Research (1968) by A. Gauld. London: Routledge & Kegan Paul. ISBN: 978 0710060679

Poltergeists (1979) by A. Gauld, & A.D. Cornell. London: Routledge & Kegan Paul. ISBN: 978 0710001856

"Report on psychokinetic activity surrounding a seven-year-old boy" (2001) by M. Grosse, & M.R. Barrington. *Journal of the Society for Psychical Research, 65*, 207-217.

"The Poltergeist of Cideville" (1904) by A. Lang. *Proceedings of the Society for Psychical Research, 18*, 454-463.

Can we explain the poltergeist? (1964) by A.R.G. Owen. New York: Garrett Publications. ASIN: B0006BMB9Q

Conjuring up Philip (1976) by I.M. Owen, & M. Sparrow. New York: Harper and Row. ISBN: 978 0060132798

The Table Rappers (1972) by R. Pearsall. London: Michael Joseph Ltd. ISBN: 978 0718106454

The Flying Cow (1975) by G.L. Playfair. London: Souvenir Press. ISBN: 978 1907661945 [Reprinted by White Crow Books]

This House is Haunted (1980) by G.L. Playfair. London: Souvenir Press. ISBN: 978 1907661785 [Available on Kindle and Reprinted by White Crow Books]

SORRAT: A history of the Neihardt psychokinesis experiments, 1961-1981 (1982) by J.T. Richards. London: Scarecrow Press. ISBN: 978 0810814912

The Poltergeist (1976) by W.G. Roll. London: Wyndham Publications Ltd. ISBN: 978 1931044691 [Available on Kindle]

"Karin: an experimental study of spontaneous rappings" (1905) by H. Wijk. *The Annals of Psychical Science*, 143-180.

Endword

Long Range Acoustic Device: http://www.lradx.com/site/ accessed 16th January, 2015.

Mosquito Acoustic Deterrent: http://www.compoundsecurity.co.uk/security-equipment-mosquito-mk4-anti-loitering-device accessed 16th January

ABOUT THE CONTRIBUTING AUTHORS

Barrie Colvin, Ph.D. – joined the Society for Psychical Research in 1973 and was co-opted to Council in 2007 and became an elected member in 2014. He has been actively involved in the investigation of mental and physical mediums, including direct-voice, transfiguration and materialisation mediumship. Past projects have included the investigation of haunted houses, the human aura, X-ray analysis of hair reported to be taken from the head of Katie King and evaluation of evidence from Gerard Croiset in a missing person case. His principal interest in recent times has been the physics of poltergeist activity, including the development of instrumentation for this branch of the subject. He developed and successfully trialled infra-red absorption equipment as well as a bespoke mid-frequency infra-red camera for poltergeist field work. His most recent project has been a study of the acoustic properties of poltergeist rapping sounds. He has formed the Poltergeist Research Group, an assembly of interested specialists, and is a member of the Spontaneous Cases Committee of the SPR.

C.R. Foley – has actively researched and investigated the paranormal since the 1960s, when he became fascinated by accounts of hauntings as well as unidentified flying objects. Since 1978, his professional work in law enforcement included 14 years as a Forensic Science investigator with the *Ontario Provincial Police* in which he investigated scenes of crime and their associated exhibits for the resolution of criminal matters. Over the years, along with other official positions held, Foley has consequently developed technical as well as the pure and applied investigative skills which have augmented his psychical research studies. In the 1990s he was a regular contributor to *The Canadian Ufologist*, as published by the *Mutual UFO Network of Ontario*. Foley was also a member of the *American Association of Electronic Voice Phenomena*. In 2012, Foley and Callum E. Cooper contributed an article detailing the similarities between certain aspects of psi and ufology in the journal *Anomaly*. Foley resides in the greater Toronto area, Canada.

Jack Hunter – a Ph.D. candidate in the Department of Archaeology and Anthropology at the University of Bristol. His research takes the form of an ethnographic study of contemporary trance and physical mediumship in Bristol, focusing on themes of personhood, performance, altered states of consciousness and anomalous experience. In 2010 he established *Paranthropology: Journal of Anthropological Approaches to the Paranormal*, as a means to promote an interdisciplinary dialogue on issues relating to paranormal beliefs, experiences, and phenomena. He is the author of Why People Believe in Spirits, Gods and Magic (Kindle ebook), a beginner's introduction to the anthropology of the supernatural, and co-editor with Dr David Luke of *Talking With the Spirits: Ethnographies from Between the Worlds* (Daily Grail Publishing).

Melvyn Willin, Ph.D. – was born in St Albans, Hertfordshire. He was educated at Francis Bacon Grammar School and then took degrees at several British universities including doctorates in musicology at Sheffield and history at Bristol. He was closely associated with Bob Morris at Edinburgh University for several years. He is the Honorary Archive Liaison Officer to the Society for Psychical Research and was the Events Officer and Editor of the *Ghost Club Magazine* for many years. In the last few years he has published several books including Music, *Witchcraft and the Paranormal* (Melrose Press, Ely) *Ghosts caught on film* (David & Charles, Exeter) and contributory chapters in specialist encyclopedias. He also co-produced a triple CD collection of auditory anomalies in conjunction with the Frieburg Institute in Germany. Recent research includes Perrott-Warrick scholarships into the study of Near-Death Experiences from the perspective of music; the efficacy of witchcraft spells in modern society and alleged paranormal demonstrations within the martial arts.

Ann Winsper – After co-founding Para.Science, Ann has for many years successfully combined the role of spontaneous case investigator with the academic pursuits of parapsychology. Ann is currently working toward her Ph.D. exploring the Psychology of the EVP experience. Additionally, Ann has found time to combine her paranormal studies with an active role within the media. She has consulted or appeared on many TV programmes and radio broadcasts for a number of major of broadcast networks in the UK and overseas. Ann has been a constant force at academic conferences and has had papers selected for presentation by the Society for Psychical Research Conference every year since 2006. Her unique insight gained from many years of 'hands-on' investigating anomalous claims and her academic credentials continue to provide a valuable contribution to both ghost hunting and parapsychology.

Paperbacks also available from White Crow Books

Elsa Barker—*Letters from a Living Dead Man*
ISBN 978-1-907355-83-7

Elsa Barker—*War Letters from the Living Dead Man*
ISBN 978-1-907355-85-1

Elsa Barker—*Last Letters from the Living Dead Man*
ISBN 978-1-907355-87-5

Richard Maurice Bucke—*Cosmic Consciousness*
ISBN 978-1-907355-10-3

Arthur Conan Doyle—*The Edge of the Unknown*
ISBN 978-1-907355-14-1

Arthur Conan Doyle—*The New Revelation*
ISBN 978-1-907355-12-7

Arthur Conan Doyle—*The Vital Message*
ISBN 978-1-907355-13-4

Arthur Conan Doyle with Simon Parke—*Conversations with Arthur Conan Doyle*
ISBN 978-1-907355-80-6

Meister Eckhart with Simon Parke—*Conversations with Meister Eckhart*
ISBN 978-1-907355-18-9

D. D. Home—*Incidents in my Life Part 1*
ISBN 978-1-907355-15-8

Mme. Dunglas Home; edited, with an Introduction, by Sir Arthur Conan Doyle—*D. D. Home: His Life and Mission*
ISBN 978-1-907355-16-5

Edward C. Randall—*Frontiers of the Afterlife*
ISBN 978-1-907355-30-1

Rebecca Ruter Springer—*Intra Muros: My Dream of Heaven*
ISBN 978-1-907355-11-0

Leo Tolstoy, edited by Simon Parke—*Forbidden Words*
ISBN 978-1-907355-00-4

Leo Tolstoy—*A Confession*
ISBN 978-1-907355-24-0

Leo Tolstoy—*The Gospel in Brief*
ISBN 978-1-907355-22-6

Leo Tolstoy—*The Kingdom of God is Within You*
ISBN 978-1-907355-27-1

Leo Tolstoy—*My Religion: What I Believe*
ISBN 978-1-907355-23-3

Leo Tolstoy—*On Life*
ISBN 978-1-907355-91-2

Leo Tolstoy—*Twenty-three Tales*
ISBN 978-1-907355-29-5

Leo Tolstoy—*What is Religion and other writings*
ISBN 978-1-907355-28-8

Leo Tolstoy—*Work While Ye Have the Light*
ISBN 978-1-907355-26-4

Leo Tolstoy—*The Death of Ivan Ilyich*
ISBN 978-1-907661-10-5

Leo Tolstoy—*Resurrection*
ISBN 978-1-907661-09-9

Leo Tolstoy with Simon Parke—*Conversations with Tolstoy*
ISBN 978-1-907355-25-7

Howard Williams with an Introduction by Leo Tolstoy—*The Ethics of Diet: An Anthology of Vegetarian Thought*
ISBN 978-1-907355-21-9

Vincent Van Gogh with Simon Parke—*Conversations with Van Gogh*
ISBN 978-1-907355-95-0

Wolfgang Amadeus Mozart with Simon Parke—*Conversations with Mozart*
ISBN 978-1-907661-38-9

Jesus of Nazareth with Simon Parke—*Conversations with Jesus of Nazareth*
ISBN 978-1-907661-41-9

Thomas à Kempis with Simon Parke—*The Imitation of Christ*
ISBN 978-1-907661-58-7

Julian of Norwich with Simon Parke—*Revelations of Divine Love*
ISBN 978-1-907661-88-4

Allan Kardec—*The Spirits Book*
ISBN 978-1-907355-98-1

Allan Kardec—*The Book on Mediums*
ISBN 978-1-907661-75-4

Emanuel Swedenborg—*Heaven and Hell*
ISBN 978-1-907661-55-6

P.D. Ouspensky—*Tertium Organum: The Third Canon of Thought*
ISBN 978-1-907661-47-1

Dwight Goddard—*A Buddhist Bible*
ISBN 978-1-907661-44-0

Michael Tymn—*The Afterlife Revealed*
ISBN 978-1-970661-90-7

Michael Tymn—*Transcending the Titanic: Beyond Death's Door*
ISBN 978-1-908733-02-3

Guy L. Playfair—*If This Be Magic*
ISBN 978-1-907661-84-6

Guy L. Playfair—*The Flying Cow*
ISBN 978-1-907661-94-5

Guy L. Playfair —*This House is Haunted*
ISBN 978-1-907661-78-5

Carl Wickland, M.D.—*Thirty Years Among the Dead*
ISBN 978-1-907661-72-3

John E. Mack—*Passport to the Cosmos*
ISBN 978-1-907661-81-5

Peter & Elizabeth Fenwick—*The Truth in the Light*
ISBN 978-1-908733-08-5

Erlendur Haraldsson—*Modern Miracles*
ISBN 978-1-908733-25-2

Erlendur Haraldsson—*At the Hour of Death*
ISBN 978-1-908733-27-6

Erlendur Haraldsson—*The Departed Among the Living*
ISBN 978-1-908733-29-0

Brian Inglis—*Science and Parascience*
ISBN 978-1-908733-18-4

Brian Inglis—*Natural and Supernatural: A History of the Paranormal*
ISBN 978-1-908733-20-7

Ernest Holmes—*The Science of Mind*
ISBN 978-1-908733-10-8

Victor & Wendy Zammit —*A Lawyer Presents the Evidence For the Afterlife*
ISBN 978-1-908733-22-1

Casper S. Yost—*Patience Worth: A Psychic Mystery*
ISBN 978-1-908733-06-1

William Usborne Moore—*Glimpses of the Next State*
ISBN 978-1-907661-01-3

William Usborne Moore—*The Voices*
ISBN 978-1-908733-04-7

John W. White—*The Highest State of Consciousness*
ISBN 978-1-908733-31-3

Stafford Betty—*The Imprisoned Splendor*
ISBN 978-1-907661-98-3

Paul Pearsall, Ph.D. —*Super Joy*
ISBN 978-1-908733-16-0

All titles available as eBooks, and selected titles available in Hardback and Audiobook formats from www.whitecrowbooks.com

www.ingramcontent.com/pod-product-compliance
Ingram Content Group UK Ltd.
Pitfield, Milton Keynes, MK11 3LW, UK
UKHW041831290726
14061UKWH00004BA/192/J